MALT
WHISKY
YEARBOOK
2010

www.maltwhiskyyearbook.com

First published in Great Britain in 2009 by
MagDig Media Limited

ISBN 978-0-9552607-6-6

Translations by Hirschfeld Media.
www.hirschfeldmedia.com

MagDig Media Limited
1 Brassey Road
Old Potts Way, Shrewsbury
Shropshire SY3 7FA
ENGLAND

E-mail: info@maltwhiskyyearbook.com
www.maltwhiskyyearbook.com

Contents

Introduction

No one can have missed the financial turmoil that started last year. The whisky industry has of course felt the pressure even if it has fared better than most other businesses. The Malt Whisky Yearbook 2010 tells you the story about this of course, but also of the careful optimism for the future, financial investments, new, exciting bottlings and a world of whisky that is still growing.

Malt Whisky Yearbook 2010 reflects on the past year but also takes a view into the future and the team of distinguished whisky writers have covered a wide array of subjects this year too;

The whisky innovators are in constant search of new expressions to dazzle us customers. *Gavin D Smith* has met with a few of them. Peated malts - some whisky drinkers reject them while others simply cannot get enough. *Ian Wisniewski* shows us why the flavour variation within that segment is so huge. Is Europe a whisky market in decline or is there a golden era around the corner? Join *Dominic Roskrow* on his investigative journey. Whisky distilleries that are forced to shut down do not always disappear completely. They can still be found on the shop shelves or in the minds of punters. *David Stirk* and friends discuss why that is so. In the last Yearbook, *Charles MacLean* searched for The Fathers of Whisky. This year he puts the light on three dynasties which laid the foundations of the modern whisky industry. And how are the whisky producers faring in the worst economy in a long time? *Ian Buxton* takes the temperature of the industry.

In Malt Whisky Yearbook 2010 you will also find the unique, detailed and much appreciated 176-page section on malt whisky distilleries. It has been thoroughly revised and updated not just in text but also including numerous new pictures and tasting notes for all the core brands. There is a list of 130 of the best whisky shops in the world with their full details and a comprehensive list of 500 new bottlings. The summary The Whisky Year That Was has been expanded again this year, in order to reflect on the exciting times. A new feature for this edition are pages describing the various steps in whisky production and you will also meet the people behind the whiskies - the distillery managers. The very latest statistics finally, gives you all the answers to questions on production and consumption.

Thank you for buying Malt Whisky Yearbook 2010. We hope that you will have many enjoyable moments reading it and we can assure you that we will be back with a new edition in 2011.

Great care has been taken to ensure the accuracy of the information presented in this book. MagDig Media Ltd can, however, not be held liable for inaccuracies.

Malt Whisky Yearbook 2011 will be published in October 2010.
To make sure you will be able to order it directly, please register at
www.maltwhiskyyearbook.com.

If you need any of the previous four volumes of Malt Whisky Yearbook, they are available
for purchase (in limited numbers) from the website www.maltwhiskyyearbook.com

Acknowledgments

First of all I wish to thank the writers who have shared their great specialist knowledge on the subject in a brilliant and entertaining way – Ian Buxton, Charles MacLean, Dominic Roskrow, Gavin D. Smith, David Stirk and Ian Wisniewski.

A special thanks goes to David and Dominic who put in a lot of effort nosing, tasting and writing notes for more than 100 different whiskies.

The following persons have also made important photographic or editorial contributions:

Tomo Akaike, Rob Allanson, Chris Allwood, Paul Aston, David Baker, Nick Ballard, Ian Bankier, Rachel Barrie, Sonia Bastian, Keith Batt, Iain Baxter, Kirsteen Beeston, Lauren Beth, Ali Bosmans, Etienne Bouillon, Stephen Bremner, Alex Bruce, Gordon Bruce, Alexander Buchholz, Bert Burger, John Campbell, Peter Campbell, Ian Chang, Ian Chapman, Stewart Christine, Marco di Ciacca, Margaret Mary Clarke, Doug Clement, Michael Cockram, Neal Corbett, Graham Coull, Jason Craig, Katherine Crisp, Keith Cruickshank, Jeremy Cunnington, Peter Currie, Jancine Davies, Stephen Davies, David Doig, Jean Donnay, Frances Dupuy, Ralph Erenzo, Graham Eunson, Joanna Fearnside, Berle Figgins Jr, Douglas Fitchett, Thomas Fleischmann, Robert Fleming, Thomas Gerber, Jess Graber, Kenny Grant, Alan Gray, Ueli Hagen, Monika Haider, Mike Haldane, Anna Hall, Diana Hamberger, Jay Harman, Michael Heads, Holger Höhler, Anne Jack, Ben Kagi, Moritz Kallmeyer, Sheila Kennedy, Ruedi Käser, Mari Laidlaw, Bill Lark, Gerhard Liebl, Aart van der Linde, Mark Littler, Doug Long, Jim Long, Alistair Longwell, Bill Lumsden, Horst Lüning, Urs Lüthy, Des McCagherty, Iain McCallum, Stephen McCarthy, Alan McConnochie, John MacDonald, Judy Macdonald, Neil Macdonald, Polly MacDonald, Barbara McEwan, Frank McHardy, Catherine Mackintosh, John MacLellan, Beth McMillan, Ian MacMillan, Grant MacPherson, Anne McQueen, Patrick Maguire, Dennis Malcolm, Stephen Marshall, Annabel Meikle, Jean Metzger, Ann Miller, Euan Mitchell, Henric Molin, Jemma Morris, Arthur Motley, Andrew Nelstrop, Stuart Nickerson, Jay Oddleifson, Linda Outterson, Richard A Pelletier, Don Poffenroth, Brett Pontoni, Warren Preston, Anssi Pyysing, Robert Ransom, Patrick Roberts, David Robertson, Brian Robinson, Caroline Rylance, Torsten Römer, Andrew Scott, Jacqui Seargeant, Andrew Shand, Rubyna Sheikh, Derek Sinclair, Sukhinder Singh, Gabriele Sponheimer, Alison Spowart, Verity Staniforth, Billy Stitchell, Thomas Sundblom, Cameron Syme, Duncan Tait, Kazuyuki Takayama, Stephen Teeling, Gerry Tosh, Alan Tough, Erkin Tuzmuhamedov, Brett Vanderkamp, Lasse Vesterby, David Vitale, Alistair Walker, Alex Wang, Andy Watts, Iain Weir, Brigitte Weutz, James Whelan, Cristina Wilkie, Anthony Wills, Allan Winchester, Patrick van Zuidam, Daniel and Ursula Zürcher

Thank you!

Ingvar Ronde
Editor

Whisky
and
Recession

It used to be said that the drinks industry was recession proof - customers would still buy their favourite tipple no matter how bad the economy got. Present circumstances beg for a more cautious attitude. Perhaps it is more likely that the industry merely is recession resilient. Ian Buxton has met with several industry heavy-weights to hear what they have to say.

In the Malt Whisky Yearbook 2008 I contributed an article entitled *Bring on the Bulls?* This looked at the then-current boom in Scotch whisky and the Roman rites of the Triumph. I noted that the successful general, returning from a victorious campaign, was accompanied by a slave to remind him of his mortality and was obliged to sacrifice several white bulls on the Capitoline Hill. This offering to Jupiter was intended to pacify the god and bring good fortune to Rome.

The article reviewed Scotch whisky's historic tendency to boom and bust and concluded that, in what appeared to some to be a 'golden age' for Scotch whisky, the industry might like to find some bulls to sacrifice to appease the whisky (or economic) gods – just in case.

I wrote:
"...recessions do happen in the best-ordered of economies – and it's a while since the world had a full-blown slump."

"If you believe in the Kondratiev Wave theory something nasty might be just round the corner. It could be driven by a surge in oil prices

as, for example, Chinese energy demand rises. After all, they've got to earn the money to pay for all the whisky we're going to sell them and that requires an increase in output and thus oil consumption."

"Or there could be a really big war in the Middle East. Perhaps the U.S.A. may decide to invade Iran. Or perhaps a resurgent Russia will once again seek to expand – by laying claim to the North Pole, for example. I don't have a crystal ball. My point is simply that the future is fraught with risk and that imponderable events larger than the whisky industry can and do happen."

It seems quite prophetic when I see those words again.

So, how is the Scotch whisky industry faring in the very different conditions now facing the world?

It's clear that no one anticipated the very rapid economic collapse that occurred in late 2008, or the severity of the decline, or the systemic nature of the underlying problems in the international banking system. A few sages

The Financial Crisis
Investor Panic
Shares Fall
Go From Bad to Worse to Ugly
Shares Fall
Headed for a De
Problems Spur Layoffs
Global Financial Crisis
Credit Crunch
Earnings Fall
Bankruptcy
wnturn
Economic Turbulence
Times
Job Cuts
Recess
Profit Falls
The Depression
Big Deficits
Worries
Jobless
Economy Takes Toll
Bailout
Jobs Crisis Forcing Thousands

may have questioned some of what was happening, but politicians, bankers and economists alike were basically caught unawares. So I don't think we can blame the whisky industry for getting caught up in the general optimism, however rash it may now appear.

However, at least for the early part of 2009 it was clear that no one knew what was happening, or seemed to have a clear idea how to deal with it. If they did, they certainly weren't saying.

It seemed to me at the time as if most of the industry was in shock for about six months – effectively pulling the bedclothes over their corporate heads and trying to ignore the world, rather as a truculent or frightened child ignores their parent and hopes they will go away.

Pounded by the recession, and beset by hysterical media reports, there was a general trend to destocking all through the global supply chain. Basically this meant that round the world retailers ran down their inventory and ordered less whisky, reasoning that it was better to risk running out of a product than be caught with unsold stock; wholesalers and distributors did the same, leading to a toxic chain reaction back to the distilleries. The result: short-time working and temporary closure of some

bottling and blending plants. And a knee-jerk reaction to cut budgets, lay off workforces and slash marketing activity. This, of course, while it seemed the appropriate course of action for any individual business that wanted to survive the threatened economic holocaust, just made the macro picture even worse.

Corporate Platitudes

It proved hard around that time to engage with the industry to get a meaningful picture of what was happening. Those who did respond did so with bland corporate platitudes about "rebalancing the business" and "reviewing priorities": hard facts proved elusive - until there was an announcement of a specific plant closure.

Take Diageo, for example. A spokesman (I won't embarrass the individual by putting a name to this particular piece of banality) told me

"At Diageo we are running our business for the long-term. We intend to emerge from the economic downturn stronger therefore none of our long-term initiatives - around supply or innovation for example - are affected, nor is our confidence for the future of our whisky portfolio. In addition, we know that consumers are united by a desire for quality brands with a

Johnnie Walker will not be walking out of the Kilmarnock packaging plant after 2011

strong sense of heritage and authenticity, and innovation – and that does not diminish in a downturn; in fact they turn towards the brands that stand for quality, integrity and that they know they can trust."

That was in early June. Less than a month later they announced a net loss of 500 jobs in Scotland and the closure of the Johnnie Walker bottling plant in Kilmarnock and the historic Port Dundas grain distillery. Evidently, not enough consumers were turning to brands that they could trust. Certainly, trust in Diageo was severely damaged in Scotland, where political reaction was shock and outrage at what many saw as a betrayal.

The decision to cut Diageo's Scottish operations came out of the blue, Scotland's First Minister Alex Salmond commenting: "I think when a company has made billions of pounds out of Scotland with the sales of Scotch whisky, at the very least when they are planning a decision of such enormity - particularly in the economy of Kilmarnock and Ayrshire - then they have an obligation to let the representatives know what is happening."

At the time of writing the position on the Diageo closures is unclear though, for all the sound and fury of the chattering classes and the workers' distress, it's hard to see Diageo changing their mind. Johnnie Walker, it seems, will soon be walking out of Kilmarnock for the last time, unless a belated effort by the Scottish Executive and their enterprise agency can persuade them otherwise.

Glasgow-based Whyte & Mackay have also announced significant job cuts – around 100 in their case. With an emphasis on 'value' brands and own-label the company has been hard hit by UK duty increases and, despite the public optimism of its Indian owners, has looked vulnerable to a downturn.

Of course, it's worth remembering that these changes aren't all about Scotch whisky. Cuts in bottling capacity, for example, may be driven by falls in demand for gin and vodka rather than any downturn in whisky sales but it doesn't bode well. In May Diageo said that net sales in the quarter to the end of March were down by 7% year-on-year, with stock reductions in the US resulting in a drop in volumes in the quarter of 1m cases. At the last count, however, the drinks giant was still forecasting profit growth of between 4% and 6% - which can't have gone down very well in Kilmarnock.

Over at the Scotch Whisky Association the message was both clear and calming – "don't panic". Which is, when you think about it, a perfectly reasonable response. Spokesman David Williamson told Malt Whisky Yearbook:

"We remain optimistic about the future prospects for Scotch Whisky. Indeed, Scotch has proved itself again to be recession-resilient if not recession-immune. To have achieved a record export value performance in 2008 in the face of such challenging conditions is an impressive achievement. The next twelve months may be challenging but distillers are looking more than a decade ahead as they plan and invest, with opportunities both in mature and emerging markets."

In fact, by the middle of 2009 it seemed clear that things weren't quite as dire as had been feared. Whilst consumers were delaying 'big ticket' purchases such as cars or house moves (or simply couldn't fund them due to a shortage of finance deals), smaller treats and special occasion purchases such as single malt seemed to be holding up.

"Well," the industry seemed to conclude "things may be bad but they could be a lot worse."

Some restocking helped pull through volume and sales, especially of some of the specialist malts, seemed to recover quite quickly.

Some honesty – and some numbers

An emphasis on the long term characterised the responses of those willing to go beyond trite and colourless corporate clichés. Mike Keiller, MD of Morrison Bowmore, was one prepared to go on the record. He told me that, in his view, there were greater problems:

"The biggest cloud on the horizon is the crazy policies of the UK and Scottish governments towards the drinks industry with minimum pricing and duty increases," he said.

"Overall our markets are holding up very well and our strategy is not changing because of the current turmoil."

Better still, he went on to confirm that "as a specialist single malt player Morrison Bowmore is particularly long term in approach. Our distillation plans remain as before."

He also commented on the strong performance of travel retail and duty free, suggesting that while travel numbers may be down, those who are travelling internationally are still spending freely.

Fraser Thornton, Managing Director of Burn Stewart Distillers, raises his glass in toast of a prosperous 2008.

There is good news too from Glenmorangie, Ian Macleod Distillers and Burn Stewart, all of whom have recently reported sharply rising profits (though boosted in Glenmorangie's case by one-off profits from the sale of Glen Moray and the Broxburn HQ).

Glenmorangie more than doubled its annual profits for the second year running, making £30.5 million in 2008, on increased turnover of £112.5m, as sales rose 34%.

Likewise, Ian Macleod Distillers announced a 51% rise in pre-tax profits to £1.5 million, boosted by investment in developing markets such as India and China and a 4% increase in group turnover in the year.
Managing Director Leonard Russell also stressed the long-term nature of their business:

"As an independent company we can focus on the longer term, rather than short-term returns for shareholders."

Finally, Burn Stewart Distillers almost doubled its full-year pre-tax profits, boosted by the success of the company's Scottish Leader whisky brand in Taiwan and South Africa.

Pre-tax profits for the year to 31 December 2008 reached £650,000 up from £380,000 in the comparable period of the previous year, and the company, which employs 250 people across its head office and three distilleries, claimed that it has seen continued growth across its core brands, with a 75% increase in volume over the last four years. The group sold more than 500,000 cases in 2008.

The distiller has experienced continued growth of Scottish Leader in Taiwan where it has maintained a 7% growth in the market, as well as 15% year-on-year growth in the South African market.

Black Bottle also witnessed new areas of growth through distribution in 20 new markets, including Denmark, Holland, Russia, South Africa and Taiwan.

Managing director Fraser Thornton said the company's primary focus is to develop and grow its core portfolio of brands.

"We have enjoyed another year of growth and have opened up new markets as well as continuing to build our brands in existing markets," he said.

"2008 was an exciting year as we invested £6m in brand marketing as well as making improvements in both our distilling and bottling infrastructure."

These figures, of course, relate to trading last year when conditions were much easier and markets relatively buoyant. For that reason, the Diageo job cuts are the most worrying because they represent the most recent reaction to a rapidly-changing situation.

Steady nerves required

And that's the problem. The situation is highly volatile and the down-turn in the last quarter of 2008 was unexpectedly fast and severe. So fast and severe, in fact, that it was all but un-precedented in the experience of most of the industry's management. In the 2008 Yearbook I quoted Diageo's Ken Robertson as follows:

"If, despite everything, we did lapse back into over-supply, someone somewhere should have access to the hand-book that tells you how to avoid the pitfalls of commoditisation and loss of brand values that have haunted us for the last twenty years."

That seemed comforting at the time, but may turn out to be little more than a sanguine hope. The industry may avoid over-supply, but only at the cost of further rationalisation and plant closures. If that scenario plays out, the Johnnie Walker closures may just be the first of many painful losses – of historic plants as well as jobs.

The last few years have protected those smaller players who may be financially vulnerable. As Ian Bankier of The Whisky Shop puts it

"The industry's problem will be managing the inevitable surpluses and this will require a strong balance sheet and steady nerves."

Persistent rumours surround Burn Stewart,

Bruichladdich, Arran and Tullibardine all of which are alleged to be 'available' to the right buyer – though it's only fair to observe that all energetically deny these stories.

But some brand owners are still determined-ly upbeat. For its critics, the launch of The Macallan's controversial Masters of Photography Rankin Edition marked the high water mark of the whisky boom. This 30 year old Macallan, normally retailing for under £300, was released in an edition of just 1,000 bottles accompanied by an original Polaroid print by well-known Scottish fashion photographer Rankin. Most of the prints, and the bottle label itself, featured a nude portrait of international model Tuuli.

That, and the £800+ price tag, caused more than a few eyebrows to be raised. Was it art, soft porn or simply a faux controversy manipu-lated to generate media coverage? Certainly Macallan needed the storm of publicity to justify the cost – estimated at £1.2m – because they will undoubtedly have lost money on the exercise.

The Masters of Photography bottle sits along-side the two previous releases of ultra-old and ultra-high priced The Macallan in Lalique decanters and, some would argue, all look increasingly uncomfortable in an age of auste-rity and global recession.

But it's about positioning The Macallan in the long-term as a global luxury icon, and that

When The Macallan Masters of Photography bottlings were launched more than one eyebrow was raised

Photo: © The Edrington Group

implies a long-term confidence in the development of the whisky market and the existence of a few super-premium consumers for whom price isn't really an issue. Exclusivity becomes the key here and the distiller's cunning plan is that the image of standard Macallan is enhanced by the so-called 'halo effect' of these super-premium offerings.

It would seem to be working: independent data from the IWSR suggests that between 2000 and 2008 The Macallan has seen stellar growth rates, increasing sales nearly 75% faster than the overall single malt market and confirming its position as the world's number 2 single malt brand by value.

So, whatever you may think about Macallan's repositioning, the pertinent question here is: do they feel confident enough, despite the recession, to press on with the strategy. And here the answer is unambiguous.

Glenfiddich 50 year old with a price tag of £10,000

It may have taken longer than they anticipated, but the distillery has all but sold out of the Rankin edition (it will have been exhausted by the time this reaches you) and definitely plans a second Masters of Photography, working with another renowned name to explore aspects of the brand's visual identity and physical heritage. This is expected in the final quarter of 2010 and presumably will be equally bold in both pricing and packaging.

Even more encouragingly a third Lalique decanter, this time containing a 57 year old Macallan, was released in September 2009. Priced at $15,000 (just over £9,000 at current exchange rates) there will be just 400 of the so-called 'Finest Cut' decanters available. That may be entirely irrelevant to you and me, but the fact that Macallan are pressing on with both these projects gives cause for optimism about the whisky market in general.

Over at Dufftown, Glenfiddich have confidently doubled the price of the latest release of their 50 year old to £10,000 for each of the 50 hand-blown, sliver labelled bottles they confidently expect to sell each year. Glenfiddich's Chairman Peter Gordon said:

"Our independence enables us to do things differently."

It may have been accidental, but this almost makes the Macallan Finest Cut look a bargain!

The third of Macallan's Lalique bottlings

14

But again, Ian Bankier confirms these trends.

"Whilst the conspicuous consumers, gene-rally rich Russians, property and finance types, seem to have dropped out of the market we're still seeing collectors interested in £500+ bottles."

Market dynamics

The IWSR kindly supplied their very latest data for the global single malt market for the pur-poses of this article - and it makes fascinating reading.

The table below compares the retail value of brands in 2008 in 000's of US$ and the growth rate of the global market between 2000 and 2008 in % with the same information for the top ten brands.

Bear in mind that the table shows IWSR's esti-mate of retail value and is ranked accordingly – it would be different if case sales were used as the basis of the table. However, according to these figures the global malt market has slightly more than doubled in value over the past 8 years.

Therefore, any brand showing growth of less than 208% has lost share of retail value and a brand showing growth of more than this has

gained share. On such figures are sales and marketing careers built.

Though it grew in value, the global malt mar-ket lost 0.4% in volume in 2008 over 2007, with virtually all the decline coming in the standard and low price categories. Just over 6.4 million 9 litre cases of malt Scotch were sold in 2008 according to the IWSR data.

What this tells us is that the winners have been Johnnie Walker Green Label (spectacular-ly so); The Macallan; The Balvenie; Laphroaig and The Glenlivet and that their growth has come at the expense of the overall losers: Glenfiddich; the Classic Malts; Glenmorangie; Cardhu and Aberlour, though every one of these brands has seen significant absolute growth.

Johnnie Walker Green Label is perhaps something of a 'one off'. Starting from a low, indeed virtually non-existent, base it benefits from Diageo's excellent global distribution and the strength of the Johnnie Walker brand franchise. Nonetheless, its growth was drama-tic and it is clearly one to watch.

Apart from that, the outstanding perfor-mance is that of The Macallan. Notwithstan-ding the critics of the Fine Oak range, this brand has consistently powered ahead of its

Rank	Brand	Retail value 2008 in 000's US$	Growth % 2000-2008	Share trend
	Total - Global Malt	2,978,429	208.6	
1	Glenfiddich	431,995	173.7	↓
2	The Macallan	295,609	360.7	↑↑
3	Diageo Classic Malts	263,778	171.8	↓
4	The Glenlivet	234,785	213.5	↑
5	Glenmorangie	188,042	176.9	↓
6	J Walker Green Label	135,952	981.5	↑↑↑
7	Cardhu	110,063	159.9	↓
8	Laphroaig	91,653	215.7	↑
9	The Balvenie	83,199	235.8	↑
10	Aberlour	80,104	179.1	↓

Source: IWSR

Ian Bankier, owner of The Whisky Shop chain, is optimistic about future sales of single malts

rivals and is now the undisputed global number 2 by value (it is still out-ranked in case sales by The Glenlivet).

All other things being equal, you would expect that those brands showing positive growth will be best placed to withstand any market downturn, as they are exhibiting the greatest dynamism and presumably are engaging best with the trade and consumer.

But to see if that picture was confirmed in the retail environment, I spoke to some key retailers about the current performance and their view of the prospects for single malt.

Ian Bankier of The Whisky Shop was quite complimentary to the distillers.

"I wouldn't criticise. In general, they've waited to see what will happen in a market that's difficult to call. There was an early over-correction but stock management has improved and we shouldn't see the 'whisky loch' again, though there may be more consolidation amongst distillers."

"Our single malt experience, bearing in mind that single malt is still a small part of the market and generally speaking a special occasion purchase, has been good. 2008 was a reasonable year for us and in the first six months of 2009 we're well up on last year." Bankier pointed to some special factors;

"The Homecoming celebrations in Scotland

Brett Pontoni of Binny's Beverage Depot says distillers have reacted intelligently

Royal Mile Whiskies is having a great year, says Managing Director Keir Sword

have helped us, as has the 'staycation' trend [UK consumers holidaying in Britain instead of going abroad, Ed.]. While our shop in the City of London had a very poor autumn it has recovered dramatically since then."

Another factor was emphasised by Royal Mile Whiskies' MD Keir Sword.

"Whisky is international. The UK looks cheap right now to international buyers, especially in Europe, and so the strength of the pound has been good for us."

Sword's feeling is that the UK market, if only for specialists and quality whiskies, remains strong.

"We haven't really seen the apocalypse that was predicted. There's been little impact on promotional activity so far as we are concerned and I feel that media hysteria about the recession has a lot to answer for. Frankly, we're having a great year in this recession!"

Over in the USA, where the recession started and has been deeply felt Brett Pontoni, Speciality Spirits Buyer for Binny's Beverage Depot, an important and influential stockist of many whiskies, told me he felt that "as a whole" the industry was holding up well.

"The high-end ($200+) is soft but we feel the distillers have reacted intelligently, holding back releases until the market improves. This isn't about people 'trading down' more that buyers of regular brands aren't trading up for special occasions. We have to work harder and help people experiment to try something new but save a few dollars."

"Having said that, the real-world impact has been on the middle-classes and the working

guy. The very wealthy may have taken paper losses but they're still looking for super-premium ($500 and up). I wouldn't want to run a bar or restaurant right now though."

So we can leave the last word, after all, to the optimists, typified by Ian Bankier, who told me confidently

"Malts are doing well across the world, carried along by their discovery by new consumers, and here in the UK consumers are enthusiastically buying single malt and will continue to do so. We have no recession."

Let's hope they're right to be bullish.

Keeper of the Quaich and Liveryman of the Worshipful Company of Distillers, Ian Buxton is well-placed to write or talk about whisky, not least because he lives on the site of a former distillery! Ian began work in the Scotch Whisky industry in 1987 and, since 1991, has run his own strategic marketing consultancy business. In addition, he regularly gives lectures, presentations and tastings on whisky and writes regular columns for Whisky Magazine, the Scottish Field website, and various other titles. He is a co-author of the recent Eyewitness Companion to Whisky *(Dorling Kindersley) and is currently working on a history of John Dewar & Sons and a history of Glenglassaugh Distillery. He established the World Whiskies Conference in 2005 and, with Neil Wilson, also established Classic Expressions to reprint facsimile editions of rare whisky classics.*

The Dynasties

- founders of the modern whisky industry

*The Scottish history is filled
with people who have contributed to create
the succesful business we see today. Charles MacLean tells
the story of the most influential.*

I n the last edition of the Yearbook, I investigated some of the 'Fathers' of Scotch whisky. Here I propose to consider three dynasties which laid the foundations of the modern whisky industry – the Forbes', the Steins and the Haigs – and one individual: Aeneas Coffey.

The Forbes' of Culloden
– First Commercial Distillers

In 1689, the year after King James VII went into exile, a substantial distillery at Ferintosh, on the Black Isle, just north of Inverness, was burnt down by Jacobite sympathisers. We know this because its owner, a staunch Presbyterian and supporter of the new regime, claimed £54,000 compensation from the Government, and was granted the right to distil duty-free in perpetuity from grains grown on his own lands. This is the first mention of distilling on a commercial scale in Scotland.

The owner of Ferintosh estate was Duncan Forbes of Culloden (1644-1704), Provost (i.e. mayor) of Inverness. We do not know when his family founded the distillery – 'around 1650' has been suggested – but the dispensation enabled his son, John, to live comfortably, even lavishly.

He was known as 'Bumper John' on account of his fondness for wine and convivial company.

Captain Edmund Burt, who began his *Letters from a Gentleman in the North of Scotland* in 1726, reported:

"There lives in our neighbourhood at a house or castle called Culloden, a gentleman whose hospitality is almost without bounds. It is the custom of that house, at the first visit or introduction, to take up your freedom by cracking his nut (as he terms it), that is a coconut shell, which holds a pint filled with champagne, or such other sort of wine as you shall choose. You may guess by the introduction, at the contents of the volume, few go away sober at any time; and for the greatest part of his guests, in the conclusion, they cannot go at all".

'Bumper John' was succeeded by his brother, another Duncan Forbes, who became Lord President of the Court of Session – Scotland's highest legal appointment – in 1737. The position was hugely influential, and when the Jacobites took to arms again in 1745, he expended great efforts and very large sums of his own money in the Government cause, including helping to pay the salaries of the army in Scotland.
Sir Walter Scott described him as "the distinguished Scotsman who saved the Kingdom for the House of Hanover". The Rising was ultimately crushed at the Battle of Culloden, which was fought close to the Forbes' family home – indeed for three nights before the battle the house was adopted by Bonnie Prince Char-

THE BATTLE
OF CULLODEN
WAS FOUGHT ON THIS MOOR
16TH APRIL 1746.

THE GRAVES OF THE
GALLANT HIGHLANDERS
WHO FOUGHT FOR
SCOTLAND & PRINCE CHARLIE,
ARE MARKED BY THE NAMES
OF THEIR CLANS.

The Forbes family fortune virtually disappeared in the aftermath of the battle of Culloden in 1746

lie as his headquarters – and following this Duncan Forbes used all his influence to plead clemency for the 'rebels'.

This did not go down well in the fevered and vengeful atmosphere of the time, and the Government conveniently used Forbes' 'support' for the defeated Jacobites as an excuse not to recompense him for his losses on its behalf – a fact which "impaired and almost ruined his private fortune" (Scott).

Duncan Forbes died next year (1747) and was succeeded by his son, John, who set about restoring the family fortunes, including opening three more distilleries on his Black Isle estate. During the middle decades of the eighteenth century the family was producing almost two-thirds of the whisky legally offered for sale in Scotland – around 90,000 gallons per annum – and making a profit of £18,000 a year, which is over £2 million in today's money.

This was too much for an avaricious Government, and by the Wash Act 1784, the Forbes's dispensation was revoked.
Robert Burns famously wrote in *Scotch Drink*:

Thee Ferintosh! O sadly lost!
Scotland lament frae coast to coast!
Now colic-grips, an' barkin hoast,
May kill us a';
For loyal Forbes' Charter'd boast
Is ta'en awa!

Robert Burns reacted in a poem when the Forbes fell out of favour with the Government

The Steins - First Industrial Distillers

The distilleries founded in Clackmannanshire by members of the Stein family during the latter part of the 18th century have been described by Professor Michael Moss as "the largest manufacturing undertakings of any kind to emerge during the first decade of the industrial revolution in Scotland".

The name Stein (pr. 'Steen') derives from the Old Scots for Steven. The earliest reference to the family in Clackmannan is from around 1200, and by 1300 the family was clearly one of substance: they owned their farms at Craigton (Alloa) and Greenyards, on the other side of the River Forth, rather than being tenants. It was at Greenyards that the English knights became bogged down during the running battle of Bannockburn in 1314.

It is supposed that the Steins extended their land-holding at the Reformation, upon the dissolution of Kennetpans Abbey, near Alloa, and there is a family tradition that they learned the art of distilling from the friars. They certainly bought land at Kennetpans in 1642 and by the 1740s, John Stein (1697-1773) was operating a distillery of the same name on the shore of the River Forth which may have been established by his father twenty years earlier.

The situation was ideal: Alloa stands in the shadow of the Ochil Hills, out of which flows a copious supply of fresh water, at the junction of the Stirling Plain and the fertile lowlands of Fife. The town had long been a centre of brewing. It was also close to some of the earliest coal pits in Scotland, and had access to the Forth for the import of coal and grain from East Lothian.

John Stein had seven children who survived into adulthood. All of them became or married distillers.

James Stein (1740-1804) founded a large distillery a few hundred yards from Kennetpans, named Kilbagie, in about 1770. It was the largest distillery in Scotland, producing 3,000 tons of spirit annually and fattening 7,000 head of cattle and 2,000 pigs on the draff and residues. A canal was built to connect it with the Forth – one of the earliest in Scotland – and Robert Burns, who visited the district in 1787, mentions 'that dear Kilbagie' in his poem *The Jolly Beggars*. Some Burns scholars maintain that the reference was inspired by James Stein having been tried by the High Court the previous year for attempting to bribe the Solicitor of the Excise, John Bonar!

On 4th Dec 1786 Stein had breakfasted with Bonar in Edinburgh, during which he complained bitterly about the recently passed Scotch Distillery Act. As he was leaving he slipped a packet into Bonar's pocket saying it was a pair of gloves. In fact it was £500 in banknotes, wrapped in a paper inscribed 'This will be repeated once every year'. Stein employed the leading advocate of the day to defend him and the jury found that although Stein had given Bonar the money, the charge of bribery was 'not proven'.

James seems to have been the leader of the family, although he was the second son: his older brother, Robert (1733-1816), founded a distillery at Kincaple, close to St. Andrews. Andrew (1741-1828), bought Hattonburn Distillery at Milnathort, not far away (reputed to make the worst whisky in Scotland!), and became Provost of St. Andrews.

John (1745-1825) took over the family concern at Kennetpans, where he built a dock and installed the first railway in Scotland, connecting the dock to his brother's distillery at Kilbagie. Alison Stein, their sister, married Richard Philp, whose brother had founded Dolls Distillery at Menstrie about 1780.

Margaret (1729-1794), John Stein's oldest child, married John Haig, and during the nineteenth century, the pioneering Steins would be eclipsed by their cousins, the Haigs, although her nephew Robert, James Stein's son and successor at Kilbagie, invented a continuous still in 1827, which would be perfected by Aeneas Coffey three years later.

Andrew Stein was Provost of St. Andrews

The Haigs – Founders of the Modern Industry

Like the Steins, the Haigs are of ancient lineage. Petrus de Hage appears as a witness to charters in 1162 and 1166. He was granted lands at Bemesyde in Roxburghshire and was described as 'likely an adventurer of noble birth and soldier-like qualities'. His descendants fought with William Wallace at Stirling Bridge, with Robert Bruce at Bannockburn, at Otterburn and Flodden, and were granted the right to wear the Saltire in their arms on account of having taken part in a Crusade.

In1623 Robert Haig, brother of the 18th laird of Bemersyde, moved to Throsk, near Alloa, Clackmannanshire, after a family row. Tradition has it that he learned the art of distilling in Holland before he arrived at Throsk; certainly, in the Session Record for St. Ninian's Parish Church dated 22nd November 1667, he is rebuked for distilling on the Sabbath.

Throsk is not far from Craigton and Kennetpans, and in 1751, John Haig (1720-1773), Robert Haig's great-great grandson, moved to The Gartlands on marrying John Stein's daughter, Margaret, who was also his first cousin. The Gartlands was an elegant farmhouse, built in 1666, and surrounded by gardens and orchards. It may be that his brother-in-law gave it to him as a dowry.

The Haig family's roots are ancient.
Some of them even fought with Robert the Bruce in the 1300s

In a short time, the Haigs had eleven children, then John died at the age of fifty-three. Margaret 'took to her bed and refused to get up – repining and inconsolable', until the ghost of her dead mother appeared to her begging her to pull herself together, saying: "Take your children and educate them, and give them a good start in life. For I am permitted to tell you that if you give heed to my words, some of your descendants shall rise to such high positions in this world as are undreamt of by you".

Her Stein nephews took the children under their wing and trained them as distillers. They would go on to surpass even their cousins.

James Haig, the oldest (1755-1833), went to Edinburgh in 1780 and built Lochrin Distillery on the edge of the Union Canal, then Canonmills Distillery two years later. Following three successive years of crop failures, on 4th June 1784 the latter was stormed by an angry, hungry mob, which believed that oats and potatoes were being used for distilling. The mob was resisted by "Mr. Haig's servants, who were armed in defence of their master's property", but the rioters returned in greater force three days later. This time they were met by militia, who opened fire, wounding several people. The ringleaders were whipped through the streets of Edinburgh and then transported to the plantations for 14 years. On 8th June, James Haig issued a printed statement rebutting absolutely the accusation that he was distilling from 'food crops':

"The genuine truth is that no other species of grain are made use of at Canonmills but barley, rye, and sometimes such parcels of wheat as happen to receive damage, or are in quality unfit for bread".

By the 1790s James Haig was the pre-eminent Lowland distiller and the spokesman for the industry. "His skill in negotiation and his highly technical knowledge of distilling did much to aid the government in trying to frame regulations which would protect the legitimate manufacturer and trader and help to eliminate the innumerable illicit stills both in the Lowlands and in the Highlands" (James Laver, House of Haig)

In 1798/99 he submitted a Memorial to the Parliamentary Committee on The Distilleries in Scotland, in which he made the excellent claim: "The less oil any Spirit contains the purer it is, and the more wholesome the Spirit. Scotch Whisky contains less oil than any other Spirit; hence the cause why the Drinkers of Whisky Punch have less Head Ach [sic] the following morning, than those who drink any other Liquor".

His brother John (1758-1819?) married his cousin Margaret Stein, moved to Edinburgh and joined James at Lochrin, then bought and expanded Leith Distillery at Bonnington in 1804.

Robert Haig (1764-c.1834) moved to Dublin, where his sister Isabella had married John Jameson. Here he established Dodderbank Distillery in 1795. Another sister, Janet, married John Philp, who had founded Dolls Distillery.

Andrew Haig (1769-1824), the fifth son, seems to have remained at Kilbagie – in an article in The Morning Chronicle (February 1810), he is listed as 'of Clackmannan', and as one of the four leading distillers in Scotland [along with James Haig (Sunbury), James Stein (Kennetpans) and Spears, Mitchell & Co (Kirkaldy)].

The youngest brother, William (1771-1847) – after marrying his first cousin Janet Stein (daughter of John of Kennetpans) – and serving an apprenticeship under his cousin Robert Stein at Kincaple (which he ultimately took over) built Seggie Distillery at Guardbridge, not far from St. Andrews – now a large paper mill. He also seems to have taken over his brother John's Bonnington Distillery between 1821-26, when it passed to Haig Bros & Co (i.e. Thomas and Robert, his sons). William and Janet's grandson was Field Marshall Earl Haig.

These were the sons and daughters of John Haig of the Gartlands, the first generation of what would become a distilling dynasty. Pre-eminent in the second generation was another John Haig (1802-1878), third son of William Haig of Kincaple, who founded Cameron Bridge Distillery at Leven in Fife in 1824.

According to family tradition in 1822 (aged 20), John was riding with a servant along the road which runs through Windygates (a posting station for travellers going to Edinburgh from the north-east, before the days of rail) on his way back to Kincaple, when his attention was drawn to the old Cameron Mills on the River Leven. For two centuries this mill had enjoyed 'thirled' privileges (i.e. local tenants were obliged to have their corn ground there). John turned to the old retainer and said: "D'ye ken Sandy. There is money to be made here – aye from whisky".

A 'level-headed and genial man', by his middle age he was a JP and a Captain in the Leven Artillery Corps, and like his uncles and his cousin, Robert Stein, he was an innovator: he installed a Stein still within a year of its invention (1828), paying the Steins 1d per gallon royalty, to make 'malt aqua'.

The introduction of the more efficient Coffey still three years later led to a glut of spirits, and as early as the mid-1830s John Haig was trying to interest the Eastern Lowland distillers in a scheme to regulate prices. By the 1850s he was the leading spokesman for the Scottish distillers in their negotiations with Government and had many interviews with Prime Minister William Gladstone, influencing the latter's important Spirit Act 1860.

His concern about over-production and price wars was recognized by his fellow Lowland distillers, and in 1865 the Scotch Distillers Association was formed to divide up the market according to their production capacity, fix

As spokeman for the Scottish distillers John Haig often negotiated with the Prime Minister of the time, William Gladstone

I use the word 'perfection' advisedly. We have seen (above) that Robert Stein of Kilbagie invented a continuous still in 1827 – used successfully in his brother's distillery at Kirkliston, near Edinburgh, and at Wandsworth Distillery in London. Others worked on, and even patented, similar designs during the 1820s, but it fell to Aeneas Coffey to solve the problems inherent in these designs and come up with a still which would be widely adopted, and which remains in its essentials the kind of still used today for the distillation of grain whisky, rum, gin, vodka and neutral spirits.

Aeneas Coffey was born about 1780, probably in Dublin, where his father was the Engineer in Charge of Waterworks and later City Engineer. At the age of twenty, Aeneas joined the Excise Service, and nine

prices and conditions of sale. But output continued to climb out of control, and in 1877 the Distillers Company Limited (DCL) succeeded the SDA. This was a combination of six leading grain whisky distillers, which together controlled 75% of production. John Haig and his sons, Hugh Veitch Haig and William Henry Haig, were appointed directors of the new company, although John died the following year.

In time, the DCL would become the largest and most powerful of all Scotch whisky companies. Its successor, Diageo plc, remains so.

Aeneas Coffey – Perfector of the Continuous Still

The Forbes', the Steins and the Haigs were the leading commercial distillers of their times; it is appropriate now to consider the achievement on a man whose contribution to commercial distilling was revolutionary – Aeneas Coffey and the perfection of the continuous still.

The modern continuous stills of today, like this one at North British Grain Distillery, builds on Aeneas Coffey's principles

years later he was appointed Surveyor for Dublin City. He was active in suppressing illicit distilling in Donegal and on one occasion in 1810 was "beaten until he was supposed to be dead" when he and five soldiers under his command were "attacked by a great number of persons" while attempting to seize illicit stills.

In 1818 he was appointed Acting Inspector General of Excise in Ireland, an appointment that was confirmed the following year, and in 1821 he was supervising experiments at Carrickfergus Distillery to devise a prototype spirit safe, in order to prevent licensed distillers drawing off spirit, and thus avoiding duty, while still being able to measure its strength and temperature. This is the first record we have of Coffey's scientific ability.

Inexplicably, Coffey resigned his position as Inspector General in 1824 and reappears three years later as a landowner in Co. Kildare, and in 1828 as founder of 'Aeneas Coffey & Co' with 'Distillery Offices and Stores' at South King Street, Dublin. In his famous patent application of 1830 entitled 'Apparatus for Brewing and Distilling', Coffey is designated as 'of the Dock Distillery, Dublin, Distiller'. The patent was granted in March 1831.

The still which bears his name (also now known simply as the 'Patent Still') operated rapidly and continuously – unlike traditional pot stills, it did not have to be charged, distilled off and recharged in a batch process. Although expensive to install, it was comparatively cheap to operate and simple to control and maintain, and it produced spirits of high strength (over 90%Vol) very rapidly: a Coffey still could produce in a week what an average sized pot still could make in an entire distilling season.

Early versions were made from wood and cast iron and, since the latter reacted with acids in the wash, the resulting spirit was fit only for rectification into gin. By 1833 he had manufactured 'about seven' stills for Irish distillers, but it seems these were returned, on account of the horrid spirit they produced, and thereafter the Irish turned their backs on the Patent Still, proudly advertising their product as 'Pure Pot Still Whiskey', in spite of the fact that Coffey was now using copper and making clean, light, high strength, potable 'whiskey'.

Coffey and his family moved to London in 1835 and began manufacturing Patent Stills in Bromley. The first to acquire the new equipment was Andrew Philp of Grange Distillery, Alloa – a cousin of the Steins and Haigs – at least one of whom, Thomas Haig of Bonnington Distillery, Leith, (now trading as Booth, Haig & Co), soon followed suit. Sir Felix Booth, the renowned gin distiller, ordered an exceptionally large still. By 1850 thirteen Coffey stills were operating in Scotland.

Aeneas Coffey died in 1852 and was succeeded by his sons, who continued trading until 1874 when, owing to a downturn in the trade, the remaining son made the firm over to his foreman, John Dore. Recovery was not long to come, and by the time of the foundation of the Distillers Company Limited three years later, grain whisky distilling was almost entirely done in Coffey stills.

Today, all the grain whisky made in Scotland comes from Coffey stills, and although there are only six operating grain whisky distilleries (and one, Loch Lomond, which makes both malt and grain whisky), these produce considerably more spirit than that produced by the hundred operational malt whisky distilleries.

Charles MacLean has spent the past twenty-five years researching and writing about Scotch whisky and is one of the leading authorities.
He spends his time sharing his knowledge around the world, in articles and publications, lectures and tastings, and on TV and radio. His first book (Scotch Whisky) was published in 1993 and since then he has published nine books on the subject, his most recent being Charles MacLean´s Whiskypedia, published in 2009. He was elected a Keeper of the Quaich in 1992, in 1997 Malt Whisky won the Glenfiddich Award and in 2003 A Liquid History won 'Best Drinks Book' in the James Beard Awards.

Whisky
Innovators
in search of new expressions

*There are strict regulations that define
what a Scotch whisky is and isn´t. But within these boundaries,
a handful of creative people strive to give the whisky drinker new
experiences based on novel methods. Gavin D Smith has
met with a few of them - the Whisky Innovators.*

"Without tradition, art is a flock of sheep without a shepherd. Without innovation, it is a corpse." Sir Winston Churchill 1874-1965.

All the best consultants will tell you that the two key functions of business are marketing and innovation. It therefore follows that in order to compete successfully, companies operating within the Scotch whisky industry must practice the art of marketing in an effective manner and they must innovate. However, when it comes to innovation, they have to work within a stringent set of legally-binding rules, enshrined in The Scotch Whisky Act 1988 and policed by the Scotch Whisky Association (SWA).

A Scotch Whisky Association spokesman says that "The law setting out how Scotch whisky must be produced has not changed in its essentials since Scotch whisky was first defined in 1933. The definition serves to stop the reputation of Scotch whisky being taken advantage of by non-traditional products. For example, if there was no protective definition it might be possible to sell a whisky at only one year of age, or to use oak essences or other flavourings to create an artificial 'Scotch whisky.' Reputations take a long time to build, but can be destroyed very quickly if care is not taken to ensure the quality and consistency of the product."

Given the creative constraints within which Scotch whisky distillers must operate, the scope for product innovation seems somewhat limited. It is, of course, possible to 'tweak' the production regime in terms of yeast types, fermentation times, distillation speed and cut points in order to give a degree of character variation to the spirit, and greater knowledge of the chemistry of whisky-making has made such measures infinitely more quantifiable. However, the most obvious scope for innovation comes with the maturation process, and the practice of 'cask finishing,' in which whisky spends a final maturation period in a secondary cask which previously contained a different type of spirit or wine, has now become widespread.

Glenmorangie was the first distillery to offer its own bottlings of 'finished' whisky, initially from ex-port casks, and the brand has remained at the forefront of the process. However, the company has also been altogether more radical in terms of its 'wood policy.' The man behind much of the company's pioneering work with wood is Head of Distilling and Whisky Creation, *Dr Bill Lumsden*.

*Dr Bill Lumsden - Head of Distilling
and Whisky Creation at Glenmorangie*

The wood is air-seasoned before being used for casks at Glenmorangie

He declares that "My philosophy on wood is that it doesn't matter how good your raw material - your new spirit - is, if you don't fill it into good quality wood which is also sympathetic to the style of your whisky. I'm surprised by the number of distillers who still don't pay attention to that. I've spent much of the last ten years refining our wood policy, and no other company has gone into such detail and aimed to make the barrel-making process as good as it possibly can be."

Lumsden's attention to detail in this respect has led the company to purchase a tract of woodland in Missouri's Ozark mountain region, from where the timber for so-called 'designer casks' is sourced.

He says that "It is all about selecting slow-growth, 'tight-grained' wood. Despite assumptions to the contrary, 'tight-grained' actually means it has a more porous internal structure, so the spirit is more influenced. This type of wood, from the Ozarks, gives a sweeter, creamier flavour than casks made from oak sourced from other locations, and we've tried quite a few."

"Critically important is the fact that the wood is air-seasoned, and for a minimum of two years. It's very mature wood and breaks down the components that give bitterness and astringency. The barrels undergo a light char and a heavy, even toasting. The whole of the staves are fully toasted. This gives incredibly full flavour."

"The spirit matured in these casks is intended to be used as a component of Glenmorangie Original but I bottled some in its own right as Astar, following on from our earlier Artisan Cask release. For me, Astar is the most perfect style of Glenmorangie. The quintessence of the Glenmorangie style of spirit."

Innovation is enlightened evolution

Lumsden is far from being the only man in the Scotch whisky industry to take wood really seriously, and Compass Box entrepreneur *John Glaser* has even found himself in conflict with the Scotch Whisky Association because of his innovative interpretation of maturation practices.

"Not being a distiller, wood is the main tool I have to influence spirit character," explains Glaser, whose Spice Tree blended malt fell foul of the SWA's reading of the laws relating to Scotch whisky."

"With Spice Tree we took the highest quality cooperage oak in the world," Glaser says. "It's hardly ever used by the Scotch whisky industry. It's fine grained, air-seasoned French oak, carefully and heavily toasted, in flat stave form. We lined the insides of old casks with these staves, the aim being to complement distillery character with flavours from oak which ordinary barrels don't provide. It was a quality initiative. We weren't flavouring up old, worn out casks with Pedro Ximinez or something, as has been known to happen!"

"However, the SWA threatened to take us to court, and we couldn't afford to fight a case, so we dropped it. The SWA is more about the law than visionary thinking. When it comes to issues like wood innovation, or evolution, as I would probably call it, I don't think they've really thought it through. To me, innovation is enlightened evolution, though you can obviously take things too far away from the core values of the product."

Far from giving up on wood-related innovation, Glaser has modified his approach; releasing Oak Cross blended malt and Canto single cask blended malt.

"These have provided another way of using the same high quality French oak we employed in Spice Tree," he notes. "We couldn't have flat staves, so we used heavily toasted cask ends. Experimenting with different levels of toasting and using both French and American oak has led to Oak Cross and the Canto. Spice Tree is returning, with a similar flavour profile, but the process is different. We are using very heavily toasted oak heads."

On the wider subject of whisky innovation per se, Glaser declares that "During the last 30 or 40 years the Scotch whisky industry has been very good at creating a consistent product at lower and lower cost. Yeasts have been changed for efficiency, not character, and fermentation and distillation regimes have been altered, perhaps bringing in shorter fermentation times. Everything has been streamlined and there has been 'flavour creep.' There is less character and complexity.

"One of the most exciting developments for me is that someone like Henric Molin has set up a distillery on the Swedish island of Hven. He has a chemical engineering background and is a great whisky aficionado. He has brought these two things together and is working

Taking meticulous notes is crucial for John Glaser - owner of Compass Box Whisky

Photo: © Compass Box Whisky

to build more character into whisky again. Remember, you don't have to be in Scotland to make great whisky! I'm excited by small companies like Henric's, set up to make more complex and interesting whisky than most on the market, to create more compelling products."

Inspiration from beer brewing

Meanwhile, in Scotland, Bill Lumsden and the Glenmorangie team have been responsible for the creation of one of the most 'compelling products' in the world of Scotch whisky for many years. Not content with 'tweaking' production processes or using cask finishes, Lumsden has been truly radical in virtually every aspect of the creation of the Signet expression, launched in 2009.

Lumsden makes the bold claim that "Signet is probably the biggest product innovation apart from wood finishes in Scotch whisky for many years. I was looking for two things, really. Firstly, something that was genuinely innovative, and secondly, when I came to think more about what sort of Glenmorangie I wanted to make, I had something altogether deeper and richer in mind, and something that would work well on ice."

When asked about the development schedule for Signet, Lumsden chuckles and says "In effect, the timescale for creating Signet was 25 years! At least, it had its origins about 25 years ago when I was studying for my PhD and I became interested in how different styles of beer were made using different types of malt. I was also a gourmet coffee fan and I was interested in the way various roasting regimes brought out a variety of flavours. I thought then that it would be interesting to apply that to malt used for whisky-making."

"Chocolate malt was available, and we distilled a batch of spirit using chocolate malt when I was Glenmorangie distillery manager in 1995. There was no 'master plan' to create Signet, but I did want to market a product at some point. We subsequently made sporadic batches every year or two, and are now doing some every year. We really developed the plan for Signet two or three years ago."

"On its own, the whisky made with chocolate malt was too full-on, too spicy and not refined enough. As it is, you can definitely taste the mocha in Signet, and whisky distilled from chocolate malt only makes up a part of the total.

"We opted for the idea of an 'assemblage' of whiskies, to borrow a term from the Champagne industry. We looked at different ages of whiskies matured in different cask types. We embraced Sherry, new charred oak, wine and some 'Astar-spec' casks. We selected casks by trial and error. From 2006 to 2008 we tried lots of different specs. Ultimately, the whisky distilled from chocolate malt makes up around 30 per cent of the recipe at present, but that will probably change from batch to batch."

"It was a huge sense of relief when Signet was finally bottled. There were lots of variables and getting it right did present a real challenge. We agonised over the recipe for years. People are wowed by the product and we plan to make the message of what exactly it is clearer in the future. It's been very challenging and satisfying – in effect it's my magnum opus!"

Glenmorangie has not been alone in embracing non-traditional distilling malts to make whisky, however, with Balvenie producing a 14-year-old Roasted Malt expression in 2006. This was the first single malt Scotch whisky to be made using a batch of dark, roasted malted barley, more commonly employed in the production of stout. In the summer of 1992, a batch of barley was germinated over 24 hours (as opposed to the usual five days) before being kiln dried. It was then heated in a roasting drum at a temperature of 200°C and mixed with traditional malted barley. The barley was completely roasted to between 1600 and 1800 European Brewing Colour (EBC) units, while 'normal' malted barley only reaches around 30 EBCs.

According to *David Stewart*, the Balvenie 'Malt Master,' "We are always looking at ways to offer consumers other taste sensations with Balvenie and we thought that using roasted malt at the start of the process might just give us something interesting. We didn't quite know at that stage how it would alter the flavour."

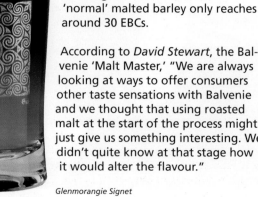

Glenmorangie Signet

Master Blender David Stewart - 45 years in the business and still an innovator

"We also tried other malt types but we thought the roasted malt really enhanced the flavours of Balvenie. It gave the whisky an additional dimension, with an increased oaky effect and hints of smoke from the roasted malt. We think that it is still very much Balvenie, with the usual vanilla fruitiness and honey, but with this added complexity."

Ireland's Bushmills distillery in County Antrim has also experimented with malt types, and Bushmills 1608 is described by the brand's owners Diageo as "…a unique blend of tradition and innovation."

The limited edition whiskey is made from crystal malt, so named because of the crystallised appearance the barley corns adopt when lightly toasted before the commencement of the distilling process. According to a Diageo spokesperson, "Crystal malt lends a sweet, toffee-like smoothness to the final spirit. The result is a whiskey with an alluring sweet aroma, mouth-filling creamy notes and a uniquely smooth finish."

Acknowledging the difficulty of being truly innovative within the legal confines of what constitutes Scotch – or Irish – whisk(e)y, Bill Lumsden says that "Now Signet has been developed I'm under pressure to follow it up with something else! I am currently working on short, medium and long-term projects, and in the long term these will focus on, shall we say,

aspects of primary production. But most of our innovations will inevitably be with maturation, as it's the easiest way of bringing new products to market."

"I have tried experimenting with different barley types, using winter barley and spring barley, but the results were fairly inconclusive. I would like to see a barley variety developed specifically to give the optimum fruity and creamy characteristics to Glenmorangie spirit."

Innovation by regression

Other distillers too have worked with 'alternative' barley varieties include Benromach and Bruichladdich, with the former launching its new 'Origins' series in 2008 with a release of 1999 spirit distilled using Golden Promise barley. This is effectively 'innovation by regression,' as Golden Promise was the distiller's barley of choice for many years, but the variety has now been abandoned by most distillers in favour of more modern and higher yielding barley types.

Keith Cruickshank, Benromach distillery manager, explains the reasoning behind this return to Golden Promise. "At Benromach we believe that making single malt whisky is a little like creating a jigsaw. Like each part of a jigsaw, each element of the whisky making process plays an important part in the overall

Keith Cruickshank, the manager of a highly innovative distillery, Benromach

Photo: © Gordon & MacPhail

picture. We feel that every stage plays an important part in the quality of the final product. Launching the Benromach Origins brand allows us to highlight how each part affects the final product."

Across on Islay, *Mark Reynier* and his Bruichladdich team are passionate innovators, and barley varieties have come under close scrutiny from Reynier and Bruichladdich's master distiller *Jim McEwan*. As at Benromach, they have indulged in 'innovation by regression,' making whisky from the primitive, six-row barley variety known as bere, once one of the staple grain crops in much of the Highlands and islands. Reynier also points out that "Fifty per cent of the barley we use is now organically grown, on the mainland; that's around 1,800 tonnes per year."

Benromach too has gone down the organic route, and is the first single malt whisky to be fully certified by the Soil Association. According to *Ian Chapman* of Benromach's parent company Gordon & MacPhail, "We launched Benromach Organic in 2006, and before we started producing it we tried to source organic Sherry or wine casks to mature it in. However, we couldn't find any, so we took the decision

to use Missouri virgin oak. Obviously using new oak casks plays a significant part in the character of the matured whisky."

Back with Bruichladdich, Mark Reynier notes that "Around half of the barley we use is now grown on Islay, and by persuading farmers on the island to grow it for us we've brought them closer to the community and helped emphasise community values. There's an excitement at harvest time, and this year sees the first bottling of single farm, single variety Bruichladdich."

Bruichladdich has also practiced triple and even quadruple distillation in recent years, while "The 'assembly' of our bottlings is also innovative," according to Reynier. "What you may call the multi-vintage concept. The selection and assembly rely absolutely on human skills, as every cask is different. Doing this gives us sufficient continuity to be able to provide volume so we can distribute all over the world."

Multi-vintages are marketed as 'Rocks,' 'Waves' and 'Peat,' and Reynier is fond of quoting Remi Krug, of Champagne fame, who declared "With a single vintage, it is God who decides on the quality. But with a multi-vintage, I am God."

One of the latest innovations from Bruichladdich is the 'Micro-provenance' range, and Mark Reynier declares that "The big distillers say that it doesn't matter where you mature whisky, it makes no difference to the spirit character. We beg to differ. We're not just talking about proximity to the sea or something like that, but proximity within the warehouse to windows, roof or ground."

"Micro-provenance is a range of single cask bottlings selected to show the difference between one variable – for example, a barrel from the very top and a barrel from the very bottom of a warehouse. We select for comparison casks that are as similar as possible in every way, except for that one aspect. Some are available in pairs. It illustrates that there really can be a hell of a difference in the whisky, depending on where exactly it is matured."

Photo: © Bruichladdich

Mark Reynier, CEO of Bruichladdich distillery, where innovation is a cornerstone

The knowledge that casks mature differently within the same warehouse is not, of course, new, but what is innovative in the Bruichladdich approach is the deliberate bottling of whisky to demonstrate and emphasise the phenomenon.

New make is the new deal

At the opposite end of the whisky maturation 'time line,' a recent innovation has been the willingness of a number of small-scale distillers to offer 'new make' spirit to consumers.

The trend was started by the Islay distillery of Kilchoman, and serves the dual purposes of bringing in revenue before the spirit is old enough to sell legally as 'Scotch whisky' and raising the distillery profile ahead of mature whisky sales.

Subsequently, the Perthshire distillery of Tullibardine began to market Pure Pot Spirit in 2009, with director *Douglas Ross* noting that "People on tours of the distillery have the option of sampling 'new make' spirit, and they often want to buy it, so we have responded to that demand."

The same dynamic prevails in the southern hemisphere, with Lark Distillery in Hobart, Tasmania selling new make under the 'Lark

Pure Malt' banner. Meanwhile, St George's distillery in Norfolk, England, offers both peated and non-peated new make spirit for sale, but has gone a stage further, and additionally sells its spirit as 'work in progress' after short periods of maturation. Similarly, the Japanese distillery of Chichibu, which came on stream in spring 2008, offers what it terms 'Chichibu Newborn.' This is also spirit that has spent a very brief period in wood.

However, the most innovative 'new make' venture has been undertaken by Glenglassaugh distillery at Portsoy on the Moray Firth coast of Scotland. Glenglassaugh reopened in 2008,

The Spirit Drink That Dare Not Speak Its Name from Glenglassaugh

Roseisle Distillery by night

after being silent since 1986, and the distillery is now selling 'The Spirit Drink That Dare Not Speak its Name.' This is a tongue-in-cheek reference to legislation that forbids a Scotch whisky distiller from using the name of his distillery in the product title unless the spirit is legally-defined Scotch whisky.

Glenglassaugh's marketing consultant *Ian Buxton* says that "This is not just new make, this is single mash new make spirit. We obviously can't offer single cask bottlings of the whisky we are distilling, so we thought that at the opposite end of the process spectrum to the cask of mature spirit is the business of mashing. Accordingly, this bottling is the result of one single mash. We also filled some new make into Californian red wine casks for six months, and we have bottled that as The Spirit Drink that Blushes to Speak its Name!"

The importance of being green

On a more serious note, one area in which Scotch whisky innovation is currently at its most fruitful is in respect of environmental responsibility. From an image-related viewpoint, distillers have to be seen to be 'green,' and there can also be long term financial benefits

Mike Jappy, Project Director for Roseisle

from embracing environmental considerations. As Scotch whisky's largest player, Diageo leads the way in high-profile green initiatives, and the company announced in August 2008 that it was to spend some £65 million developing a bio-energy facility at its Cameronbridge grain distillery in Fife.

According to a Diageo spokesperson, "The facility will for the first time integrate sustainable technologies – including anaerobic digestion and biomass conversion – on a commercial scale. It is set to reduce annual CO_2 emissions at the site by approximately 56,000 tonnes, equivalent to taking 44,000 family cars off the road."

Diageo has invested in similar state-of-the-art technology at its vast, £40 million Roseisle malt whisky distillery on the Moray Firth coast, which came on stream during 2009. Project Director *Mike Jappy* declares that "Our aim was to make this plant as carbon-neutral and water-neutral as we could. We already have malted barley on site at our adjacent maltings, which immediately takes lots of road miles out of the equation. We have quantities of hot water from the distillery condensers, and the maltings can receive waste heat and utilise it in the barley dryer and the kilns."

A biomass burner helps the distillery achieve its goal of being as fossil fuel-neutral as possible, and Jappy notes that "Additionally, there is a water reclamation plant which takes pot ale and spent lees and puts them through a three-stage process, along with water from steeps in the maltings. At the end of the process you have clean water which goes back into the maltings for steeping. Methane is created during the first stage of the water reclamation process, which provides another source of energy for the distillery. This, plus the burning of draff in the biomass plant, offsets some 63/66 per cent of our requirement for steam which would otherwise require burning oil or using gas."

Meanwhile, most other Scottish distillers have also been putting in place their own measures to advance environmental responsibility. *David Hume* of William Grant & Sons Ltd says of the company's Girvan distilling and blending complex in Ayrshire that "The site is at the forefront of the company's renewable energy development. William Grant & Sons continues to invest significantly in energy management and reduction across its distillation operations, and has commenced commissioning its most significant project to date with two on-site anaerobic reactors."

However, arguably the most interesting environmental-related Scotch whisky innovation concerns a project run by scientists at Aberdeen University. They have taken distillery residue and used it to develop a ground-breaking method of cleaning up contaminated land and polluted water. Secrecy currently surrounds DRAM (Device for the Remediation and Attenuation of Multiple Pollutants) as the commercial possibilities for this development are obviously highly significant.

Innovative failures

Inevitably, anyone innovating within the Scotch whisky industry will have their share of failures as well as successes, and Bill Lumsden admits that "We have had a couple of Glenmorangies that didn't see the light of day. One was matured in normal oak barrels for 10 years then filled into Brazilian cherry wood."

"The legislation says that Scotch whisky must be matured in oak for a minimum of three years, so we weren't breaking any rules and could have argued if the SWA had objected. However, it didn't come to that because it tasted like furniture polish and marzipan! It was a salutary lesson on why oak is used. It does give good flavours. I've also used other ex-wine barrels at times and just didn't like the result."

Some innovative products that did get past 'quality control' and were intended to help boosts sales of Scotch whisky among younger and 'non-traditional' whisky drinkers have enjoyed only comparatively short life spans.

These included the now highly collectable Loch Dhu 'black whisky,' a 10-year-old Mannochmore Speyside single malt, matured in double-charred casks. Introduced by United Distillers in 1996, Loch Dhu did at least survive for slightly longer than its stable mate Red Devil, a concoction of 8-year-old Bell's whisky, red chilli peppers and other spices. Launched at the same time as Loch Dhu, it was discontinued just two years later.

Undeterred, by these failures, a decade later, United Distillers' successor company Diageo introduced J&B -6°C, an almost clear blended whisky, chill-filtered to minus six degrees celsius. It failed to woo its target market of younger white spirits drinkers and was abandoned after a briefer existence than Red Devil.

Meanwhile, The Edrington Group bravely entered the 'youth market' fray in 2008 with The Snow Grouse. Presented in a frosted-effect bottle, redolent of Scandinavian premium vodka, it is a blended grain whisky, which has undergone a process described by its producers as 'Smoothchill filtered.'

So what does the future hold for innovation within the Scotch whisky industry?

It seems certain that environmental concerns will continue to drive developments in terms of energy creation and use, while potentially cost-cutting measures will always prove attractive to producers.

As one anonymous insider puts it, "There are undoubtedly a lot of things going on behind the scenes which are designed with economics in mind. How to make whisky quicker and cheaper. It's not a qualitative thing. I'm talking about stuff like high density fermentation. Using twice the yeast theoretically halves the fermentation time, cutting costs and improving productivity and overall output."

There are even dark murmurings of possible experiments involving vast, stainless steel vats filled with spirit, to which oak essence or oak chips are added, reducing cost by removing the need for casks. Oak essence, a distillate of oak, has long been used in the Cognac business, and oak chips are common in the wine industry, so perhaps such experimentation is not so far-fetched after all.

And what seems to be the most far-fetched innovation possible is actually being trialled by Diageo right now.

One of the 'Holy Grails' for distillers is to find a way of reducing spirit loss by evaporation – the so called 'angels' share.' In the summer of 2008, Diageo announced that it had been conducting experiments which involved wrapping some casks in 'cling film' over a five-year period.

Obviously it is always a matter of concern that spirit quality may be sacrificed in the name of profit, but apparently,

THE
SNOW
GROUSE
SMOOTH CHILL FILTERED
BLENDED GRAIN
SCOTCH WHISKY

The newest member of the Famous Grouse family

enveloping a cask in cling film does not have a negative effect on the matured character of its contents, and can save up to 50 litres of spirit that would otherwise have evaporated over a period of 10 years. It has been estimated that the company could save at least £1 million per annum just by wrapping 20,000 barrels of single malt in cling film.

"Over a number of years the industry has studied the way whisky matures in oak casks," says a Diageo spokesperson. "This has included the evaporation loss known as the 'angel's share'. As a custodian of the rich heritage of our industry, Diageo fully recognises the importance of understanding the complex maturation process and its key role in the production of high-quality Scotch whisky.

"We are therefore continuously developing our knowledge of maturation and, in so doing, conduct a wide range of small-scale trials, of which this is one. At this stage the technologies under trial in this long-term project are not proven and we are continuing our research into this very interesting area."

Innovation is the life blood of competitive business and standing still is rarely an option. Nevertheless, in the perpetual rush to move 'onwards and upwards' perhaps we should also be mindful of the words of iconic French fashion designer Coco Chanel: "Innovation! One cannot be forever innovating. I want to create classics."

Gavin D Smith is one of Scotland's leading whisky writers and Contributing Editor to www.whisky-pages.com He hosts whisky presentations and tastings and produces feature material for a wide range of publications, including Whisky Magazine, The Malt Advocate *and* Whisky Etc. *He is the author of more than 20 books, including* Whisky, Wit & Wisdom, The A-Z of Whisky, Worts, Worms & Washbacks, The Secret Still, The Whisky Men, Ardbeg: A Peaty Provenance *and* Goodness Nose *(with Richard Paterson). Most recently he has collaborated with Dominic Roscrow to produce a new edition of the iconic title* Michael Jackson's Malt Whisky Companion. *He is a Keeper of the Quaich and lives on the Fife coast in Scotland.*

Innovation does not mean abandoning traditions

Gone but not forgotten

*The fire under the stills may have gone out
but passion still burns intensely in the heart of many whisky lovers.
David Stirk presents three distilleries that continue
to fascinate long after they were closed.*

Rosebank 25 year old - released in 2007

Port Ellen 30 year old - released in 2009

Brora 30 year old - released in 2009

Over the centuries, since distilling began in an industrial manner in Scotland, hundreds of distilleries have come and gone (around 34 in Campbeltown alone). It is possible today to purchase whisky from approximately 32 of these lost distilleries (depending upon how much you would like to spend). In this article I am going to look at three distilleries that have obtained cult status; Brora, Port Ellen and Rosebank.
A quartet of knowledgeable and experienced whisky aficionados help me out:

Dr Nicholas Morgan (DM)
Scotch Knowledge and
Heritage Manager, Diageo

Serge Valentin (SV)
Malt Maniac
www.whiskyfun.com

Carsten Ehrlich (CE)
Co-founder Limburg Whisky
Fair & Mara Malt Rarities

Bert Bruyneel (BB)
Malt Maniac
www.weedram.be

Port Ellen, UDV (Diageo)
Opened: 1825   Closed: 1983
Expect to pay in excess of £100 for any bottle of Port Ellen regardless of age (and up to £1,000 for some of the rare ones).

Mention the words 'Port' and 'Ellen' in the same breath near a whisky drinker and it is likely someone will start to lament its loss. Being located on Islay is the first plus for Port Ellen; but for many distillery-seekers it is the first Islay distillery they see due to its location in the main port in the town of the same name. Countless hearts have sank at finding out that the remaining pagodas are purely for show and the huge bluey-grey building behind is just a maltings (albeit an important one).

SV: " ...I was moving to glance at the old buildings through the slightly opaque windows... we also walked around the premises before they were demolished, looking for ghosts (or forgotten casks and bottles)."

The decision to close Port Ellen was purely a tactical one. Lagavulin was the home of the White Horse blend (still going strong in the early 80s) and Caol Ila had only been reopened after a complete rebuild in the late 60s. Due to the recession, the abundant supply of whisky (at the time referred to as the 'Whisky Loch') and the need to cut costs, the Distillers Company Limited had to close one of their three Islay whiskies. At the time, Port Ellen's whisky was not in the same class as Lagavulin's or Caol Ila's (remember, we are not talking about whiskies destined to be bottled as single malts) and as **DM** states;

"Some people also recall that there were issues around the availability of adequate quantities of process water at Port Ellen, given the competing demands of the Maltings."

Thus, in May 1983 (along with a great number of other distilleries), Port Ellen was mothballed never to distil again.

Port Ellen is almost beyond cult status – it is likely in one hundred years whisky drinkers will be discussing it as if it were an old departed friend whilst, perhaps, more important distilleries have come and gone.
The main reason for this affinity is that there are still a fair few bottlings of Port Ellen circulating (and emerging) meaning that other distillates from Islay such as Malt Mill (good luck trying to find one of those) are really only in the minds of those that can remember the actual distillery – and they are increasingly few and far between.

What's interesting with Port Ellen is how long it seems to have been at the forefront of Islay malt lovers.

BB: "One of my favourites was a Signatory bottling from 1976 bottled in 1999... I had heard and read a lot about the distillery; it was legendary even back then."

Photo: Diageo

When Port Ellen closed in 1983 it had four stills and a production capacity of 800,000 litres per year

SV: "There were numerous bottlings by Gordon & MacPhail in the 80s which went unnoticed when first bottled but are much sought after these days. The first bottlings that really brought Port Ellen to everyone's attention were the two Rare Malts bottlings (both from 1972) from UDV; two extremely powerful malts that took no prisoners."

And it seems that Port Ellen whisky seems to have been running out of stock forever.

CE: "Everyone keeps talking about Port Ellen and how long it might take until stocks dry out and prices sky rocket. For a while there was plenty of Port Ellen available from independent bottlers such as Cadenhead's, Signatory and Gordon & MacPhail and there are still several bottlings available from Douglas Laing, in particular several heavily sherried expressions."

SV: "Many said a few years ago that the stocks of Port Ellen were exhausted, which wasn't exactly the case since clearly so many casks have been bottled over the last five years."

Brora Distillery, UDV (Diageo)
Opened: 1825   Closed: 1983
It is still possible to find Brora's around £70 although there aren't many at this price. Expect to pay around £100 - £350 depending upon age and rarity of the bottle.

Originally called Clynelish, the name was permanently changed in 1969 when it was deemed that two distilleries could not share a name; a new Clynelish Distillery was built a couple of hundred metres from the old one. Thus any whisky called Clynelish made before 1968/69 was in fact made at the Brora Distillery.

It is ironic that the new Clynelish was built due to the whisky boom of the 1960s (several other distilleries such as Caol Ila and Craigellachie were also re-built at this time to increase production) and yet just over a decade later the recession of the 80s caused the closure of the original distillery. At the time it was quite an easy decision to make; "do we close the old

Most of the equipment is still in place at Brora and the buildings have been listed and saved for posterity

inefficient plant or the new, rather modern, expensive and efficient one?"

DM: "...if you exclude the now celebrated heavily-peated Brora, the spirit character produced by the old distillery was regarded by the blenders to be more than adequately replaced by that from the new [Clynelish Distillery]."

There are other peaty whiskies made on the mainland (like Ardmore, Glenisla made at Glen Keith and Longrow etc) but Brora seems to be the one that can sit closest to an Islay style malt although geographically it is as far removed from Islay as it is almost possible to be.

CE: "Brora was always heavier and more oily in style than the new Clynelish, and although the style seemed much lighter in the 70s, and again much heavier in its final years it was always considered the Islay of the Highlands."

SV: "Brora hasn't got the fame like Port Ellen and malt drinkers took a little while longer to realise its ultra-high quality. Less 'sexy' than Port Ellen and not on Islay, but actually an Islay whisky since it was the first attempt by some distillers to replicate the Islay style of whisky on Mainland Scotland."

Although UDV released no less than 13 Brora's as part of the Rare Malts Series it is the much pricier Special Releases at 30 years of age that have really revved up the cult status of the whisky. These releases have shown an enormous depth to the whisky and created a strong following.

BB: "My most memorable Brora is without doubt the Brora 30yo bottled by Diageo in 2004 (56.6%)"

CE: "There have been great bottlings from Diageo (from 2002-2007, all more or less of exceptional quality). The new 25yo Special Release still needs to find its way onto collectors shelves and drinkers hearts."

SV: "No other malt whisky has a profile like Brora; very old school that I enjoy so much. Sometimes, the new Clynelish comes close though."

Rosebank Distillery, UDV (Diageo)

Opened: 1840   Closed: 1993

There are plenty of bottlings of Rosebank for the time being. Expect to pay £40-£50 from the more commonly available independent bottlers and for the Flora & Fauna bottling that is still available. The older expressions and rare ones from the 60s and 70s etc will set you back £150-£450.

Other than the region of Campbeltown, no region has been more affected by distillery closures than the Lowlands. Several grain distilleries that were closed down in the Lowlands also housed pot still for malt whisky production; the likes of Glen Flagler (Moffat Distillery) and Inverleven (Dumbarton Distillery). Ladyburn Distillery (1966-1975) was housed within Girvan Grain Distillery and Kinclaith Distillery (1958-1975) was housed within Strathclyde Grain Distillery, whilst both grain distilleries are still in the production neither produce malt whisky. Rosebank was not situated in a grain distillery and its demise was not due to a recession, over production, or the fact that the distillery was not as attractive as Glenkinchie (also owned by UDV), or even that there was something wrong with the spirit made there:

DM: "Delightful though Rosebank's spirit character was, our blenders were convinced that the absence of this distillery would have no impact on our ability to maintain the character and quality of our blended Scotch whiskies."

CE: "Rosebank never fit into the cliché of Lowland whiskies; it wasn't light mellow or to be enjoyed particularly young. It was instead sometimes smoky, aged well and appeared more like a Highland whisky than the typical Lowlander."

Rosebank appears to have gained a lot of popularity not just because of the quality of the whisky but because it was from the Lowland's and for a time, there was precious little whisky being bottled as a Lowland single malt whisky. Rosebank though, was advertised quite heavily from the 60s onwards although when UDV were creating their Six Classics, Glenkinchie, an even more robust malt than Rosebank, was chosen to represent the Lowlands;

DM: "The issue at Rosebank related to the feasibility of continuing to operate at the required scale on a site where compliance issues were becoming increasingly onerous. This in particular involved the disposal of effluent and other by-products. There were also compliance and Health & Safety issues relating to the number of traffic movements on and around a very constricted site with limited access for large vehicles."

Sometimes, floral, sometimes citrusy but nearly always an olfactory delight it is no wonder that it was considered to be the 'Queen of the Lowlands'.

SV: "Do I miss Rosebank? Hard to say. The revived Bladnoch Distillery makes a spirit that can be wonderfully citrusy as was Rosebank's and it is still quite easy to find Rosebank bottlings here and there."

BB: "My most memorable Rosebank was 1981 bottling in the Rare Malts (UDV) Series. At the time people were quite dismissive of Lowland whisky but on blind tasting the Rosebank would invariably sweep all against it aside."

CE: "For me the 20yo 57% bottling from the Distillers Agency was as close to perfection as you can get although when tasted blind no-one believes it is from the Lowlands."

These are, arguably, the three most unforgettable lost distilleries in living memories. Sadly there is little chance of any of them being revived.

Port Ellen only has a few remnants of its distilling days left; the pagodas from its silent kilns being the most stark reminder.

Brora is riddled with health and safety issues and is unlikely to be sold for distilling purposes – would Diageo really want competition on its doorstep.

As for Rosebank, its warehouses have been converted into a restaurant and the main buildings have been sold to the British Waterways Board – there are allegedly still plans to turn it into flats as was the fate of another lost Lowland Distillery St Magdalene in Linlithgow.

But do we lament their loss too much? Afterall there has never been a time in the history of the world when more malt whisky was available. Independent bottlers release expression after expression of tantalising whiskies from closed and little-heard of distilleries when just a couple of decades ago you would be hard pressed to walk into a decent retailer and leave with more than half a dozen malt whiskies whereas to try that today you would need to have won a large lottery.

The distillation equipment was in place at Rosebank until Christmas 2008 when copper thieves removed most of it

Photo: Diageo

So would we bring the distilleries back to life given the chance?

BB: "I would bring back Rosebank, without a doubt. I only really miss Rosebank out of the three. I've been lucky enough to try lots of peaty whisky but to find a Lowlander that kind of signature and quality is quite rare."

SV: "I would revive Brora, if I could remove all of the Health & Safety issues."

CE: "Brora should never have been closed, from a malt whisky drinker's perspective – although it has to be said that the new Clynelish consistently makes high quality spirit with some stellar bottlings from the early 70s. It is very difficult for me to choose which of the three I would revive as each had periods of production that were outstanding;
Port Ellen from '69 – '74, Brora from '65 – '76 and Rosebank from '65 – '76."

The final word comes from Dr Morgan:
"It is ironic that these whiskies, which were not especially highly regarded by experts 20 or 30 years ago have now obtained such a cult status among whisky enthusiasts and collectors. I might even speculate that, had the distilleries remained open, interest in them would have been relatively low."
"As it is, I am delighted that we are still

able to continue to fuel the passion of enthusiasts and collectors for these wonderful old whiskies, if only on a small scale."
"Although we never disclose details of our stock position, I can confirm that we have limited supplies of Port Ellen, Brora and Rosebank in our inventory. Competition for these stocks between our blenders developing super-premium products and the single malts team is very intense. But we will continue to bottle small quantities of Brora and Port Ellen as stocks allow, and we may also see more very limited Rosebank bottlings in the future."

David Stirk started hosting tastings over a decade ago before working for Whisky Magazine and writing 'The Malt Whisky Guide' and 'The Distilleries of Campbeltown'. He has spent time working in several distilleries and travelling the world as a Brand Ambassador for Wm Cadenhead Ltd. He nows runs his own whisky company www.creativewhisky.co.uk and is co-owner of The Chester Whisky & Liqueur Co Ltd www.chesterwhisky.com. David has contributed to each edition of The Malt Whisky Yearbook.

Peated Malts

not just a smoky whisky

*For many people, a peated dram
brings all the joy they are looking for in a whisky.
But within that segment of single malt Scotch, the variations
are huge. To find out why that is, Ian Wisniewski
had to dig down deep to a molecular level.*

Choice is a wonderful thing, and with a wider range of malts available than ever before, there are various ways of dividing up the category: regionalism, the style (special finishes, single barrel, organic, etc), or the age statement, with a more practical approach being affordable and unaffordable malts, depending on individual budget. But for some whisky fans the category divides into two essential options. There are peated malts, and there are unpeated malts.

"If you look at markets around the world there's a strong following for peated malts in the US, UK, Scandinavia, France and Germany, but also significant spikes of interest in the Far Eastern markets like Taiwan. And an awful lot of people from their late 20s - early 30s are coming straight into this sector, which is evident in the people who come to whisky fairs, and who visit Ardbeg distillery," says Hamish Torrie of The Glenmorangie Company.

Beyond flavour delivery, peated malts also offer additional details for the technically-minded to explore, whether it's the origin and composition of the peat, how different peating levels are achieved, and how the phenolic level, as well as individual phenolic compounds, are influenced by the production process and maturation.

With the majority of malted barley supplied by commercial maltsters, floor maltings are limited to several distilleries, including The Balvenie, Bowmore, Highland Park, Laphroaig and Springbank. The peating level quoted, referring to malt at the beginning of the production process, is expressed in terms of 'ppm' (parts per million).

Colourimetry is the longest established method for measuring the peating level, although this method is unable to measure individual phenolic compounds.

"Most maltsters do this in their own lab, which involves steam stripping the phenolic compounds from the malt. When this condenses you have a liquid that can be analysed by adding a chemical that reacts with the phenolics. It's a colour reaction, and the higher the phenolic level the darker the colour. In the lab we take the main compounds that are found in peated malts, and make up standard solutions of 10, 15, 20 ppm etc, and do tests," says Mark Kinsman of Baird's Malt.

Two other methods are HPLC (High Performance Liquid Chromatography) and SPME (Solid Phase Micro Extraction), which both re-quire more sophisticated equipment in order to measure individual phenolic compounds that have been extracted from the malt, in addition to the total peating level. Both methods are based on the principle that different phenolic compounds (either in a liquid or gas phase) move through a column at different speeds, which enables the individual levels to be calculated.

While peating levels can be accurately measured, peating malt to a particular specification on a consistent basis is altogether more challenging.

"The peating level can vary by 5-10% from batch to batch, we try to maintain the same peating regime for each batch, differences occur when individual operators tend the peat fire. The difference in phenolic content is mainly due to the peat flaming rather than creating peat reek," says Stuart Robertson of Springbank distillery.

Different phenolic characteristics

Whether malt at higher and lower peating levels also includes different phenolic characteristics, rather than just being a more intense, or less intense version of each other, is another consideration.

"I personally believe there would be slightly different characteristics coming across at 40 ppm compared to 80 ppm. The way we pro-

Photo: © Glenmorangie Co.

Hamish Torrie - Ardbeg Brand Director

Burning peat at Laphroaig

duce whisky for Ardbeg 10 year old and Supernova is the same, but the range of flavour characteristics isn't the same," says Dr Bill Lumsden of The Glenmorangie Company.

One way of maintaining precise peating levels is to blend different batches of malt. "We can blend malt with batches of say 30, 40 or 50 ppm, and work out how much is needed to make a batch of malt at 35 ppm, then we can check the level in the lab," says Mark Kinsman.

Meanwhile, the peating level may also include a contribution from the malt, as even unpeated malt can contain 'background' phenolics.

"Unpeated malt can have background phenolics at around 0.6-0.8 ppm. Phenolics may be present in very small quantities when measured scientifically, but can also have a disproportionate effect when you nose it," adds Mark Kinsman.

Whether, and to what extent, individual barley varieties can influence the character of new make spirit has long been (and continues to be) debated, with opinions varying significantly depending on who you ask. But another aspect of this issue is whether the barley variety can have any influence on peating levels.

"Smaller varieties take on more phenolic compounds compared to larger varieties. Locally-grown optic seeds are generally smaller than East coast grown barley and take on more phenolic character in comparison. The smaller the corn the greater the phenolic content," says Stuart Robertson.

Peat from different regions of Scotland, and even from different parts of the same peat bog, can certainly have varying characteristics. But whether these differences can influence the character of the new make spirit is the real question. However, trying to answer this question means considering additional factors, and not just the composition of the peat.

"Peat from different areas does have a different make-up, but how it's been cut, how long it's been lying, the moisture level, and how you burn the peat are also key factors," says Mark Kinsman.

Stuart Robertson adds, "If you change the source of the peat I think there'd be a slight

The kiln at Springbank

Photo: © Glenmorangie Co.

Mickey Heads, Distillery Manager of Ardbeg

moisture of the malt. A vast range of phenols are absorbed from 40-20% moisture, the first hours are about drying off moisture from the surface of the grain and replacing it by peat smoke," says Russell Anderson of Highland Park.

A typical cut off point for peating is when the moisture level of the malt reaches around 20 -18 -16%. Although peat smoke is essentially absorbed by the husk, the interior of the malt is not exempt from the process. "Smoke also gets into the embryo as the rootlets act like a conduit," says Stuart Robertson.

Once the peating stage is concluded, the malt is dried further (using heat rather than smoke). Drying is a vital stage, in order to avoid the risk of pre-germination during storage, and a consequent reduction in the yield of alcohol.

"Longrow malt is peated heavily to create loads of peat reek until the corns contain approximately 16% moisture, we then gene-rate heat to get the moisture down to 4% for storage, that's the curing stage, and you get different flavour compounds in the malt, sugars are encapsulated by the drying so you're creating a flavour profile if you like. Curing also changes the way the malt is broken down by hot water in the mash tun," says Stuart Robertson.

Commercial maltsters have varying opportuni-ties to conduct the process compared to floor maltings, and also compared to each other.

"Different maltsters have different methods

difference but not enough to register it in the new make spirit, as the biggest influence is the way you run your stills."

Nevertheless, peat can contribute specific cha-racteristics to the new make spirit. "The peat we use is cut here on Islay near the beach, we've got more of a moss peat with more heather and elements of seaweed. I think seaside peat is more intense, and I think the sea salt character comes from the peat," says Mickey Heads of Ardbeg distillery.

How peat smoke is absorbed

Achieving different peating levels is in one sense a straightforward formula: using larger amounts of peat over a longer period produces a higher peating level. However, that's just one aspect of a more complicated equation, with the moisture level of the malt another vital consideration.

"The green malt has a moisture level of 40-45% at the start of the kilning process, al-though some steam is also produced from the peat, so you can slightly increase the surface

Photo: © The Edrington Group

Russel Anderson, Distillery Manager of Highland Park

of peating, we can peat within the kiln cycle if we wish, we can also extend the peating because we don't have to remove the malt as each vessel is a Steeping Germination Kilning vessel. Peating malt to 2-5 ppm can take up to 5-6 hours of actual peating time, 10-15 ppm can take 12-15 hours, 50 ppm can take 48 hours peating time," says Mark Kinsman.

While various stages of the production process result in the peating level, and the range of phenolic characteristics being reduced, this doesn't apply to the first stage of production, milling.

The milling spec promotes processability and drainage in the mash tun, with a typical spec being 20% husk, 70% grits (or 'middles,' i. e. medium ground) and 10% flour. As the mashing water is able to access every element of the malt, changing the milling spec wouldn't affect the level, or range of phenolics that the water can extract.

Distilleries typically use three waters for mashing at progressively higher temperatures, starting at around 63-64 degrees centigrade and peaking at around 85-90 degrees centigrade. Whether the different temperature of each water extracts slightly different phenolic characteristics is one consideration. Another is the level of phenolics extracted, and consequently how much is lost in the draff (i.e. residue grist).

"There is a distinct possibility that different waters extract different phenolics, with a huge amount of peatiness lost during mashing. Essentially all the husk ends up in the draff, what you loose in draff are phenols which are not solubilised," says Dr Bill Lumsden.

Consequently, the wort shows a different balance of flavour active compounds compared to the preceeding stage, while also undergoing further significant changes during fermentation. It's not only the choice of yeast, the pitching temperature (i. e. the temperature of the wort when the yeast is added), and the length of fermentation that influence the range of flavours created. The choice of washbacks, whether stainless steel or wood, is another factor. Wooden washbacks have a higher level

Three distinguished peated whiskies - Longrow 10 yerar old 100 Proof, Ardbeg Supernova and Laphroaig Quarter Cask

of bacteria which means lactic acid in the latter stages of fermentation, adding another dimension to flavour creation.

With so much happening during fermentation, how are the phenolics affected?

"I don't think the phenolic character changes during fermentation, it's that other flavours start, you get fruity esters starting to evolve. For a heavily peated malt you have a longer fermentation, as the yeast takes longer to get going," says John Campbell of Laphroaig.

Kenny Gray, a retired distillery manager for Diageo, raises another consideration;

"Analytically peated malts generally produce a slightly lower yield of alcohol compared to unpeated malt, that's down to yeast not being as happy in the peated malt wort."

Fine-tuning the phenols during distillation

Distillation sees another reduction in peating levels, which can mean a loss of up to half of the original level, while also providing the distiller with an opportunity to select which phenolic characteristics to retain in the spirit cut.

"The first distillation defines the flavours, the second distillation refines the flavours. Phenolic character gets richer and more intense as the spirit cut continues," says John Campbell of Laphroaig.

While the character of the new make spirit is an obvious focus, this also raises the issue of how the phenolics evolve during the overall spirit run.

"There are very light, volatile phenolics even at the start of the spirit run, showing notes such as embers, then it becomes heavier, so that mid-way through the spirit run you'd start getting notes like creosote, then end up with a freshly laid tar aroma," says Stuart Robertson.

Mickey Heads adds, "Phenolics come through right from the start of the spirit run, the aromas are light and fruity with some lighter phenols. They build and become more intense towards the back of the distillation run, with heavier, oilier phenols coming through at the back end."

The profile of the new make spirit also depends of course on the size and shape of the stills, the rate of distillation, and type of condensers (either shell and tube, or worms). As ever, it's a case of various details all making

an individual contribution, together with the consequences of those details, such as the degree of reflux.

"The slower the distillation rate the better, as this maximises reflux and you can promote more volatile phenolics, as the condensate comes back into the pot and it's like getting a syrup that's getting richer, so at the end you will get heavier phenolics. We have one worm and two condensers, worms give a heavier character than a condenser, Springbank and Longrow both go through the worm," says Stuart Robertson.

The peat character changes during maturation

The character of the new make spirit is of course a vital factor, but then again it's also a starting point for a malt's eventual flavour profile, following maturation.

"Ardbeg's new make spirit has aromas of embers, ash, creosote, baked apples and pine forest," says Mickey Heads.

John Campbell describes the aromas of Laphroaig's new make spirit as, "Initially a light smoke becoming deeper, then tar, pears, and the next layer is a bit of spiciness, floral, black pepper."

The way the spirit matures is essentially determined by the choice of cask. An initial choice is between bourbon barrels, typically giving vanilla, creme brulee and coconut notes, among others, while sherry casks are characterised by richer fruitcake, dried fruit notes. The fill (i. e. how many times the cask has previously been filled with new make spirit) is another factor, with second and third fill casks exerting a progressively milder influence in terms of the oak extractives, while oxidation and evaporation play a relatively greater role.

With the vast majority of casks used for aging malt whisky being bourbon barrels, comparing the manner in which two Islay malts, Ardbeg and Laphroaig evolve in this type of cask provides an interesting test case.

"Over the first 3 years in first fill bourbon barrels you get an initial wave of oak with vanilla, and fruit notes in the spirit are joined by fruit notes from the wood. You also notice saltyness as it's in the new make spirit, Islay peat gives some saltyness. At 10-15 years the wood influence increases, you have a bit of vanilla but it's not pronounced, with toffee and fudge notes

Even the cask itself contributes during maturation to the peaty taste

coming through, as well as banana and citrus notes developing. At 20-25 years vanilla notes become dominant, and the phenols don't show as clearly as other characteristics have built up," says Mickey Heads of Ardbeg distillery.

So, how does this compare to the way in which Laphroaig evolves during maturation?

"After two years in first fill bourbon barrels the character of the new make spirit softens slightly and there's a hint of colour. At 3-5 years there's a bit more cask influence with more colour, a softer flavour, more body and a little vanilla sweetness. After 5-6 years there's much more cask influence, and at 6-10 years saltyness starts to come through, this comes from the Islay peat and the atmosphere must also influence it. After 15, 20, 25 years in bourbon barrels you get more vanilla and wood influence, more balance, and there's a different level of details, with citrus flavours coming through, and a bit of dryness. With longer aging you tend to get the subtleness of wood flavours first, and peatyness in the second phase, and the saltyness is mainly in the finish," says John Campbell.

Meanwhile, aging in sherry casks means altogether different parameters.

"A sherry cask gives much more fruityness upfront with dried fruit, grape, raisin and Christmas cake notes, with smoke coming through at the end," says John Campbell.

Casks are constantly 'multi-tasking' during aging, with the toasted layer (i. e. beneath the surface layer of char in bourbon barrels) releasing a range of extractives. As bourbon and sherry casks both have a toasted layer, this means that (depending on the heating regime) both cask types potentially provide the same level of extractives, which includes phenolic compounds. However, the phenolics a cask contributes are a fraction of the total present within the spirit when distilling peated malt. And rather than providing any additional types of phenolic compounds, it's thought that casks add more of the same phenolics as the malt.

"Casks will contribute some phenolics, as you can pick up a hint of phenolics from the cask with unpeated malts, but isolating exactly what phenolics a cask contributes is very difficult. I think phenolic compounds also show more clearly when the level of sulphurous compounds is reduced, through absorption by the charred layer of the cask," says Mickey Heads.

Two other key influences during maturation are oxidation and evaporation. The rate of evaporation, typically around 2% of the cask's contents per annum includes water and alcohol. While the exact role evaporation plays in aging is still being researched, this process is instrumental in helping the spirit to loose immaturity.

Meanwhile, the process of oxidation (i. e. fresh air being 'inhaled' into the cask, while saturated air is 'exhaled') plays a vital role in flavour development, particularly fruit notes. But how does evaporation and oxidation affect the phenolics?

"Evaporation and oxidation have to make the phenolics more complex, I would suggest phenolics also evaporate but that's not a scientific opinion," says Stuart Robertson.

Russell Anderson adds, "I think some phenolics can be volatile and evaporate during maturation, there are phenols there all the time, though some will be masked organoleptically through extraction from the wood."

With a growing number of longer aged malts having become more available, it's easier to conduct a 'compare and contrast' exercise to see how phenolics show after spending different periods in a cask. Aging can make phenolic character appear significantly mellower, compared to a younger version. But rather than phenolic levels diminishing during aging, phenolic levels are believed to remain consistent, and merely appear milder as other characteristics become more intense, and so alter the balance in a malt's flavour profile.

Ian Wisniewski is a food, drink and travel writer and broadcaster specialising in spirits.
He contributes to various publications, including Whisky Magazine, and has written 8 books on drinks, including Classic Malt Whisky. *He is a regular visitor at malt whisky distilleries in Scotland, and also distilleries in various other countries, as he is fascinated by the production process. He is also chairman of the white spirits judges for the International Spirits Challenge, and frequently conducts tutored tastings.*

Is Europe worth caring about?

Is the whisky axis changing beyond all recognition and are some traditional European whisky markets no longer worth pursuing? Or are flat-lining markets or ones in decline just 'resting' before surging forward again in the future? Dominic Roskrow investigates.

Running a major whisky business as we enter the second decade of the Millennium must feel a little bit like playing a complicated version of the military strategy game Risk.

In Risk the object of the game is to move your armies across the world to conquer new territories while protecting territories you control from attack from rival players.

And so it is with the whisky industry. For as the reputation of malt spreads ever further a plethora of potentially lucrative new territories have sprung up. Existing whisky companies, limited by how much whisky they can produce and the time it takes to produce it, have to make decisions as to which markets to pursue and which to ignore. And as new distilleries open up and new players enter the market, they must decide which territories to try and conquer and establish a foothold in, and which ones to ignore, pull out of, or risk being overwhelmed in as other acquisitive companies further seek to consolidate their positions.

Those decisions have become ever more complex as new markets have emerged, keen to taste and discover whisky but with a low knowledge level and starting from relatively low or non existent sales levels. Meanwhile the biggest, most established markets, particularly some of those of Europe, have stopped growing to any great extent or are witnessing volume falls.

Undoubtedly the world of whisky is changing. It is well documented that the Scotch whisky markets in the so-called BRIC nations – Brazil, Russia, India and China – have been growing phenomenally and although the current recession has slowed progress down, the figures still make remarkable reading. Between 2000 and 2008, for instance, the volume of Scotch whisky consumed in them grew by 208 per cent, from 7.15 million litres to 22.04 million. China, admittedly from a negligible base, has seen consumption grow by a staggering 3915 per cent. Brazilians drink almost as much whisky as the Greeks and Germans, an amazing statistic when you consider that both European countries are top 10 export markets for Scotch.

And it's not just the BRIC nations that are keen to taste Scotch. South America excluding Brazil has seen a 44 per cent increase in consumption. In 2008 the region consumed 25.9 million litres of whisky, almost the same as the United Kingdom. The Far East as a whole, which 10 years ago consumed far less than the United Kingdom, has grown by 58 per cent and now consumes more than 15 million litres more Scotch than the British do.

Indeed, the growth in emerging markets across many regions of the world is in stark contrast to Europe as a whole, which grew in volume terms by a virtually insignificant 0.8 per cent between 2000 and 2007. Nor does that figure tell the whole story. In performance terms Europe is split between North and South. In the countries which constitute Southern Europe – France, Spain, Italy, Greece and Portugal – only France bucked the trend and didn't suffer from a fall in volume. In Spain, not so long ago the world's leading market for Scotch by volume and value and long seen as a whisky cash cow, and in neighbouring Portugal, the decline has been dramatic.

In stark contrast the rest of northern Europe excluding Great Britain and Northern Ireland grew by a healthy nine per cent in the same period. Three markets – France, Spain and the United Kingdom – dominate Europe in sales terms. Only France has continued to perform well in volume terms.

Is targeting Europe a waste of money?

So have parts of Europe reached a level of whisky saturation that excludes the possibility of further growth? Are they now at a point where there is no point whisky makers targeting them significantly, and would resources be better employed elsewhere?

It depends which country you're talking about. Spain, for instance, may well have peaked, but a combination of factors may have conspired to ensure that the whisky boom period is well and truly over, at least for the foreseeable future.

Spain's problems, it seems, are unique. The market for Scotch there grew up after the Franco era and with the arrival of Spain as a member of the European Union. Scotch – both blended and single malt – became the style drink for a new generation of fashionistas reveling in new found freedom and independence. Sales grew extraordinarily quickly and for the better part of a quarter of a century whisky was the drink to be seen with, so much so that when the new Millennium dawned it was by some way the biggest volume market in the world, with a weighty 44.49 million litres of Scotch whisky consumed that year. Its value was even greater because unlike the markets of France or the United Kingdom, Spain enjoyed its whisky in bars and restaurants rather than in the home.

There are a number of reasons why the

decline in the last decade has been so marked and dramatic. Michael Cockram, director for Scotch at Beam Global, says the country has been hit by the perfect storm.

"It may well be that Spain has reached that point in its development where the next generation is now rejecting what the previous generation drank and whisky is a victim of that," he says.

"But Spain is under increasing pressure for other reasons too. It's been hit by a change in drinking culture because the brutal decline of the Spanish economy has meant less money to go out in a country where going out is important. Also the economic pressures mean that there is more pressure on working culture. Traditionally Spaniards went out late and stayed out until very late, catching up with sleep by having a traditional siesta during the day. But the economic situation has put the siesta under threat as people are encouraged to work harder."

Ken Grier, director of malts at Edrington, owner of The Macallan and Highland Park agrees, but points out that the volume figures hide another trend in Spain.

"The global recession has had a huge impact on Spain's economy with huge unemployment

Ken Grier, Director of Malts at Edrington

and a huge decrease in tourism," he says.

"With less money being spent in the market and new legislation such as the clamp down on drink driving, drinking habits have changed. "But even so Spain has been showing fantastic growth in the single malt category. Generally

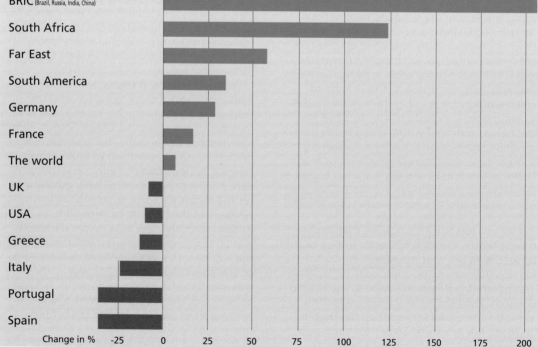

Some producers fear that supermarket price cuts on whisky have damaged the market for years to come

while Europe as a whole is 'mature' when it comes to whisky, there are still pockets of great potential and Spain would fall in to this category. There is a widespread knowledge of Scotch, a trend towards premium drinking, and the single malt category is still relatively underdeveloped."

The effects of the economic climate and a change in drinking habits may underlie the large fall in volume in Portugal and the smaller but significant declines in Italy and Greece. John Glaser, owner of bespoke whisky company Compass Box, picks up on the point made by The Macallan's Ken Grier about value over volume.

"While there have been general declines in volume of Scotch whisky you have to split the market up and look at blends and single malts separately," he says. "In markets where knowledge levels are high, as in Europe, we have seen the growth of premium and super premium single malts. In volume terms these may not be very large but they have high value."

"And even within these markets there are lesser known brands that are still being discovered. My view on this would be that we don't see any country in Europe where the market is saturated and things are stalling."

UK market hit by supermarket discounting

So what of the United Kingdom, Scotch whisky's home market and one fought over, certainly in Scotland, by the drinks companies just for 'bragging rights'? After all, nothing quite matches the boast that your brand is popular in the country which makes it.

Here, though, volumes are declining. Are these temporary or the result of a longer term refocusing away from a market that offers less incentive to a whisky maker because of supermarket discounting and the dominance of many big names?

Although the Spanish situation is different in many ways to that of the UK, there are some parallels. The issue of volume as opposed to value is one, and the growth of the single malt category at the expense of blends is another. It is perfectly possible for overall volumes of Scotch whisky to be declining but the value of the market going up as consumers switch from cheap blends to higher priced single malts.

"When you look at the UK you're looking at a market that is well established," says Iain Baxter, senior brand manager for Inver House Distillers, owners of Old Pulteney and Balblair.

"The anecdotal view is that the market is established by blends and then consumers move to single malts as they moved from quantity to quality. The question is, is the UK at the end of that process and the market has gone as far as it can?

"I would be very surprised if that was the case and there was no potential for further value growth. We're seeing people moving to more complex tastes and back towards brown spirits and both those trends favour whisky."

Beam's Michael Cockram agrees, arguing that UK whisky figures aren't bad at all.

"I don't think we should be depressed by the figures. The UK remains a very big market and value-wise it's great. There might not be explosive growth in single malt whisky sales but it's been steady, especially when you look at value over volume," he says.

"There may have been a bump in the road in the UK because there has been pressure on prices caused by supermarkets and discounting. But the general move to quality products rather than cheap mass volume ones is good for malt whisky."

"I think in the UK we are seeing the esta-

blishment of a high quality premium product at a fair price after years and years of deflation. There are two parts to this. The customer might want low prices but as an industry the aim must be to try and build the brand and establish it as a consistent and high quality product. Perhaps it is possible that we will return to whisky lakes and poor quality as the industry cuts corners and slashes prices but no one wants that. We want to build long term brands that are respected across the world and are sought after because of their quality."

Cockram's comments with regard to supermarkets raise another issue. With world whisky sales booming and single malt in demand, are the UK's declining figures a symptom of a lack of effort by the whisky makers as they pursue lucrative new markets and lose interest in a market where discounting has long been the norm and where customers expect to pay far less for a malt than a fair and justifiable price? Once people have a price for a given brand in their heads, runs the argument, it's hard to change it. Perhaps easier to just move the brand to another territory entirely?

"Consumers have very long memories when it comes to price," says Iain Baxter. "Research shows that where there has been sustained and constant discounting it can take five to ten years to change perceptions. But it's not that easy just to move to another market because people travel a lot and we live in a globalised world."

A mature market but not necessarily exhausted

The concept of different markets being at different points on the economic cycle is also pertinent when it comes to looking at what is going on in the UK. Arguably the most mature market for whisky in the world, it follows that what it is facing is new, whereas other markets such as Spain are experiencing what the UK experienced a couple of decades ago or in the case of the very newest markets, considerably longer. According to Neil Macdonald, Brand Director at Chivas Brothers, it's actually more complex than that and it doesn't follow that every country will follow the same economic cycle as the UK.

"Different countries have different experiences," he says. "If you look at South Africa, which is starting to do really well, it's because traditionally Scotch whisky was consumed by white people in the Apartheid era and now

Neil Macdonald, Brand Director Royal Salute,
The Glenlivet and Single Malt Whiskies

*In some markets young people reject whisky
because it is perceived as "Dad's drink"*

there is a growing black middle class who are discerning and cultivated and want the best. No-one knows where that may lead. And look at China. How big can that be? It's been having problems but the growth there is still eight per cent and in terms of economic potential we haven't even started yet. There has been nothing like it before."

"It makes for a very complex picture, made all the more complex by the fact that different whisky companies are having different experiences with malts doing well in different countries – Glenmorangie in the United Kingdom, Glenfiddich and Aberlour in France, The Macallan in Taiwan, Cardhu in Spain and so on. It makes for a very complex overall picture."

Key to understanding where the European whisky market is going is the question of maturity. The argument goes that if Europe is considered a mature market it may offer no growth potential for the future and therefore it isn't worth the drinks companies trying to revive it when they can focus their resources elsewhere.

Everyone accepts that Europe is a relatively mature market. The question is, is it an exhausted and saturated one? Not necessarily. Indeed, maturity might work in its favour. While blended Scotch may once have been considered 'dad's drink' and was rejected by the next generation, a further generation has come up and is removed from the baggage associated with Scotch. Furthermore, while the tag might burden blended Scotch, single malt whisky falls outside the 'dad's drink' association anyway.

"It's possible that some parts of Europe are a generation past being seen as an old man's drink and this may help it," says Michael Cockram.

"But more importantly they are moving towards having an older population and if it's the case that people move to malt whisky in their 30s then there will be a natural move to it in the near future, so growth will take care of itself."

Neil Macdonald identifies something else, too – the trend towards environmental awareness. He points at the huge effort made by the Scotch Whisky Association in 2009 to draw up a blueprint for a green future for the whisky industry in the future.

"The overall move to high quality premium products will work in favour of single malt," he says. "It's a relatively natural product and it tends to be consumed in small and sensible quantities and as such it fits well in to a society which is health conscious. This will benefit it more and more in the future, along with the issues of credibility and provenance. People know what they are drinking and they know it is made with the finest natural materials."

Helping each other promote the whisky category

But there isn't universal agreement over whether the natural market trends will benefit single malt. Derek Scott, global marketing director of Burn Stewart, whose distilleries include Bunnahabhain and Tobermory, believes that some European countries may have reached full maturity. Further growth will only be achieved with a great deal of help and effort from the whole industry.

"Perhaps it has reached the point where the consumer is fully aware of whisky. It's possible that there could be a retro trend among young people to turn back to Scotch where it does not have negative connotations but while it's not impossible to engineer that, it's very difficult."

"I think there's a need to build up a broad understanding of Scotch as a concept. In the

Derek Scott, Global Marketing Director of Burn Stewart

Iain Baxter, Senior Brand Manager for Inver House Distillers

Scotland is whisky's spiritual home. There has most certainly been a shift in the axis of whisky in the last five to ten years towards the East but that doesn't mean we will stop taking the UK market very seriously. Far from it."

Not everyone in the industry agrees with the view of Scott and Baxter. Indeed some smaller companies argue the opposite, pointing out they do not have the leverage of a Diageo or Pernod Ricard in the big, mature European markets and that rather than try and carve out an identity in their home market their longer term future will be secured elsewhere. The new territories of Eastern Europe and Southern Africa, for instance, are proving to be fertile hunting grounds for the owners of BenRiach and Glendronach, for instance.

It's a complicated and confusing picture then, but it's fair to conclude that North and South Europe, which still accounts for a whopping 150 million litres of Scotch whisky, remains important for whisky producers. Some believe it can take care of itself naturally, others argue that certainly in terms of malt whisky there is little to be concerned about. It may even be in reasonably good health.

old world markets Scotch is not seen as appealing or as special. There's a big opportunity for us as a business to build the credibility of whisky to compete with other categories – to grow together the overall size of the whisky category pie rather than each company try and increase their share of the existing pie. If we don't do that and make whisky relevant in the old established markets, there will be companies abandoning them and focusing on markets elsewhere. We have already seen it. For a company like us there is a need to focus on our home land because we want to be seen here and we want to be able to go out to other markets and tell them that Scottish people drink our whiskies. That's very important to our credibility but I'm not sure that's true for all whisky makers."

This is a point picked up by Inver House's Iain Baxter who argues that companies such as his will continue to work hard to ensure that the UK market remains an important and growing one.

"The bigger companies are under different pressures to us and have to make decisions in a more global capacity. This is very hard because there are difficult choices to be made and they must make them for business and not emotional reasons.

"We are not one of the big, big players and the UK whisky market remains a very big category for us. Scotland is particularly important because there is a tourist issue to consider and

Certainly the industry's not about to abandon these vast mature markets any time soon. Move all the troops to new territories and leave the older mature markets open to challenge?

That wouldn't just be risky – it would be plain stupid.

Dominic Roskrow is a freelance whisky writer and former editor of Whisky Magazine, which he edited for four years. He writes regularly for Whisky Magazine and Malt Advocate, has columns in magazines in America, China and Ireland and has contributed to leading drinks titles such as Harpers Food & Wine, Imbibe, Decanter and Morning Advocate. He is the business development director for The Whisky Shop chain, and his business is based at the company's shop in Norwich. He has been writing about drinks for 15 years and is the author of Whiskies: From Confused to Connoisseur published by Harper Collins, and the new Collins Gems Whisky, published in 2009. He is currently working on updating Michael Jackson's Companion to Whisky, for publicaton in March 2010. He lives in Norfolk, home of England's first malt whisky distillery, and is married with three children.

Malt distilleries
of Scotland and Ireland

O n the following pages, 128 Scottish and Irish distilleries are described in detail. Most are active, while some are mothballed, decommissioned or demolished.

Long since closed distilleries from which whisky is very rare or practically unobtainable are described at the end together with four new and upcoming distilleries.

Japanese malt whisky distilleries and distilleries in other countries are covered on pp. 204-237.

Just a brief explanation with regards to where in the book the different distilleries are placed.

I have decided that the owners must have released at least one bottling of single malt whisky (not just new make spirit) to warrant a place of its own in the alphabetical part of the distillery directory of Scottish and Irish distilleries. That is why Kilchoman and Glengyle are to be found in that part this year while, for example, Kilbeggan is not but instead mentioned under Cooley Distillery since they share the same owner.

Distilleries that are about to be built or have not left the planning phase yet are treated in the part The Whisky Year That Was (pp. 238-251).

Explanations

Owner:
Name of the owning company, sometimes with the parent company within brackets.

Region/district:
There are four formal malt whisky regions in Scotland today; the Highlands, the Lowlands, Islay and Campbeltown. Where useful we mention a location within a region e.g. Speyside, Orkney, Northern Highlands etc.

Founded:
The year in which the distillery was founded is usually considered as when construction began. The year is rarely the same year in which the distillery was licensed.

Status:
The status of the distillery's production. Active, mothballed (temporarily closed), closed (but most of the equipment still present), dismantled (the equipment is gone but part of or all of the buildings remain even if they are used for other purposes) and demolished.

Visitor centre:
The letters (vc) after status indicate that the distillery has a visitor centre. Many distilleries accept visitors despite not having a visitor centre. It can be worthwhile making an enquiry.

Address:
The distillery's address.

Tel:
This is generally to the visitor centre, but can also be to the main office.

website:
The distillery's (or in some cases the owner's) website.

Capacity:
The current production capacity expressed in litres of pure alcohol (LPA).

History:
The chronology focuses on the official history of the distillery and independent bottlings are only listed in exceptional cases. They can be found in the text bodies instead.

Tasting notes:
For all the Scottish and Irish distilleries that are not permanently closed we present tasting notes of what, in most cases, can be called the core expression (mainly their best selling 10 or 12 year old).

We have tried to provide notes for official bottlings but in those cases where we have not been able to obtain them, we have turned to independent bottlers.

The whiskies have been tasted by *Dominic Roskrow* (DR) and *David Stirk* (DS), well-known whisky profiles and contributors to Malt Whisky Yearbook over four years now. We have strived to have both gentlemen's comments for each distillery but in a few cases, only one of them has been able to provide notes.

The notes have been prepared especially for Malt Whisky Yearbook 2010.

Brief distillery glossary

A number of terms occur throughout the distillery directory and are briefly explained here. We can recommend for example *A to Z of Whisky* by Gavin D Smith for more detailed explanations.

Blended malt
A type of whisky where two or more single malts are blended together. The term was introduced a few years ago by SWA to replace the previous term vatted malt. The term is controversial as those who oppose the use of it are of the opinion that it can be confused with 'blended whisky' where malt and grain is blended.

Cask strength
It has become increasingly common in recent times to bottle malt whisky straight from the cask without reducing the alcohol contents to 40, 43 or 46%. A cask strength can be anything between 40 to 65% depending on how long the cask has been matured.

Chill-filtering
A method used for removing unwanted particles and, especially used to prevent the whisky from appearing turbid when water is added. Some producers believe that flavour is affected and therefore avoid chill-filtering.

Continuous still
A type of still used when making grain whisky. The still allows for continuous distillation and re-distillation. Can also be called column still, patent still or Coffey still.

Cooling
The spirit vapours from the stills are cooled into liquids usually by a shell and tube condenser, but an older method (worm tubs) is still in use at some distilleries.

Dark grains
The draff and pot ale from the distillation process is used for making fodder pellets, so-called dark grains.

Drum maltings
The malting method used on all major malting sites today.

Dunnage warehouse
Also called traditional warehouse. The walls are made of stone and the floors of earth. The casks (up to three) are piled on top of each other.

Floor maltings
The traditional method of malting the barley on large wooden floors. This method is only used by a handful of distilleries today.

Lyne arm
The lyne arm leads the spirit vapours from the wash or spirit still to the condenser. The angle of the lyne arm has great significance for reflux and the final character of the whisky.

Mash tun
The procedure after the malt has been milled into grist is called the mashing. The mash tun is usually made of cast iron or stainless steel, but can sometimes be made of wood. The grist is mixed with hot water in order to release the sugars in the barley. The result is the wort which is drawn off through a perforated floor into the underback. The mashed grains in the mash tun are called draff and are then used for making animal feed.

Pagoda roof
A roof shaped as a pagoda which was built over the kiln to lead the smoke away from the drying peat. The pagoda roof was invented by the famous architect Charles Doig. These days pagoda roofs provide mainly aesthetical value as the majority of distilleries usually buy their malt elsewhere.

Peat
A soil layer consisting of plants which have mouldered. Used as fuel in drying the green malts when a more or less peaty whisky is to be produced. In other cases the kiln is usually heated by oil or gas.

PPM
Abbreviation for Parts Per Million. This is used to show the amount of phenols in the peated malt. Peated Islay whisky usually uses malt with 40-60 ppm, which is reduced to 10-20 ppm in the new make spirit.

Purifier
A device used in conjunction with the lyne arm which cools heavier alcohols and lead them back to the still. A handful of distilleries use this technique to make a lighter and cleaner spirit.

Racked warehouse
A modern warehouse with temperature control and built-in shelves. Casks can be stored up to a height of 12.

Reflux
When the heavier vapours in the still are cooled and fall back into the still as liquids. The amount of reflux obtained depends on the shape of the still and the angle of the lyne arm. A distillation process with high reflux gives a lighter, more delicate spirit while a small amount of reflux gives a more robust and flavour-rich whisky.

Saladin box
A method of malting barley which replaced floor maltings. It was invented by the Frenchman Charles Saladin in the late 19th century and was introduced in Scottish distilleries in the 1950s. The only distillery using the method today is Tamdhu.

Shell and tube condenser
The most common method for cooling the spirit vapours. It is a wide copper tube attached to the lyne arm of the still. Cold water is led through a number of smaller copper pipes and cools the surrounding vapours.

Spirit still
The second still, usually a little smaller that the wash still. The low wines are collected in the spirit still for redistilling. Alcohol increases to 64-68% and unwanted impurities disappear. It is only the middle fraction of the distillate (the cut) which is utilized.

Vatted malt
See blended malt.

Washback
Large tubs of stainless steel or wood in which fermentation takes place. Yeast is added to the worts and the sugars change into alcohol. The result is a wash with an alcoholic content of 6-8% which is then used for distillation.

Wash still
The first and usually largest of the stills. The wash is heated to the boiling point and the alcohol is vaporized. The spirit vapours are cooled in a condenser and the result is low wines with an alcohol content of c 21%.

Worm tub
An older method for cooling the spirit vapours in connection with distilling. This method is still used in approximately ten distilleries. The worm tub consists of a long, spiral-shaped copper pipe which is submerged in water in a large wooden tub, usually outdoors. The spirit vapours are led through the copper spiral so they can condense.

Aberfeldy

Owner:
John Dewar & Sons
(Bacardi)

Region/district:
Eastern Highlands

Founded: **Status:** **Capacity:**
1896 Active (vc) 3 500 000 litres

Address: Aberfeldy, Perthshire PH15 2EB

Tel:
01887 822010 (vc)

website:
www.dewarswow.com

History:
1896 – John and Tommy Dewar embark on the construction of the distillery, a stone's throw from the old Pitilie distillery which was active from 1825 to 1867. Their objective is to produce a single malt for their blended whisky - White Label.

1898 – Production starts in November.

1917-19 – The distillery closes.

1925 – Distillers Company Limited (DCL) takes over.

1930 – Operations are transferred to Scottish Malt Distillers (SMD).

1972 – Reconstruction takes place, the floor maltings is closed and the two stills are increased to four.

1991 – The first official bottling is a 15 year old in the Flora & Fauna series.

1998 – Bacardi buys John Dewar & Sons from Diageo at a price of £1,150 million. Five malt distilleries and Bombay Sapphire Gin are included in the purchase.

2000 – A visitor centre opens and a 25 year old is released.

2005 – A 21 year old is launched in October, replacing the 25 year old.

2009 – Chris Anderson's Cask from 1990 is released.

Aberfeldy 12 year old

DR – The nose is a mix of fresh and clean barley, honey and a hint of smoke. The honey carries through to the palate and the pleasant finish is shaped by a touch of smoke and peppery spice.

DS – Apples, honey and caramel with a hint of champagne on the nose. The palate is sweet and firm with some herbal, vanilla flavours and the finish is sugary.

Dewar's is not known for marketing its distilleries as own brands. The exceptions are Glen Deveron (Macduff Distillery) and Aberfeldy. Still, beautifully situated by the longest river in Scotland, the River Tay, Aberfeldy is more about the blended whisky Dewar's than about single malt. This is of course enforced by Dewar's World of Whiskies, a brilliant visitor centre which opened in 2000 and attracts 40,000 visitors every year. Dewar's White Label is the seventh most sold blended Scotch in the world and in the USA it has been number one for several years. Over 17 million bottles were sold in the USA in 2008 which means that White Label's market share is 15% compared to number two Johnnie Walker Black Label which has a share of 9%. Every second bottle of White Label is thus sold on the American market. Other expressions of Dewar's blended Scotch include the 12 and 18 year old and Signature.

The equipment at Aberfeldy consists of a stainless steel mash tun, eight washbacks made of Siberian larch, two stainless steel washbacks placed outdoors and two pairs of stills. There are six warehouses on site though they are no longer used for storage. Instead, the spirit is tankered to Stirling for filling in casks (mostly ex-bourbon) and maturation. A new pot ale plant has recently been built to take care of residues from the distilling. The core range consists of a *12 year old* and a *21 year old*. Limited editions are rare but several *Single Casks* were announced for release in autumn 2009, the first being a refill hogshead distilled in 1990. It was titled *Chris Anderson's Cask* to commemorate the distillery manager's retirement after 40 years in the whisky industry.

Independent bottlings have been very rare in recent years but at least a couple were released in 2009 - a 13 year old from 1996 by Cadenheads and a 1997 released by Blackadder.

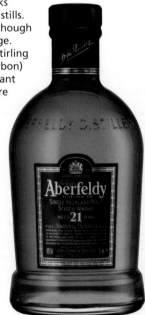

21 years old

Aberlour

Owner:
Chivas Brothers Ltd
(Pernod Ricard)

Region/district:
Speyside

Founded: **Status:** **Capacity:**
1826   Active (vc)   4 200 000 litres

Address: Aberlour, Banffshire AB38 9PJ

Tel:
01340 881249

website:
www.aberlour.com

History:

1826 – James Gordon and Peter Weir found the first Aberlour Distillery.

1827 – Peter Weir withdraws and James Gordon continues alone.

1879 – A fire devastates most of the distillery. The local banker James Fleming constructs a new distillery a few kilometres upstream the Spey river.

1892 – The distillery is sold to Robert Thorne & Sons Ltd who expands it.

1898 – Another fire rages and almost totally destroys the distillery. The architect Charles Doig is called in to design the new facilities.

1921 – Robert Thorne & Sons Ltd sells Aberlour to W. H. Holt & Sons, a brewery near Manchester.

1945 – S. Campbell & Sons Ltd buys the distillery.

1962 – Aberlour terminates floor malting.

1973 – Number of stills are increased from two to four.

1975 – Pernod Ricard buys Campbell Distilleries.

2000 – Aberlour a´bunadh is launched. A limited 30 year old cask strength is released.

2001 – Pernod Ricard buys Chivas Brothers from Seagrams and merges Chivas Brothers and Campbell Distilleries under the brand Chivas Brothers.

2002 – A new, modernized visitor centre is inaugurated in August.

2008 – The 18 year old is also introduced outside France.

Aberlour 12 year old

DR – The nose combines horse chestnut casing then sweet melon and fresh spearmint, the taste is beautifully fresh and clean, with mint and gentle fruit.

DS – Rich dried fruits and spices with star of anise on the nose. Citrusy and rich-caramel flavours in the mouth with a fruity, sherried finish.

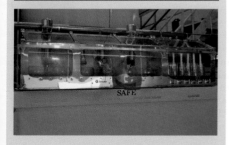

SAFE

For a decade now, Aberlour has been amongst the top ten selling single malts. In early 2009, the owner announced that it had reached not one but two milestones - the past year the 200,000 cases limit was passed and it gained category leadership in terms of volume on main market France. The struggle over that position has been between Aberlour and Glenfiddich. One of the reasons for these successes is thought to be the introduction of a 10 year old sherry cask finish on the French market and the 18 year old now being sold globally.

James Fleming, the man who built the new Aberlour Distillery back in 1879, was a man of great importance to the town of Aberlour. A succesful grain merchant and banker, he was also a large-scale philanthropist. He financed the building of the town hall and the installation of street lamps. He died in 1895, leaving a legacy which helped fund the building of a public school and a hospital for those unable to pay for health care.

The distillery is equipped with one semi-lauter mash tun, six stainless steel washbacks and two pairs of stills. There are five warehouses on site (three racked and two dunnage) but only two racked are used for maturation with a total of 27,000 casks. About half of the production is used for single malts.

The core range of Aberlour includes a *10 year old* (sherry/bourbon), a *12 year old Double Cask Matured*, a *16 year old Double Cask matured* and *a'bunadh*, of which there are 26 batches launched up to and including summer 2009. A new expression in spring 2008 was the *18 year old*, previously sold exclusively in France. In France, a *10 year old Sherry Cask Finish* and the *15 year Cuvée Marie d'Ecosse* are available. Two 'exclusives' are available for the duty free market – *12 year old sherry matured* and *15 year old double cask matured*.

Recent independent bottlings include two from Duncan Taylor (1992 and 1995) and a 1996 from Dewar Rattray.

12 years old

Allt-a-Bhainne

Owner:
Chivas Brothers Ltd
(Pernod Ricard)

Region/district:
Speyside

Founded: **Status:**   **Capacity:**
1975   Active   4 000 000 litres

Address: Glenrinnes, Dufftown,
Banffshire AB55 4DB

Tel:
01542 783200

website:
-

History:
1975 – The distillery is founded by Chivas
Brothers, a subsidiary of Seagrams, in order to
secure malt whisky for its blended whiskies. The
total cost amounts to £2.7 million.

1989 – Production has doubled.

2001 – Pernod Ricard takes over Chivas Brothers
from Seagrams.

2002 – Mothballed in October.

2005 – Production restarts in May.

Deerstalker 12 year old

DR – Autumn fields and damp hay on the
nose, a richer, sweeter earth and heathery
taste on the palate and a gentle rounded
finish.

DS – Pine and anise on the nose with biscuit
and lemon grass. Sweet and perfumed on
the palate. Sugary and spiky with a medium,
sweet finish.

Allt-a-bhainne, halfway between Dufftown and Glenlivet in a
remote and beautiful part of the Highlands, was built in 1975
and belongs to one of the more modern distilleries in Scotland
today. Despite this, it was closed soon after Pernod Ricard assumed ownership and production stopped for three years before
the distillery was back in production in 2005.

The production novelty called the lauter mash tun was introduced about a decade before Allt-a-bhainne distillery was built.
In use in breweries for many years, its operating principle is
that rotating knives cut through the malted barley in order
to facilitate the extraction of soluble starch. (In the traditional mash tun, rakes and ploughs performed this function).
One would have thought that in a modern distillery such as
Allt-a-bhainne, this new invention would
have been obvious but that was far from
the case. The Distilleries Director of Chivas
Brothers at the time, Stuart McBain, was not
in favour of this innovation and decided that
traditional mash tuns should be installed at
both Allt-a-bhainne and its sister distillery
Braeval. These tuns, built by R G Abercrom-
bie of Alloa, are still used. The rest of the
equipment consists of eight stainless steel
washbacks and two pairs of stills. The
wash stills are of the traditional broad-
necked versions but the two spirit stills
have rather unusual long necks with
parallel sides which increase reflux and
thus produce a lighter spirit. There is
capacity for 25 mashes per week. The
whisky is not filled in casks on site but
transported by lorry to a facility in
Keith.

There are no official bottlings of Allt-a-
bhainne and according to Chivas Brothers there are no plans for any either.
Independent bottlings can be found
though in the form of Deerstalker 12
year old from Aberko. Recently there
have also been a couple from 1991
with a finish in Amarone casks released
by Murray McDavid and a 14 year old
Medoc finish by Ian MacLeod.

Deerstalker 12 year old

In Focus...

Barley | Malting | Mashing | Fermentation | Wash still | Spirit still | Maturation | Oak & Casks

Barley (*Hordeum vulgare*) is the fourth most important cereal crop in the world after wheat, maize and rice and it is one of three raw materials needed to produce malt whisky. The other two are water and yeast. Barley is grown all over the world and is mainly used for feeding animals or for producing beer and spirits. The total barley production in Scotland in 2008 was 1.9 million tonnes (of which 75% was spring barley and the rest winter barley). The Scottish whisky industry is using about 500,000 tonnes of barley per year and the major part comes from Scottish farms. In 2005, the share grown in Scotland was 90% but it has decreased since then and an increasing share is imported from, e. g. Denmark, Germany, France and Australia not to mention England.

There are two forms of barley that are of interest to producers of beer and whisky: *two-row* and *six-row* barley, with the names alluding to how the kernels are arranged on the plant. Furthermore, barley can be divided into *spring barley* (planted in spring and harvested in late summer or early autumn) and *winter barley* (planted in autumn and harvested the following autumn). Finally, through continuous improvement, there are probably over 100,000 different varieties of barley today. At the ICARDA (International Center for Agricultural Research in the Dry Areas) barley nursery in Syria alone, 25,000 different varieties are sown each year.

The most common barley for distilling malt whisky is two-row spring barley. This form can be divided into many different varieties, each more or less suitable for whisky production. Until the early 1800s, the traditional *Bere barley*, a six-row variety, was used for making whisky in Scotland but through plant refinement new kinds with better characteristics were developed. Despite that, both Bruichladdich and Springbank have tried Bere for whisky production recently albeit with mixed results.

In modern times, new varieties were introduced such as Golden Promise in 1966. It was replaced by Prisma and Chariot in the early nineties. The dominating barley strain today is Optic which was introduced in 1995. Recent varieties include Forensic (which can be used both for malt and grain distilling), Cocktail and Oxbridge.

Research is ongoing to find new and better varieties by hybridising and refining existent varieties. The key factors to take into consideration when searching for new varieties are:

• High content of starch which can be transformed into sugar and finally alcohol. This is measured as *spirit yield* (litres of alcohol/tonne of barley). A yield considered good today will be around 405-420 litres per tonne compared to older varieties with a spirit yield of 380 litres. It varies, however, whether peated or unpeated whisky is produced. Figures will be a little lower with peated whiskies, as they will when

using floor malted barley rather than malt from commercial maltsters.

• Resistance to diseases like mildew, brown rust and leaf spotting.

• Good capability to germinate which is a prerequisite for malting.

• A high yield (from the farmer's point of view) from the fields. The yield of the old variety Golden Promise was about two tonnes per acre whereas Optic has a yield of three tonnes.

A recent sidetrack has been to find varieties that do not produce *epiheterodendrin (EPH)* during the malting process. This is a precursor chemical which, in reaction with the copper in the stills, produces *ethyl carbamate (EC)* which is a potential carcinogen. EC can also be found in beer and other spirits as well as in different kinds of fermented food. The EC side effect was discovered already in the eighties and the Canadian Government placed a maximum level of 150 micrograms of EC per litre. There are currently no set limits in the EU but a survey in 2000 showed an average of 29 microgram/litre in Scotch whisky with levels being considerably lower in samples from the nineties compared to those produced in the seventies and eighties. One major reason for this is that whisky producers nowadays are addressing the issue by using barley varieties that do not produce EPH or, at the most, low levels of the compound. The most important of these new barley strains is Decanter but also Troon and Oxbridge.

The harvested grain is laboratory-tested when it arrives at the maltings and before the consignment is accepted and brought to the barley store. Thereafter, it is dried by warm air and screened which also functions as purification. It is then cooled to ca 15°C and can subsequently be stored for months before use. The barley is now dormant and it will take several weeks before it wakes up and can germinate (see malting page 89).

Ardbeg

Owner:
Glenmorangie Co
(Moët Hennessy)

Region/district: The
Islay

Founded: 1815
Status: Active (vc)
Capacity: 1 000 000 litres

Address: Port Ellen, Islay, Argyll PA42 7EA

Tel:
01496 302244 (vc)
website:
www.ardbeg.com

History:

1794 – First record of a distillery at Ardbeg. It was founded by Alexander Stewart.

1798 – The MacDougalls, later to become licensees of Ardbeg, are active on the site through Duncan MacDougall.

1815 – The current distillery is founded by John MacDougall, son of Duncan MacDougall.

1853 – Alexander MacDougall, John's son, dies and sisters Margaret and Flora MacDougall, assisted by Colin Hay, continue the running of the distillery. Colin Hay takes over the licence when the sisters die.

1888 – Colin Elliot Hay and Alexander Wilson Gray Buchanan renew their license.

1900 – Colin Hay's son takes over the license.

1959 – Ardbeg Distillery Ltd is founded.

1973 – Hiram Walker and Distillers Company Ltd jointly purchase the distillery for £300,000 through Ardbeg Distillery Trust.

1974 – Widely considered as the last vintage of 'old, peaty' Ardbeg. Malt which has not been produced in the distillery's own maltings is used in increasingly larger shares after this year.

1977 – Hiram Walker assumes single control of the distillery. Ardbeg closes its maltings.

1979 – Kildalton, a less peated malt, is produced over a number of years.

1981 – The distillery closes in March.

Today's Ardbeg is a brand of iconic proportions with followers all over the world. Still, it was not an easy task for Glenmorangie to assume ownership in 1997. The distillery was rather run-down and for certain years there was an inconsistency in stock both in terms of quality and quantity. Production ceased between 1982 and 1989 and thereafter only took place for two months a year until 1996. Some casks from the 60s and 70s were included in the acquisition while there were very few from the 80s, plenty from 1990 but then fewer and fewer in the years until 1996. One of the first actions of Glenmorangie became to turn all stones in the whisky market to locate Ardbeg casks and those that could be found were bought from, e. g. Allied, Diageo and William Grant. The owners have not furnished independent bottlers with Ardbeg spirit since 1997. The distillery is equipped with a stainless steel mash tun, six washbacks made of Oregon pine and one pair of stills. In the spirit still, installed as recently as in 2001, lies a large part of the secret of Ardbeg's taste; compared to neighbours Laphroaig and Lagavulin the peatiness is supplemented by a fruitiness which gives Ardbeg its own very special style and sometimes the nickname "the peaty paradox". The character is achieved by a purifier attached to the spirit still and increasing the reflux. The distillery is producing at full capacity which funnily enough is the same volume (1 million litres) as it produced already back in 1887. An unpeated Ardbeg known as Kildalton is produced a few weeks a year since 1999 and was released in 2004. The peated malt is bought from Port Ellen and the unpeated from the mainland. The specification of Ardbeg's malt is 55 ppm which gives c 23 ppm in the finished spirit.

The visitor centre was reconstructed in 2008 while the announced new warehouse has been put on hold.

The core range consists of the *10 year old*, *Uiegedail* (with 20% sherry casks) and *Corryvreckan* (French oak and bourbon casks), which was first released as a Committee bottling in late 2008 but then came on general release September 2009. In 2008 the lightly peated (8 ppm) *Blasda* was released. The peatiest ever release from Ardbeg, at the opposite end of the scale from Blasda, is called *Supernova* and was released in early 2009. Its phenol level is well in excess of 100ppm. This whisky is from 2001 and has been matured in first fill bourbon casks (70%) and sherry butts (30%). A total of 550,000 bottles of Ardbeg were sold in 2008.

A couple of young expressions were recently released by Adelphi Distillery and a 15 year old (1994) came from Cadenheads.

History (continued):

1987 – Allied Lyons takes over Hiram Walker and thereby Ardbeg.

1989 – Production is restored with Iain Henderson as Manager. All malt is taken from Port Ellen.

1996 – The distillery closes in July and Allied Distillers decides to put it up for sale during the autumn.

1997 – Glenmorangie plc buys the distillery for £7 million (whereof £5.5 million is for whisky in storage). On stream from 25th June. Ardbeg 17 years old and Provenance are launched

1998 – A new visitor centre opens.

2000 – Ardbeg 10 years is introduced. The Ardbeg Committee (a worldwide forum for Ardbeg fans) is launched and has 30 000 members after a few years.

2001 – Lord of the Isles 25 years and Ardbeg 1977 are launched.

2002 – Ardbeg Committee Reserve and Ardbeg 1974 are launched.

2003 – Uigeadail is launched.

2004 – Very Young Ardbeg (6 years) and a limited edition of Ardbeg Kildalton (1300 bottles) are launched. The latter is an un-peated cask strength from 1980.

2005 – Serendipity is launched.

2006 – Ardbeg 1965 and Still Young are launched. Distillery Manager Stuart Thomson leaves Ardbeg after nine years. Almost There (9 years old) and Airigh Nam Beist are released.

2007 – Michael Heads becomes the new distillery manager. Ardbeg Mor, a 10 year old in 4.5 litre bottles is released.

2008 – The new 10 year old, Corryvreckan, Rennaisance, Blasda and Mor II are released.

2009 – Supernova is released, the peatiest expression from Ardbeg ever.

Ardbeg 10 year old

DR – Intense smoke and tar on the nose but with some distinctive sweet lemon notes, a mouth-coating palate with honeyed but firey peat, completely balanced and impressive, and a long smoke tail at the finish.

DS – Sweet peat smoke with apples in syrup on the nose. Strong, spiky peat with a searing hot hit of salt and pepper. Long, peppery finish.

Uigeadail   Blasda   Supernova

10 years old   Corryvreckan

Ardmore

Owner:
Beam Global
Spirits & Wine

Region/district:
Highland

Founded: **Status:** **Capacity:**
1898 Active 5 200 000 litres

Address: Kennethmont,
Aberdeenshire AB54 4NH

Tel: **website:**
01464 831213 www.ardmorewhisky.com

History:
1898 – Adam Teacher, son of William Teacher, starts the construction of Ardmore Distillery which eventually becomes William Teacher & Sons' first distillery. Adam Teacher passes away before it is completed.

1955 – Stills are increased from two to four.

1973 – A visitor centre is constructed.

1974 – Another four stills are added, increasing the total to eight.

1976 – Allied Breweries takes over William Teacher & Sons and thereby also Ardmore. The own maltings (Saladin box) is terminated.

1999 – A 12 year old is released to commemorate the distillery's 100th anniversary. A 21 year old is launched in a limited edition.

2002 – Ardmore is one of the last distilleries to abandon direct heating (by coal) of the stills in favour of indirect heating through steam.

2005 – Jim Beam Brands becomes new owner when it takes over some 20 spirits and wine brands from Allied Domecq for five billion dollars.

2007 – Ardmore Traditional Cask is launched.

2008 – A 25 and a 30 year old are launched.

Ardmore Traditional

DR – Unique and remarkable mix of burnt meat savouriness on the nose, and a delicatessen of flavours on the palate, smoked vanilla, burnt fruit and a distinctive and highly addictive sweet and savoury mix towards the peated finish

DS – Burnt toffee and caramel with spiky peat on the nose. Sweet and mushy with sweet peat flavours and some fruitiness in the earthy finish.

Ardmore distillery has become considerably better known in whisky circles since Ardmore Traditional was released in 2007. This was the first official bottling for several years and firm proof that the new American owner was more interested in the distillery than Allied Domecq ever was. Beam Global also decided to use quarter casks as part of the maturation process just as Laphroaig had done a few years earlier. But in all honesty, it was actually Allied who started re-racking whisky into the smaller (circa 100 litres) casks. In fact they tried it with all of their distilleries but only Laphroaig and Ardmore developed well.

Ardmore is an important part of the Teacher's blend and 35% of the 36 different malts (corresponds to 15% of the total quantity) which are included in this blend is Ardmore. A new expression of Teacher's is in the pipeline; the 36 single malts are re-vatted in used quarter casks for a second maturation of 2-3 years. The grain blend receives the same treatment, but in ex-bourbon casks, and the two are married together. The new expression, named Teacher's Origin, will be launched in India this year and in Europe in 2010. The distillery is also equipped with a castiron mash tun, 14 Douglas fir washbacks and four pairs of stills equipped with sub-coolers to give more copper contact. Ardmore has always been known to use peated malt (12-14 ppm) but for 18 of the 47 production weeks an unpeated version called Ardlair is produced. There will probably be a release of this unpeated version in the future but for the time being it is used mainly by other companies as a blending malt. At the moment, Ardmore is doing 23 mashes per week resulting in 5.2 million litres. Mostly ex-bourbon barrels are filled but also a few Pedro Ximenez sherry, port and cognac are in use in the warehouses.

The core range is the *Traditional* but last year a *25 year old* was launched as a duty free exclusive while a *30 year old* went to the American market. The most recent independent bottling was an 11 year old released in 2009 by Cadenheads.

Ardmore Traditional Cask

Meet the Manager

ALISTAIR LONGWELL
DISTILLERY MANAGER, ARDMORE DISTILLERY

When did you start working in the business and when did you start at Ardmore?

I started with William Teacher & Sons in 1987 and have worked for Teacher's, and their subsequent parent companies ever since. In 2004 I became distillery manager for Ardmore.

What kind of education or training do you have?

During my first years at Teacher's, I completed a Higher National Certificate in Electrical and Electronic Engineering. As well as on-the-job training and development, I have also undertaken further education including a Diploma in Management Studies and Associate Membership of the Institute of Environmental Management and Assessment.

Describe your career in the whisky business.

I was working at Allied Distillers Kilmalid Blending and Bottling site with maturation, filling and blending. This was a great education and I was able to learn from many knowledgeable people, including our own Master Blender, Mr Robert Hicks. After that I headed for the only part of the production business that I hadn't experienced – malt distilling. Between 2000 and 2004 I worked at all ten distilleries within the Allied estate. In 2005, my career turned full circle when I was made manager at Ardmore!

What are your main tasks as a manager?

Maintaining the high standards whilst maximising distillery output. The principal focus of my role is the day-to-day operation, but I also support our Sales and Marketing teams both in the UK as well as abroad.

What are the biggest challenges of being a distillery manager?

The barley harvests in recent years have meant that malt quality (and availability) has been variable to say the least! There have also been severe commercial challenges to our distillery budgets from both malt prices and utility/energy prices.

What would be the worst that could go wrong in the production process?

The one problem we all fear is not having the raw materials to work with. Touch wood, both quality and supply is looking a lot better this year compared to 2007 and 2008. The other principal raw material is water and restriction on availability of water is giving many distillers headaches, and this will only increase over the years to come.

How would you describe the character of Ardmore single malt?

Ardmore has an intriguing mix of highland malty/cereal tones, allied to a lightly peated, dry, earthy smoke balanced nicely by some rich dried fruits and citrus flavours which are more apparent in the older expressions. There is also an inherent sweetness which counteracts the smoke.

What are the main features in the distillation/maturation process at Ardmore, contributing to this character?

We only use local peat from our source at St Fergus which imparts the unique Ardmore peat notes. The distillation regime is also fairly balanced which helps to produce a consistent middle cut and the shape of the stills and the use of condensers and sub-coolers increase the distillate's exposure to copper, removing a lot of the unwanted, sulphury flavours. High quality ex-bourbon barrels contribute to the flavour profile, and the use of Quarter Casks help to generate a lot of the creamy caramel notes on the nose and the spicy, peppery finish on the palate.

What is your favourite expression of Ardmore and why?

We have some casks here that escaped under the radar for blending into Teacher's and one parcel of casks in particular holds my current favourite Ardmore! The spirit is 31 years old and the extremely slow maturation in the hogsheads has given us a spirit which is still indicative of the original distillation flavours and not dominated by overt wood flavours.

If it were your decision – what new expression of Ardmore would you like to see released?

I would like to see an Ardmore which has spent some, or all, of its life within the custom-built European Oak Puncheons that the full flavoured and robust Ardmore malt we use as the base for Teacher's Highland Cream is matured in.

If you had to choose a favourite dram other than Ardmore, what would that be?

If I couldn't have an Ardmore then I would have to take a Teacher's. With its exceptionally high malt content, it can truly be said to be a malt drinker's blend!

What are the biggest changes you have seen the past 10-15 years in your profession?

The adoption of new plc and computer technologies to automate and control distillery processes and associated plant. Although there has been huge benefit in reducing manual handling hazards, explosion risks etc, as well as improving consistency and quality, I think that there is a lot to be said for maintaining a 'hands-on' approach to whisky making.

Do you see any major changes in the next 10 years to come?

The industry has recently pledged itself to some extremely stretching environmental targets. This will accelerate the adoption of new technologies to harness the potential of distillery co-products – draff and pot ale. Where currently we normally use fairly energy intensive processes to convert distillery co-products into animal feeds, we will see distilleries exploiting the energy potential of the co-products to either raise steam or generate green electricity.

What are the implications of distilling both peated and unpeated spirit?

The major challenge is ensuring that everything is kept separated from malt intake and storage right through to the spirit receivers. Obviously this is more important when changing over from traditional Ardmore to Ardlair (unpeated spirit) as the slightest hint of peat will show in the unpeated spirit. The spirit cut for the Ardlair is radically different to the Ardmore cuts as we are looking to collect a different flavour profile and the Stillman needs to keep his wits about him as the wash stills will tend to perform differently depending on the malt type.

It must be rewarding for you to see Ardmore being recognised also as a single malt.

The launch of Ardmore Traditional Cask has been a source of immense satisfaction to both myself and the entire team here at Ardmore. We've always known that we distill a very special malt and it has been unbelievably frustrating to have had to wait 108 years for Ardmore to be made available as a proprietary single malt! The most rewarding aspect has been the reaction from the public. Some are initially put off when we tell them that it is peated – they are expecting a full West Coast Iodine hit and most are pleasantly surprised by the controlled, dry earthy highland peat smoke that Ardmore delivers.

Arran

Owner:
Isle of Arran Distillers

Region/district:
Islands (Arran)

Founded: **Status:** **Capacity:**
1993 Active (vc) 750 000 litres

Address: Lochranza, Isle of Arran KA27 8HJ

Tel: **website:**
01770 830264 www.arranwhisky.com

History:
1993 – Harold Currie founds the distillery.

1995 – Production starts in full on 17th August.

1996 – A one year old is released with the text '1 year old spirit' on the label as it is not, in legal terms, whisky.

1997 – A visitor centre is opened by Her Majesty the Queen.

1998 – The first release is a 3 year old (1,000 bottles).

1999 – The Arran 4 years old is released.

2002 – Single Cask 1995 is launched.

2003 – Single Cask 1997, non-chill filtered and Calvados finish is launched.

2004 – Cognac finish, Marsala finish, Port finish and Arran First Distillation 1995 are launched.

2005 – Arran 1996 is launched (6,000 bottles). Two more finishes are launched - Chateau Margaux and Grand Cru Champagne.

2006 – After an unofficial launch in 2005, Arran 10 years old is released as well as a couple of new wood finishes.

2007 – Arran is named Scottish Distiller of the Year by Whisky Magazine. Four new wood finishes and Gordon's Dram are released.

2008 – The first 12 year old is released as well as four new wood finishes.

2009 – Peated single casks, two wood finishes and 1996 Vintage are released.

Arran 10 year old

DR – Creamy barley, toffee and citrus notes on the nose then creamy, full and chunky fruit centre. The finish is rich and full.

DS – Honey, malt and biscuit on the nose. A malty, honeyed palate – not a robust whisky but flavourful. The finish is biscuity and sweet.

Establishing a new distillery and brand of whisky is a tough task but the owner of Arran distillery must be pleased. The first official 10 year old was launched in 2006 and already 150,000 bottles a year of its various malt expressions are sold.

The semi-lauter mash tun, the four Oregon pine washbacks and the two stills all stand in one room which allows the production to be easily overviewed by the 60,000 annual visitors to the distillery. One dunnage warehouse holds 3,000 casks and a new racked warehouse completed in summer 2007 is of a similar capacity. Total capacity is 750,000 litres but current production only amounts to just around 125,000. Of that, 8,000-10,000 litres has since 2004 been a peated version with a phenol content of 12ppm.

The owner's long-term plan is to have three core expressions - 10, 14 and 18 years old. The 14 year olds were re-racked from sherry casks to bourbon this year and are due for release in June 2010.

The current core range of Arran consists of *10 year old*, *12 year old* (a new addition to the range released in October 2008), *100 Proof* and *Robert Burns*. The latter is a single malt usually bottled as a 5 year old. A limited edition (6000 bottles) of Robert Burns was launched around the same time to commemorate the 250th anniversary of the poet's birth. Other limited editions include yearly bottlings of *single casks*, either *sherry matured* or *bourbon matured*. There used to be quite a few wood finishes every year but for 2009 there are only two - *Pinot Noir* and *Pomerol*. Exciting limited releases in the beginning of 2009 were the first *peated versions of Arran*. Four casks (three bourbon and one sherry) were bottled as 4 year olds. Finally, in August a *1996 Vintage* was released as a part of the new Icons of Arran Distillery series.

Independent bottlings are not that common but both Dewar Rattray and Duncan Taylor have recently released bottlings from 1996 and from Murray McDavid came a 12 year old Margaux finish.

12 years old

Auchentoshan

Owner:
Morrison Bowmore
(Suntory)

Region/district:
Lowlands

Founded: 1823
Status: Active (vc)
Capacity: 1 750 000 litres

Address: Dalmuir, Clydebank, Glasgow G81 4SJ

Tel: 01389 878561
website: www.auchentoshan.com

History:

1800 – First mention of the distillery Duntocher, which may be identical to Auchentoshan.

1823 – An official license is obtained by the owner, Mr. Thorne.

1903 – The distillery is purchased by John Maclachlan.

1923 – G. & J. Maclachlan goes bankrupt and a new company, Maclachlans Ltd, is formed.

1941 – The distillery is severely damaged by a German bomb raid and reconstruction does not commence until 1948.

1960 – Maclachlans Ltd is purchased by the brewery J. & R. Tennant Brewers.

1969 – Auchentoshan is bought by Eadie Cairns Ltd who starts major modernizations.

1984 – Stanley P. Morrison, eventually becoming Morrison Bowmore, becomes new owner.

1994 – Suntory buys Morrison Bowmore.

2000 – A cask strength 31 year old is launched in a limited edition.

2002 – Auchentoshan Three Wood is launched in May.

2004 – More than a £1 million is spent on a new, refurbished visitor centre. The oldest Auchentoshan ever, 42 years, is released.

2006 – Auchentoshan 18 year old is released.

2007 – A 40 year old and a 1976 30 year old are released.

2008 – New packaging as well as new expressions - Classic, 18 year old and 1988.

Auchentoshan 12 year old

DR – Toffee, rose water and Milk Chocolate Crisp on the nose, grape and crisp apple on the palate before a spicy fruity interplay in a lengthy finish.

DS – Sweet straw and icing sugar on the nose with heavy sherry notes. Sweet and sherried – slightly bitter with grape skin flavours in the aftertaste.

Except for Hazelburn produced at Springbank Distillery, Auchentoshan is the only triple distilled whisky in Scotland. The distillery is equipped with a semi-lauter mash tun, four Oregon pine washbacks which have been doubled in size and three stills. There are another four washbacks which are not in use at the moment. The spirit matures in three dunnage and two racked warehouses which currently house 18,000 hogsheads. Unlike many other Scottish distilleries, Auchentoshan is not running at full capacity. A five-day week with eight mashes per week results in 850,000 litres which is about half of maximum output. Even if Auchentoshan sales have been steady at the same level in recent years, the brand has advanced nicely in total sales during the last decade increasing from 120,000 to 420,000 bottles, of which 85% of are exported.

Morrison Bowmore´s range of single malts under the name McClelland sell double that figure. The company T & A McClelland was bought already in 1970 and the range of un-aged (around 5 years old) single malts consists of Highland, Islay, Lowland and the most recently introduced Speyside. In addition to that, a 12 year old of the latter was launched in 2008. Key markets for McClelland are the USA, Canada, Japan and France.

The core range of Auchentoshan was completely overhauled in 2008 and now consists of *Classic, 12 years, Three Wood, 18 years* and *21 years. Select* (no age statement) has been moved to the duty free range. Apart from *Auchentoshan 1988*, a Bordeaux finish exclusive for the duty free market, 2008 also saw the re-release of the *1957 Vintage* (171 bottles). The first release was in November 2007. Recent independent bottlings include a 9 year old by Duncan Taylor, a 17 year old by Douglas Laing and an 18 year old from 1990 released by Cadenheads.

Three Wood

Auchroisk

Owner:
Diageo

Region/district:
Speyside

Founded: 1974

Status: Active

Capacity: 3 580 000 litres

Address: Mulben, Banffshire AB55 6XS

Tel: 01542 885000

website: www.malts.com

History:
1972 – Building of the distillery commences by Justerini & Brooks (which, together with W. A. Gilbey, make up the group IDV) in order to produce blending whisky. In February the same year IDV is purchased by the brewery Watney Mann which, in July, merges into Grand Metropolitan.

1974 – The distillery is completed and, despite the intention of producing malt for blending, the first year's production is sold 12 years later as single malt thanks to the high quality.

1986 – The first whisky is marketed under the name Singleton.

1997 – Grand Metropolitan and Guinness merge into the conglomerate Diageo. Simultaneously, the subsidiaries United Distillers (to Guinness) and International Distillers & Vintners (to Grand Metropolitan) form the new company United Distillers & Vintners (UDV).

2001 – The name Singleton is abandoned and the whisky is now marketed under the name of Auchroisk in the Flora & Fauna series.

2003 – Apart from the 10 year old in the Flora & Fauna series, a 28 year old from 1974, the distillery's first year, is launched in the Rare Malt series.

Auchroisk 10 year old

DR – Young and zesty and citrusy on the nose, warming tangerine and citrus fruits and a touch of salt on the palate, medium long malty finish.

DS – Malt loaf with raisins and vanilla on the nose. The palate is oily and sweet with fortified wine flavours. A long, oily finish.

Auchroisk was built as late as 1974 by Justerini & Brooks, with the purpose of producing malt whisky for their main blend J&B. Eventually, Justerini & Brooks became a part of Diageo and today J&B is their second best selling whisky after Johnnie Walker and number three in the world after Ballantine´s. J&B has shown a weakening trend, or at best zero growth, since the late nineties but recent years have seen an increase after several lavish campaigns launching the blend as the "party whisky".

Auchroisk is a fairly large distillery with one stainless steel mash tun, eight stainless steel washbacks and four pairs of stills. Fermentation in the washbacks can often be quite vigorous and to prevent overflow most distilleries have rotating blades to keep the wash away. At Auchroisk, however, each washback is equipped with four stainless steel bars containing a fibre-based solution to prevent frothing.

The huge warehouses at Auchroisk which can store 250,000 casks have a special role in Diageo´s production of blended whiskies. New make comes by tanker from many other distilleries, especially Knockando, Glen Spey and Strathmill. They are all, in common with Auchroisk, vital parts of J&B and filled into casks for maturation. Mature malt whisky from different distilleries are blended at Auchroisk and then shipped to any of the bottling plants where the final blending with grain spirit as well as bottling takes place. This blend of malt whiskies is called part blend. In 1986, a 12 year old was launched as Singleton as Auchroisk was considered too difficult to pronounce. It was however discontinued and the name Singleton is now used for single malts from Dufftown, Glendullan and Glen Ord. Today the core range consists of a *10 year old Flora & Fauna* under the name Auchroisk. Independent bottlings occur now and then. Some of the more recent ones are an 18 year old released by Blackadder and a really old one from 1975 by Douglas Laing.

Flora & Fauna
10 years old

Aultmore

Owner:
John Dewar & Sons
(Bacardi)

Region/district:
Speyside

Founded: 1896

Status: Active

Capacity: 2 900 000 litres

Address: Keith, Banffshire AB55 6QY

Tel: 01542 881800

website: -

History:
1896 – Alexander Edward, owner of Benrinnes and co-founder of Craigellachie Distillery, builds Aultmore.

1897 – Production starts.

1898 – Production is doubled; the company Oban & Aultmore Glenlivet Distilleries Ltd manages Aultmore.

1923 – Alexander Edward sells Aultmore for £20,000 to John Dewar & Sons.

1925 – Dewar's becomes part of Distillers Company Limited (DCL).

1930 – The administration is transferred to Scottish Malt Distillers (SMD).

1971 – The stills are increased from two to four.

1991 – UDV launches a 12-year old Aultmore in the Flora & Fauna series.

1996 – A 21 year old cask strength is marketed as a Rare Malt.

1998 – Diageo sells Dewar's and Bombay Gin to Bacardi for £1 150 million.

2004 – A new official bottling is launched (12 years old).

Aultmore 12 year old

DR – Orange blossom and flowers on the nose, lemon and lime Starburst on the palate, with late sherbet spicy and drying and more-ish finish. Altogether, zesty and very pleasant.

DS – Fresh and crisp on the nose with a herbal, green tea aroma. The palate is soft and sweet with oatmeal and malt flavours which linger on the finish.

John Dewar & Sons owns and operates five distilleries in Scotland and, apart from Aberfeldy which was founded by the Dewar brothers themselves in 1896, Aultmore was the first which came into their ownership (already in 1923). Today, virtually nothing of the old Aultmore Distillery is left and the visitor encounters rather traditionally industrial buildings which were erected in the early seventies.

Since 2008 production has been running seven days a week which means full capacity of 2.9 million litres. A Steinecker full lauter mash tun, six washbacks and two pairs of stills are operated. The stillhouse control system has also been modernised in 2008. All the warehouses were demolished in 1996; in fact Dewar's no longer has any maturation capacity at any of its distilleries. Instead the company has redeveloped its headquarters at Westthorn in Glasgow where another five warehouses have been constructed. A new site at Pontiel has been bought with plans for a new maturation centre to be opened in 2009/2010.

Aultmore was one of the first distilleries to build a dark grains plant in order to process pot ale and draff into cattle feed. It was commissioned in 1977 but closed in 1985. It then reopened in 1989 but was finally taken out of production in 1993. Most of these distillation by-products are still to this day converted to either fodder or fertilizer, but a new use has recently been found for them - producing electricity. Basically it is done in the same way as a biomass power plant would do. Diageo's new distillery at Roseisle, for example, will use whisky by-products to generate the majority of its power needs.

Most of the output is, above all, used in Dewar's blended whiskies, but a *12 year old* official bottling appeared on the market in 2004. Three different versions of Aultmore 1997 were released by Ian MacLeod in 2009 (Medoc, Sherry, Manzanilla) and from Blackadder came an older version distilled in 1989.

12 years old

Balblair

Owner:
Inver House Distillers
(Thai Beverages plc)

Region/district:
Northern Highlands

Founded: 1790   **Status:** Active   **Capacity:** 1 330 000 litres

Address: Edderton, Tain, Ross-shire IV19 1LB

Tel: 01862 821273

website: www.balblair.com

History:

1790 – The distillery is founded by John Ross.

1824 – The son Andrew Ross starts taking over, but moves to Brora after a couple of years and John Ross takes over again.

1836 – The founder John Ross dies and Andrew Ross takes over with the help of his sons.

1872 – New buildings replace the old.

1873 – Andrew Ross dies and his son James takes over.

1894 – Balnagowan Estate signs a new lease for 60 years with Alexander Cowan. He builds a new distillery, a few kilometres from the old.

1911 – Cowan is forced to cease payments and the distillery closes. The staff sell out the whole stock in the 20-year period until 1932.

1941 – Balnagowan Estate goes bankrupt and the distillery is put up for sale.

1948 – The lawyer Robert Cumming from Keith buys Balblair for £48,000.

1949 – Production restarts.

1970 – Cumming sells Balblair to Hiram Walker. A third still is installed.

1988 – Allied Distillers becomes the new owner through the merger between Hiram Walker and Allied Vintners.

1996 – Allied Domecq sells the distillery to Inver House Distillers.

2000 – Balblair Elements and the first version of Balblair 33 years are launched.

2001 – Thai company Pacific Spirits (part of the Great Oriole Group) takes over Inver House.

2004 – Balblair 38 years is launched.

2005 – 12 year old Peaty Cask, 1979 (26 years) and 1970 (35 years) are launched.

2006 – International Beverage Holdings acquires Pacific Spirits UK.

2007 – Three new vintages replace the entire former range.

2008 – Vintage 1975 and 1965 are released.

2009 – Vintage 1991 and 1990 are released.

Balblair 1997

DR – Crystal clear and clean barley and vanilla nose, vanilla ice cream and soft yellow melon on the palate, and a gentle oakiness towards the finish.

DS – Juniper berries with sherry notes and hazelnuts on the nose. The palate is sweeter than expected, earthy, oily and complex and the apple turnover in the finish is sublime.

Looking back, the complete relaunch of Balblair single malt in the beginning of 2007 seems to have been beneficial. Sales soared by 23% to 4,200 cases in 2008 and although the figures are still lower than in 2005, one must remember that the new range is a high premium one, consisting of vintages rather than the "ordinary" 10 or 12 year olds.

The equipment at Balblair consists of a stainless steel mash tun, six Oregon pine washbacks and one pair of stills. There is actually a third still but it has not been used since 1969. The spirit is matured in eight dunnage warehouses with a capacity of 26,000 casks. Some 12-15% of the production is bottled as single malt which is filled and stored on site. Currently, a six-day week is in place with 17 mashes per week and the target for 2009 is to produce 1.3 million litres of alcohol. The water is drawn from Ault Dreag more than 4 miles from the distillery and is pumped to a tank, equipped with a copper filter, on the other side of the road.

The owner of Balblair, Inver House, has been well backed-up financially by its Thai parent company, Thai Beverages. A £1m investment resulted in a new bottling hall, opened in spring 2009 at its headquarters in Airdrie, creating 10 new jobs.

In 2007 the old expressions were all discontinued and replaced by three vintages - *1979, 1989* and *1997*. All three had been matured in first or second fill bourbon casks. The 1979 was replaced by the *1975*, this time from second filled sherry butts. 2008 also saw the launch of a *1986* for duty free, a *1985 single cask* for Maison du Whisky and *Balblair 1965*. In 2009, *Balblair 1990* was released as a duty free exclusive and early autumn saw the launch of the bourbon matured *Balblair 1991*. Independent bottlings have become rarer lately, but one of the few recent ones was a Cadenhead 18 year old.

Balblair 1991

Balmenach

Owner:
Inver House Distillers
(Thai Beverages plc)

Region/district:
Speyside

Founded: 1824   **Status:** Active   **Capacity:** 2 000 000 litres

Address: Cromdale, Moray PH26 3PF

Tel: 01479 872569   **website:** www.inverhouse.com

History:

1824 – The distillery is licensed to James MacGregor who operated a small farm distillery by the name of Balminoch for decades.

1897 – Balmenach Glenlivet Distillery Company is founded.

1922 – The MacGregor family sells to a consortium consisting of MacDonald Green, Peter Dawson and James Watson.

1925 – The consortium becomes part of Distillers Company Limited (DCL).

1930 – Production is transferred to Scottish Malt Distillers (SMD).

1941 – The distillery closes.

1947 – The distillery reopens.

1962 – The number of stills is increased to six.

1964 – Floor maltings replaced with a Saladin box

1992 – The first official bottling is a 12 year old.

1993 – The distillery is mothballed in May.

1997 – Inver House Distillers buys Balmenach from United Distillers.

1998 – Production recommences.

2001 – Thai company Pacific Spirits takes over Inver House at the price of £56 million. The new owner launches a 27 and a 28 year old.

2002 – To commemorate the Queen's Golden Jubilee a limited edition of 800 bottles of 25-year old Balmenach is launched.

2006 – International Beverage Holdings acquires Pacific Spirits UK.

Deerstalker 18 year old

DR – Pine needles, lemon and grapefruit and flu powder on the nose, rich sherry and a trace of sulphur on the palate, with savoury lemon and a traces of peat. A medium and citrusy finish.

DS – One of the most intense and curious noses I've ever come across; juniper berries, eucalyptus, fino sherry and trifle. The palate is more subdued but very peaty with oodles of strangely delicious smoke on the finish.

The owner of Balmenach, Inver House Distillers, sells the equivalent of more than 8.4 million bottles per year but only 15% of them are single malts. The lion's share of the sales is blended Scotch with brands like MacArthur's, Catto's and Hankey Bannister. The latter goes back to 1757 when Hankey Bannister established itself as supplier of wines and spirits. To celebrate the 250th anniversary of the foundation, a 40 year old expression was launched in 2007. It was blended already in 1966 and had been maturing in Spanish oak since then. Some of the ingredients were single malts which today are extremely rare like Killyloch and Glen Flagler. Hankey Bannister 40 year old was voted Best Blended Whisky in the World at the World Whiskies Awards 2009.

Balmenach distillery is equipped with a mash tun made of cast iron, six wooden washbacks and three pairs of stills. A traditional feature still remains - a worm tub with a 94 metre long worm used for cooling the spirit vapours. The three dunnage warehouses have space for 14,000 casks. Production in 2009 was 15 mashes per week which is full capacity.

We are still waiting for an official bottling of Balmenach from the current owner. When Inver House Distillers took over from United Distillers there was no maturing whisky included in the deal, so they had to start from scratch. This means that the oldest whisky will be around 10 years old, so with luck, we may soon see the first Inver House-produced Balmenach on the shelves. There has also been indications from Inver House implying that un-aged versions (like Speyburn Bradan Orach) from other distilleries in the group may be launched.

The only "official" bottling so far is the 12 year old Flora & Fauna from the previous owner and this is now becoming increasingly difficult to find. There are however other Balmenach on the market. One is produced by an independent company called Aberko in Glasgow under the name Deerstalker 18 years.

Deerstalker 18 years

Balvenie

Owner:
William Grant & Sons

Region/district:
Speyside

Founded: **Status:**
1892   Active (vc)

Capacity:
5 600 000 litres

Address: Dufftown, Keith,
Banffshire AB55 4DH

Tel:
01340 820373

website:
www.thebalvenie.com

History:
1892 – William Grant rebuilds Balvenie New House to Balvenie Distillery (Glen Gordon was the name originally intended). Part of the equipment is brought in from Lagavulin and Glen Albyn.

1893 – The first distillation takes place in May.

1955 – The distillery is modernized.

1957 – The two stills are increased by another two.

1965 – Two new stills are installed.

1971 – Another two stills are installed and eight stills are now running.

1973 – The first official bottling appears.

1982 – Founder's Reserve, in an eye-catching Cognac-reminiscent bottle, is launched.

1990 – A new distillery, Kininvie, is opened on the premises.

1996 – Two vintage bottlings and a Port wood finish are launched.

2001 – The Balvenie Islay Cask, with 17 years in bourbon casks and six months in Islay casks, is released.

2002 – Balvenie releases 83 bottles of a 50 year old that has been in sherry casks since January 1952. Recommended price £6,000 a bottle.

2004 – The Balvenie Thirty is released to commemorate Malt Master David Stewart's 30th anniversary at Balvenie.

2005 – The Balvenie Rum Wood Finish 14 years old is released.

2006 – The Balvenie New Wood 17 years old, Roasted Malt 14 years old and Portwood 1993 are released.

2007 – Vintage Cask 1974 and Sherry Oak 17 years old are released.

2008 – Signature, Vintage 1976, Balvenie Rose and Rum Cask 17 year old are released.

2009 – Vintage 1978, 17 year old Madeira finish, 14 year old rum finish and Golden Cask 14 years old are released.

The Balvenie Doublewood 12 year old

DR – Red fruits and berries, a hint of smoke on the nose, on the palate mouth filling, rich and fruity and, surprisingly, with a peat presence. Lots of sherry and some toffee in the finish.

DS – A sherried and malty nose with rich honey and fruitcake. The most honeyed palate there is with rich spice and fruit. The finish is akin to a honey liqueur.

Balvenie distillery is unique because it is the only Scottish distillery where all the stages of whisky production take place at the distillery, including growing barley and malting. The man-in-the-know may claim that this is also the case at Kilchoman on Islay. True, but added to the fact that Balvenie also has its own copper smith (Dennis McBain who has been with the distillery for 49 years) and its own cooperage, then it becomes clear that Balvenie is indeed special in this respect.

Thirty tonnes of malt, corresponding to 10% of requirements, are produced in the maltings every week. For the first six hours the malt is dried using peat and for the remaining 42 hours it is dried with coal. The malted barley is used exclusively for Balvenie single malt and not for the other two malt distilleries in the group - Glenfiddich and Kininvie. The distillery has a full lauter mash tun, nine wooden and five stainless steel washbacks. The number of wash stills was increased to five and spirit stills to six, divided into two still rooms, in 2008 when the facilities were expanded. This means that 28 mashes per week with an annual capacity of 5.6 million litres of alcohol is now possible. Both bourbon and sherry casks are used, stored in a total of 44 dunnage, racked or palletised warehouses shared with Kininvie and Glenfiddich. The distillery opened up for visitors only recently, but instead of catering to the masses, a quality tour for smaller groups is on offer.

Balvenie is one of the Top Ten malts in terms of sales and sold 170,000 nine litre cases in 2008.

The core range consists of *Doublewood 12 years old*, *Signature 12 years*, *Single Barrel 15 years*, *Portwood 21 years* and the *30 year old*. New limited releases during 2009 are this year's *vintage* from *1978*, a *17 year old* finished in *Madeira* casks and, for the French market, a *14 year old rum finish* called *Cuban Selection*. A new duty free exclusive, *Golden Cask 14 years old* with a finish in Carribean rum, was also launched.

There are no independent bottlings of Balvenie.

17 year old Madeira cask

Ben Nevis

Owner:
Ben Nevis Distillery Ltd
(Nikka, Asahi Breweries)

Region/district:
Western Highlands

Founded: **Status:** **Capacity:**
1825 Active (vc) 2 000 000 litres

Address: Lochy Bridge, Fort William PH33 6TJ

Tel:
01397 702476

website:
www.bennevisdistillery.com

History:

1825 – The distillery is founded by 'Long' John McDonald.

1856 – Long John dies and his son Donald P. McDonald takes over.

1878 – Demand is so great that another distillery, Nevis Distillery, is built nearby.

1908 – Both distilleries merge into one.

1941 – D. P. McDonald & Sons sells the distillery to Ben Nevis Distillery Ltd headed by the Canadian millionaire Joseph W. Hobbs. He has already bought Bruichladdich, Glenesk and Glenury Royal and he opens Lochside in 1957.

1955 – Hobbs installs a Coffey still which makes it possible to produce both grain and malt whisky.

1964 – Joseph Hobbs dies.

1978 – Production is stopped.

1981 – Joseph Hobbs Jr sells the distillery back to Long John Distillers and Whitbread.

1984 – After restoration and reconstruction totalling £2 million, Ben Nevis opens up again.

1986 – The distillery closes again.

1989 – Whitbread sells the distillery to Nikka Whisky Distilling Company Ltd.

1990 – The distillery opens up again.

1991 – A visitor centre is inaugurated.

1996 – Ben Nevis 10 years old is launched.

2006 – A 13 year old port finish is released.

Ben Nevis 10 year old

DR – Grape skins, over-ripe pear on the nose, baked apple and liquorice roots on the palate, pleasant malty finish.

DS – Pine nuts with a malty sweetness on the nose. The palate is full of bittersweet bread and nut flavours – warm dough. The finish is short and yeasty.

Since the foundation by "Long" John MacDonald in 1825, Ben Nevis distillery has had a long and colourful history, especially under the ownership of the eccentric Joseph Hobbs. He was, among other things, responsible for introducing the Coffey still so the distillery could produce both malt and grain spirit. A period of melancholy followed during the eighties when the distillery was under the ownership of Whitbread. Despite some investments it was primarily used during most of the decade for warehousing and trial production and it was only during 1984-1986 that there was commercial production. Japan with Nikka Whisky Distilling was the saviour when it acquired Ben Nevis, installed a new mash tun and replaced the concrete washbacks Joseph Hobbs had installed.

Ben Nevis is currently equipped with one lauter mash tun, eight stainless steel washbacks and two pairs of stills. A combination of bourbon and sherry casks is used for maturation.

Around one million litres are produced annually and most of it is sold either as blended whisky or as single malt in Japan where Ben Nevis ranks seventh among most sold single malts. It also sells well in the Nordic countries, Germany and France.

Since 1996 the core of the range has been a *10 year old*. Some one-off bottlings have appeared at regular intervals such as the *13 year old Port finish* released in 2006 and the *1992 single cask* released in 2007. There have also been some interesting *26 year olds*, the first released in the early nineties and the last, distilled in 1975, a couple of years ago. The blended whisky Dew of Ben Nevis, which occurs in several varieties, is the main seller. Glencoe, a vatted malt which was introduced in the late sixties by Rory McDonald, one of Long John McDonald's descendants, is also produced.

Recent independent bottlings include a couple from 1999 by Duncan Taylor, a 12 year old from Cadenhead and a Grenache finish from Murray McDavid distilled in 1999.

10 years old

BenRiach

Owner:
Benriach Distillery Co

Region/district:
Speyside

Founded: 1897
Status: Active
Capacity: 2 800 000 litres

Address: Longmorn, Elgin, Morayshire IV30 8SJ

Tel: 01343 862888
website: www.benriachdistillery.co.uk

History:
1897 – John Duff & Co founds the distillery.

1899 – Longmorn Distilleries Co. buys the distillery.

1903 – The distillery is mothballed. The maltings is kept running to supply Longmorn with malt.

1965 – The distillery is reopened by the new owner, The Glenlivet Distillers Ltd.

1978 – Seagram Distillers takes over ownership.

1983 – Seagrams starts producing a peated Benriach.

1985 – The number of stills is increased to four.

1994 – The first official bottling is a 10 year old.

1999 – The maltings is decommissioned.

2001 – Pernod Ricard takes over Chivas Brothers.

2002 – The distillery is mothballed in October.

2004 – Intra Trading, buys Benriach together with the former Director at Burn Stewart, Billy Walker. The price is £5.4 million including stock.

2004 – Standard, Curiositas and 12, 16 and 20 year olds are released.

2005 – Four different vintages are released in limited editions - 1966, 1970, 1978 och 1984.

2006 – Sixteen new releases, among them a 25 year old, a 30 year old and 8 different vintages.

2007 – A 40 year old and three new heavily peated expressions are released.

2008 – New expressions include a peated Madeira finish, a 15 year old Sauternes finish and nine single casks. Benriach Distillery Co buys Glendronach distillery from Chivas Brothers.

2009 – Two new wood finishes (Moscatel and Gaja Barolo) and nine different single casks are released.

BenRiach Curiositas

DR – Complex nose with sooty smoke, cocoa powder and lemon. Lots of charcoal smoke and heavy peat on the palate, but melon and peach too. A long finish mixing sweet fruit with an acerbic wood fire smokiness.

DS – Ash and tar on the nose with a hint of salty rubber. The palate is sweet and salty with a hint of Turkisk pepper and carob. A finish akin to chewing peat grist.

BenRiach 12 year old

DR – Classic Speyside nose, with a rich blend of fruits, vanilla and honey. On the palate ripe fruits are balanced by crisp barley and sweet honey, and the finish is balanced, rounded and pleasant.

DS – A sweet and spicy nose with heather and pine notes. Round and malty on the palate with cloves and nutmeg and a finish like an Autumnal day in the Highlands.

It can be difficult for small producers to take shares in established markets as the large whisky giants' marketing efforts overshadow them. Easier then, like BenRiach, to explore new export markets such as Kazakhstan. In 2009 the first 500 cases were sent to what is the world´s ninth biggest country and which, according to owner Billy Walker, has a huge potential both for standard bottlings and deluxe items.

BenRiach experienced an exciting period during the seventies and eighties as an experimental laboratory. Trials with peated whiskies and maturation in virgin oak were made and these are now launched by the new owner. Triple distillation, using a now removed fifth still, was also performed and some of these distilled in 1998 still remain in the warehouses.

The distillery is equipped with a traditional cast iron mash tun, eight washbacks made of stainless steel and two pairs of stills. The annual production of this independent distillery has increased from year to year and has now reached 1.8 million litres. Some of this is still earmarked for the old proprietor Chivas Brothers.

The core range of BenRiach is *Heart of Speyside* (no age), *12, 16* and *20 years old* in what the distillery itself calls Classic Speyside style and *Curiositas 10 year old, Authenticus 21 year old* and the four *12 year olds* named *Fumosus* - heavily peated whiskies with different finishes and launched 2007/2008 as the peated varieties. Four different *15 year olds* with different finishes were supplemented in 2008 with a *16 year old Sauternes finish* and in August 2009 with *Moscatel* and *Gaja Barolo*, both *18 year olds*. According to tradition, the distillery also launched a batch (the sixth) in July 2009 of no less than nine different *single casks* ranging *from 1970 to 1994*. Some old BenRiachs of between *25-40 years* of age complete the range.

Independent bottlings are becoming rare. Recent releases include a 42 year old from Signatory, a 23 year old from Cadenhead and a 1996 by Duncan Taylor.

Curiositas 10 year old

Benrinnes

Owner: Diageo
Region/district: Speyside

Founded: 1826
Status: Active
Capacity: 2 540 000 litres

Address: Aberlour, Banffshire AB38 9NN

Tel: 01340 872600
website: www.malts.com

History:

1826 – The first Benrinnes distillery is built at Whitehouse Farm by Peter McKenzie.

1829 – A flood destroys the distillery.

1834 – A new distillery, Lyne of Ruthrie, is constructed a few kilometres from the first one. The owner, John Innes files for bankruptcy and William Smith & Company takes over.

1864 – William Smith & Company goes bankrupt and David Edward becomes the new owner.

1896 – Benrinnes is ravaged by fire which prompts major refurbishment and rebuilding including electrification. David Edward dies and his son Alexander Edward takes over. Alexander also founds the distilleries Dallas Dhu, Aultmore and Craigellachie and purchases Oban.

1922 – John Dewar & Sons takes over ownership.

1925 – John Dewar & Sons becomes part of Distillers Company Limited (DCL).

1930 – DCL transfers management and operations to Scottish Malt Distillers (SMD).

1955/56 – The distillery is completely rebuilt.

1964 – Floor maltings is replaced by a Saladin box.

1966 – The number of stills doubles to six.

1984 – The Saladin box is taken out of service and the malt is purchased centrally.

1991 – The first official bottling from Benrinnes is a 15 year old in the Flora & Fauna series.

1996 – United Distillers releases a 21 year old cask strength in their Rare Malts series.

2009 – A 23 year old (6,000 bottles) is launched as a part of this year's Special Releases.

Benrinnes 15 year old

DS – Heavily sherried nose with figs in syrup. Rich and sweet in the mouth like a dark rum. Sweet and rich throughout with figs on the finish.

Benrinnes Distillery has been subjected to at least three major refurbishings since its inception in 1826. The first entailed rebuilding a completely new distillery after a serious flooding and the most recent, in the fifties, gave it the current, rather charmless, appearance. The surroundings at the foot of the mountain Ben Rinnes are however unrivalled.

The distillery is equipped with a stainless steel lauter mash tun, eight washbacks made of larch and six stills. Instead of running the stills in three pairs, they are grouped three and three resulting in a partial triple distillation similar to that of Springbank. This technique was probably adopted in connection with rebuilding the distillery in 1955. Worm tubs are used for condensation and, up to the 1880s, worm tubs were the only cooling method in practice. During his trip in 1885-86, the famous whisky author Alfred Barnard saw only eight distilleries not using worm tubs and it was not until the 1960s, when many of the distilleries were refurbished, that the modern shell and tube condensers took over.

Being the biggest player in the Scotch whisky business, Diageo is sometimes accused of thinking more of production efficiency than of traditional methods. However, it is in at least one respect a defender of traditions: maintaining worm tubs for cooling the spirit vapours. Only 13 distilleries still use this technique and no less than nine of these are owned by Diageo.

The lion part of Benrinnes is used in blended whiskies, especially A & A Crawford but also in J&B and Johnnie Walker. The only official bottling has so far been *Flora & Fauna 15 years old*. In autumn 2009 however, a surprise appeared in Diageo´s annual Special Releases when a new bottling of Benrinnes was launched - a *23 year old* from 1985.

Independent bottlings are quite rare. Three of the most recent are a 12 year old from Cadenheads, an 11 year old Tokay-finish from 1996 by Ian MacLeod and a 14 year old from 1994 by the same bottler.

23 years old

Benromach

Owner:
Gordon & MacPhail

Region/district:
Speyside

Founded: 1898

Status: Active (vc)

Capacity: 500 000 litres

Address: Invererne Road, Forres,
Morayshire IV36 3EB

Tel: 01309 675968

website: www.benromach.com

History:

1898 – Benromach Distillery Company starts the distillery. Duncan McCallum is one of the owners.

1909 – The distillery operates under the name Forres Distillery for a few years.

1911 – Harvey McNair & Co buys the distillery.

1919 – John Joseph Calder buys Benromach and sells it to recently founded Benromach Distillery Ltd owned by several breweries.

1931 – Benromach is mothballed.

1937 – The distillery reopens.

1938 – Joseph Hobbs buys Benromach through Associated Scottish Distillers and sells it on to National Distillers of America (NDA).

1953 – NDA sells Benromach to Distillers Company Limited (DCL).

1966 – The distillery is refurbished.

1968 – Floor maltings is abolished.

1983 – Benromach is mothballed in March.

1993 – Gordon & McPhail buys Benromach from United Distillers.

1998 – The distillery is once again in operation. A 17 year old is released to commemorate this and the distillery's 100th anniversary.

1999 – A visitor centre is opened.

2004 – The first bottle distilled by the new owner is released under the name 'Benromach Traditional' in May. Other novelties (although distilled in UD times) include a 21 year Tokaji finish and a Vintage 1969.

2005 – A Port Wood finish (22 years old) and a Vintage 1968 are released together with the Benromach Classic 55 years.

2006 – Benromach Organic is released.

2007 – Peat Smoke, the first heavily peated whisky from the distillery, is released.

2008 – Benromach Origins Golden Promise is released.

2009 – Benromach 10 years old is released.

The owner of Benromach, Gordon & MacPhail (G&M), has been a well-known company in Morayshire since 1895 and just a few months ago it won the prestigious Queens Award for Enterprise for International Trade. However, in November 2008 relations with Moray Council became strained. A planned, new flood alleviation scheme could disrupt the distillery's water supply and G&M's calculation for future losses until 2016, £184m, was sent to the Council on request but was perceived by the members as a legal compensation claim. Negotiations will follow.

Benromach is the smallest working distillery in Speyside and is equipped with a semilauter mash tun, four washbacks made of larch and one pair of stills. Only two people are employed in the production, and although it has the capacity to produce 500,000 litres per annum, the current output is approximately 200,000 litres or five mashes per week.

There is a filling store on site and some of the production is stored in the three warehouses while the rest is taken to the owner's facilities in Elgin.

The biggest news came in autumn 2009 when *Benromach 10 year old* was launched. This is the first Benromach distilled by Gordon & MacPhail to carry an age statement since they purchased the distillery in 1993. The 10 year old will be the core expression in a range that otherwise consists of *Traditional* (around 6 years old), *21 years old, 25 years old, Cask Strength 1981* and *Vintage 1968*. There is also *Organic*, the first single malt to be fully certified organic by the Soil Association, *Peat-smoke*, produced using barley peated to 55 ppm, and *Origins* (batch 2), which is made using Golden Promise barley and matured in first and second fill sherry casks. Limited editions include *Benromach Classic 55 years* and *Madeira Wood Finish* (replacing last years Marsala).

10 year old

Benromach 10 year old

DR – Lemon custard creams, apricots and then pine table polish on the nose, spicy virgin oak, refreshing sharp barley and pine needles on the palate, and a complex and intriguing spicy and wood shaving finish.

DS – Sweet heather, cloves and honeycomb - slightly malty. Soft and delicately sweet with hints of malt and earth. Lots of vanilla and sherbet in the finish.

Meet the Manager

KEITH CRUICKSHANK
DISTILLERY MANAGER, BENROMACH DISTILLERY

When did you start working in the whisky business and when did you start at Benromach?

I started working in the whisky business in 1990. I came to Benromach in 1998 and trained under the previous manager, Bob Murray for 2 years and then I took over as manager.

Have you been working in other lines of business before whisky?

I worked in the textile industry.

What kind of education or training do you have?

I have been on numerous courses relating to the whisky industry. These include sensory analysis training and various health & safety and environmental courses. I am currently working through a diploma in distilling.

Describe your career in the whisky business.

I started with William Grant in their bottling line before moving to Chivas Brothers and into warehousing. I was then transferred to Glen Grant and Caperdonich where I worked as a shift operator.

What are your main tasks as a manager?

Ultimately I am responsible for ensuring the highest quality production of spirit at Benromach. I also look after the bulk management of casks and provide help for Benromach Visitors Centre, including delivering Managers Tours, tutorials and our "bottle your own Benromach" experience. I also ensure the distillery complies with Health & Safety, Revenue & Customs and SEPA regulations.

What are the biggest challenges of being a distillery manager?

Trying to keep on top of the every changing legislation including Health & Safety/Environmental issues.

What would be the worst that could go wrong (your worst nightmare) in the production process?

I am quite a positive person and try to think on the bright side on every situation. Benromach is Speyside's smallest working distillery, where only two men – myself included! – hand craft Benromach using traditional working practices. We know the distillery inside out and we instinctively know which lever to turn or button to push throughout the process. We can even pick up sounds and detect small changes in the production process – this allows us to react very quickly and minimise the chances of anything happening.

How would you describe the character of Benromach single malt?

The character of Benromach new make spirit can best be described as fruity, slightly floral, with malt and a touch of smoke.

What are the main features in the distillation/maturation process at Benromach, contributing to this character?

At Benromach we consider that each part of the whisky making process, however small, contributes to the final character. Even if it contributes just a small part to the final character we want to grab it. That said focusing in on a couple of specifics we utilise a long fermentation which helps to contribute to the fruity character of the new make spirit. We always use the highest quality casks. Our sherry casks are made in Spain and seasoned before they are shipped to Benromach to enter our filling programme.

What is your favourite expression of Benromach and why?

Difficult to say. Every expression offers something different. Benromach Traditional is a versatile whisky which can be enjoyed whenever and whatever the occasion.

If it were your decision alone – what new expression of Benromach would you like to see released?

Benromach Distillery has been back in production since 1998, so it would be great to see the first aged product distilled by Gordon & MacPhail at Benromach released into the market.

If you had to choose a favourite dram other than Benromach, what would that be?

Working for Gordon & MacPhail I am spoiled for choice! Gordon & MacPhail bottles whiskies from distilleries throughout Scotland. For me it depends on the type of occasion or the mood I am in. That said my favourite style is typically Speyside – elegant and fruity, with some complexity.

What are the biggest changes you have seen the past 10-15 years in your profession?

Throughout the industry the whisky production process has been increasingly automated. At Benromach we hand craft our product by retaining traditional working practises.

Do you see any major changes in the next 10 years to come?

The need for all businesses to be pro-active in response to an ever changing environment is definitely high on the agenda. The SWA recently published The Scotch Whisky Industry Environmental Strategy and G&M was involved in the consultation to develop this document. We continually assess our processes to find out new ways of improving our efficiency.

Do you have any special interests or hobbies that you pursue?

I am a member of the Buchan Pipe Band and we compete in Scotland and beyond. In the past our pipe band has won the World Pipe Band Championship.

Benromach released Origins last year, focusing on the raw material and especially the barley being used. Do you think that wood finishes now will be less important in the future?

Benromach is a small, boutique distillery and innovation is always high on our agenda. We introduced Benromach Origins in 2008 to illustrate how different parts of the production process impacts on the final product. We have received very good feedback from the consumer regarding this approach. Answering a question about the future of wood finishes is a difficult one, but ultimately the whisky drinker will shape the way distillers develop their portfolio in the future.

Bladnoch

Owner:
Co-ordinated
Development Services

Region/district:
Lowlands

Founded: 1817 **Status:** Active (vc) **Capacity:** 100 000 litres

Address: Bladnoch, Wigtown,
Wigtonshire DG8 9AB

Tel: 01988 402605 **website:** www.bladnoch.co.uk

History:

1817 – Brothers Thomas and John McClelland found the distillery.

1825 – The McClelland brothers obtain a licence.

1878 – John McClelland's son Charlie reconstructs and refurbishes the distillery.

1905 – Production stops.

1911 – Dunville & Co. from Ireland buys T. & A. McClelland Ltd for £10,775. Production is intermittent until 1936.

1937 – Dunville & Co. is liquidated and Bladnoch is wound up. Ross & Coulter from Glasgow buys the distillery after the war. The equipment is dismantled and shipped to Sweden.

1956 – A. B. Grant (Bladnoch Distillery Ltd.) takes over and restarts production with four new stills.

1964 – McGown and Cameron becomes new owners.

1966 – The number of stills is increased from two to four.

1973 – Inver House Distillers buys Bladnoch.

1983 – Arthur Bell and Sons take over.

1985 – Guiness Group buys Arthur Bell & Sons which, from 1989, are included in United Distillers.

1988 – A visitor centre is built.

1993 – United Distillers mothballs Bladnoch in June.

1994 – Raymond Armstrong from Northern Ireland buys Bladnoch in October.

2000 – Production commences in December.

2003 – The first bottles from Raymond Armstrong are launched, a 15 year old cask strength from UD casks.

2004 – New varieties follow suit: e. g. 13 year olds 40% and 55%.

2008 – First release of whisky produced after the take-over in 2000 - three 6 year olds.

2009 – An 8 year old of own production and a 19 year old are released.

Bladnoch 6 year old - lightly peated

DR – Korma chicken tin and butter with traces of pepper on the nose, dark spicy chili chocolate and prickly smoke on the palate, oil and pepper finish.

DS – Strong malt and cheddar cheese flavours on the nose. Again slightly cheesey with a hard hit of bitter earth and oak in the long finish.

Bladnoch is the southernmost of the Scottish distilleries and lies almost isolated down at Wigtown Bay. It was owned by United Distillers (later Diageo) and was planned to be decommissioned in the beginning of the nineties due to overproduction. A total of 1.3 million litres was produced in 1992 and the following year it was mothballed. In 1994, Raymond Armstrong, a builder from Northern Ireland bought it with the reservation from Diageo that it should not be used for whisky production. In 2000, after lobbying from the local community and Armstrong, Diageo gave permission for Bladnoch to produce 100,000 litres of alcohol per year.

The distillery is equipped with a stainless steel semi-lauter mash tun, six washbacks made of Oregon pine (of which only two are in use) and one pair of stills. Unusually enough, both stills were originally wash stills. There used to be two pairs of stills and when the spirit stills were due for replacement, it was decided not to renew them but to turn one of the wash stills into a spirit still. The whisky is mainly matured in ex-bourbon casks in one of the 11 warehouses where 3,000 casks are currently stored.

The distillery has an excellent visitor centre which attracts 25,000 visitors per year.

Up until recently, all official bottlings have come from the previous owner's production. These included 13 to 18 year olds but recently a couple of *19 year olds* have also been released; the latest, which is matured in ex-bourbon casks, in August 2009. In April 2008 the first release from stock distilled under the current ownership appeared. Three *6 year old* cask strengths were released - a *bourbon* matured, a *sherry* matured and one *lightly peated* from a bourbon barrel. One of them, the lightly peated was released again in 2009 as a *7 year old*. The release of a new *8 year old* was planned for early October. Raymond Armstrong is also known for bottling whiskies from other distilleries and among them a series of 36 and 37 year old single grains from Invergordon deserve mention. Recent independent bottlings include a 15 year old from 1992 by Douglas Laing.

6 year old sherry matured

Blair Athol

Owner:
Diageo

Region/district:
Eastern Highlands

Founded: 1798

Status: Active (vc)

Capacity: 2 500 000 litres

Address: Perth Road, Pitlochry, Perthshire PH16 5LY

Tel: 01796 482003

website: www.malts.com

History:
1798 – John Stewart and Robert Robertson found Aldour Distillery, the predecessor to Blair Athol. The name is taken from the adjacent river Allt Dour.

1825 – The distillery is expanded by Robert Robertson and takes the name Blair Athol Distillery.

1826 – The Duke of Atholl leases the distillery to Alexander Connacher & Co.

1832 – The distillery closes.

1860 – Elizabeth Connacher runs the distillery.

1882 – Peter Mackenzie & Company Distillers Ltd of Edinburgh (future founder of Dufftown Distillery) buys Blair Athol and expands it.

1932 – The distillery is mothballed.

1933 – Arthur Bell & Sons takes over by acquiring Peter Mackenzie & Company.

1949 – Production restarts.

1973 – Stills are expanded from two to four.

1985 – Guinness Group buys Arthur Bell & Sons.

1987 – A visitor centre is built.

2003 – A 27 year old cask strength from 1975 is launched in Diageo's Rare Malts series.

Blair Athol 12 year old

DR – The nose is rich and full, with orange and citrus fruit. The palate, too, is big and chunky, with some tannin and spice in the mix, and with water, parma violet notes.

DS – Stewed fruits and cider on the nose. Rich and fruity on the palate with raisins and cinnamon. Dry, fruity finish that lingers.

Blair Athol is the spiritual home of Bell's and has been a vital part of the blended whisky for years together with the likes of Caol Ila, Glenkinchie, Inchgower and Dufftown. The share of the spirit which goes into Bell's and other blends (90-95%) is matured mainly in bourbon casks while the rest is matured in sherry casks. Bell's Original (around 8 years old) is once again the number one blended Scotch in the UK after having been surpassed by The Famous Grouse in 2006. The interest among blended whisky producers to also produce blended malts has increased in recent years. Bell's presented its version in 2005 - Bell's Special Reserve. In spring 2009 Diageo launched a new packaging in a malt whisky-style bottling and this relaunch was part of a £2m investment in the brand.

Blair Athol is one of the oldest distilleries in Scotland. It was founded in 1798 as Aldour distillery even though most of the buildings we see today are from 1825 when it was expanded and renamed Blair Athol. A visitor centre was built already in 1987 and during the 90s when the tour on offer was rather simple and free of charge there were up to 100,000 visitors per year. Today the excellent centre has been upgraded offering a quality tour at a fee and the number of annual visitors is now around 40,000. The distillery is equipped with a semi-lauter mash tun, four washbacks of stainless steel and four of larch, and two pairs of stills. The wooden washbacks, half the size of the stainless steel ones, are 75 years old and were brought in from Mortlach. In 2008, the distillery was running seven days a week giving a production of 2.5 million litres of spirit. The malt is acquired from Diageo's own Roseisle maltings.

Currently there is only one official bottling, the 12 year old Flora & Fauna. Independent bottlings are also rare. One of the most recent is a 19 year old from 1989 by Cadenhead.

Flora & Fauna 12 years old

Bowmore

Owner: **Region/district:**
Morrison Bowmore   Islay
Distillers (Suntory)

Founded: **Status:**   **Capacity:**
1779   Active (vc)   2 000 000 litres

Address: School Street, Bowmore, Islay,
Argyll PA43 7GS

Tel: **website:**
01496 810441   www.bowmore.com

History:
1779 – Bowmore Distillery is founded by John Simpson and becomes the oldest Islay distillery.

1837 – The distillery is sold to James and William Mutter of Glasgow.

1892 – After additional construction, the distillery is sold to Bowmore Distillery Company Ltd, a consortium of English businessmen.

1925 – J. B. Sheriff and Company takes over.

1929 – Distillers Company Limited (DCL) takes over.

1950 – William Grigor & Son takes over.

1963 – Stanley P. Morrison buys the distillery for £117,000 and forms Morrison Bowmore Distillers Ltd.

1989 – Japanese Suntory buys a 35% stake in Morrison Bowmore.

1993 – The legendary Black Bowmore is launched. The recommended price is £100 (today it is at least ten times that if it can be found). Another two versions are released 1994 and 1995.

1994 – Suntory now controls all of Morrison Bowmore.

1995 – Bowmore is nominated 'Distiller of the Year' in the International Wine and Spirits competition.

Despite the economic downturn in 2008, the balance sheets of Bowmore Distillery showed how profits leaped up 13%. The development shows the same pattern as for other major owners where turnover is slipping (-7% for Morrison Bowmore) while profit is increasing. The reason is premiumisation of the range where standard expressions give way for more exclusive bottlings which are often destined for sale in the Far East.

The strategy of decreasing the presence of Bowmore malts in supermarkets that was implemented a few years ago in order to spend effort on the more lucrative travel retail has been important for Morrison Bowmore. Sales increased to 146,000 cases during 2008 which places Bowmore at number 2 of Islay malts behind Laphroaig.

Bowmore is one of few Scottish distilleries with its own malting floor, with as much as 40% of the malt requirement produced in-house. The distillery has a stainless steel semi-lauter mash tun, six washbacks of Oregon pine and two pairs of stills. 27,000 casks are stored in two dunnage and one racked warehouse. The twelve men in production work three shifts five days a week which, for 2008, resulted in 12 mashes per week, i. e. 1.6 million litres per year.

A now legendary limited bottling of Bowmore called *Black Bowmore*, distilled in 1964, was launched in 1993-1995. This expression made a surprising comeback as a 42 year old in 2007. The year after, *White Bowmore* appeared followed by *Gold Bowmore* in autumn 2009, both distilled in 1964. Apart from these very rare bottlings the range of Bowmore is divided into core domestic markets and travel retail. The former includes *Legend* (no age), *12 years, Darkest 15 years, 18 years* and *25 years*. The duty free line-up contains *Surf, Enigma, Mariner* (15 years old), *17 year old* and *Cask Strength*. Among more recent limited bottlings, the *1992 Vintage*, a 16 year old with a finish in Bordeaux casks, and a *1991 Vintage* (16 year old) Port matured should be mentioned. A new range called *Craftman's Collection* was introduced in the beginning of 2009 and the first to be launched was the *Maltmen's Selection*, a sherry matured 13 year old. May 2009 also saw the release of *Laimrig*, an exclusive for the Swedish market, with 10 years in a bourbon barrel and 5 years in an Oloroso cask. In autumn finally, *Bowmore Tempest*, a limited 10 year old cask strength matured in first fill Bourbon casks, was released. There are also a number of recent independent bottlings. Among others there is a 36 year old from Signatory, a 10 year old Syrah finish from 1999 by Murray McDavid and a 1991 from Dewar Rattray.

History (continued):

1996 – A Bowmore 1957 (38 years) is bottled at 40.1% but is not released until 2000.

1999 – Bowmore Darkest with three years finish on Oloroso barrels is launched. A Claret cask strength is also released in 12,000 bottles.

2000 – Bowmore Dusk with two years finish in Bordeaux barrels is launched.

2001 – Bowmore Dawn with two years finish on Port pipes is launched. A bottle from 1890 is sold at an auction in Glasgow and brings in £14,300 which is a new world record. The Manager Jim McEwan moves to Bruichladdich.

2002 – A 37 year old Bowmore from 1964 and matured in fino casks is launched in a limited edition of 300 bottles (recommended price £1,500).

2003 – Another two expressions complete the wood trilogy which started with 1964 Fino - 1964 Bourbon and 1964 Oloroso.

2004 – Morrison Bowmore buys one of the most outstanding collections of Bowmore Single Malt from the private collector Hans Sommer. It totals more than 200 bottles and includes a number of Black Bowmore.

2005 – Bowmore 1989 Bourbon (16 years) and 1971 (34 years) are launched.

2006 – Bowmore 1990 Oloroso (16 years) and 1968 (37 years) are launched. A new and up-graded visitor centre is opened.

2007 – Dusk and Dawn disappear from the range and an 18 year old is introduced. New packaging for the whole range. 1991 (16yo) Port and Black Bottle are released.

2008 – White Bowmore and a 1992 Vintage with Bourdeaux finish are launched.

2009 – Gold Bowmore, Maltmen´s Selection, Laimrig and Bowmore Tempest are released.

Bowmore 12 year old

DR – Rich peat and seaweed and the merest hint of characteristic palma violets on the nose, smoked fish in butter, menthol cough sweets and lemon on the palate, sweet peat in the finish.

DS – Fresh peat with a hint of fruity sweetness on the nose. Sweet and peaty, perfumed and oily on the palate with a fruity, yet smoky finish.

Maltmen´s Selection

Gold Bowmore

Bowmore Tempest

12 years old

15 years old Darkest

18 years old

Braeval

Owner:
Chivas Brothers Ltd
(Pernod Ricard)

Region/district:
Speyside

Founded: **Status:**
1973   Active

Capacity:
3 800 000 litres

Address: Chapeltown of Glenlivet,
Ballindalloch, Banffshire AB37 9JS

Tel: **website:**
01542 783042   -

History:
1973 – The Chivas and Glenlivet Group founds
Braes of Glenlivet, the name which will be used
for the first 20 years. The Glenlivet, Tomintoul
and Tamnavulin are the only other distilleries
situated in the Livet Glen valley. Production
starts in October.

1975 – Three stills are increased to five.

1978 – Five stills are further expanded to six.

1994 – The distillery changes name to Braeval.

2001 – Pernod Ricard takes over Chivas Brothers.

2002 – Braeval is mothballed in October.

2008 – The distillery starts producing again in
July.

Deerstalker 10 year old

DR – Grass and violin bow on the nose, zippy
sherbet and citrus fruit on the palate, with a
clean and refreshing finish.

DS – Apple skin and melon balls on the
green nose. Green and appley on the palate
– bittersweet with a malty-fresh finish and
herbal aftertaste.

Scotch whisky boomed from the mid-fifties onwards and no less
than 16 new distilleries were founded in the fifties and sixties.
The momentum was maintained into the seventies even if the
oil crisis of 1973 started to slow down the economy. Four distilleries were built during the seventies before the next decade
entered with all its closures. Braeval (or Braes of Glenlivet as it
was called then) was one of these distilleries. Braeval is situated
in a very remote part of the Highlands with Tamnavulin as
its closest distillery neighbour and it is both impressive and
surprisingly handsome despite that it was built to function as a
typical working distillery.

When Braeval was reopened last summer, after having been
mothballed for six years, not so much work had to be done
in order to once again start production. A
new boiler was installed and an upgrade of
still venting and control systems was made.
The distillery is equipped with a stainless
steel traditional mash tun. One peculiarity
sometimes mentioned in books is the copper
dome which used to be raised a few inches
above the edge of the tun. This was Stuart
McBain's decision, Distilleries Director of
Chivas Brothers at the time, as he was of
the opinion that it would help draw the
air off the top of the mash tun. The
dome was lowered onto the mash tun
(just as it has been at Allt-a-bhainne)
before Pernod Ricard took over, but
this arrangement can still be seen at
Strathisla and Glen Keith. There are
also fifteen washbacks made of stainless steel and six stills. There used to
be four pairs but now each of the two
wash stills serve two spirit stills. The
capacity is 25 mashes per week.

There are no official bottlings of Braeval but Aberko Ltd have two versions
from the distillery in their range of
Deerstalker single malts - a 10 year old
and a 15 year old. Recently there has
also been a release of a 19 year old
from 1989 by Cadenhead.

Deerstalker 10 year old

Malting is the process during which the barleycorn is modified so that it is possible to extract the sugar in the next step - the *mashing*. This process is used for producing both beer and whisky but when making malt for whisky, low protein barley with a high starch content is chosen which can be turned into sugar and then alcohol. About 96% of the malt produced in the world is used to make beer while only 3% is used for whisky production (the remaining percentage goes into food).

The barleycorn consists of three parts - the *husk* which is wrapped around a piece of *starch* to which the *embryo* (or germ) is attached. By consuming the starch the embryo will, if not controlled, develop into the roots and shoots of a new barley plant. So what malting is all about is controlling the germination process.

The harvested barley is dormant between six to sixteen weeks before germination can begin. To determine if the barley is ready a viability test is performed. If the barley has wakened it is sent to the *steepings* which is where the barley is immersed in water in order to raise moisture content so that the germination can begin. Dry barley has a water content of less than 12%. The first steeping water has a temperature of 14-17 degrees and after eight hours the barley has absorbed and contains 32-35% water. At that time the water is drained off and the barley rests in air for 12 hours. Water is once again added and finally after another 16 hours the water content has reached the optimal 46%.

During the steeping, a variety of enzymes have become active. *Cytase* starts breaking down the cell walls exposing the starch and *amylase* invades the starch itself, breaking it down into smaller parts. The moist malt is left to germinate either on traditional malting floors or in modern vessels (more about that later).

The germination process will take about 7-10 days on a malting floor and 2-4 days at a modern, commercial maltings. Germination produces heat so at this stage it is vital to turn the barley so that air is allowed to pass through the grains in order to control temperature. Also, if it is left unturned the roots tend to grow into each other leaving a rug of entangled grain that can weigh up to 500 tonnes.

During the germination process the enzymes awakened by the steeping continue to do their job but the germ also starts feeding on the modified starch. In order not to "lose" too much starch which will then be converted into sugar and in the end alcohol, the maltster needs to terminate the germination at the correct time. This process, known as *kilning*, entails drying the *green malt* (as it is now called) with the help of heat.

At this time we can take a look at the different types of maltings. The traditional way is *floor malting* where, after steeping, the grain is spread out on a floor made of stone or concrete in a layer 30 cm thick. Two to three times a day for about a week, the green malt has to be turned with *shiels* (wooden shovels). After that time the malt is brought to the kiln where it is spread out on a perforated metal floor. Here it is dried, either directly fired when the smoke from the furnace below passes through the malt bed, or indirectly when heated air passes from a radiator through the malt. If a peated whisky is desired, dried peat will be thrown into the furnace during the first part of the process when the temperature is around 60 degrees. At the end of the kilning the temperature is increased to about 75 degrees. The whole process takes between 24 and 48 hours depending on the size of the kiln and the amount of malt. There are only a handful of distilleries left using this traditional method and when they do it is generally only for a small part of their requirements. Commercial maltsters use any of three techniques - *Saladin box*, *Drums* or *SGKV*

(Steeping, Germination and Kilning Vessel).

The *SGKV*, which was developed in the seventies, is the most recent and can process up to 500 tonnes in one batch, performing all the steps in one process.

Saladin boxes can be found at Tamdhu distillery and also at Baird's in Inverness and Crisp in Alloa. They were invented by Frenchman Charles Saladin in the late 19th century and can handle up to 200 tonnes.

The third method is *drum maltings* which came into use in the late 1960s. The drums are reliable and easy to use but have a disadvantage in that only 30 to 50 tonnes of barley can be loaded at a time.

Apart from different varieties of peated and unpeated malt, some distilleries have recently started experimenting with malt types usually developed for the brewing industry - *chocolate malt* and *crystal malt* - adding new flavours to the whisky. From 100 kilos of barley, 80 kilos of malt is produced, and when the malting process is finished, the malt is taken to the mill and then to the *mash tun* (see page 113).

Bruichladdich

Owner: **Region/district:**
Bruichladdich Distillery Co   Islay

Founded: **Status:**   **Capacity:**
1881   Active (vc)   1 500 000 litres

Address: Bruichladdich, Islay, Argyll PA49 7UN

Tel: **website:**
01496 850221   www.bruichladdich.com

History:

1881 – Barnett Harvey builds the distillery with money left by his brother William III to his three sons William IV, Robert and John Gourlay. The Harvey family already owns the distilleries Yoker and Dundashill.

1886 – Bruichladdich Distillery Company Ltd is founded and reconstruction commences.

1889 – William Harvey becomes Manager and remains on that post until his death in 1937.

1929 – Temporary closure.

1936 – The distillery reopens.

1938 – Joseph Hobbs, Hatim Attari and Alexander Tolmie purchase the distillery for £23 000 through the company Train & McIntyre.

1938 – Operations are moved to Associated Scottish Distillers.

1952 – The distillery is sold to Ross & Coulter from Glasgow.

1960 – A. B. Grant buys Ross & Coulter.

1961 – Own maltings ceases and malt is brought in from Port Ellen.

1968 – Invergordon Distillers take over.

1975 – The number of stills increases to four.

1983 – Temporary closure.

1993 – Whyte & Mackay buys Invergordon Distillers.

1995 – The distillery is mothballed in January.

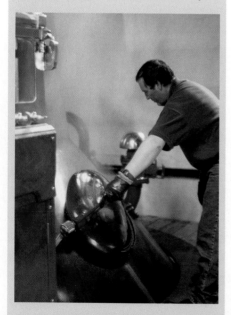

Independently owned Bruichladdich Distillery defied the expected bad times and showed a 15% rise in sales for 2008. Pre-tax profits rose even more with 42% to just over £1m which will come in handy when building the new Port Charlotte Distillery on the site of the Old Lochindaal distillery. It was initially thought that 2009 would be the inauguration year of this new venture but the start has been delayed until 2010 or 2011 to allow for enough time to obtain all the necessary permissions. Bruichladdich distillery is equipped with a cast iron, open mash tun, six washbacks of Oregon pine and two pairs of stills. All casks are stored either at Bruichladdich or at the old Port Charlotte site. The yearly production at Bruichladdich increased by 15% in 2009 to 800,000 and all whisky produced is based on Scottish barley. Twenty-three farmers are contracted and eight of these grow the barley organically. The latter are responsible for 50% of the annual requirements.

There are three main lines in Bruichladdich's production; lightly peated Bruichladdich, moderately peated Port Charlotte and the heavily peated Octomore. In addition to these, experiments with triple-distilled (Trestarig) and quadruple distilled (Perilous) spirit have been made. Bruichladdich was, as usual, a source of joy for its many fans with plenty of new bottlings in 2009. *Bruichladdich Classic*, a multi vintage which will become a permanent member of the core range, was described by the distillers themselves as "an Audrey Hepburn rather than a Marilyn Monroe, with a natural elegance". *Bruichladdich Organic*, the first ever organic Islay single malt, was distilled in 2003 from Chalice barley grown on Culblair Farm. The first 19 year old from the distillery was named *Black Art* and this sherry matured cask strength is a follow-up to last year's *Blacker Still*. Furthermore, the third edition of *Infinity*, *Port Charlotte 8 year old* and the second edition of *Octomore* (5 years), a peat monster at 140ppm (!) were also released. There was also a series of *17 year olds*, matured in bourbon barrels but each with a different enhancement (or finish) in *rum*, *Fino sherry* and *PX sherry* casks. A very unusual release was *X4+3* at 63.5%, the world's first quadruple-distilled single malt. It was distilled in 2006 and has matured in both ex-bourbon and virgin oak.

Apart from all these new releases, there is the previous core range of Bruichladdich *10, 12, 15, 17* and *20 years old*. Limited releases from last year include Multi Vintage Trilogy (*Waves, Rocks* and *Peat*), *Golder Still*, the 36 year old *DNA* and seven *16 year olds*, each with a different enhancement.

History (continued):

1998 – In production again for a few months, and then mothballed.

2000 – After several years of attempts, Murray McDavid buys the distillery from JBB Greater Europe (previously Whyte & Mackay Group) for £6.5 million. 1.4 million litres of whisky from 1964 and younger is included in the purchase.

2001 – Jim McEwan from Bowmore becomes Production Director. The first distillation (Port Charlotte) is on 29th May and the first distillation of Bruichladdich starts in July. In September the owners' first bottlings from the old casks are released, 10, 15 and 20 years old.

2002 – The world's most heavily peated whisky is produced on 23rd October when Octomore (80ppm) is distilled.

2003 – Bruichladdich becomes the only distillery on Islay bottling on-site. It is awarded Distillery of the Year for the second time and launches the golf series, Links, 14 years old.

2004 – Second edition of the 20 year old (nick-named Flirtation) and 3D, also called The Peat Proposal, are launched.

2005 – Several new expressions are launched - the second edition of 3D, Infinity (a mix of 1989, 1990, 1991 and Port Charlotte), Rocks, Legacy Series IV, The Yellow Submarine and The Twenty 'Islands'.

2006 – Included in a number of new releases in autumn is the first official bottling of Port Charlotte; PC5.

2007 – New releases include Redder Still, Legacy 6, two new Links, PC6 and an 18 year old.

2008 – More than 20 new expressions including the first Octomore, Bruichladdich 2001, PC7, Golder Still and two sherry matured from 1998.

2009 – New releases include Classic, Organic, Black Art, Infinity 3, PC8, Octomore 2 and X4+3 - the first quadruple distilled single malt.

DNA   Black Art   17 year old rum

Classic

Bruichladdich 12 year old

DR – Very welcoming mix of melon, grape and pear on the nose, and over-ripe peach, soft melon and other sweet fruits on the palate, with a delightful clean and fresh finish.

DS – Sweet and fruity on the nose with icing sugar and tangerine peel. Round and pleasant on the palate it is again fruity and slightly buttery. The long finish is creamy with a hint of spice.

Port Charlotte PC6

DR – Peat with the volume turned up, intense smoke and soot. On the palate quite stunning mix of candy sweets in intense barbecue smoke, with a long sweet and sooty finish that will delight Islay fans.

DS – Icing and fruit cake with champagne sorbet on the nose. Smoked meat flavours on the palate with a thunderous hit of peat and salt. Long, smoky, cheesy finish.

Organic 2003   X4+3

Bunnahabhain

Owner:
Burn Stewart Distillers
(CL Financial)

Region/district:
Islay

Founded: **Status:** **Capacity:**
1881 Active (vc) 2 500 000 litres

Address: Port Askaig, Islay, Argyll PA46 7RP

Tel:
01496 840646

website:
www.bunnahabhain.com

History:
1881 – William Robertson of Robertson & Baxter, founds the distillery together with the brothers William and James Greenless. The Greenless brothers co-founded the Islay Distillers Company Ltd in 1879 with James Ford.

1883 – Production starts in earnest in January.

1887 – Islay Distillers Company Ltd merges with William Grant & Co. in order to form Highland Distilleries Company Limited.

1930 – The distillery closes.

1937 – The distillery reopens.

1963 – The two stills are augmented by two more.

1982 – The distillery closes.

1984 – The distillery reopens. A 21 year old is released to commemorate the 100th anniversary of Bunnahabhain.

1999 – Edrington takes over Highland Distillers and mothballs Bunnahabhain but allows for a few weeks of production a year.

2001 – A 35 year old from 1965 is released in a limited edition of 594 bottles during Islay Whisky Festival.

2002 – As in the previous year, Islay Whisky Festival features another Bunnahabhain – 1966, a 35 year old in sherry casks. Auld Acquaintance 1968 is launched at the Islay Jazz Festival.

2003 – In April Edrington sells Bunnahabhain and Black Bottle to Burn Stewart Distilleries (C. L. World Brands) at the princely sum of £10 million. A 40 year old from 1963 is launched.

2004 – The first limited edition of the peated version is a 6 year old called Moine.

2005 – Three limited editions are released - 34 years old, 18 years old and 25 years old.

2006 – 14 year old Pedro Ximenez and 35 years old are launched.

2008 – Darach Ur is released for the travel retail market and Toiteach (a peated 10 year old) is launched on a few selected markets.

2009 – Moine Cask Strength is released during Feis Isle.

Bunnahabhain 12 year old

DR – Ginger and barley candy on the nose, then sweet and sour mix on the palate, lots of sweetness but with a distinctive savoury and earthy undertow.

DS – A sweet, smoky and scented nose with hints of sherry. Delicate smoke and touches of oakiness are on the palate and the finish is peaty and malty.

Burn Stewart´s big seller is without doubt Scottish Leader, a blended whisky selling almost 6 million bottles in, above all, Asia and South Africa. Among the single malts, however, Bunnahabhain is the star with 225,000 bottles sold yearly. The distillery is equipped with a stainless steel mash tun, six washbacks made of Oregon pine and two pairs of stills. The spirit destined for single malt bottling and for the Black Bottle blend is stored on site in six dunnage and one racked warehouse (totally 21,000 casks) while the rest is shipped to other sites for maturation. Last year production increased to 2 million litres but for 2009 the reduction to 5 mashes per week will result in circa 1.2 million litres. The lion's share of this is of course the traditional unpeated version but 125,000 litres will be peated (38 ppm).

Similarly with his experiments with Ledaig at Tobermory distillery, Master Blender Ian MacMillan has attempted to recreate the style of whisky produced at Bunnahabhain until the 1960s when the maltings were closed. The peated version *Moine* (Gaelic for peat) and primarily used as a part of the blend Black Bottle, has also been released as a single malt a couple of times. The last occasion was during Feis Isle 2009 when two hogsheads were bottled.

The core range consists of *12, 18* and *25 years old*. In September 2008 a special 10 year old version of the peated Bunnahabhain, this time called *Toiteach* (smoky in Gaelic), was released in France, Germany and The Netherlands. Since summer 2009 it was also available in other markets. Late 2008 also saw the first release of a travel retail exclusive from the distillery. The non-chill filtered *Darach Ur* has no age statement but contains whiskies up to 20 years of age. The name is Gaelic for "new oak".

Recent independent bottlings include a 35 year old from Adelphi Distillery, a 29 year old from Ian MacLeod and a 31 year old from Murray McDavid.

Darach Ur

Meet the Manager

JOHN MACLELLAN
DISTILLERY MANAGER, BUNNAHABHAIN DISTILLERY

When did you start working in the whisky business and when did you start at Bunnahabhain?

I started work in the whisky business at Bunnahabhain in May 1989.

Have you been working in other lines of business before whisky?

I worked as a fisherman immediately prior to starting at Bunnahabhain and previously did various other jobs on Islay.

What kind of education or training do you have?

I attended school on Islay up to age 16 and then at Oban High School to age 18. I did consider going to college or university but instead decided to stay on Islay.

Describe your career in the whisky business.

My career in the business has been quite varied as I have risen from the "shop floor" to management and during that time have been in charge through a sale of the distillery which was fairly traumatic.

What are your main tasks as a manager?

Main tasks as a manager would involve day to day running, overseeing all production matters, dealing with members of the public and also with enquiries from the media etc. You never really know when you arrive in the morning exactly how your day will develop.

What are the biggest challenges of being a distillery manager?

Biggest challenge nowadays would be trying to keep ahead of bureaucracy.

What would be the worst that could go wrong in the production process?

Apart from injury of any sort to my workforce the worst thing to happen would be a major loss of either wort or spirit as the implications regarding cost are so enormous with the tax element added in.

How would you describe the character of Bunnahabhain single malt?

Bunnahabhain Single Malt for me has many characteristics which make it special. Its softness, its unique nutty malty flavour and its point of difference against all the other famous Islay Malts. I believe it holds its own place well in the rightly celebrated Islay pantheon of world class malts.

What are the main features in the distillation/maturation process at Bunnahabhain, contributing to this character?

Low phenolic content of malted barley used on site. Slow mashing cycle. Undercharging of the stills which helps produce a very light spirit. The people who produce it and the length of time they have been doing so.

What is your favourite expression of Bunnahabhain and why?

My favourite expression from the current range is the 18 year old as it has that soft, sherried flavour which I believe Bunnahabhain lends itself to so very well. My all time favourite however would be the "Auld Acquaintance" 1968 which was so well put together by John Ramsay and was a real example of the blenders art.

If it were your decision alone – what new expression of Bunnahabhain would you like to see released?

There are lots of good casks here just crying out to be bottled and I would like to see a selection of these released as limited edition bottlings. I would also like to see a peated version of Bunnahabhain running in tandem with the standard.

If you had to choose a favourite dram other than Bunnahabhain, what would that be?

I enjoy many different drams on many different occasions and am very much a "horses for courses" type drinker, i. e. on a cold wet night I might enjoy a particular whisky and at another time something completely different. I am very partial to Black Bottle 10 year old which is sadly being phased out. I love Highland Park and Glenrothes also and Ardbeg and Caol Ila from nearer home.

What are the biggest changes you have seen the past 10-15 years in your profession?

Unfortunately not so much trust and honesty in the industry, people watching their backs and others trying to get on at the expense of their colleagues.

Do you see any major changes in the next 10 years to come?

Hopefully we will see more small players come into the business, there needs to be more of the Glengoynes, Benriachs, Bruichladdichs etc which have fresh ideas and the means to be innovative. This does not mean that I don't admire the bigger companies; I have personal experience of how supportive some of these can be.

Do you have any special interests or hobbies that you pursue?

I am an enthusiastic though largely unskilled golfer. I enjoy walking, nature and socialising and am never happier than when with my family and friends on Islay.

What does it mean to you being an Ileach and managing an Islay distillery?

To be an Ileach managing an Islay distillery has been a fantastic experience especially as I have been able to be part of the group of Ileachs who currently manage all the Islay distilleries. I believe it is the first time in documented memory that this has ever happened.

Running a distillery on Islay has its implications (water supply, transports etc). Do you and the other distillery managers on Islay work together trying to tackle these issues?

As a group on Islay we do work together to tackle common issues. We all as distilleries (large and small) bring our own unique skills to the forum and use these skills as best we can for the common good. We are all different but I feel that Islay as a unit more than holds its own against other industry areas .

You produce a peated spirit for part of the year. How does that differ from the ordinary production and what special considerations have to be made?

Our peated spirit is made using barley peated to approx 35 - 40 ppm against normal Bunnahabhain using barley peated to less than 2 ppm. There are of course also changes made to cutting levels when separating middle-cut from other components.

Bushmills

Owner:
Diageo

Region/district:
N Ireland (Co. Antrim)

Founded: 1784

Status: Active (vc)

Capacity: 3 000 000 litres

Address: 2 Distillery Road, Bushmills,
Co. Antrim BT57 8XH

Tel:
028 20731521

website:
www.bushmills.com

History:
1608 – James I issues Sir Thomas Philips a licence for whiskey distilling.

1784 – The distillery is formally registered.

1885 – Fire destroys part of the distillery.

1890 – S.S. Bushmills, the distillery's own steamship, makes its maiden voyage across the Atlantic to deliver whiskey to America and then heads on to Singapore, China and Japan.

1923 – The distillery is acquired by Belfast wine and spirit merchant Samuel Wilson Boyd. Anticipating the end of US prohibition, he gears Bushmills up for expansion and increases production.

1939-1945 – No distilling during the war. The distillery is partly converted to accommodate American servicemen.

1972 – Bushmills joins Irish Distillers Group which was formed in 1966. Floor maltings ceases.

1987 – Pernod Ricard acquires Irish Distillers.

1996 – Bushmills 16 years old is launched.

2005 – Bushmills is sold to Diageo at a price tag of €295.5 million as a result of Pernod Ricard's acquisition of Allied Domecq.

2007 – The 40 year old cast iron mash tun is replaced by a new one of stainless steel at a cost of £1.4m.

2008 – Celebrations commemorate the 400th anniversary of the original license to distil, granted to the area in 1608.

Bushmills 10 year old

DR – Autumn orchard of over-ripe apples on the nose, soft red apples and pear on the palate, soft sweetie finish.

DS – Dried citrus fruit with apricot and peach on the nose. Malty sweet with herbal barley flavours and bubblegum. A tasty, fruity finish.

Bushmills is the second biggest selling Irish whiskey in the world behind Jameson, but while Jameson (produced by Pernod Ricard) is a giant with 60% of global Irish whiskey sales selling 2.75 million cases in 2008, Bushmills sells less than a fifth of that which translates into 450,000 cases. Diageo, who became owner of the distillery in 2005, decided early on to increase sales and the bold aim is to more than double the figures by the end of 2012. Over £6m have been invested in, among other things, a new mash tun, a new still (the 10th) and a new warehouse. Since 2008 production takes place seven days a week which means, in conjunction with the refurbishings, that it has tripled in just three years. More investments were made in 2009 when a new bottle design of the big seller Bushmills Original was marketed for a Northern Ireland launch in November and a global release in the beginning of 2010. The investment totalled £1.75m including the advertising campaign.

Bushmills uses two kinds of malt, one unpeated and one slightly peated. The distillery uses triple distillation, which is the traditional Irish method, contrary to Cooley which uses double distillation. There are five wash stills and five spirit stills and the whiskey is matured and bottled on site. Bushmills' core range of single malts consists of a *10 year old*, a *16 year old Triple Wood* with a finish in Port pipes for 6-9 months and a *21 year old* finished in Madeira casks for two years. There is also a *12 year old Distillery Reserve* which is sold exclusively at the distillery.

Black Bush and Bushmills Original are the two main blended whiskeys in the range. To celebrate the 400th anniversary, a Bushmills 1608 Anniversary Edition was launched in 2008. The malt whiskey part for that expression was distilled using a proportion of crystal malt which gave the blend distinct toffee/chocolatey notes. The grain whiskey used for Bushmills blended whiskeys is bought from Midleton Distillery in Cork which is owned by arch rival Pernod Ricard. Bushmills is open to the public and the visitor centre receives more than 100,000 visitors per year.

21 years old

Caol Ila

Owner:
Diageo

Region/district:
Islay

Founded: 1846
Status: Active (vc)
Capacity: 3 800 000 litres

Address: Port Askaig, Islay, Argyll PA46 7RL

Tel: 01496 302760
website: www.malts.com

History:

1846 – Hector Henderson founds Caol Ila.

1852 – Henderson, Lamont & Co. is subjected to financial difficulties and Henderson is forced to sell Caol Ila to Norman Buchanan.

1863 – Norman Buchanan encounters financial troubles and sells to the blending company Bulloch, Lade & Co. from Glasgow.

1879 – The distillery is rebuilt and expanded.

1920 – Bulloch, Lade & Co. is liquidated and the distillery is taken over by Caol Ila Distillery.

1927 – DCL becomes sole owners.

1930 – DCL transfers administration to Scottish Malt Distillers (SMD). The distillery closes.

1937 – Operations recommence.

1972 – All the buildings, except for the warehouses, are demolished and rebuilt.

1974 – The renovation, which totals £1 million, is complete and six new stills are installed.

1999 – Experiments with a completely unpeated malt are performed.

2002 – The first official bottlings since Flora & Fauna/Rare Malt appear; 12 years, 18 years and Cask Strength (c. 10 years).

2003 – A 25 year old cask strength is released.

2005 – A 25 year old Special Release is launched.

2006 – Unpeated 8 year old and 1993 Moscatel finish are released.

2007 – The second edition of the unpeated 8 year old is released.

2008 – The third edition of unpeated 8 year old is released.

2009 – The fourth edition of the unpeated version (10 year old) is released.

Caol Ila 12 year old

DR – Barbecued fish and seaweed on the nose, oily bacon-fat, squeezed lemon and sweet smoke on the palate, immensely satisfying citrusy seaside barbecue of a finish.

DS – Sweet toasted tar and peat on the nose. The peatiness and maltiness are immediate on the palate and continue into the after-taste which is slightly burnt.

Diageo has a reputation of letting its distillery managers rotate between different distilleries and some of them have held positions at more than 15 facilities. The manager of Caol Ila is, however, an exception; Billy Stitchell started here in 1974 and has served as manager the last ten. And that is not all: his father, both of his grandfathers and his great grandfather all worked at Caol Ila!

Caol Ila is by far the biggest distillery on Islay and with a cast iron mash tun that can take 13 tonnes of grist per mash it runs 16 mashes a week which is its full capacity. The distillery is also equipped with eight washbacks made of Oregon pine and three pairs of stills in a still room with a beautiful view of Jura across the Sound of Islay. There is a three-storey warehouse on site but today's production is sent by lorry to the mainland for filling and maturation.

The whisky from Caol Ila is peated but trials with low phenol started already in the 1980's. The result, destined for blended whisky, was that unpeated Caol Ila was produced annually until 2005. In recent years the increasing demand for peated whisky has put an end to the production of the unpeated, so called Highland, Caol Ila. This variety was bottled for the first time in 2006.

The main mission for Caol Ila is to be part of Johnnie Walker blended whiskies but despite that it has become more and more visible as a single malt.

The core range consists of *12* and *18 years old* and *Cask Strength*. Limited editions have included *25 years old* and a *1993 Distiller's Edition Moscatel finish*. The fourth edition of the unpeated, a *10 year old*, was released in autumn 2009. In connection with the Islay Festival in May 2009, the first-ever *single cask* (ex-sherry), bottling by the owners of Caol Ila was released.

The number of independent bottlings is huge. Recent releases include a 1982 by Blackadder, an 18 year old Single Malts of Scotland, a 1982 from Duncan Taylor, an 18 year old matured in German oak by Ian MacLeod and from Murray McDavid, a 28 year old with a finish in a Sauternes cask.

10 year old unpeated

Caperdonich

Owner:
Chivas Brothers
(Pernod Ricard)

Region/district:
Speyside

Founded: 1897
Status: Mothballed
Capacity: 2 200 000 litres

Address: Rothes, Aberlour, Banffshire AB38 7BN

Tel: 01542 783000
website: -

History:
1897 – The distillery is founded by James Grant and is named Glen Grant Number 2 Distillery after the neighbouring sister distillery Glen Grant.

1902 – The Pattison crash shakes the industry and the distillery closes.

1965 – It reopens with The Glenlivet & Glen Grant Distilleries as owner. According to law two distilleries cannot bear the same name so it is changed to Caperdonich.

1967 – The number of stills are increased from two to four.

1977 – Seagrams buys The Glenlivet Distilleries Ltd (the new, shortened name) and forms Chivas and Glenlivet Group. Longmorn, Benriach, Glen Grant and The Glenlivet are also included in the deal.

2001 – Pernod Ricard and Diageo take over Seagram Spirits & Wine, the Chivas Group becomes part of Pernod Ricard.

2002 – The distillery is mothballed.

2005 – A 16 year old from 1988 is launched.

Caperdonich 16 year old 55,8%

DS – Lemony and earthy with icing sugar on the nose. Sweet and fruity on the palate. Dry. Long, hot finish and again very dry.

Every year there are rumours about the closed Caperdonich distillery being sold. A few years ago, adjacent Forsyths in Rothes was rumoured a potential buyer and word got around again during 2009. It is perhaps not so far-fetched even if it may mean that the distillery will not be used for whisky production. Forsyths, founded in 1890, is a coppersmith and fabricator world famous for its copper pot stills for the distilling industry. Besides most Scottish distilleries, distilleries all over the world such as Mackmyra, Teerenpeli, Hakushu, Yamazaki and Glenora can be found among their clients. Aside from new production of pot stills, Forsyths work a great deal with maintenance and renovation of existing stills. Clan Forsyths´ motto, which they were granted after their services at the battle of Dykes, is *Instaurator Ruinae* (Restorer of the Ruins) which seems more than just a coincidence! Richard Forsyth acquired his elder brother´s share of the company for £2.15m in spring 2009. Caperdonich was founded under the name Glen Grant No 2 in 1897 but had to close five years after its inception. It was not reopened until 1965 with investment in another two pot stills and the very latest in modern technology enabling the whole process to be controlled by only two men.

The distillery is equipped with a cast iron mash tun, eight washbacks made of stainless steel and two pairs of stills. Even though most of the equipment remains in place, some of it has been dismantled and sent to other distilleries in the group. The condensers for example have all been removed.

Almost all the production was used for different blended whiskies, e. g. 100 Pipers, Chivas Regal and Passport. The only official bottling ever launched was a *16 year old cask strength* released in 2005.

There are, however, more to be found among independent bottlings. Some more recent ones are two 38 year old from Adelphi Distillery and Signatory, three from Duncan Taylor (1968, 1970 and 1972) and a 12 year old from Cadenhead.

16 years old

Cardhu

Owner:		Region/district:
Diageo		Speyside

Founded:	Status:	Capacity:
1824	Active (vc)	2 980 000 litres

Address: Knockando, Aberlour, Moray AB38 7RY

Tel:	website:
01340 872555 (vc)	www.malts.com

History:

1811 – The whisky smuggler John Cumming founds an illicit distillery.

1824 – John Cumming applies for and obtains a licence for Cardhu Distillery.

1846 – John Cumming dies and his son Lewis takes over.

1872 – Lewis dies and his wife Elizabeth takes over.

1884 – A new distillery is built to replace the old.

1893 – John Walker & Sons purchases Cardhu for £20,500 but the Cumming family continues operations. The whisky changes name from Cardow to Cardhu.

1908 – The name reverts to Cardow.

1930 – Administration is transferred to Scottish Malt Distillers (SMD).

1960-61 – Reconstruction and expansion of stills from four to six.

1981 – The name changes to Cardhu once again.

1998 – A visitor centre is constructed.

2002 – Diageo changes Cardhu single malt to a vatted malt with contributions from other distilleries in it.

2003 – The whisky industry protests sharply against Diageo's plans.

2004 – Diageo withdraws Cardhu Pure Malt.

2005 – The 12 year old Cardhu Single Malt is relaunched and a 22 year old is released.

2009 – Cardhu 1997, a single cask in the new Manager's Choice range is released.

Cardhu 12 year old

DR – Honeycomb and chocolate Crunchie bar on the nose, fluffy over-ripe apples, toffee, boiled sweets on the palate, delightful clean and crisp finish.

DS – A spicy and floral nose coupled with a honeyness that is also on the spicy palate. The finish is also honeyed and lingers.

Cardhu is by far the biggest selling of the Diageo single malts (and number six in the world) with annual sales totalling more than 3 million bottles. That is twice the volume of number two of the Diageo distilleries, Talisker. Furthermore, there are probably few malts that are so concentrated to a single country as Cardhu is to Spain where 75% of sales occur. The increase from 1993 ten years onwards was over 2000%! But being so exposed to one single market (even if the brand is also selling well in France and Greece) makes it vulnerable. The current recession has weakened the Spanish market considerably and Cardhu has decreased accordingly.

Cardhu was sold as pure malt, i. e. mixed with malt whisky from other distilleries, for almost a year. The reason for that was above all the increased interest from especially Spain and the fact that the distillery was closed during part of the nineties when a new still house was built. In spring 2004 it returned to being sold as a single malt.

But Cardhu is not just single malt. It is also one of the most important ingredients of Johnnie Walker and c. 70% of production goes to the various versions of that blend.

Cardhu distillery's location is unrivalled; situated on a small hill it overlooks Ben Rinnes, with Knockando and Tamdhu as closest neighbours. The distillery is equipped with one stainless steel full lauter mash tun, eight washbacks made of Scottish larch and three pairs of stills. At least until 2008, Cardhu was working a seven-day week with a production of almost 3 million litres of alcohol.

The core range consists of the *12 year old* and a *22 year old Special Release* which was released for the Spanish and French markets in 2005. In October 2006, a *Special Cask Reserve* with no age statement was released in Spain. A *single cask* from *1997* was released in autumn 2009 as part of the new series Manager's Choice.

12 years old

Clynelish

Owner: Diageo

Region/district: Northern Highlands

Founded: 1967 **Status:** Active (vc) **Capacity:** 4 200 000 litres

Address: Brora, Sutherland KW9 6LR

Tel: 01408 623003 (vc) **website:** www.malts.com

History:

1819 – The 1st Duke of Sutherland founds a distillery called Clynelish Distillery.

1827 – The first licensed distiller, James Harper, files for bankruptcy and John Matheson takes over.

1834 – Andrew Ross takes over the license.

1846 – George Lawson & Sons become new licensees.

1896 – James Ainslie & Heilbron takes over.

1912 – James Ainslie & Co. narrowly escapes bankruptcy and Distillers Company Limited (DCL) takes over together with James Risk.

1916 – John Walker & Sons buys a stake of James Risk's stocks.

1931 – The distillery is mothballed.

1939 – Production restarts.

1960 – The distillery becomes electrified.

1967 – A new distillery is built adjacent to the first one. It is also named Clynelish and both operate in parallel from August.

1968 – 'Old' Clynelish is mothballed in August.

1969 – 'Old' Clynelish is reopened as Brora and starts using a very peaty malt.

1983 – Brora is closed in March.

2002 – A 14 year old is released.

2006 – A Distiller's Edition 1991 finished in Oloroso casks is released.

2009 – A 12 year old is released for Friends of the Classic Malts.

Clynelish 14 year old

DR – Fresh green fruit and unripe melon on the nose, sweet almost fizzy lemon sherbet on the palate, a wispy hint of peat and pepper, and satisfying and balanced finish.

DS – Sweet rubber and mustard married with tar and alcohol. The palate also has a hint of mustard the goes long into the peppery finish.

In recent years, more and more women have started to work in the domain of the whisky industry which traditionally has been reserved for men, i. e. the distillery itself. More women are assuming positions as distillery managers as at Glenkinchie and Mannochmore. A third such situation exists since September 2008 when Sarah Burgess was appointed Manager of Clynelish. Sarah has been with Diageo for 11 years, including at Dailuaine and Glen Spey distilleries and most recent as Operations Manager of Northern Warehousing at Auchroisk.

Clynelish is actually the site of two distilleries - the closed Brora which was originally founded as Clynelish in 1819 and the operating distillery which was built in 1967. The old buildings are still there but only the warehouses are used for maturation of Clynelish. The mash tun, washback and the two old stills are intact in the old still house, although not in the best of shape due to holes in the roof. Bottlings of Brora are still released and are highly sought after by whisky buffs. A 30 year old was released in 2009 as a part of the Special Releases from Diageo.

The distillery we today call Clynelish lies on the other side of the small road and is a modern creation made of glass, steel and concrete. It is equipped with a cast iron mash tun, eight wooden washbacks, two stainless steel washbacks installed in 2008 and three pairs of stills. The spirit distillation is unusually slow with a 5 hour run for the middle cut. In 2008 production was increased to full capacity which is 4.2 million litres. The spirit from Clynelish is stored in its own warehouses or in the old warehouses of Brora. The whisky is much less peated than Brora.

Official bottlings include a *14 year old* and a *Distiller's Edition 1992*. The first distillery shop exclusive, a *cask strength*, was released in 2008. In 2009 another addition was made to the range, a *12 year old* for Friends of the Classic Malts.

Lately, there have been plenty of independent bottlings: a 16 year old from 1992 from Single Malts of Scotland, a 15 year old from 1993 by Adelphi Distillery and Dewar Rattray released one distilled in 1982.

14 years old

Cooley

Owner: | **Region/district:**
Cooley Distillery plc | Ireland (County Louth)

Founded: | **Status:** | **Capacity:**
1987 | Active | 3 250 000 litres

Address: Riverstown, Cooley, Co. Louth

Tel: | **website:**
+353 (0)42 9376102 | www.cooleywhiskey.com

History:
1987 – John Teeling purchases Ceimici Teo Distillery in Dundalk. Previously it has produced spirits in column stills (e. g. vodka) and is now renamed Cooley Distillery.

1988 – Willie McCarter acquires part of A. A. Watt Distillery and the brand Tyrconnell and merges with Teeling. Teeling simultaneously buys decommissioned Locke's Kilbeggan Distillery.

1989 – A pair of pot stills is installed for production of both malt and grain whiskey.

1992 – Locke's Single Malt, without age statement, is launched as the first single malt from the distillery. Cooley encounters financial troubles and Irish Distillers offers to purchase the company for £24.5 million.

1994 – The Competition Authority establishes that Irish Distillers cannot acquire Cooley as they then would be dominating the Irish whiskey market.

1995 – Finances improve and production resumes.

1996 – Connemara is launched.

2000 – Locke's 8 year old single malt is launched.

2003 – The Connemara 12 year old is launched.

2006 – Five Connemara Single Casks from 1992 are released.

2007 – Kilbeggan distillery is reopened.

2009 – New packaging for the Connemara range and release of the first in The Small Batch Collection.

Connemara 12 year old

DR – Soft fruit and tarry peat on the nose, then fluffy red apples, toffee and smoke intriguingly mixed into an unusual and very enticing whole. Smoke in the finish.

DS – Fresh, melon and apple on the nose with aniseed and herbs. A mix of tropical fruit, mild peat and herbs swims about on the palate into the long, lingering finish.

The old Locke's distillery (now Kilbeggan)

The Kilbeggan Distillery, re-opened by the owner of Cooley in 2007 after having been silent for 50 years, entered a new phase in 2009. When starting up, the distillery only had one pot still (albeit almost 170 years old) and the first distillation was made at Cooley Distillery. In April 2009, however, a second pot still was installed, fabricated by Forsyths of Scotland. It is slightly larger than the first still - 3,000 litres compared to 2,000 litres - and at least for the time being, mashing and fermentation will continue at Cooley. The Kilbeggan Distillery has a capacity of producing 100,000 cases per year and at the moment they are triple distilling contrary to Cooley. The first whiskey will be available in late 2010 but a year before that Spirit of Kilbeggan (from 1 month to two years) will be released.

The owner has recently invested in new bottling equipment at Cooley, a new warehouse (with another one potentially being added) and embarked on maintenance work on both the grain and malt distilleries. There is a production capacity of 250,000 cases of malt whisky and 800,000 cases of grain whisky. The company was not hit by the economic downturn in 2008 but instead reported an increase in sales by 50% and a doubling of the profit before tax to just over €3.3m instead.

The range of Connemara single malts obtained a new design in summer 2009 and now consists of a *no age*, a *12 year old*, a *cask strength*, a *single cask* and a *sherry finish*. The latter is new and the first in a series of limited expressions called The Small Batch Collection. The idea is to replace it after 18 months with a new bottling. The Connemara brand comes peated but experiments have been made with a heavily peated version and this could well be the next "small batch". The rest of Cooley's single malt range includes *Tyrconnel no age*, *Tyrconnel 15 year old single cask* and *Tyrconnel wood finishes* (Port, Madeira and sherry) as well as *Locke's 8 years old*.

A number of blended whiskeys are also produced as is a single grain called Greenore.

Connemara 12 years old

Cragganmore

Owner: Diageo

Region/district: Speyside

Founded: 1869

Status: Active (vc)

Capacity: 1 520 000 litres

Address: Ballindalloch, Moray AB37 9AB

Tel: 01479 874700

website: www.malts.com

History:

1869 – John Smith, who already runs Ballindalloch and Glenfarclas Distilleries, founds Cragganmore.

1886 – John Smith dies and his brother George takes over operations.

1893 – John's son Gordon, at 21, is old enough to assume responsibility for operations.

1901 – The distillery is refurbished and modernized with help of the famous architect Charles Doig.

1912 – Gordon Smith dies and his widow Mary Jane supervises operations.

1917 – The distillery closes.

1918 – The distillery reopens and Mary Jane installs electric lighting.

1923 – The distillery is sold to the newly formed Cragganmore Distillery Co. where Mackie & Co. and Sir George Macpherson-Grant of Ballindalloch Estate share ownership.

1927 – White Horse Distillers is bought by DCL which thus obtains 50% of Cragganmore.

1964 – The number of stills is increased from two to four.

1965 – DCL buys the remainder of Cragganmore.

1988 – Cragganmore 12 years becomes one of six selected for United Distillers' Classic Malts.

1998 – Cragganmore Distillers Edition Double Matured (port) is launched for the first time.

2002 – A visitor centre opens in May.

2006 – A 17 year old from 1988 is released.

Cragganmore 12 year old

DR – The nose has honey, soft fruits and sweet spring meadow notes and is very inviting, and on the palate soft barley, summer fruits and a sweetness lead up to an almost tangy finish.

DS – Soft and buttery at first with a hint of mild, perfumed smoke. A spicy palate carries on the short but sweet finish.

Cragganmore has enjoyed a solid reputation among blenders for more than a century and the first to help it establish that position was James Watson & Co, a blending and bottling company established in Dundee in 1815. From the very beginning it bought the entire output from Cragganmore in order to use it in its famous No. 10 blend which was renowned as far away as Australia in the beginning of the 1900s. James Watson & Co was also the owner of Glen Ord, Parkmore, Pulteney and Balmenach distilleries until 1923 when these were bought by a trio of bigger companies - Walker, Dewars and Lowrie. What the big companies really were after was one of the biggest stocks of mature whisky of that time - 150,000 casks.

Cragganmore is one of the original six Classic Malts selling around 350,000 bottles per year (of the six, only Glenkinchie sells less). However, it is also an important part of two blended whiskies: Old Parr and White Horse.

The distillery is equipped with a stainless steel full lauter mash tun which was installed in 1997. There are also six washbacks made of Oregon Pine and two pairs of stills (where the spirit stills have flat tops!) attached to cast iron worm tubs. Part of the production matures in three dunnage warehouses on site.

The core range is made up of a *12 year old* and a *Distiller's Edition 1997*. The latter version was introduced for all six Classics in 1997 and entails maturation in refill bourbon casks with a finish in another cask. For five of the whiskies, different varieties of sherry finishing was chosen but port pipes were selected for Cragganmore. There has also been five limited bottlings since 2000: a *14 year old* destined for 'Friends of Classic Malts', a *1973 29 year old*, a *10 year old cask strength* in 2004, a *1993 Bodega Cask* the same year and, finally, a *17 year old* released in 2006.

Recent independent bottlings include a Duncan Taylor from 1993 and a 1989 from Blackadder.

12 years old

Craigellachie

Owner:
John Dewar & Sons
(Bacardi)

Region/district:
Speyside

Founded: 1891
Status: Active
Capacity: 3 600 000 litres

Address: Aberlour, Banffshire AB38 9ST

Tel: 01340 872971
website: -

History:
1891 – The distillery is built by Craigellachie–Glenlivet Distillery Company which has Alexander Edward and Peter Mackie as part-owners. The famous Charles Doig is the architect.

1898 – Production does not start until this year.

1916 – Mackie & Company Distillers Ltd takes over.

1924 – Peter Mackie dies and Mackie & Company changes name to White Horse Distillers.

1927 – White Horse Distillers are bought by Distillers Company Limited (DCL).

1930 – Administration is transferred to Scottish Malt Distillers (SMD), a subsidiary of DCL.

1964 – Refurbishing takes place and two new stills are bought, increasing the number to four.

1998 – United Distillers & Vintners (UDV) sells Craigellachie together with Aberfeldy, Brackla and Aultmore and the blending company John Dewar & Sons to Bacardi Martini.

2004 – The first bottlings from the new owners are a new 14 year old which replaces UDV's Flora & Fauna and a 21 year old cask strength from 1982 produced for Craigellachie Hotel.

Craigellachie 14 year old

DR – Intriguing and deep mix of light fruits on the nose, a spicy bite then clean and smooth mouth feel, and a soft finish.

DS – Mild spice with vanilla and honeycomb on the nose. More honey on the palate with malt and fruit flavours. The finish is short but sweet.

Craigellachie distillery enjoys a magnificent and central location in the heart of whisky country - it stands at the confluence of the famous rivers Spey and Fiddich and at the intersection of the A95 from Keith to Aberlour and the A941 from Rothes to Dufftown. To the west lies Macallan Distillery, to the north Speyside Cooperage and to the south the famous Craigellachie Hotel. Huge glazed curtain walls make the stills easy to see from the main road and it feels natural to attach a visitor centre to the distillery. However, the owners keep it purely as a working distillery producing malt for, among others, the Dewar's blends and the sale of Craigellachie single malt is minimal.

In 2007 the owner, Bacardi, decided to invest £125m in a new whisky storage and blending facility for Dewars. Forty three acres of land at Poniel in South Lanarkshire, 25 miles outside of Glasgow where the Dewar's head office lies, was acquired. In February 2009, the first two palletised warehouses, each with a capacity of 72,000 casks, were ready to be used and a third will be built before the end of the year. At least another eight warehouses are needed to store casks for Diageo and at full capacity the plant will employ 30 people. Malted barley is bought from Glenesk Maltings and the distillery has a very modern Steinecker full lauter mash tun, installed in 2001, which replaced the old open cast iron mash tun. There are also eight washbacks made of larch wood and two pairs of stills, each of them connected to a cast iron worm tub. Since 2008 a seven-day working week is in place at the distillery which means that it is now producing at full capacity, 3.6 million litres.

Bacardi launched a *14 year old* in 2004 and this is, so far, the only official bottling. Recent independent bottlings include a 14 year old from Cadenhead and a 15 year old from Single Malts of Scotland.

14 years old

Dailuaine

Owner: Diageo

Region/district: Speyside

Founded: 1852

Status: Active

Capacity: 3 370 000 litres

Address: Carron, Banffshire AB38 7RE

Tel: 01340 872500

website: www.malts.com

History:

1852 – The distillery is founded by William Mackenzie.

1865 – William Mackenzie dies and his widow leases the distillery to James Fleming, a banker from Aberlour.

1879 – William Mackenzie's son forms Mackenzie and Company with Fleming.

1884 – Rebuilding transforms the distillery into one of the largest in the Highlands.

1889 – Charles Doig builds his and Scotland's first pagoda roof on Dailuaine.

1891 – Dailuaine-Glenlivet Distillery Ltd is founded.

1898 – Dailuaine-Glenlivet Distillery Ltd merges with Talisker Distillery Ltd and forms Dailuaine-Talisker Distilleries Ltd. Imperial Distillery, built by Thomas Mackenzie the previous year, and a grain distillery in Aberdeen are also incorporated.

1915 – Thomas Mackenzie dies without heirs.

1916 – Dailuaine-Talisker Company Ltd is bought by the previous customers John Dewar & Sons, John Walker & Sons and James Buchanan & Co.

1917 – A fire rages and the pagoda roof collapses. The distillery is forced to close.

1920 – The distillery reopens.

1925 – Distillers Company Limited (DCL) takes over.

1960 – Refurbishing. The stills increase from four to six and a Saladin box replaces the floor maltings.

1965 – Indirect still heating through steam is installed.

1983 – On site maltings is closed down and malt is purchased centrally.

1991 – The first official bottling, a 16 year old, is launched in the Flora & Fauna series.

1996 – A 22 year old cask strength from 1973 is launched as a Rare Malt.

1997 – A cask strength version of the 16 year old is launched.

2000 – A 17 year old Manager's Dram matured in sherry casks is launched.

Dailuaine Distillery is a fine example of an entrepreneur and a financier working hand in hand. Thomas Mackenzie, whose father William founded the distillery, teamed up with local banker James Fleming in the late 19th century and founded, what was considered at the time, a very modern distillery. Simultaneously, Fleming found time to establish the new Aberlour Distillery and Mackenzie (already part-owner of Talisker) constructed Imperial as a second distillery to Dailuaine.

Apart from distilling whisky which principally becomes a part of Johnnie Walker, Dailuaine has also turned into an "environmental hub" to seven distilleries nearby. On the site lies one of two dark grains plants in the Diageo group. It was built in 1960 to process draff and pot ale into cattle feed. The capacity of the plant is 900 tonnes per week (Glenlossie is the other plant and three times as big). There is also an effluent treatment plant just below the other buildings, which treats spent lees and wastewater using various filters. The effluent is discharged into the river when the BOD level (biological oxygen demand) is less than 20 ppm.

The distillery is equipped with a stainless steel full lauter mash tun installed in 1993, eight washbacks made of larch and three pairs of stills. There are also eight magnificent granite warehouses but they are no longer used for storing whisky. Instead the spirit is tankered away to Cambus for filling and then to the Diageo warehouses in Blackrange. Except for a *16 year old* in the *Flora & Fauna* series, only a couple of limited versions have been released by the owners.

Independent bottlings are rare but there have been a couple of interesting ones recently; a 34 year old from 1973 by Douglas Laing and an 11 year old with a Tokay-finish from Ian MacLeod.

Flora & Fauna 16 years old

Dailuaine 16 year old

DS – Heavy chocolate and syrup flavours on the nose with cheese-cake notes. The palate is soft at first with a burst of sherry and raisins in Cointreau. An aggressive finish.

Dalmore

Owner:
Whyte & Mackay Ltd
(United Spirits)

Region/district:
Northern Highlands

Founded: 1839
Status: Active (vc)
Capacity: 4 200 000 litres

Address: Alness, Ross-shire IV17 0UT

Tel: 01349 882362
website: www.thedalmore.com

History:

1839 – Alexander Matheson founds the distillery and lets it to the Sunderland family.

1867 – The brothers Charles, Andrew and Alexander Mackenzie run the distillery.

1874 – The number of stills is increased to four.

1886 – Alexander Matheson dies.

1891 – Sir Kenneth Matheson sells the distillery for £14,500 to the Mackenzie brothers.

1917 – The Royal Navy moves in to start manufacturing American mines.

1920 – The Royal Navy moves out and leaves behind a distillery damaged by an explosion.

1922 – The distillery is in production again. Andrew Mackenzie and the Royal Navy disagree on compensation for the damages.

1956 – Floor malting is replaced by a Saladin box.

1960 – Mackenzie Brothers (Dalmore) Ltd merges with Whyte & Mackay and forms the company Dalmore-Whyte & Mackay Ltd.

1966 – The number of stills is increased from four to eight.

1982 – The Saladin box is abandoned.

1990 – American Brands buys Whyte & Mackay.

1996 – Whyte & Mackay changes name to JBB (Greater Europe).

2001 – Through management buy-out, JBB (Greater Europe) is bought from Fortune Brands and changes name to Kyndal Spirits.

2002 – A 62 year old Dalmore is sold at McTear's auction for £25,877.50 and becomes the world's so far most expensive bottle of whisky. Kyndal Spirits changes name to Whyte & Mackay.

2004 – A new visitor centre opens.

2007 – United Spirits buys Whyte & Mackay. 15 year old, 1973 Cabernet Sauvignon and a 40 year old are released.

2008 – 1263 King Alexander III and Vintage 1974 are released.

2009 – New releases include an 18 year old, a 58 year old and a Vintage 1951.

Dalmore 12 year old

DR – Orange jelly and squidgy fruit on the nose, an impressive full confectionery and fruit salad taste on the softest of peat beds, and a wonderful and warming finish.

DS – Cherries with fruitcake and hints of marzipan on the nose. The palate is softer and quite oily-rich. Bitter fruitcake dominates and continues onto the finish.

For eight years now, production at Dalmore has taken place around the clock and amounted to 3.6 million litres of alcohol. The actual capacity is slightly over four million litres but water availability is a problem every summer and production has to be reduced by one third in the hottest period. In 2009 the aim is to reach 3.2 million because the closure will be for a little longer. The reason for this is a refurbishment of the millroom. Among other equipment a Buhler aspirator will be installed for the malt handling. In order to get the malted barley as clean as possible before it reaches the rollers of the mill it first passes a dresser to remove any small stones and similar objects and then proceeds through the aspirator with air currents removing all remaining lighter impurities.

The distillery is equipped with a semi-lauter mash tun, eight washbacks made of Oregon Pine and four pairs of stills. Four of the stills were installed in the sixties and are twice the size of the old ones. The spirit stills have water jackets, a peculiar device that cannot be seen anywhere else. This allows cold water to circulate between the reflux bowl and the neck of the stills, thus increasing the reflux.

Two weeks per year a heavily peated spirit is produced using 400 tonnes of malt peated at 50 ppm.

The core range consists of a *12 year old* (since 2008 a 50/50 combination of sherry and bourbon), a *15 year old* and *Gran Reserva*. Another addition to the core range was an 18 year old released in autumn 2009. Limited editions released in 2008 included *1263 King Alexander III* and *Vintage 1974*. In autumn 2009 some really rare expressions were launched - *1981 Matusalem, 1981 Amoroso*, a *58 year old* (30 decanters) and the rarest, a *1951 Vintage* (just 12 decanters). Among the latest independent bottlings are a 12 year old rum finish by Ian MacLeod, an 18 year old Sauternes finish by Cadenhead and an 18 year old from 1990 by Signatory.

Gran Reserva

Dalwhinnie

Owner:
Diageo

Region/district:
Speyside

Founded: 1897 **Status:** Active (vc) **Capacity:** 2 200 000 litres

Address: Dalwhinnie, Inverness-shire PH19 1AB

Tel: 01540 672219 (vc) **website:** www.malts.com

History:

1897 – John Grant, George Sellar and Alexander Mackenzie from Kingussie commence building the facilities. The first name is Strathspey and the construction work amounts to £10,000.

1898 – Production starts in February. The owner encounters financial troubles after a few months and John Somerville & Co and A P Blyth & Sons take over in November and change the name to Dalwhinnie. The architect Charles Doig is called in to make some improvements.

1905 – America's largest distillers, Cook & Bernheimer in New York, buys Dalwhinnie for £1,250 at an auction. This marks the first time a foreign company takes ownership of a Scottish distillery. The administration of Dalwhinnie is placed in the newly formed company James Munro & Sons.

1919 – Macdonald Greenlees & Williams Ltd headed by Sir James Calder buys Dalwhinnie.

1926 – Macdonald Greenlees & Williams Ltd is bought by Distillers Company Ltd (DCL) which licences Dalwhinnie to James Buchanan & Co.

1930 – Operations are transferred to Scottish Malt Distilleries (SMD).

1934 – The distillery is closed after a fire in February.

1938 – The distillery opens again.

1968 – The maltings is decommissioned.

1986 – A complete refurbishing takes place.

1987 – Dalwhinnie 15 years becomes one of the selected six in United Distillers' Classic Malts.

1991 – A visitor centre is constructed.

1992 – The distillery closes and goes through a major refurbishment costing £3.2 million.

1995 – The distillery opens in March.

1998 – Dalwhinnie Distillers Edition 1980 (oloroso) is introduced for the first time. The other five in The Classic Malts, each with a different finish, are also introduced as Distillers Editions for the first time.

2002 – A 36 year old is released.

2003 – A 29 year old is released.

2006 – A 20 year old is released.

Dalwhinnie 15 year old

DR – Full honey and sweet peat on the nose, a rich creamy mouthfeel and a delicious honey and exotic fruits mix all layered on soft peat foundations.

DS – A light and grassy nose with hints of heathery-sweetness. Light palate with malty flavours. Warming and slightly oaky finish.

One of the worst nightmares for a distiller is an unwanted change in the character of the spirit caused by a change in the equipment. That is why, for example, any new copper still being replaced at a distillery is an exact replica of the old one. Dalwhinnie´s owner experienced this dreaded scenario that involved the cooling device of the spirit vapours. The old worm tubs were replaced by tube condensers in the eighties. After some time it was discovered that the tubes, with more copper contact than the worm tubs, resulted in a new character and the worms were then reinstalled. Worm tubs usually produce a robust and powerful whisky but it is compensated at Dalwhinnie by striving for a clear wort giving a smooth and fruity spirit. In 1923 Dalwhinnie became the first Scottish distillery to have an American owner, Cook & Bernheimer, a large spirits wholesaler from New York who bought it for £1,250 at an auction. It would take at least another 15 years before more American influence in the form of National Distillers of America entered the scene.

Dalwhinnie is equipped with a full lauter mash tun, six wooden washbacks and just the one pair of stills. From the stills, the lyne arms lead out through the roofs to the wooden wormtubs outside. During 2008 the distillery speeded up production to full capacity. That means 15 mashes per week instead of 10, resulting in 2.2 million litres per year. Two racked warehouses are able to store approximately 5,000 casks.

Diageo has done a good job in positioning Dalwhinnie on the market, and the whisky is among the top 15 most sold single malts worldwide.

The core range is made up of a *15 year old* and a *Distiller's Edition*. Some older versions have also been released in recent years. It is very difficult to find an independently bottled Dalwhinnie.

15 years old

Deanston

Owner:
Burn Stewart Distillers
(C L Financial)

Region/district:
Eastern Highlands

Founded: 1965
Status: Active
Capacity: 3 000 000 litres

Address: Deanston, Perthshire FK16 6AG

Tel: 01786 841422
website: www.burnstewartdistillers.com

History:
1965 – A weavery from 1785 is transformed into Deanston Distillery by James Finlay & Co. and Brodie Hepburn Ltd (Deanston Distillery Co.). Brodie Hepburn also runs Tullibardine Distillery.

1966 – Production commences in October.

1971 – The first single malt is named Old Bannockburn.

1972 – Invergordon Distillers takes over.

1974 – The first single malt bearing the name Deanston is produced.

1982 – The distillery closes.

1990 – Burn Stewart Distillers from Glasgow buys the distillery for £2.1 million.

1991 – The distillery resumes production.

1999 – C L Financial buys an 18% stake of Burn Stewart.

2002 – C L Financial acquires the remaining stake.

2006 – Deanston 30 years old is released.

2009 – A new version of the 12 year old is released.

Deanston 12 year old (new bottling)

DR – Fresh and young crystallized barley on the nose with some cut hay and grass. On the palate it's a fruit sandwich, with orange and yellow fruits at first, then a cough candy honey and aniseed centre, and orange marmalade late on. The finish is intensely fruity with some spice.

DS – Mild aniseed mixed with tropical fruit (pineapple rind) – bittersweet. Sweeter than expected but quickly bittersweet with a quite hot finish and mildly oaky aftertaste.

When CL Financial bought Burn Stewart Distillers, owner of Deanston, five years ago, exports were only 50% of the sales and a large part of the production went to supermarkets and own-label brands. Today the exports have risen to 80% and of the major chains it is only Marks & Spencer that is sold to. This means that volumes have increased and profits even more so. After nine years in a row with red figures, 2006 and 2007 became profitable.

Part of the profit has been invested in Deanston where the two wash stills were replaced in spring 2008 and new bases were fitted onto the spirit stills. In early 2009, the traditional cast iron mash tun was refurbished and the distillery did not start production until March. This, in combination with moving back to a five day working week, means that it will produce 1.5 million litres of alcohol compared to 2.2 million last year. There are two warehouses, one modern racked and one listed building from the old mill which altogether can contain 45,000 casks with the oldest dating back to 1971.

No more than 24,000 bottles of Deanston single malt were sold last year but the aim for 2009 is 60,000. The figures for Scottish Leader, the blend where Deanston plays a part, are of a quite different dimension. Last year 5.3 million bottles were sold and it is hoped that the 500,000 cases (6 million bottles) barrier will be broken in 2009 thanks to a strong growth in Asia and South Africa. This would give Deanston a place on the top 30 list.

Deanston is one of six surviving distilleries in Perthshire, a region where, at one time, there were 140 active distilleries.

The official range from Deanston consists of the new version of the *12 year old* (non-chill filtered and at a higher strength), a *12 year old* for *Marks & Spencer* and the *30 year old* which was released in 2006. A *17 year old* M&S exclusive (800 bottles) is due for release in October 2009.

12 years old

Dufftown

Owner: Diageo

Region/district: Speyside

Founded: 1896 **Status:** Active **Capacity:** 5 800 000 litres

Address: Dufftown, Keith, Banffshire AB55 4BR

Tel: 01340 822100 **website:** www.malts.com

History:
1895 – Peter Mackenzie, Richard Stackpole, John Symon and Charles MacPherson build the distillery Dufftown-Glenlivet in an old mill.

1896 – Production starts in November.

1897 – The distillery is owned by P. Mackenzie & Co., who also owns Blair Athol in Pitlochry.

1933 – P. Mackenzie & Co. is bought by Arthur Bell & Sons for £56,000.

1968 – The floor maltings is discontinued and malt is bought from outside suppliers. The number of stills is increased from two to four.

1974 – The number of stills is increased from four to six.

1979 – The stills are increased by a further two to eight.

1985 – Guinness buys Arthur Bell & Sons.

1997 – Guinness and Grand Metropolitan merge to form Diageo.

2006 – The Singleton of Dufftown is launched as a special duty free bottling.

2008 – The Singleton of Dufftown is made available also in the UK.

Singleton of Dufftown

DR – Honeycomb and tinned peach and apricot in syrup on the nose, sharp and spicy clean barley on the palate, with some bitter orange notes towards the finish.

DS – A malty, sherried nose with heavy spices and mulled wine notes. A heavy, mouth coating whisky – very oily and full of sherry flavours. Oily, hot finish.

Two years ago Diageo did some extensive research trying to establish what style of whisky newcomers to the drink would appreciate. The word "smooth" kept recurring. An idea was born; some of their lesser known malts could be relaunched in a new, smoother style in the Singleton series. The name Singleton had previously been used in connection with the marketing of another distillery, Auchroisk. Glen Ord, Dufftown and Glendullan were launched in this series and each of them was targeted towards a specific market. Singleton of Dufftown was first ear-marked for Duty Free but it is also for sale in the UK since autumn 2008, backed up by a £800,000 marketing campaign. Dufftown distillery is a giant in terms of production. It was in fact the biggest of all Diageo's 27 working distilleries before Roseisle was built.

Dufftown also has one of the biggest mash tuns in the industry, with a capacity of no less than 13 tonnes. It is a full lauter model and was installed in 1979. There are twelve stainless steel washbacks which replaced old wooden ones in 1998 when the distillery closed for four months for refurbishing. No less than £3m were invested in the distillery during 1998-2000. Throughout the years stills have been added and it is a bit of a mystery how all of them have managed to fit into such small premises. The still house, with its three pairs of stills, must certainly be one of Scotland's most cramped.

About 97% of the production goes into blended whiskies, especially Bell's. The only official bottling of Dufftown used to be the 15 year old in the Flora & Fauna series. Since 2006 there is Singleton of Dufftown which, compared to the 15 year old, contains a larger share of ex-sherry European oak casks.

Independent bottlings turn up now and then. One of the most recent was a Cadenhead from 1978, 31 years old.

The Singleton of Dufftown

Edradour

Owner:
Signatory Vintage
Scotch Whisky Co. Ltd

Region/district:
Eastern Highlands

Founded: 1825
Status: Active (vc)
Visitor centre: 90 000 litres

Address: Pitlochry, Perthshire PH16 5JP

Tel: 01796 472095
website: www.edradour.com

History:

1825 – Probably the year when a distillery called Glenforres is founded by farmers in Perthshire.

1837 – The first year Edradour is mentioned.

1841 – The farmers form a proprietary company, John MacGlashan & Co.

1886 – The American company J. G. Turney & Sons acquires Edradour through its subsidiary William Whitely & Co.

1922 – William Whiteley buys the distillery. The distillery is renamed Glenforres-Glenlivet.

1975 – Pernod Ricard buys Campbell Distilleries.

1982 – Campbell Distilleries (Pernod Ricard) buys Edradour and builds a visitor centre.

1986 – The first single malt (10 years) is released.

2002 – Edradour is bought by Andrew Symington from Signatory Vintage Scotch Whisky for £5.4 million. The product range is expanded with a 10 year old and a 13 year old cask strength.

2003 – A 30 year old and a 10 year old that are non-chill filtered are released. As an experiment a heavily peated variety (50ppm) is also distilled.

2004 – A number of wood finishes are launched as cask strength.

2006 – James McGowan becomes the new distillery manager. The first bottling of peated Ballechin is released.

2007 – A Madeira matured Ballechin is released.

2008 – A Ballechin matured in Port pipes and a 10 year old Edradour with a Sauternes finish are released.

2009 – Fourth edition of Ballechin (Oloroso) is released.

Edradour 10 year old

DR – Lemon and lime, rich fruits and some mint on the nose, sharp grape, berries and honey on the palate, and a lingering and pleasant fruity finish with hints of smoke.

DS – Rich malt infused with orange peel and cloves. Heavy perfume (musky). Sweet and scented, fresh fruit in a sweet liqueur with a soft, sherried aftertaste.

Ballechin No 3 Port matured

DR – Peat, plum and a nutty nose, with apricot and peach on the palate, a delicious spiciness and assertive peat. The finish is medium, spicy and peaty.

DS – Mature cheddar mixed with a rich peat all in an expensive olive oil. Again viscous and peaty with an earthy flavour mixed with some obvious heavy wine notes from the Port cask. Long cheddary finish.

Edradour distillery has been a busy place for many years now. Not so much because of a huge production (they only do 90,000 litres per year) but because of almost 100,000 visitors attracted by one of the most picturesque distilleries in Scotland. Since 2007 is has become even busier when the owner, independent bottler Signatory, moved from Edinburgh to a purpose-built bottling hall and warehouse next to the distillery. There are now two bottling lines as well as hand bottling equipment used for filling the "Straight From The Cask" bottlings.

The equipment at Edradour consists of an open, cast iron mash tun (1.15 tonnes per mash), two Oregon pine washbacks and one pair of stills with a purifier connected to the spirit still. The vapours are cooled in a wormtub from 1910. Edradour is the only distillery still using a Morton refrigerator to cool the worts. The original one, dating back to 1934, was replaced by a replica in 2009. The grist used to be bought in bags but in 2007 a 4 roller mill was installed. The existing warehouse with room for only 700 casks will be demolished and a new one built to store 6,000 casks.

All of the production today is reserved for single malts. The core expression is the *10 year old*. A large number of single casks, vintages and wood finishes have been released in addition to this. A series of wood finishes tapped on 50 cl bottles was commenced in 2004. Most have been around 10-11 years but older versions have also been launched. The most recent ones have been *Sauternes, Moscatel, Sassicaia, Madeira* and *Rum*. Distilled in *2003*, a bottling fully matured on *port pipes* was released at the end of 2008 and a *Straight From The Cask Chateau Neuf du Pape* was launched in July 2009.

An exciting experiment got under way in 2003 with the first distilling of a heavily peated (no less than 50 ppm) malt. The first bottling of *Ballechin*, as it is called, appeared on the market in 2006. In July 2009 the fourth edition was released, fully matured in *Oloroso sherry butts*.

10 years old

Fettercairn

Owner:
Whyte & Mackay Ltd
(United Spirits)

Region/district:
Eastern Highlands

Founded: | **Status:** | **Capacity:**
1824 | Active (vc) | 2 300 000 litres

Address: Fettercairn, Laurencekirk,
Kincardineshire AB30 1YB

Tel:
01561 340205

website:
www.whyteandmackay.co.uk

History:
1824 – Sir Alexander Ramsay, owner of Fasque Estate, founds the distillery.

1825 – The first licensee is James Stewart & Co.

1830 – Sir Alexander Ramsay sells Fasque Estate and the distillery to Sir John Gladstone.

1887 – A fire erupts and the distillery is forced to close for repairs.

1890 – Thomas Gladstone dies and his son John Robert takes over. The distillery reopens after the fire.

1912 – The company is close to liquidation and John Gladstone buys out the other investors.

1926 – The distillery is mothballed.

1939 – The distillery is bought by Associated Scottish Distillers Ltd. Production restarts.

1960 – The maltings discontinues.

1966 – The stills are increased from two to four.

1971 – The distillery is bought by Tomintoul-Glenlivet Distillery Co. Ltd owned by W. & S. Strong & Co. and Hay & McLeod & Co.

1973 – Tomintoul-Glenlivet Distillery Co. Ltd is bought by Whyte & Mackay Distillers Ltd.

1974 – The mega group of companies Lonrho buys Whyte & Mackay.

1988 – Lonrho sells to Brent Walker Group plc.

1989 – A visitor centre opens.

1990 – American Brands Inc. buys Whyte & Mackay for £160 million.

1996 – Whyte & Mackay and Jim Beam Brands merge to become JBB Worldwide.

2001 – Kyndal Spirits, a company formed by managers at Whyte & Mackay, buys Whyte & Mackay from JBB Worldwide.

2002 – The whisky undergoes a major makeover including new bottle, new packaging and the name which is changed from Old Fettercairn to Fettercairn 1824.

2003 – Kyndal Spirits changes name to Whyte & Mackay.

2007 – United Spirits buys Whyte & Mackay. A 23 year old single cask is released.

Fettercairn 1824 12 year old

DR – The nose is quite light and honeyed, the palate oily, artichoke, nutty and with some clean barley. The finish is short with a hint of ginger.

DS – A spicy, malty and woody nose overshadowed by a sweeter, malty palate. There is oakiness in the finish which is short but pleasantly nutty.

Whyte & Mackay was founded in 1881 as a blending company but is was not until 1960 that they acquired their first distillery, Dalmore. Fettercairn was incorporated in 1973 and Invergordon grain distillery, Jura and Tamnavulin in 1993. The last two were included in the acquisition of Invergordon Distillers together with Bruichladdich, Tullibardine and Tomintoul. The latter three were, however, resold in the beginning of the 21st century. Fettercairn lies just a few miles off the A90 between Dundee and Aberdeen with Glencadam in Brechin as the closest distillery neighbour. The distillery is equipped with a traditional mash tun made of cast iron, eight washbacks made of Douglas fir and two pairs of stills. One feature makes it unique among Scottish distilleries: cooling water is allowed to trickle along the spirit still necks and is collected at the base for circulation towards the top again in order to increase reflux and thereby produce a lighter and cleaner spirit. The stills are then connected to copper condensers where the spirit vapours turn to liquid. This is the common way of doing it but until 1995, these condensers were made of stainless steel which probably will result in a heavier, more sulphury spirit. There are 14 dunnage warehouses on site holding 32,000 casks with the oldest from 1962.

In 2009 the working week is five days, allowing for 19 mashes per week which equals 1.5 million litres of alcohol. The core range of Fettercairn simply consists of a *12 year old*. Some older, limited versions exist such as *Stillmans Dram 26* and *30 years* respectively. There is also a *19 year old* which the owner hopes to bottle during 2009. Visitors to the distillery are offered to fill their own bottle from two casks of 15 year old whisky.

Independent bottlings are very rare but turn up occasionally.

12 years old

Glenallachie

Owner:
Chivas Brothers
(Pernod Ricard)

Region/district:
Speyside

Founded: **Status:** **Capacity:**
1967 Active 3 000 000 litres

Address: Aberlour, Banffshire AB38 9LR

Tel:
01542 783042

website:
-

History:
1967 – The distillery is founded by Mackinlay, McPherson & Co., a subsidiary of Scottish & Newcastle Breweries Ltd. William Delmé Evans is architect.

1985 – Scottish & Newcastle Breweries Ltd sells Charles Mackinlay Ltd to Invergordon Distillers which acquires both Glenallachie and Isle of Jura.

1987 – The distillery is decommissioned.

1989 – Campbell Distillers (Pernod Ricard) buys the distillery, increases the number of stills from two to four and takes up production again.

2005 – The first official bottling for many years becomes a Cask Strength Edition from 1989.

Glenallachie 16 year old 56,7%

DS – Intense sherry with raisins and brown sugar on the nose. The palate is powerful with sherry and coffee liqueur flavours. Long finish with a coffee aftertaste.

Just outside Aberlour in the shadow of Ben Rinnes, from where the distillery obtains its water, lays Glenallachie. It was constructed by the famous architect William Delmé Evans with the purpose of functioning as a gravity fed distillery. This means that a flow of liquids run naturally through the distillery at different levels as opposed to requiring pump action. Delmé Evans had plans for such a distillery already in 1940 but it took until 1967 before he could realise them.

The distillery is equipped with a semi-lauter mash tun, six stainless steel lined washbacks and two pairs of stills. The wash stills are lantern-shaped while the spirit stills are of the onion model. All four stills are unusually connected to horizontal tube condensers rather than vertical ones and the capacity is 18 mashes per week. The spirit is filled into bourbon casks and matured in 12 racked and two palletised warehouses.

The trickle of Glenallachie reaching the market as single malt is feeble. It is used instead in, among others, Pernod Ricard´s fourth largest (after Ballantine´s, Chivas Regal and 100 Pipers) blended Scotch - Clan Campbell. It is also important to another blend which is not especially well-known in the rest of the world but very popular in Australia where it sells 1 million bottles per year, namely White Heather. This was the standard blend of Campbell Distillers, a company which was bought by Pernod Ricard in 1975.

Currently the only official bottling is a *16 year old cask strength* matured in first fill Oloroso casks and released in 2005. Independent bottlings have also been scarce even if single versions have appeared in the Netherlands and Germany. Duncan Taylor recently released a bottling distilled in 1995 and from Cadenhead came a 16 year old distilled in 1992.

1989 16 years old

Glenburgie

Owner: Chivas Brothers (Pernod Ricard)

Region/district: Speyside

Founded: 1810

Status: Active

Capacity: 4 200 000 litres

Address: Glenburgie, Forres, Morayshire IV36 2QY

Tel: 01343 850258

website: -

History:

1810 – William Paul founds Kilnflat Distillery. Official production starts in 1829.

1870 – Kilnflat distillery closes.

1878 – The distillery reopens under the name Glenburgie-Glenlivet, Charles Hay is licensee.

1884 – Alexander Fraser & Co. takes over.

1925 – Alexander Fraser & Co. files for bankruptcy and the receiver Donald Mustad assumes control of operations.

1927 – James & George Stodart Ltd buys the distillery which by this time is inactive.

1930 – Hiram Walker buys 60% of James & George Stodart Ltd.

1936 – Hiram Walker buys Glenburgie Distillery in October. Production restarts.

1958 – Lomond stills are installed producing a single malt, Glencraig. Floor malting ceases.

1981 – The Lomond stills are replaced by conventional stills.

1987 – Allied Lyons buys Hiram Walker.

2002 – A 15 year old is released.

2004 – A £4.3 million refurbishment and reconstruction takes place.

2005 – Chivas Brothers (Pernod Ricard) becomes the new owner through the acquisition of Allied Domecq.

2006 – The number of stills are increased from four to six in May.

Glenburgie 10 year old G&M

DR – Classic sherry, barley and prickly wood on the nose, sweet and gentle red berry on the palate, and a warming mouth-filling soft and pleasant finish.

DS – Rich with raisins and sherry notes on the nose. Hint of burnt rubber. Again sweet and slightly sulphury. Raisins and fruit-cake on the finish.

Glenburgie distillery must be a distillery manager's dream! When the old distillery was knocked down in 2003, a new purpose-built and highly efficient distillery was built just behind it. All the equipment fits on one level in one gigantic room. Most of the equipment is new but four stills, the mill and the boiler were brought in from the old distillery. The only remaining building of the old distillery is the customs house which is now used as a tasting room. A huge lawn fills up the rest of the view. The distillery is equipped with a full lauter mash tun, 12 stainless steel washbacks and three pairs of stills. Thermal compressors are attached to the condensers and although not a unique method of recovering heat, the way it is constructed at Glenburgie makes it the most efficient in the business during this part of the production process. Another production feature is the water treatment plant. Because Glenburgie uses hard water, reversed osmosis is used at the plant in order to soften the water.

The majority of production is filled into bourbon casks and part of them are matured in four dunnage, two racked and two palletised warehouses.

Since April 2009 a five-day week has been implemented which means that 2.6 million litres of alcohol will be produced in the year. Glenburgie is, together with Miltonduff, one of the cornerstones in the Ballantine blend. Unlike Chivas Regal, which is a blend of malt whiskies exclusively from Speyside, Ballantine's contains malts from Speyside, Islay, Highlands and Lowlands. A single malt from Glenburgie named Glencraig can still be found on the market. It came into being by Hiram Walker's experimenting with Lomond stills in the fifties. Glenburgie's first Lomond still was a small model, originating in Dumbarton. It was replaced in 1958 by a pair of full-size Lomond stills and it is the make from these stills that received the name Glencraig. An official *15 year old cask strength* Glenburgie appeared in 2008. Apart from Gordon & MacPhail 10 year old, independent bottlings are rare. A recent one is a 15 year old Cadenhead with a port finish.

Gordon & MacPhail Glenburgie 10 years old

Glencadam

Owner:
Angus Dundee Distillers

Region/district:
Eastern Highlands

Founded: 1825
Status: Active
Capacity: 1 400 000 litres

Address: Brechin, Angus DD9 7PA

Tel: 01356 622217
website: www.glencadamdistillery.co.uk

History:

1825 – George Cooper founds the distillery.

1827 – David Scott takes over.

1837 – The distillery is sold by David Scott.

1852 – Alexander Miln Thompson becomes the owner.

1857 – Glencadam Distillery Company is formed.

1891 – The blending company Gilmour, Thompson & Co Ltd takes over.

1954 – Hiram Walker takes over.

1959 – Refurbishing and modernization of the distillery.

1987 – Allied Lyons buys Hiram Walker Gooderham & Worts.

1994 – Allied Lyons changes name to Allied Domecq.

2000 – The distillery is mothballed.

2003 – Allied Domecq sells the distillery to Angus Dundee Distillers.

2005 – The new owner releases a 15 year old.

2008 – A re-designed 15 year old and a new 10 year old are introduced.

2009 – A 25 and a 30 year old are released in limited numbers.

Glencadam 15 year old

DR – Very delicate nose with pineapple notes, with water a touch of grapefruit and wispy smoke. On the palate exotic fruits, cocoa powder, pineapple and a touch of smoke. The finish is attractive, full and warming.

DS – A rich and herbal nose with vanilla and fudge. The palate is full of toffee and caramel flavours and the finish is rich and sweet.

The town of Brechin would probably not have had a distillery today if it had not been for the fact that Angus Dundee Distillers bought Glencadam in 2003. The former owner, Allied Domecq, mothballed the distillery in 2000 and plans were to close it for good. Today it is not only a busy distillery but also hosts a huge filling and bottling plant with 16 large tanks for blending malt and grain whisky. Owner Angus Dundee is responsible for 4-5% of the total export of Scotch and 3.8 million litres per year can be blended at Glencadam.

There is a traditional cast iron mash tun from the 80s and the mashing time is quite long - nine hours. There are six stainless steel washbacks (four with wooden tops and two with stainless steel ones) and one pair of stills with ascending lyne arms, increasing the reflux which adds to the gentle and mellow taste of the whisky. The external heat exchanger on the wash still is from the fifties and perhaps the first in the business. In full production 16 mashes a week can be made but from July 2009 it will be down to a five-day week production.

On site are three dunnage warehouses from the 50s and one racked. Another two dunnage warehouses from 1825 were debonded in the sixties but rebonded in 2009. There are 23,000 casks maturing, the oldest from 1978. Most of the spirit is matured in bourbon casks, some in sherry butts and there are also plans to fill some port pipes. Unusually enough the casks are filled at still strength (around 68%) rather than watered down to the more common 63.5%.

The first official bottling appeared in 2005, a *15 year old*, which has now been redesigned and is bottled at 46% and without chill filtration. This also goes for the *10 year old*, introduced in autumn 2008. Two very limited releases appeared in the beginning of 2009 - a *25 year old* from 1983 and a *30 year old* from 1978, both bottled in elegant glass decanters. Independent bottlings are scarce but one appeared in 2008 - a 19 year old Signatory distilled in 1989.

10 years old

Glendronach

Owner: Benriach Distillery Co   **Region/district:** Speyside

Founded: 1826   **Status:** Active (vc)   **Capacity:** 1 400 000 litres

Address: Forgue, Aberdeenshire AB54 6DB

Tel: 01466 730202   **website:** www.glendronachdistillery.com

History:

1826 – The distillery is founded by a consortium. James Allardes is one of the owners.

1837 – The major part of the distillery is destroyed in a fire.

1852 – Walter Scott (from Teaninich) takes over.

1887 – Walter Scott dies and Glendronach is taken over by a consortium from Leith.

1920 – Charles Grant buys Glendronach for £9,000 and starts production three months later.

1960 – William Teacher & Sons buys the distillery.

1966-67 – The number of stills is increased to four.

1976 – A visitor centre is opened.

1976 – Allied Breweries takes over William Teacher & Sons.

1996 – The distillery is mothballed.

2002 – Production is resumed on 14th May.

2005 – Glendronach 33 years old is launched. The distillery closes to rebuild from coal to in-direct firing by steam. Reopens in September. Chivas Brothers (Pernod Ricard) becomes new owner through the acquisition of Allied Domecq.

2008 – Pernod Ricard sells the distillery to the owners of BenRiach distillery.

2009 – Relaunch of the whole range - 12, 15 and 18 year old including limited editions of a 33 year old and five single casks.

Glendronach Original 12 year old

DR – Sherry, red berries, vanilla and traces of mint-flavoured toffee on the nose, an intriguing palate of cranberry and blueberry, a peaty carpet and some pepper, and a medium savoury and peaty finish.

DS – Creamy toffee and custard – bread and butter pudding. Sweet and creamy with some peatiness/earthiness and lots of vanilla and malt. The finish is also slightly peaty/peppery.

The sherried whisky from Glendronach has always had a faithful following around the world and many were probably relieved when BenRiach took over ownership in summer 2008. The distillery was in production before but it was never one of the more obvious distilleries in the Pernod Ricard group. Forty years ago Glendronach was amongst the top five most popular malts in the world and the new owner has ambitious plans to restore the brand's former status. A £5m investment in sherry casks over the next four years and another £2m on brand promotion and extra staff was announced in September 2009. When Ben-Riach bought Glendronach it sold 20,000 bottles in a year and in 2009 it is expected to sell around 150,000.

The equipment consists of a cast iron mash tun with rakes, eight Oregon pine washbacks, two wash stills with heat exchangers and two spirit stills. Glendronach was the last Scottish distillery to fire the stills with coal. This old, traditional process continued until September 2005 when indirect heating using steam coils replaced it.

The new owners took over 9,000 casks of maturing whisky when they bought the distillery and the oldest expression in the three dunnage and three racked warehouses is from 1968. Most of the casks are ex-sherry but for some reason the previous owners filled a lot of bourbon casks since the reopening in 2002. There are also some Sauternes casks as well as red wine casks and the latter will probably be released as a finish in 2010 or 2011.

This year there will be an average of 18 mashes a week resulting in 1.1 million litres of alcohol. Some 50% are aimed for own releases and the rest will be sold to Pernod Ricard for its blended whiskies. The core expression from the new owner is the *12 year old* (a mix of Oloroso casks and Pedro Ximenez) whereas the "old" 12 year old received a six months finish in bourbon casks. The range is supplemented by a *15 year old Revival* and an *18 year old Allardice*, both of which are matured in Oloroso casks. There is also a limited *33 year old* and in July 2009 five *single casks* were released, the oldest from 1971.

Original 12 years old

Before it is possible to start extracting soluble sugars from the malted barley during the mashing, it has to be crushed in a mill. The passage from the malt bin leads through a dressing machine where unwanted parts (rootlets etc.) are removed and into the mill. There are different types of mills but the basic concept is that rollers crack the husks of the barleycorn and grinds them to grist.

The most common type is the *Porteus* two or four roll mill but some distilleries use a more modern version called *Bühler-Miag* with up to seven rolls. A few distilleries still use an old but reliable mill called *Boby mill*. During the milling it is vital that the size of the particles is perfect in order to have an as efficient as possible mashing process. The optimum distribution is 10% *flour*, 70% *grits* and 20% *husk*. With too much flour, the filter in the mash tun can become clogged and with too much husk the water will flow through too quickly.

The *grist* (as the milled barley malt is called) flows from the mill to the grist hopper where it is stored before taken to the *mash tun*. The latter is a large circular vessel made either of stainless steel or (more uncommon) cast iron. Just one distillery (Glenturret) still uses a wooden mash tun. Most mash tuns are covered with a dome

but some that are open are still operated. The sizes vary a great deal, from Glenturret where the mash tun holds 1 tonne of grist to the giants at Glenfarclas; 10 metres in diameter and loaded with 15 tonnes of grist per mash.

The grist is then mashed with hot water in order to extract sugars from the barley. The enzymes, amylase, that were awakened during the malting process but deactivated during the kilning, now start to transform starch to sugars. Two to five (but usually three) waters are used in the mashing.

The *first water* (which is actually the third water from the previous mashing) is heated to about 65 degrees. The temperature is crucial - too warm and the enzymes are killed. During the process it is important to keep in mind that certain enzymes are most active at 50 degrees while others are active at higher temperatures.

After the water has been mixed with the grist it is stirred to increase the extraction of sugars. In the old days this was done manually with large wooden spades. The only distillery which practices that method today is Glenturret. Today, when talking about *traditional mash tuns*, it refers to the ones where revolving mechanical rakes stir the mash. Many distilleries have switched to the more modern *lauter mash tuns* commonly used in breweries. In this newer version, a rotating arm is equipped with blades that cut through the

mash. Two varieties exist: *semi-lauter* and *full lauter*. In the latter, the knives can be moved not only horizontally but also vertically. After about 30 minutes the first batch of *wort*, as the mash is now called, is drained off through the perforated floor into the underback or wort receiver.

The *second water* is now filled into the mash tun, this time heated to anywhere between 70 and 85 degrees, depending on the distillery's different preferences. The same procedure follows and the wort is drained off after 30 minutes. At this time, 90% of the starches have been converted into fermentable sugars but there is still some soluble starch left in the mash and in order to make use of it a *third water* is added. The temperature of this water will typically vary between 80 and 95 degrees and after 15 minutes it is drained off. Since this water only contains about 1% sugar, it should not be mixed with the wort already collected so it is pumped to the hot water tank to be used as part of the first water in the next mashing.

The resulting residue in the mash tun is now called *draff*, consisting of husks and spent grains, which is collected, processed and used for cattle feed. Sometimes it is mixed with the pot ale from the distillation and transformed into pellets, so called *dark grains*. Before the collected wort in the wort receiver goes into the *washbacks* for fermentation (se page 147) the temperature has to be reduced to 18-20 degrees, otherwise the yeast would be destroyed.

The whole mashing procedure will take about three hours in a modern lauter mash tun and, in the case of Glenfarclas, a batch of 15 tonnes of grist will produce around 75,000 litres of wort. One thing which is important to measure before the fermentation starts is the *Original Gravity* (OG) of the wort, i. e. how rich the wort is in sugars. This will determine the amount of yeast that can be used during the next phase - fermentation. The density of water at 20 degrees is 1000 and when whisky is produced the OG of the wort will be around 1050.

Glendullan

Owner: Diageo

Region/district: Speyside

Founded: 1897 **Status:** Active **Capacity:** 3 360 000 litres

Address: Dufftown, Keith, Banffshire AB55 4DJ

Tel: 01340 822100 **website:** www.malts.com

History:
1896-97 – William Williams & Sons, a blending company with Three Stars and Strahdon among its brands, founds the distillery.

1902 – Glendullan is delivered to the Royal Court and becomes the favourite whisky of Edward VII.

1919 – Macdonald Greenlees buys a share of the company and Macdonald Greenlees & Williams Distillers is formed.

1926 – Distillers Company Limited (DCL) buys Glendullan.

1930 – Glendullan is transferred to Scottish Malt Distillers (SMD).

1962 – Major refurbishing and reconstruction.

1972 – A brand new distillery, accommodating six stills, is constructed next to the old one and both operate simultaneously during a few years.

1985 – The oldest of the two distilleries is mothballed.

1995 – The first launch of Glendullan in the Rare Malts series becomes a 22 year old from 1972.

2005 – A 26 year old from 1978 is launched in the Rare Malts series.

2007 – Singleton of Glendullan is launched in the USA.

Glendullan 12 year old

DR – The nose has a mix of fruits including grapefruit melon and even banana, the taste is more-ish, with the citrus and melon notes coming through. Warm and pleasant finish.

DS – Strong sherry notes on the nose with prune juice and oak. The palate is sweet with strong sherry flavours and malty. A fine finish with some oakiness in the aftertaste.

To find a distillery is easy in Dufftown. Just a mile from Glenfiddich for example lies Glendullan. It is on the right hand side, in the glen, if standing at the railway bridge which crosses the river Fiddich. Looking left from the bridge instead, the decommissioned Parkmore distillery is visible. It has not been in use since 1931 and all equipment is gone. The magnificent buildings remain intact though and Edrington uses them today for storing spirit from, among others, Macallan.

The American market is often reached by new releases of single malts much later than the European market and sometimes releases never even get that far. Therefore, it must feel satisfying for American consumers when some expressions are exclusively targeted towards them. Recently there has been Ardmore 30 year old, Oban 18 year old, Glenlivet Nadurra Cask Strength and Singleton of Glendullan. The latter is one of three in the newly created Singleton family of whiskies, the others being Glen Ord and Dufftown.

Glendullan is one of the largest distilleries in the Diageo group with one stainless steel mash tun, eight washbacks made of larch and three pairs of stills. It is one of the original seven distilleries of Dufftown and the last of them to open. However, the distillery that opened in 1896 is not the one distilling today; a new Glendullan was built in 1972 next to the old one. The two were operated in parallel for a few years until 1985 when the old distillery closed. It is now used as a workshop for Diageo's malt distillery engineering team. The old distillery was equipped with one pair of stills with a capacity of 1 million litres a year. The core range consists of *Singleton of Glendullan*. Previously there has also been a *12 year old* in the *Flora & Fauna* series generally available. Recent independent bottlings include a 12 year old from Cadenhead and a 15 year old Rioja finish from Murray McDavid.

The old distillery

The Singleton of Glendullan

Glen Elgin

Owner:
Diageo

Region/district:
Speyside

Founded: 1898

Status: Active

Capacity: 1 830 000 litres

Address: Longmorn, Morayshire IV30 3SL

Tel: 01343 862100

website: www.malts.com

History:

1898 – The bankers William Simpson and James Carle found Glen Elgin.

1900 – Production starts in May but the distillery closes just five months later.

1901 – The distillery is auctioned for £4,000 to the Glen Elgin-Glenlivet Distillery Co. and is mothballed.

1906 – The wine producer J. J. Blanche & Co. buys the distillery for £7,000 and production resumes.

1929 – J. J. Blanche dies and the distillery is put up for sale again.

1930 – Scottish Malt Distillers (SMD) buys it and the license goes to White Horse Distillers.

1964 – Expansion from two to six stills plus other refurbishing takes place.

1992 – The distillery closes for refurbishing and installation of new stills.

1995 – Production resumes in September.

2001 – A 12 year old is launched in the Flora & Fauna series.

2002 – The Flora & Fauna series malt is replaced by Hidden Malt 12 years.

2003 – A 32 year old cask strength from 1971 is released.

2008 – A 16 year old is launched as a Special Release.

2009 – Glen Elgin 1998, a single cask in the new Manager's Choice range is released.

Glen Elgin 12 year old

DR – Ginger, crystallised barley sweet and a complex array of fruit on the nose, a beautiful balanced taste with light fruit, sweet spice and a zesty freshness and mouth filling finish.

DS – Soft honey, heather and malt on the nose with some fruitiness. The palate is much sweeter and quite delicate. An appealing finish with honey lozenge in the aftertaste.

Just a few miles south of Elgin along the A941 lies the small village of Fogwatt. It takes a mere minute to drive through it which is why it is easy to miss Glen Elgin Distillery that also happens to lie in a side street. The distillery belongs to the Diageo group of distilleries called Speyside West with the others being Glen Spey, Benrinnes, Dailuaine, Glenlossie, Mannochmore and Linkwood.

The architect behind Glen Elgin was the famous Charles Cree Doig (1855-1918). He alone designed 56 Scottish distilleries and was probably involved in co-designing a similar number. His most recognisable contribution was the familar pagoda roof which was first constructed at Dailuaine Distillery. The purpose of it was to improve the efficiency of drawing off peat smoke from the kiln.

The distillery is equipped with a Steinecker full lauter mash tun, six washbacks made of larch and three pairs of stills. The stills are connected to six wooden worm tubs placed in the yard. They were installed in 2004 replacing six old worm tubs. Spirit from the new production is stored at Glenlossie and Auchroisk while the older production is stored in dunnage warehouses on site. Despite its small size, it has a great capacity for storing malted barley with 36 malt bins holding 400 tonnes.

In 2001 Glen Elgin was launched as a part of the Flora & Fauna series but was replaced the year after by a new *12 year old* in what was then called "Hidden Malts". Three limited editions have also been released: a *19 year old* in 2000, a *32 year old* in 2003 and finally a *16 year old* was launched in 2008. In autumn 2009 a *single cask* from *1998* was released as part of the new series Manager´s Choice. Recent independent bottlings include two 30 year old from Cadenhead and Adelphi Distillery, a 16 year old from Signatory and a 1991 from Blackadder.

16 years old

Glenfarclas

Owner:
J. & G. Grant

Region/district:
Speyside

Founded:
1836

Status:
Active (vc)

Capacity:
3 000 000 litres

Address: Ballindalloch, Banffshire AB37 9BD

Tel:
01807 500257

website:
www.glenfarclas.co.uk

History:
1836 – Robert Hay founds the distillery on the original site since 1797.

1865 – Robert Hay passes away and John Grant and his son George buy the distillery for £511.19s on 8th June. They lease it to John Smith at The Glenlivet Distillery.

1870 – John Smith resigns in order to start Cragganmore and J. & G. Grant Ltd takes over.

1889 – John Grant dies and George Grant takes over.

1890 – George Grant dies and his widow Barbara takes over the license while sons John and George control operations.

1895 – John and George Grant take over and form The Glenfarclas-Glenlivet Distillery Co. Ltd with the infamous Pattison, Elder & Co.

1898 – Pattison becomes bankrupt. Glenfarclas encounters financial problems after a major overhaul of the distillery but survives by mortgaging and selling stored whisky to R. I. Cameron, a whisky broker from Elgin.

Glenfarclas is the second oldest family-owned malt distillery in Scotland. The Grant family bought it in 1865 and now the fifth generation is involved in the business with George Grant as the Brand Ambassador of the company.

The distillery is equipped with a semi-lauter mash tun which measures ten metres in diameter and holds 15 tonnes of grist, twelve stainless steel washbacks and three pairs of stills. There are 28 dunnage warehouses on site which hold 52,000 casks. All the stills at Glenfarclas are directly fired by North Sea gas.

Glenfarclas was one of the first distilleries to open a visitor centre. "The Ship's Room", where each tour ends with a dram, is unique and very beautiful. The decorations were taken from an ocean liner, the "Empress of Australia", which had a colourful history from 1913 to 1952.

One of the biggest successes for Glenfarclas was the launch of the first commercially available cask strength whisky of modern age, Glenfarclas 105. It started back in 1968 when George S. Grant, fourth generation of the Grants, bottled a single cask from the warehouse and sent bottles to family and friends as a Christmas gift. In January, the recipients requested further bottles and thus the 105 became a permanent member of the range. The "105" in the name relates to the old way of measuring spirit strength called proof. It was abandoned in Europe in 1980 and replaced by today's system – percentage of alcohol. 105 is 5 overproof indicating a strength of 60%. For a while the strength created a problem on the US market as regulations deemed it too strong. Hence it was bottled as Glenfarclas 104 until the laws had changed.

Glenfarclas has a number of expressions in its core range: 10, 12, 15, 21, 25 and 30 years old. Furthermore, there is (as mentioned above) Glenfarclas 105, a limited version of 105 which is 40 years old and was released in autumn 2008 and limited editions of 40 and 50 years old.

In 2007, Glenfarclas presented a unique collection of bottlings called Family Casks. No less than 43 single casks from 43 different years were launched simultaneously. To add to the uniqueness it turned out that this was an unbroken series of vintages from 1952 to 1994. Some of these have now sold out and in spring 2009 a third edition of new bottlings were released from some of the years (1952, 1957, 1959, 1960, 1961, 1962, 1969, 1978, 1979 and 1987) and a fourth release is already planned for (1959, 1969, 1975 and 1979).

History (continued):

1914 – John Grant leaves due to ill health and George continues alone.

1948 – The Grant family celebrates the distillery's 100th anniversary, a century of active licensing. It is 9 years late, as the actual anniversary coincided with WW2.

1949 – George Grant senior dies and sons George Scott and John Peter inherit the distillery.

1960 – Stills are increased from two to four.

1968 – Glenfarclas is first to launch a cask-strength single malt. It is later named Glenfarclas 105.

1972 – Floor maltings is abandoned and malt is purchased centrally.

1973 – A visitor centre is opened.

1976 – Enlargement from four stills to six.

2001 – Glenfarclas launches its first Flower of Scotland gift tin which becomes a great success and increases sales by 30%.

2002 – George S Grant dies and is succeeded as company chairman by his son John L S Grant

2003 – Two new gift tins are released (10 years old and 105 cask strength).

2005 – A 50 year old is released to commemorate the bi-centenary of John Grant's birth.

2006 – Ten new vintages are released.

2007 – Family Casks, a series of single cask bottlings from 43 consecutive years, is released.

2008 – New releases in the Family Cask range. Glenfarclas 105 40 years old is released.

2009 – A third release in the Family Casks series.

Glenfarclas 10 year old

DR – Creamy sherry and bitter oranges on the nose, rich fruit cake and red berries on the palate with a pleasant spice and barley interplay and long and warming finish.

DS – Lots of malt and sherry notes on the nose that continue on the palate with an added creaminess – full bodied. The finish is long and sweet.

105 Cask Strength (Duty Free version)   10 years old   105 Cask Strength 40 years

The Family Casks 1978   12 years old   The Family Casks 1959

Glenfiddich

Owner:
William Grant & Sons

Region/district:
Speyside

Founded: **Status:** **Capacity:**
1886   Active (vc)   10 000 000 litres

Address: Dufftown, Keith, Banffshire AB55 4DH

Tel:
01340 820373 (vc)

website:
www.glenfiddich.com

History:
1886 – The distillery is founded by William Grant, 47 years old, who had learned the trade at Mortlach Distillery. The equipment is bought from Mrs. Cummings of Cardow Distillery. The construction totals £800.

1887 – The first distilling takes place on Christmas Day.

1892 – William Grant builds Balvenie.

1898 – The blending company Pattisons, largest customer of Glenfiddich, files for bankruptcy and Grant decides to blend their own whisky. Standfast becomes one of their major brands.

1903 – William Grant & Sons is formed.

1957 – The famous, three-cornered bottle is introduced.

1958 – The floor maltings is closed.

1963 – Glennfiddich becomes the first whisky to be marketed as single malt in the UK and the rest of the world.

1964 – A version of Standfast's three-cornered bottle is launched for Glenfiddich in green glass.

1969 – Glenfiddich becomes the first distillery in Scotland to open a visitor centre.

1974 – 16 new stills are installed.

2001 – 1965 Vintage Reserve is launched in a limited edition of 480 bottles. Glenfiddich 1937 is bottled (61 bottles).

It can be questioned whether the single malt segment of Scotch whisky had been so large today had not Glenfiddich existed. In 1964 they set the snowball rolling by consistently selling single malts on the international market. That year 48,000 bottles were sold and just 10 years later that had increased to 1.4 million. That is more than what, for example, Highland Park sells today, 35 years later. Glenfiddich's total sales in 2008 was almost 12 million bottles meaning that almost every fifth bottle of Scotch single malt is Glenfiddich. The distillery has been owned by the same family since commissioning in 1886 and since 2008 Peter Gordon, the great great grandson of William Grant, is Chairman of the Board while his father Charles Gordon has become Life President of the company.

The distillery is equipped with two big, stainless steel, full lauter mash tuns (11.2 tonnes), each with copper domes and a capacity of 4 mashes per day, i. e. 56/week. There are 24 Douglas fir washbacks with a fermentation time of 66 hours. One still room holds 5 wash and 10 spirit stills and the other 5 plus 8. The wash stills are all onion-shaped while half of the spirit stills are of the lantern model and the rest have a boiling ball. All the stills are directly fired using gas. Some 90% of the casks are bourbon and the rest first or refill sherry butts. Forty four warehouses on site (of which 6 are dunnage) are shared with Balvenie and Kininvie.

Close to Glenfiddich lies Parkmore distillery which has been dormant since 1931. The equipment is gone but all the buildings are intact and rumour has it that William Grant was interested in buying it from Edrington (who uses it for warehousing) but nothing has happened so far.

Glenfiddich's core range consists of *12, 15, 18* and *21 years old* as well as Glenfiddich *30 years old* and *Caoran Reserve 12 years old*. The *15 year old*, sometimes called *Solera*, was introduced in 1997 by Master Blender David Stewart. Whisky that has been maturing in bourbon barrels, new hogsheads and sherry butts are emptied into a huge (700 litres) "solera vat" made of Douglas fir. The whisky is allowed to marry for three to six months before half of the vat is emptied and bottled. The *15 year old cask strength* (Distillery Edition), previously a duty free exclusive, can now be found in key markets worldwide. Recent limited bottlings include a new vatting of both the *40* and the *50 year old*. Finally this year's *Vintage Reserve*, a sherry cask from 1975, was released in autumn.

History (continued):

2002 – Glenfiddich Gran Reserva 21 years old, finished in Cuban rum casks is launched. Sales in the USA are not possible due to the trade embargo between the USA and Cuba. Caoran Reserve 12 years, an attempt to recreate the peaty Glenfiddich produced during the war years, is launched. Glenfiddich Rare Collection 1937 (61 bottles) is launched at a recommended price of £10,000 each and becomes the oldest Scotch whisky on the market.

2003 – 1973 Vintage Reserve (440 bottles) is launched.

2004 – 1991 Vintage Reserve (13 years) and 1972 Vintage Reserve (519 bottles) are launched.

2005 – Circa £1.7 million is invested in a new visitor centre.

2006 – 1973 Vintage Reserve, 33 years (861 bottles) and 12 year old Toasted Oak are released.

2007 – 1976 Vintage Reserve, 31 years is released in September.

2008 – 1977 Vintage Reserve is released.

2009 – A 50 year old and 1975 Vintage Reserve are released.

15 years old (Solera)   *18 years old*   *Glenfiddich 30 years old*

Glenfiddich 12 year old

DR – Classic rich fruit and peerless clean barley nose, fruit bowl and sharp malt palate and pleasant and warming lengthy finish.

DS – A green nose with sweet heather honey notes. The palate is wave upon wave of soft honey and a hint of spice. A short and bittersweet finish.

12 years old   *Caoran Reserve 12 years old*   *1975 Vintage Reserve*

Glenglassaugh

Owner: **Region/district:**
Glenglassaugh Distillery Co   Speyside
(Scaent Group)

Founded: **Status:**   **Capacity:**
1875   Active   1 100 000 litres

Address: Portsoy, Banffshire AB45 2SQ

Tel: **website:**
01261 842367   www.glenglassaugh.com

History:

1873-75 – The distillery is founded by Glenglassaugh Distillery Company.

1887 – Alexander Morrison embarks on renovation work.

1892 – Alexander Morrison, the sole survivor of the original founders, sells the distillery to Robertson & Baxter. They in turn sell it on to Highland Distilleries Company for £15,000.

1908 – The distillery closes.

1931 – The distillery reopens.

1936 – The distillery closes.

1957-59 – Substantial reconstruction, including acquisition of new stills, takes place. Own maltings are abandoned and the malt is bought from Tamdhu Distillery instead.

1960 – The distillery reopens.

1986 – Glenglassaugh is mothballed.

2005 – A 22 year old is released.

2006 – Three limited editions are released - 19 years old, 38 years old and 44 years old.

2008 – The distillery is bought by the Scaent Group for £5m and the first distillation takes place on 24th November. Three bottlings are released - 21, 30 and 40 year old.

2009 – New make spirit (6 months old) is released.

The Spirit Drink
that dare not speak its name

DR – Cereal, summer fruits and spearmint toffee on the nose, strong menthol and sharp apple taste, highly palatable, and a clean, sweet mint toothpaste of a finish.

DS – A fruit/barley cocktail mixed with honeycomb and a hint of orange. A touch of that new-make fieriness but there is unexpected caramel and caraway especially in the finish.

It always feels good to see a mothballed distillery starting up again and especially so when it happens to be one that everyone thought was doomed for good. During the seventies and eighties, Highland Distillers wanted to see if they could produce a Glenrothes style of whisky at Glenglassaugh but then decided to expand Glenrothes instead and Glenglassaugh closed. Twenty two years later the distillery came back to life when it was bought by the Dutch Scaent Group for £5m. Most of the old equipment could be used again but an investment of £1m, mainly to build a new boiler room, was required in order to be ready for the inauguration on 24th November 2009. The equipment consists of a rare Porteus cast iron mash tun with rakes, four wooden washbacks and two stainless steel ones (although the last two are not being used) and, finally, one pair of stills. The first year there will be six mashes per week which corresponds to 200,000 litres of alcohol. It is vital to build up stock because only 400 casks of maturing Glenglassaugh (from 1963 to 1986) were included in the deal. The whisky is matured in a combination of dunnage and racked warehouses. There is no final decision on which casks to use and there is still much experimenting going on.

The distillery is beautifully situated near the village of Portsoy with the North Sea just behind and the owners have plans to build a visitor centre offering quality tours, to be ready in 2010.

The first limited releases from the new owner were *21, 30* and *40 year olds*. In summer 2009, 8,160 (the entire output from a single mash) 50 cl bottles of new make spirit (6 months old) was released under the title *"The Spirit Drink that dare not speak its name"*. Around the same time the distillery offered customers to buy a cask of maturing Glenglassaugh spirit for £500. The size was called Octave and contains circa 50 litres.

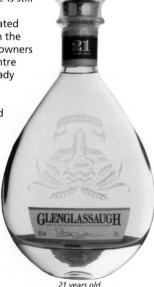

21 years old

Meet the Manager

GRAHAM EUNSON
DISTILLERY MANAGER, GLENGLASSAUGH DISTILLERY

When did you start working in the whisky business and when did you start at Glenglassaugh?

September 1990 at Scapa and joined Glenglassaugh April 2008.

Have you been working in other lines of business before whisky?

Started as an apprentice carpenter but was forced to give this up due to a badly broken leg, I then worked for 7 years in the parts dept of a Ford franchised garage – probably not the most obvious of routes into whisky!

What kind of education or training do you have?

Secondary school up to "higher" level but learned "on the job" in the whisky industry - starting in warehouse operations and then on to shifts in distillery production. I then trained as a brewer before transferring to another distillery as brewer. I changed companies to become an assistant manager and 18 months later was promoted to the position of distillery manager.

Describe your career in the whisky business.

Working as a Mashman and Stillman at Scapa Distillery I eventually became a Brewer at Glendronach. I then worked as Distillery Manager at Glenmorangie before joining Glenglassaugh in 2008.

What are your main tasks as a manager?

Man management, quality control, scheduling production including raw materials supplies, communicating with relevant bodies and ensuring compliance. Conducting tours & PR work – talks, tastings etc.

What are the biggest challenges of being a distillery manager?

Trying to balance complying with all the regulations whilst running the plant cost effectively and efficiently. Add to this keeping your boss, employees and the whisky drinking public happy.

What would be the worst that could go wrong in the production process?

A fire in the warehouses – this could wipe out all the maturing stock and destroy the brand for many years to come. Anything in the distillery that goes wrong is usually easily fixed and at worst you'd only lose one batch. Even fire in the distillery buildings would only lose a few months production

How would you describe the character of Glenglassaugh single malt?

Obviously each expression is different but in general the "house style" is typically Highland rather than Speyside with fruity notes prominent more so than floral ones. Toffee sweetness and rich liquorice combine with a common theme of boiled fruit sweets. The older expressions have an amazing balance and complexity despite their age and remain quite fresh with no hint of "woodiness" or over-aging.

What are the main features in the process at Glenglassaugh, contributing to this character?

As with most whiskies the whole is greater than the sum of its parts and it's the combination of features rather than any individual ones that make the difference. That said, we have very hard water, a traditional cast iron mash tun, wooden washbacks, uniquely sized stills and condensers and a temperate, marine climate on the shores of the Moray Firth for the maturation.

What is your favourite expression of Glenglassaugh and why?

Of the expressions released to date I'd have to choose the 40 year old which has a tremendous balance of flavour and no hint of over-aging. It has made me drastically re-think my views on older whiskies.

If it were your decision alone – what new expression of Glenglassaugh would you like to see released?

Given that our youngest maturing stock is 22 years old, I can't wait to see our new production when it reaches its 12 year anniversary.

If you had to choose a favourite dram other than Glenglassaugh, what would that be?

It's only natural to have a soft spot for the places I've worked previously and I'd probably have to choose the Scapa 16 yo or Glenmorangie 15 yo. Outwith these I'm partial to the odd Highland Park and have been known to kick start my palate at the end of a night with a Laphroaig or Ardbeg.

What are the biggest changes you have seen the past 10-15 years in your profession?

Probably the changing ownership of distilleries with more small / independent companies operating them rather than the big multi-nationals. This has lead to more "niche" brands becoming available to the consumer and can only help create more interest in single malts.

Do you see any major changes in the next 10 years to come?

The only thing for sure is that changes will happen, they've constantly happened over the last few hundred years and I don't see that trend stopping.

Do you have any special interests/hobbies that you pursue?

DIY - doing projects around the house - probably takes me back to my time as an apprentice and having just bought a house last year there are plenty to keep me going.

How does it feel coming from one of the best known and best selling distilleries, Glenmorangie, to one that has been closed for 22 years?

Two of my previous distilleries had been mothballed and the opportunity to breathe life back into one, after such a long closure, appealed to my romantic side – not that Margaret believes I have one! The jobs are remarkably similar in a number of ways although I'd have to say that running a distillery 24/7 year round was in some ways much easier than starting one up on relatively low production levels – efficiencies of scale etc. The brands PR side was probably easier also as the name was already well known and product was plentiful at a range of ages – Glenglassaugh's youngest being 22 years old and all extremely rare creates its own unique problems.

What were the biggest challenges opening up the distillery after such a long time?

Other than the obvious (time and money) it was probably trying to combine old and new plant. We tried to keep as much of the original equipment as possible to help maintain the quality of the spirit. If I had to pick out one memorable "challenge" during the project, it would probably be the day that we discovered that ground conditions weren't suitable for our new chimney foundations – this led to a few frantic days of running around demolishing the old draff hopper, complete with concrete roof, excavating, shuttering and pouring the new foundations and then hoping that the weather would stay warm to help the concrete cure – we made it with just hours to spare.

121

Glen Garioch

Owner:
Morrison Bowmore
(Suntory)

Region/district:
Eastern Highlands

Founded: **Status:** **Capacity:**
1797   Active (vc)   1 000 000 litres

Address: Oldmeldrum, Inverurie,
Aberdeenshire AB51 0ES

Tel:
01651 873450

website:
www.glengarioch.com

History:
1797 – Thomas Simpson founds Glen Garioch.

1837 – The distillery is bought by John Manson
& Co., owner of Strathmeldrum Distillery.

1884 – The distillery is bought by J. G. Thompson.

1908 – Glengarioch Distillery Company, owned
by William Sanderson, buys the distillery.

1933 – Sanderson & Son merges with the gin
maker Booth's Distilleries Ltd.

1937 – Booth's Distilleries Ltd is acquired by
Distillers Company Limited (DCL).

1968 – Glen Garioch is decommissioned.

1970 – It is old to Stanley P. Morrison Ltd.

1973 – Reconstruction and production starts
again. A more peaty whisky is produced.

1978 – Stills are increased from two to four.

1982 – Becomes the first distillery to use gas
from the North Sea for heating.

1994 – Suntory controls all of Morrison
Bowmore Distillers Ltd.

1995 – The distillery is mothballed in October.

1997 – The distillery reopens in August.

2004 – 336 bottles of the oldest ever Glen
Garioch is released, a 46 year old from 1958.

2005 – 15 year old Bordeaux Cask Finish is launched. A visitor centre opens in October.

2006 – An 8 year old is released.

2009 – Complete revamp of the range - 1979
Founders Reserve (unaged), 12 year old, Vintage 1978 and 1990 are released.

Glen Garioch 1797 Founder's Reserve

DR – Butterscotch, blood orange and citrus
fruits on the nose, a gentle mix of citrus
fruits, honey and spice on the palate, and a
soft rounded fruity finish.

DS – Malt extract - rich spices and deep European oak notes - raisins, carob, coffee bean.
Oily and rich at first before trifle flavours
(custard and fruits of the forest) lots of vanilla
especially in the finish. Rich and moreish.

In 2007 the entire range of Bowmore whiskies was revamped,
one year later it was Auchentoshans' turn and in 2009 the third
of the Morrison Bowmore distilleries, Glen Garioch, underwent
the same treatment. This charming distillery in the village of
Oldmeldrum west of Aberdeen has not experienced the same
attention as the others, although a visitor centre did open in
2005. It does, however, seem like the owner has decided to
spend effort on it. Not just through the new range but there
is also talk about increasing capacity by recommissioning the
third still which has not been used for some years now.
Today, Glen Garioch is equipped with a full lauter mash tun,
eight stainless steel washbacks and one pair of stills. The owner
is explicitly interested in starting the maltings again, dormant
since 1979. The spirit is tankered to Glasgow, filled into casks
and returned to be stored in the distillery's four warehouses.
Current capacity is 1 million litres and in
2009 there will be 10 mashes per week
which corresponds to 700,000 litres.
Sales have decreased from 250,000 bottles
in 2005 to 175,000 in 2008 so a review of
the range seems in store.
Until now the core range has consisted
of 8, 12, 15 and 21 years old. The new
range will be two core expressions: *1797
Founder's Reserve* (without age statement) and a *12 year old*, both of
them bottled at the rather unusual
strength of 48% and non-chill
filtered. There will also be two limited *cask strength vintages* released
every year, the first two being *1978*
and *1990*. Finally, the Founders
Reserve will also be available in
1 litre bottles reserved for Duty
Free. The entire range was released
in Europe in September except for
the 12 year old which will be launched in early 2010. The new range
will not appear in Asia and North
America until January 2010.
Recent independent bottlings
include a 1988 from Duncan Taylor
and a 17 year old from Signatory.

1797 Founder's Reserve

Glengoyne

Owner:
Ian Macleod Distillers

Region/district:
Southern Highlands

Founded: 1833

Status: Active (vc)

Capacity: 1 100 000 litres

Address: Dumgoyne by Killearn,
Glasgow G63 9LB

Tel: 01360 550254 (vc)

website: www.glengoyne.com

History:

1833 – The distillery is licensed under the name Burnfoot Distilleries by the Edmonstone family.

1851 – George Connell is replaced as licensee by John MacLelland.

1867 – Archibald C. McLelland takes over.

1876 – Lang Brothers buys the distillery and changes the name to Glenguin.

1905 – The name changes to Glengoyne.

1910 – Own floor maltings ceases.

1965-66 – Robertson & Baxter takes over Lang Brothers and the distillery is refurbished. The stills are increased from two to three.

2001 – Glengoyne Scottish Oak Finish (16 years old) is launched.

2003 – Ian MacLeod Distillers Ltd buys the distillery plus the brand Langs from the Edrington Group for £7.2 million.

2004 – A 12 year old cask strength is released.

2005 – Relaunch of Scottish Oak Finish. Limited editions of a 19 year old, a 32 year old and a 37 year old cask strength are launched.

2006 – Nine "choices" from Stillmen, Mashmen and Manager are released. The 10 and 17 year olds are relaunched.

2007 – A new version of the 21 year old, two Warehousemen´s Choice, Vintage 1972 and two single casks are released.

2008 – A 16 year old Shiraz cask finish, three single casks and Heritage Gold are released.

2009 – A 40 year old, two single casks and a new 12 year old are launched.

Glengoyne 12 year old

DR – Tinned pear and peach on the nose, crystallised barley, lemon and grapefruit on the palate, and a fruity and peppery finish.

DS – Rich honey mixed with creamy oak notes and mandarins in syrup. Surprisingly dry and bittersweet with honeycomb and pepper on the palate. Perfumed in the finish which is hot and tongue-tingling.

The owner of Glengoyne, Ian Macleod Distillers, is not among those complaining over poor times. It reported a 53% rise in pre-tax profits for the fiscal year ending September 2008. On the other hand, whisky industry problems did not crop up until the beginning of 2009 so it remains to be seen what the final outcome will be this year. The portfolio is well composed; apart from Glengoyne single malt selling almost 400,000 bottles per year, there is King Robert II, a Scotch blend which is the number one whisky in Duty Free India, the own single malt Islay Smokehead as well as Rostov Vodka and London Hill Gin. A total of 1 million cases of which 85% are exported to over 65 markets worldwide are produced.

Glengoyne distillery is equipped with a traditional mash tun, six Oregon pine washbacks, one wash still and two spirit stills. The high quality visitor centre receives some 40,000 visitors annually who are offered the opportunity of cask tasting and creating their own whisky blend. The core range consists of *10, 12 (cask strength), 17* and *21 years old*. An addition to this line-up, a *12 year old* bottled at 43%, was launched in October 2009.

In October 2008 three single casks were released: a *1997 European Oak Sherry hogshead (11 years)*, a *1992 refill hogshead (16 years)* and a *1989 Oloroso hogshead (19 years)*. They were followed by *single casks* from *1986* and *1995* in October 2009.

The owner has developed a five-year strategy to strengthen its prominence in duty free outlets and in October 2008 the *Glengoyne 14 year old Heritage Gold* supplemented the un-aged *Burnfoot* (the original name of the distillery). A one litre bottling of the *12 year old cask strength* was also released for duty free in autumn 2009. But the bottling that recently got the most attention was the *40 year old*, announced already in 2008 but not released until autumn 2009. The 250 crystal decanters represent the oldest bottling ever from the distillery and the oldest still left in the warehouses. Independent bottlings are not common.

12 years old

Glen Grant

Owner: **Region/district:**
Campari Group   Speyside

Founded: **Status:**   **Capacity:**
1840   Active (vc)   5 900 000 litres

Address: Elgin Road, Rothes,
Banffshire AB38 7BS

Tel: **website:**
01340 832118   www.glengrant.com

History:
1840 – The brothers James and John Grant, managers of Dandelaith Distillery, found the distillery.

1861 – The distillery becomes the first to install electric lighting.

1864 – John Grant dies.

1872 – James Grant passes away and the distillery is inherited by his son, James junior (Major James Grant).

1897 – James Grant decides to build another distillery across the road; it is named Glen Grant No. 2.

1902 – Glen Grant No. 2 is mothballed.

1931 – Major Grant dies and is succeeded by his grandson Major Douglas Mackessack.

1953 – J. & J. Grant merges with George & J. G. Smith who runs Glenlivet distillery, forming The Glenlivet & Glen Grant Distillers Ltd.

1961 – Armando Giovinetti and Douglas Mackessak found a friendship that eventually leads to Glen Grant becoming the most sold malt whisky in Italy.

1965 – Glen Grant No. 2 is back in production, but renamed Caperdonich.

A meeting in 1961 between Douglas Mackessack of Glen Grant and Italian entrepreneur Armando Giovinetti quickly resulted in Glen Grant becoming the most sold single malt in Italy. The position was strengthened year after year and eventually half of the turn-over was on the Italian market. But there is also a risk involved in being too dependent upon one market. Between 2006 and 2007 sales of Scotch whisky decreased by 30% in Italy and the decline continued during 2008. This is also reflected in Glen Grant's sales figures which decreased by 37% to 3 million bottles during 2008.

However, the new owner since 2006 (Campari) claims to be happy with the results so far and it is quite clear that Campari has done more with the brand than Chivas Brothers did during its time as owner. Among the changes are new packaging of the core range and the release of some interesting limited editions. Also, casks between 15 and 35 years old have been bought back for future special releases.

The distillery is equipped with a semi-lauter mash tun, ten Oregon pine washbacks and four pairs of stills. The stills are somewhat peculiar in that they have vertical sides at the base of the neck and are all fitted with purifiers. This gives an increased reflux and creates a light and delicate whisky. There were discussions last year of a possible capacity expansion by adding another four pairs of stills but these plans have now been put on hold. Production for 2009 is expected to be 4.6 million litres. Bourbon casks are used for maturation and the share of sherry butts is less than 10% (mainly used for the 10 year old). The previous owner, Chivas Brothers, still owns most of the warehouses, but in 2008 Glen Grant bought eleven warehouses in Rothes. They were all refurbished in summer 2009 with new roofs and rewiring at a cost of £3m. A reconstruction of the visitor centre took place in late 2008 at a cost of £500,000 with The Major's Coachmans House being converted into a new visitor centre.

Some 50% of the production goes into blended whisky, especially Chivas Regal. The Glen Grant core range of single malts consists of a *no age statement* for the UK and Europe, a *5 year old*, and a *10 year old*. Recent limited editions include *Cellar Reserve 1992* which will continue in 2010 with a 1993. There is also a cask strength, non-chill filtered *17 year old* for sale at the distillery only. In the beginning of 2010 a *16 year old* will be launched, initially as a limited release.

Some of the most recent independent bottlings include a 23 year old from Adelphi Distillery, a 41 year old from Signatory and three (1970, 1972 and 1974) released by Duncan Taylor.

History (continued):

1972 – The Glenlivet & Glen Grant Distillers merges with Hill Thompson & Co. and Longmorn-Glenlivet Ltd to form The Glenlivet Distillers. The drum maltings ceases.

1973 – Stills are increased from four to six.

1977 – The Chivas & Glenlivet Group (Seagrams) buys Glen Grant Distillery. Stills are increased from six to ten.

2001 – Pernod Ricard and Diageo buy Seagrams Spirits and Wine, with Pernod acquiring the Chivas Group.

2006 – Campari buys Glen Grant for €115 million in a deal that includes the acquisition of Old Smuggler and Braemar for another €15 million.

2007 – The entire range is re-packaged and re-launched and a 15 year old single cask is released. Reconstruction of the visitor centre.

2008 – Two limited cask strengths - a 16 year old and a 27 year old - are released.

2009 – Cellar Reserve 1992 is released.

Glen Grant 10 year old

DR – Sweet banana and toffee, vanilla and pear on the nose, sweet barley, crystallised pineapple on the palate with a touch of honey and finally a cinnamon and spice note at the finish.

DS – An earthy, boiled sweet nose. The palate is creamy and bittersweet – light and delicate. The finish is also light and quite elegant.

Cellar Reserve 1992

10 years old   5 years old   unaged

125

Glengyle

Owner:
Mitchell's Glengyle Ltd

Region/district:
Campbeltown

Founded: **Status:**
2004 Active

Visitor centre:
750 000 litres

Address: 85 Longrow, Campbeltown,
Argyll PA28 6EX

Tel:
01586 552009

website:
www.kilkerran.com

History:
1872 – The original Glengyle Distillery is built by William Mitchell who already owns also Springbank Distillery at this time.

1919 – The distillery is bought by West Highland Malt Distilleries Ltd.

1925 – The distillery is closed.

1929 – The warehouses (but no stock) are purchased by the Craig Brothers and rebuilt into a petrol station and garage.

1941 – The distillery is acquired by the Bloch Brothers, already owner of Campbeltown distillery Glen Scotia. The plans for reopening are not realized.

1957 – Campbell Henderson applies for planning permission with the intention of reopening the distillery.

2000 – Hedley Wright, owner of Springbank Distillery and related to founder William Mitchell, acquires the distillery.

2004 – The first distillation after reconstruction takes place in March.

2007 – The first limited release - a 3 year old.

2009 – Kilkerran "Work in progress" is released.

Kilkerran Work in Progress

DR – Pine forest and zesty floral and citrus notes on the nose, forest floor, honey and spice on the palate, and an earthy and grungey finish.

DS – Grappa-like nose with grape skin and heavy oils - slightly citrus. Again oily with a dry heat and earthiness the citrus is slightly dirty. Sweet and raw finish. Clearly young but showing promise.

Glengyle Distillery was the first distillery to open in the new millennium as well as the first to open in Campbeltown for 125 years. Despite this its heritage is ancient. Founded already in 1872 by William Mitchell it closed in 1925. Nearly 80 years later Hedley Wright, owner of Springbank and great great nephew of William Mitchell, founded a new company, acquired the run-down buildings and embarked on painstaking renovations. Stills were bought from the closed Ben Wyvis Distillery in 2002 and were rebuilt to increase the reflux. The wash still has a capacity of 18,000 litres and the spirit still 11,000 litres. Spirit safe and spirit receivers also came from Ben Wyvis, and a left-over malt mill from Craigellachie's expansion was purchased and installed. A new semi-lauter mash tun and four washbacks made of larch were installed and on 25th March 2004 the new Glengyle was finally inaugurated.

The owner is now working on a five-year plan where new warehouses and a bottling plant will be constructed and in ten years time the distillery will also have its own maltings. Today the malt is brought over from neighbouring Springbank whose staff also run operations.

The spirit is filled on a variety of different casks: sherry, bourbon, Madeira, Marsala and Port. When Springbank closed temporarily in 2008, this also put a stop to production at Glengyle. A short period of production took place in spring 2009 but the next distillation is not planned until March 2010.

The name Kilkerran is used for the whisky as Glengyle was already in use for a vatted malt produced by Loch Lomond Distillers. In 2007 a limited *3 year old* matured in Port pipes was for sale at the distillery. A more widely available *5 year old*, named *Kilkerran "Work in progress"*, was released in summer 2009. The standard Kilkerran 12 years will be released first in 2016.

*Kilkerran
- Work in Progress*

Glen Keith

Owner:
Chivas Brothers
(Pernod Ricard)

Region/district:
Speyside

Founded: **Status:** **Capacity:**
1957 Mothballed 3 500 000 litres

Address: Station Road, Keith,
Banffshire AB55 3BU

Tel: **website:**
01542 783042 -

History:
1957 – The Distillery is founded by Chivas Brothers (Seagrams).

1958 – Production starts.

1970 – The first gas-fuelled still in Scotland is installed, the number of stills increases from three to five.

1976 – Own maltings (Saladin box) ceases.

1983 – A sixth still is installed.

1994 – The first official bottling, a 10 year old, is released as part of Seagram's Heritage Selection.

2000 – The distillery is mothballed.

2001 – Pernod Ricard takes over Chivas Brothers from Seagrams.

Glen Keith 10 year old
DS – Soft heather and honey on the nose with a hint of banana. The palate is quite flat and light and the finish is soft and smooth with a honeyed aftertaste.

Glen Keith and Strathisla distilleries are situated just a few hundred yards from each other in Keith. Although Glen Keith has not produced whisky since 2000, the two have strong ties. Not just literally, but also in practice as pipes run between them; the boiler at Glen Keith is used for Strathisla's production and the spirit from Strathisla is pumped to Glen Keith for filling. Also, effluent from Strathisla is stored and then transferred to the Keith Water Treatment works from the Glen Keith distillery. The tanks used for the effluent holding, started life as storing Liquid Petroleum Gas, as Glen Keith was the first malt distillery to try gas for direct firing of the stills. Another historical reason for tying the two together is that Glen Keith, until 1976, operated its own Saladin maltings and also supplied Strathisla with malted barley which was blown through pipes to the distillery.

There are no signs that current owner, Chivas Brothers, will recommission the distillery again. All the equipment is however still there: one stainless steel, infusion mash tun, nine washbacks made of Oregon Pine and three pairs of stills visible through the large windows. The distillery accommodates a technical centre and the laboratory from Miltonduff was moved there when Allieds' distilleries were taken over.

When Glen Keith was built in the late 1950s on the site of the old Mill of Keith corn mill, the decision was made to triple distil the spirit. Triple distillation was abandoned in the early 70s but innovation did not cease. Some heavily peated whiskies were made (later released as Craigduff and Glenisla although some sources claim these were made at nearby Strathisla), malt whisky was distilled using a column still, new strains of yeast were tried out in the process and microprocessors were installed to control mashing, milling and distilling.

The official *10 year old* is difficult to obtain nowadays but there are independent bottlings. The latest is a 14 year old rum finish from 1995 released by Ian MacLeod.

10 years old

Glenkinchie

Owner:
Diageo

Region/district:
Lowlands

Founded: 1837

Status: Active (vc)

Capacity: 2 500 000 litres

Address: Pencaitland, Tranent, East Lothian EH34 5ET

Tel: 01875 342004

website: www.malts.com

History:

1825 – A distillery known as Milton is founded by John and George Rate.

1837 – The Rate brothers are registered as licensees of a distillery named Glenkinchie.

1840 – James Gray takes over operations.

1852 – John Rate is once again licensee.

1853 – John Rate sells the distillery to a farmer by the name of Christie who converts it to a sawmill.

1881 – The buildings are bought by a consortium from Edinburgh made up of wine merchants, whisky blenders and brewers.

1890 – Glenkinchie Distillery Company is founded with Major James Gray as General Manager. Reconstruction and refurbishment is on-going for the next few years.

1914 – Glenkinchie forms Scottish Malt Distillers (SMD) with four other lowland distilleries.

1925 – Distillers Company Limited buys SMD.

1939-45 – Glenkinchie is one of few distilleries allowed to maintain production during the war.

1968 – Floor maltings is decommissioned.

1969 – The maltings is converted into a museum.

1988 – Glenkinchie 10 years becomes one of selected six in the Classic Malt series.

1998 – A Distiller's Edition with Amontillado finish is launched.

2007 – A 12 year old and a 20 year old cask strength are released.

Glenkinchie 12 year old

DR – The nose is light and flowery, with wet meadow notes and cucumber, the palate is pure barley with a touch of star anise spice and an earthy note.

DS – A powerful heather and honey nose with brown sugar. Soft sherry and spice comes through on the heavy palate and a rather sticky after-taste

---

Glenkinchie is situated in a small depression surrounded by farmland in the village of Peastonbank east of Edinburgh. The proximity to the city is one reason why as many as over 40,000 visitors find their way to the excellent visitor centre each year. By the time Glenkinchie was founded in 1837, 115 licensed distilleries were recorded in the Lowlands but now only five producing malt whisky remain (Auchentoshan, Bladnoch, Daftmill and Ailsa Bay in addition to Glenkinchie).

Glenkinchie is equipped with a full lauter mash tun, six wooden washbacks and one pair of stills. A cast iron worm tub is used for cooling the spirits. The wash still is one of the largest in the industry (30,963 litres) and the neck was replaced in 2008.

Glenkinchie is a typical light and fresh lowland malt and one would think that the distiller would try to get as much copper contact as possible to create this. Despite that the lyne arms descend quite steeply creating little reflux. On the other hand a clear wort is produced and the cut point on the spirit run is unusually high (around 65%), so as to avoid the heavier aromas. Currently a seven-day week is enforced resulting in 14 mashes per week which produces 2.5 million litres of alcohol. Filling was on site until 2001 and since then it has been done centrally. Bourbon barrels are mostly used and of the three dunnage warehouses on site, one has three floors which is quite unusual. They contain around 10,000 cases maturing, the oldest from 1952.

The core range consists of a *12 year old* (which used to be a 10 year old) and a *Distiller's Edition* 14 years old since 2007. Autumn 2007 it appeared in the Special Release series as a *20 year old cask strength*. Independent bottlings are extremely rare but two have been released recently: a 21 year old from Cadenhead distilled in 1987 and a 1975 from Dewar Rattray.

20 year old cask strength

New Books We Enjoyed

The most important book on whisky published this past year was *Beer Hunter, Whisky Chaser* - a tribute to whisky (and beer) icon, the late Michael Jackson. Edited by Ian Buxton, the book has new contributions by amongst others Dave Broom, John Hansell, Charles MacLean and Gavin D Smith. All profits from the publication are donated to the Parkinson's Disease Society (UK).

The highly productive Dutch author Hans Offringa likes to find new angles on whisky. This year he has merged his two big interests in *Whisky & Jazz*. The result is both exciting and refreshing and the pictures are absolutely stunning. Equally productive is Charles MacLean who recently published *Charles MacLean's Whiskypedia*. It is a reference guide to Scottish distilleries but this time with emphasis on the flavour and character of the whisky and the impact of equipment and distillation techniques. Excellent images and amusingly well written.

Jim Murray has published his *Whisky Bible 2010* (the 7th edition) and as always his very personal tasting notes will be a talking piece amongst whisky lovers. Another book solely concentrated on tasting notes was published in autumn 2008. *Whisky Magazine Tastings* is a compilation of all tasting notes published in the Magazine the first 10 years. An excellent initiative to gather all these and as an extra bonus you get the opinion of two experts on all the whiskies.

Finally, one can only hope that *Skotsk Whisky* (Scotch Whisky) by Swedish Per Ellsberger will be translated into English some time soon. This is probably the most comprehensive book on the subject ever written.

Ber Hunter, Whisky Chaser
ISBN 978-1906000042

Whisky & Jazz
ISBN 978-0615281551

Charles MacLean's Whiskypedia
ISBN 978-1841585567

Jim Murray's Whisky Bible 2010
ISBN 978-0955472947

Whisky Magazine Tastings
ISBN 978-1903872239

Skotsk Whisky
ISBN 978-9151845340

Recommended Magazines

Whisky Magazine
www.whiskymag.com

Malt Advocate
www.maltadvocate.com

Whisky Time
www.whiskytime-magazin.com

Der Whisky-Botschafter
www.whiskybotschafter.com

Whisky Watch
www.whiskywatch.de

Allt om Whisky
www.alltomwhisky.nu

Glenlivet

Owner: **Region/district:**
Chivas Brothers   Speyside
(Pernod Ricard)

Founded: **Status:**   **Capacity:**
1824   Active (vc)   8 700 000 litres

Address: Ballindalloch, Banffshire AB37 9DB

Tel: **website:**
01340 821720 (vc)   www.theglenlivet.com

History:

1817 – George Smith inherits the farm distillery Upper Drummin from his father Andrew Smith who has been distilling on the site since 1774.

1840 – George Smith buys Delnabo farm near Tomintoul and leases Cairngorm Distillery. His son William takes over operations at Upper Drummin.

1845 – George Smith leases three other farms, one of which is situated on the river Livet and is called Minmore.

1846 – William Smith develops tuberculosis and his brother John Gordon moves back home to assist his father. Sales of Smith's Glenlivet increases steadily and neither Upper Drummin nor Cairngorm Distillery can meet demand.

1858 – George Smith buys Minmore farm, which he has leased for some time, and obtains permission from the Duke of Gordon to build a distillery.

1859 – Upper Drummin and Cairngorm close and all equipment is brought to Minmore which is renamed The Glenlivet Distillery.

1864 – George Smith cooperates with the whisky agent Andrew P. Usher and exports the whisky with great success.

1871 – George Smith dies and his son John Gordon takes over.

Glenlivet is situated in a part of the Highlands which was a famous haunt for smugglers and hundreds of illicit stills in the early 1800s. The Illicit Distillation Act of 1822 and the Excise Act of 1823 tried to put a stop to these activities and George Smith, founder of Glenlivet, was one of the first distillers to obtain a license. He received death threats from some of his neighbours and was required to ask for assistance from the military to protect his business. George Smith won the struggle and the family continued to be involved with the distillery until 1978 when it was acquired by Seagrams.

The unrivalled most important market for Glenlivet is the USA. Sales increased by 5% during 2008 to reach 286,000 cases which means that 45% of all Glenlivet is sold in the USA. The ten-year long downward sales trend of Scotch whisky in the USA was brought to an end in 2007 and the increase accelerated in 2008 which gives some hope for the future. Glenlivet's turning point came in 2004 when a complete relaunch of the brand was made. From 1998 to 2004 sales only increased by 15% but from 2004 to 2008 they increased by 70% - the biggest increase of all the top ten single malts during that time.

In early 2008, Pernod Ricard submitted plans to Moray Council to increase with three pairs of stills. The plans were revised and in August 2009 another two pairs of stills were commissioned (bringing the total to six pairs) but space has been reserved for yet a further pair of stills. The capacity has now increased to 8.5 million litres of spirit. Presently there are two equally large mash tuns, the first a semi-lauter and the new a full lauter, and eight new washbacks which supplement the earlier eight. Around 62,000 casks are stored on site in both dunnage and racked warehouses.

Glenlivet's core range is the *12 year old*, matured in bourbon casks, the *French Oak 15 years* (with 6-9 months finish in new Limousin Oak casks) and the *18 year old* (matured in ex-sherry casks). Limited editions include the re-launched *21 year old Archive*, *1969 Cellar Collection* and *Glenlivet XXV*, a 25 year old which has spent its last two years in Oloroso casks, launched in spring 2007.

Three expressions are earmarked for the Duty Free market: *First Fill Sherry Cask 12 years old*, *15 years old* and *Nadurra* (16 years old and non-chill filtered). A *cask strength version of Nadurra* was released in the USA in 2006 and in November 2009 yet another variety, *Nadurra Triumph 1991*, appeared. It is 18 years old (two years older than the cask strength version) and the name derives from the Triumph barley that was used in the distillation.

History (continued):

1880 – John Gordon Smith applies for and is granted sole rights to the name The Glenlivet. Only Glenlivet Distillery may thus use the name. All distilleries wishing to use Glenlivet in their names must from now hyphenate it with their brand names.

1890 – A fire breaks out and some of the buildings are replaced.

1896 – Another two stills are installed.

1901 – John Gordon Smith dies.

1904 – John Gordon's nephew George Smith Grant takes over.

1921 – Captain Bill Smith Grant, son of George Smith Grant, takes over.

1953 – George & J. G. Smith Ltd merges with J. & J. Grant of Glen Grant Distillery and forms the company Glenlivet & Glen Grant Distillers.

1966 – Floor maltings closes.

1970 – Glenlivet & Glen Grant Distillers Ltd merges with Longmorn-Glenlivet Distilleries Ltd and Hill Thomson & Co. Ltd to form The Glenlivet Distillers Ltd.

1978 – Seagrams buys The Glenlivet Distillers Ltd. A visitor centre opens.

1996/97 – The visitor centre is expanded, and a multimedia facility installed.

2000 – French Oak 12 years and American Oak 12 years are launched

2001 – Pernod Ricard and Diageo buy Seagram Spirits & Wine. Pernod Ricard thereby gains control of the Chivas group.

2004 – This year sees a lavish relaunch of Glenlivet, the objective is to overtake Glenfiddich as number one on the sales lists. French Oak 15 years replaces the previous 12 year old.

2005 – Two new duty-free versions are introduced – The Glenlivet 12 year old First Fill and Nadurra, a 16 year old non-chill filtered matured in first-fill bourbon casks. The 1972 Cellar Collection (2,015 bottles) is launched.

2006 – Nadurra 16 year old cask strength and 1969 Cellar Collection are released. Glenlivet sells more than 500,000 cases for the first time in one year.

2007 – Glenlivet XXV is released.

2009 – Four more stills are installed and the capacity increases to 8.5 million litres. Nadurra Triumph 1991 is released.

Glenlivet 12 year old

DR – Freshly chopped apple, rhubarb and crisp barley on the nose, soft rounded and beautiful mouth feel with green fruit and gooseberries and a delicate, rounded and medium long finish.

DS – Floral and malty on the nose with vanilla and soft fruits. The palate is bittersweet and creamy with a hint of fudge. The finish is long and nutty.

Glenlivet XXV

Nadurra Triumph 1991

First Fill Sherry Cask 12 years old

12 years old

18 years old

15 years old French Oak Reserve

Glenlossie

Owner:
Diageo

Region/district:
Speyside

Founded: **Status:**
1876 Active

Capacity:
2 140 000 litres

Address: Birnie, Elgin, Morayshire IV30 8SS

Tel: **website:**
01343 862000 www.malts.com

History:
1876 – John Duff, former manager at Glendronach Distillery, founds the distillery. Alexander Grigor Allan (to become part-owner of Talisker Distillery), the whisky trader George Thomson and Charles Shirres (both will co-found Longmorn Distillery some 20 years later with John Duff) and H. Mackay are also involved in the company.

1895 – The company Glenlossie-Glenlivet Distillery Co. is formed. Alexander Grigor Allan passes away.

1896 – John Duff becomes more involved in Longmorn and Mackay takes over management of Glenlossie.

1919 – Distillers Company Limited (DCL) takes over the company.

1929 – A fire breaks out and causes considerable damage.

1930 – DCL transfers operations to Scottish Malt Distillers (SMD).

1962 – Stills are increased from four to six.

1971 – Another distillery, Mannochmore, is constructed by SMD on the premises. A dark grains plant is installed.

1990 – A 10 year old is launched in the Flora & Fauna series.

Glenlossie 10 year old

DS – A fresh, herbal and grassy nose with sweet mint notes. Chewy in the mouth with sweet caramel and bitter chocolate flavours. A long finish with a herbal aftertaste.

The Glenlossie site is a busy place! Right next to the still house lies another distillery, Mannochmore. There are also ten warehouses with a capacity of 250,000 casks known as Glenlossie Bonds. These are used by many other Diageo distilleries just as the dark grains plant is. That is where the residues from distilling draff and pot ale are converted to cattle fodder. Almost 3,000 tonnes are handled each week. Diageo has a similar yet smaller facility at Dailuaine. The unit by the former distillery of Pittyvaich is sometimes referred to as a dark grains plant but is actually a bio-plant treating spent lees and washing waters. The distillery is equipped with a stainless steel full lauter mash tun (8.2 tonnes) installed in 1992, eight washbacks made of larch and three pairs of stills. The spirit stills are also equipped with purifiers between the lyne arms and the condensers to increase the reflux which gives a light and clean spirit.

The workforce used to alternate between Glenlossie and its sister distillery Mannochmore with each of them being in production for half a year at a time. In 2007 this was changed and both distilleries are now producing simultaneously. During 2009 a five-day week with 12 mashes is implemented. Glenlossie malt whisky has been a part of the Haig blend for many years along with other malts like Linkwood and Glenkinchie. It is safe to say that Haig had its great period during the twenties and thirties. It sells around 5.2 million bottles annually today which puts it at around place 30 on the sales list. Haig is still, however, a very popular brand in Greece and on the Canary Islands.

The only official bottling available today is a *10 year old* in the Distillery Malts (Flora & Fauna) series.

Glenlossie´s high quality has, on the other hand, inspired several independent bottlers. The three most recent are a 1993 Tokaji finish from Duncan Taylor, a 20 year old from 1988 released by Blackadder and 14 year old port finish from Cadenheads.

Flora & Fauna 10 years old

New Websites To Watch

www.whiskyreviews.blogspot.com

A video blog where Glaswegian Ralfy takes us around whisky shows, visits distilleries, talks about different whisky glasses and reviews the latest bottlings. Ralfy knows his stuff, is easy going and thoroughly entertaining to listen to. Also has a tradtional blog called www.whiskystuff.blogspot.com

www.whiskyforeveryone.com

This website actually started as a blog, whiskyforeveryone. blogspot.com where the founders, Matt Chambers and Karen Taylor reviewed whiskies affordable and available to anyone. The blog was later supplemented by the website with the ambitious goal of presenting the world of whisky in an understandable and easy-to-grasp way. They are aiming at beginners but here is something for everyone - just as the name says. The site is still developing so expect plenty of more information as time passes.

www.whiskymerchants.co.uk

Web sites trying to cover all the aspects of the whisky subject are not that common these days, probably because it takes a lot of work collecting all the information and keeping it up to date. Martin and Andrew Long were not deterred by that and developed this encyclopaedic website along with their ordinary jobs running a whisky shop in York. Contains an amazing amount of information on just about every whisky distillery in the world.

blog.thewhiskyexchange.com

A blog obviously connected with the famous London and on-line whisky retailer - The Whisky Exchange. Tim Forbes is writing about new bottlings as well as the whisky industry in general. Let us hope for more freguent postings though as it sometimes takes long for new postings to appear.

www.edinburghwhiskyblog.com

Lucas and Chris had both been working as tour guides at The Scotch Whisky Experience in Edinburgh when they decided to start this blog. It is about reviewing new bottlings but they also cover news from the industry, interview whisky personalities and recommend books and other websites. If you happen to visit or live in Edinburgh you will find it an excellent and useful guide to great whisky bars in the city.

Some of Our Old Favourites

www.maltmadness.com

Our all-time favourite with something for everyone. Managed by malt maniac Johannes van den Heuvel.

www.maltmaniacs.org

A bunch of knowledgeable whisky lovers dissect, debate, attack and praise the varying phenomena of the whisky world.

blog.maltadvocate.com

John Hansell is well situated with his unique contacts in the business to write a first class blog on every aspect of whisky.

www.whiskyfun.com

Serge Valentin, one of the Malt Maniacs, is almost always first with well written tasting notes on new releases.

www.nonjatta.blogspot.com

A blog by Chris Bunting with a wealth of interesting information on Japanese whisky as well as Japanese culture.

www.thescotchblog.com

One of the first blogs on whisky and Kevin Erskine has managed to keep the quality at the highest level.

drwhisky.blogspot.com

Sam Simmons delivers tasting notes that include exciting stories and reflections about distilleries, people and events.

www.caskstrength.net

Joel and Neil won a Drammie Award for this blog and deservedly so. Initiated, entertaining and well written reports.

www.whiskycast.com

The best whisky-related podcast on the internet and one that sets the standard for podcasts in other genres as well.

www.whisky-news.com

Apart from daily news, this site contains tasting notes, distillery portraits, lists of retailers, whisky clubs, events etc.

www.spiritofislay.net

This site is of course about the famous Islay whiskies but Gordon Homer also covers many other aspects of the island.

www.whiskyforum.se

Swedish whisky forum with more than 1,800 enthusiasts. Excellent debate as well as more than 2,000 tasting notes.

www.whisky-pages.com

Top class whisky site with features, directories, tasting notes, book reviews, whisky news, glossary and a forum.

www.thewhiskychannel.com

A gateway by Ian Buxton to just about anything whisky related. Check out www.whiskipedia.org. as well.

www.whiskynyt.dk

A Danish whisky site with emphasis on an active members' forum. Updated news on whisky is also presented.

www.whiskymag.com

The official website of the printed 'Whisky Magazine'. A very active whisky forum with over 3000 registered members.

www.thewhiskystore.de

German whisky dealer with more than 7 500 photos of 168 distilleries on the site.

www.whisky.de

German site managed by Dr. Clemens Dillman, author of 'W wie Whisky' who also produces the newsletter Whisky Flash.

www.whisky-distilleries.info

A great site that is absolutely packed with information about distilleries as well as history and recent bottlings.

www.whiskyguiden.se

An excellent Swedish site with thorough descriptions of most distilleries as well as continuously updated whisky news.

Glenmorangie

Owner:
The Glenmorangie Co
(Moët Hennessy)

Region/district:
Northern Highlands

Founded: | **Status:** | **Capacity:**
1843 | Active (vc) | 6 000 000 litres

Address: Tain, Ross-shire IV19 1BR

Tel:
01862 892477 (vc)

website:
www.glenmorangie.com

History:

1843 – William Mathesen applies for a license for a farm distillery called Morangie, which is rebuilt by them. Production took place here in 1738, and possibly since 1703.

1849 – Production starts in November.

1880 – Exports to foreign destinations such as Rome and San Francisco commence.

1887 – The distillery is rebuilt and Glenmorangie Distillery Company Ltd is formed.

1918 – 40% of the distillery is sold to Macdonald & Muir Ltd and 60 % to the whisky dealer Durham. Macdonald & Muir takes over Durham's share by the late thirties.

1931 – The distillery closes.

1936 – Production restarts in November.

1980 – Number of stills increases from two to four and own maltings ceases.

1990 – The number of stills is doubled to eight.

1994 – A visitor centre opens. September sees the launch of Glenmorangie Port Wood Finish which marks the start of a number of different wood finishes.

1995 – Glenmorangie´s Tain I´Hermitage (Rhone wine) is launched.

In October 2008 Glenmorangie was closed in order for a major refurbishment to take place which would allow for expansion. When it opened again in March 2009, some substantial changes estimated at £4.5m had taken place. Another two pairs of stills, exact replicas of the tall, gin type of stills that have been used since 1843, had been fitted into the magnificent still room with the other four pairs. A new building, blending in perfectly with the old style despite its recent construction, was erected and houses four new stainless steel washbacks (bringing the total to ten now) and a new, full lauter mash tun (13 tonnes) has been installed. The new capacity is six million litres but due to the expansion work only 3.6 million was produced in 2008 and 4.5 million are expected in 2009 with 32 mashes per week.

Glenmorangie has always been very particular with the casks that are used. American oak is preferred and a part of them, known as designer casks, come from slow growth woods in the Ozarks, Missouri. They are air-dried for a minimum of two years and when water content is down to 17% they are dried further through mechanical means. Then the casks are made, heavily toasted using infrared technology and then lightly charred. After having been filled with bourbon for four years, they are emptied and brought to Scotland. This programme started already in 1985 and today designer casks are used mainly for the Astar expression but since two years, also for Original.

The entire range was revised in 2007 and the core range now consists of *Original* (the former 10 year old), *18 years old* and *25 years old*. The wood finishes which a decade ago became the characteristic attribute have been reduced to three: *Quinta Ruban* (port), *Nectar D´Or* (Sauternes) and *Lasanta* (sherry). They are all non-chill filtered and bottled at 46% instead of the earlier 43%. The Burgundy was discontinued because of difficulties keeping the continuity of quality and the Madeira disappeared as it became virtually impossible to find good Madeira casks.

There have been several limited editions throughout the years. Two of the more recent are *Astar* (a follow-up to *Artisan Cask*) and the *Signet*. The latter is an unusual piece of work which has been crafted by the distillery's two whisky creators, Bill Lumsden and Rachel Barrie. A portion of the whisky (20%) has been made using chocolate malt which is normally used to produce porter and stout. The Signet also contains single malts from the seventies, eighties and nineties and will become a permanent member of the range. A new series called Private Collection aimed at the duty free market was launched in February 2009 with *Sonnalta PX* as the first expression.

History (continued):

1996 – Two different wood finishes are launched, Madeira and Sherry. Glenmorangie plc is formed.

1997 – A museum opens.

2001 – A limited edition of a cask strength port wood finish is released in July, Cote de Beaune Wood Finish is launched in September and Three Cask (ex-Bourbon, charred oak and ex-Rioja) is launched in October for Sainsbury's.

2002 – A Sauternes finish, a 20 year Glenmorangie with two and a half years in Sauternes casks, is launched.

2003 – Burgundy Wood Finish is launched in July and a limited edition of cask strength Madeira-matured (i. e. not just finished) in August.

2004 – Glenmorangie buys the Scotch Malt Whisky Society which has 27,000 members worldwide. The Macdonald family decides to sell Glenmorangie plc (including the distilleries Glenmorangie, Glen Moray and Ardbeg). Bidding is frantic and the buyer is Moët Hennessy (owned by Diageo and LVMH) at £300 million. A new version of Glenmorangie Tain l'Hermitage (28 years) is released and Glenmorangie Artisan Cask is launched in November.

2005 – A 30 year old is launched.

2007 – The entire range gets a complete makeover with 15 and 30 year olds being discontinued and the rest given new names as well as new packaging.

2008 – An expansion of production capacity is started. Astar and Signet are launched.

2009 – The expansion is finished and Sonnalta PX is released for duty free.

Glenmorangie Original

DR – Rounded honey and light tangerine on the nose, much weightier on the palate, with vanilla, honey, oranges and lemons nudging alongside some tannins and soft peat, all coming together in a rich and warming finish.

DS – Pear drops, floral and buttery on the stunning nose. The palate is slightly spicy and zesty with some fruitiness and the finish is short but very moreish.

Signet   Astar   Sonnalta PX

Nectar D´Or   Original (10 years old)   Quinta Ruban

Glen Moray

Owner:
La Martiniquaise

Region/district:
Speyside

Founded: 1897

Status: Active (vc)

Capacity: 2 100 000 litres

Address: Bruceland Road, Elgin, Morayshire IV30 1YE

Tel: 01343 542577

website: www.glenmoray.com

History:

1897 – West Brewery, dated 1828, is reconstructed as Glen Moray Distillery.

1910 – The distillery closes.

1912 – The distillery reopens, but soon closes again.

1920 – Financial troubles force the distillery to be put up for sale. Buyer is Macdonald & Muir.

1923 – Production restarts.

1932 – No whisky is produced this year.

1958 – A reconstruction takes place and the floor maltings are replaced by a Saladin box.

1978 – Own maltings are terminated.

1979 – The number of stills is increased from two to four.

1992 – Two old stills are replaced by new.

1996 – Macdonald & Muir Ltd changes name to Glenmorangie plc.

1999 – Three wood finishes are introduced - Chardonnay (no age) and Chenin Blanc (12 and 16 years respectively).

2004 – Louis Vuitton Moët Hennessy buys Glenmorangie plc for £300 million. A new visitor centre is inaugurated and 276 bottles of Glen Moray 1986 cask strength are released. A 20 and a 30 year old are released late in the year. Wood finishing ceases.

2005 – The Fifth Chapter (Manager's Choice from Graham Coull) is released.

2006 – Two vintages, 1963 and 1964, and a new Manager's Choice from Graham Coull are released.

2007 – The second edition of Mountain Oak is released.

2008 – The distillery is sold to La Martiniquaise.

Glen Moray 12 year old

DR – Maltesers and soft vanilla ice cream on the nose, full and rich sweet malt, a touch of vanilla and hints of tannin on the palate and a pleasant and pleasing finish.

DS – Soft fruits and vanilla on the nose. Light and sweet on the palate – strawberry essence. A short and sweet finish.

After having played second fiddle for quite a few years within the Glenmorangie group, Glen Moray was sold in September 2008. This was a result of their decision to withdraw from the blending market and concentrate on the two high-profile brands of Glenmorangie and Ardbeg. The new owner, Paris-based La Martiniquaise, was established already in 1934 but it is first in recent years that this company has been considered a force. La Martiniquaise has a huge plant called Glen Turner Distillery set up in 2004, near Bathgate, West Lothian. There, for example, Label 5, a blend hugely popular in France, and also Glen Turner, a vatted malt, are matured, blended and bottled. Glen Turner is the leading malt whisky in France. The company has also been granted planning permission to build a distillery within their site with a capacity of five million litres malt whisky and 25 million litres of grain spirit.

It remains to be seen if Glen Moray will receive some well-deserved attention with its new owner. The goal is to sell 25% of the production as single malt and have the distillery running at full capacity. Equipped with a stainless steel mash tun, five stainless steel washbacks and two pairs of stills the whisky is matured to 99% in bourbon casks. In the eight dunnage and two palletised warehouses (holding 63,000 casks), there are also some sherry butts and the odd Madeira, Burgundy and rum casks, as well as a few made of new French oak. The oldest casks are from 1971 and the rest are from the eighties and forward. The core range consists of *Classic (8 years old)*, *12* and *16 years old*. Limited editions include *Signature*, a *first fill bourbon from 1989*, a *30 years old* as well as several *vintages*. Two new expressions are planned for release end of 2009 - a *14 year old* with 6 months finish in a port pipe and an *8 year old* that has been maturing in red wine casks. Recent independent bottlings are rare but there is a 16 year old Madeira finish released by Murray McDavid.

1995 Manager's Choice

Meet the Manager

GRAHAM COULL
DISTILLERY MANAGER, GLEN MORAY DISTILLERY

When did you start working in the whisky business and when did you start at Glen Moray?

I started working in the whisky business in 1994 and joined Glen Moray in August 2005.

Have you been working in other lines of business before whisky?

I started my career making beer! I worked at a brewery called Webster's Brewery in Halifax, England.

What kind of education or training do you have?

I went to school in Forres (12 miles from Elgin). Then studied Chemistry at Edinburgh University.

Describe your career in the whisky business.

I worked for William Grants at Glenfiddich Distillery in Dufftown. During my time there I worked in all areas – Malting, Distilling and Bottling.

What are your main tasks as a manager?

Ensuring that the Distillery produces high quality consistent spirit as cost effectively as possible.

What are the biggest challenges of being a distillery manager?

Probably ensuring that the Distillery remains compliant with all changes on regulations and legislation. It seems never-ending!

What would be the worst that could go wrong (your worst nightmare) in the production process?

The worst thing that could possibly happen is losing valuable matured sprit. Although great care is taken some casks can become very fragile whilst maturing in the dunnage warehouses. It has been known for them to collapse and fall apart on removal and to see lovely golden mature spirit being lost is possibly the saddest sight anyone could witness! A very unlikely event which nonetheless would be catastrophic would be a fire in a warehouse. This does not bear thinking about!

How would you describe the character of Glen Moray single malt?

It is well balanced with a lovely sweet flavour and dry finish.

What are the main features in the distillation/maturation process at Glen Moray, contributing to this character?

Glen Moray operates a balanced distillation in small onion shaped stills. This gives the whisky good character and body. A lesser known fact is that Glen Moray has been in continuous 7 day production for over 20 years and this delivers a consistency which distilleries that have spells on 5 day production cannot match. The casks are stored in low lying warehouses close to the River Lossie creating cool damp conditions perfect for maturing whisky.

What is your favourite expression of Glen Moray and why?

Glen Moray 12 year old. It is wonderfully sweet and smooth and can be enjoyed at any time. It has a perfect balance of sweet spirit character and vanilla oak tones.

If it were your decision alone – what new expression of Glen Moray would you like to see released?

I would like to see a Portwood Finish released. The sweetness of Glen Moray combines beautifully with the flavours from the Port.

If you had to choose a favourite dram other than Glen Moray, what would that be?

Having worked there also, I would choose Balvenie.

What are the biggest changes you have seen the past 10-15 years in your profession?

There is far more automation in the Industry now but Glen Moray has remained very traditional. The influence of cask type and quality has also been given much more focus.

Do you see any major changes in the next 10 years to come?

I think the main areas of focus will be improving energy efficiency and reducing the impact on the environment.

Do you have any special interests or hobbies that you pursue?

I enjoy cycling and hill-walking.

You have recently changed owners. How has that affected your work?

We are in control of everything at the Distillery now from purchasing malt through to wood management and selection of whisky for bottling. It means we can ensure the quality and consistency of Glen Moray whisky for years to come.

What are your hopes for the future with the new owners?

The new owners are keen to develop the Glen Moray brand. I hope that now the Distillery is independent many more people will be able to experience Glen Moray and find out for themselves how good it is!

When looking from the outside, you always had the feeling that Ardbeg and Glenmorangie got all the attention from the previous owners in terms of investments, bottlings, marketing etc. Did you ever have the feeling that there could have been more focus on Glen Moray?

The success of Glen Moray has traditionally been because of the demand for blending. Being partnered with the established brand of Glenmorangie it was always unlikely that Glen Moray would have been able to reach a wider audience as a single malt in its own right. However I have always had confidence in the quality of the Glen Moray whisky and I look forward to see Glen Moray flourish as a single malt.

I believe you recently made a special bottling for Forres Academy. What is the distillery's role in the community today and what would you like to see in the future?

Several years ago (too many to mention!) I attended Forres Academy and when they were looking for ideas to mark their 40th anniversary I suggested a special bottling. This will be available during the school year which finishes in June 2010. This has been a great success with former pupils, teachers and collectors.

We try very hard to help the local community. We help sponsor the local football team Elgin City and also many other events and organisations in the local area. We also have many school groups visiting the distillery to better understand the science and business of whisky making.

I believe very strongly that local people are the best ambassadors that any Distillery can have.

Glen Ord

Owner:
Diageo

Region/district:
Northern Highlands

Founded: **Status:**   **Capacity:**
1838   Active (vc)   5 000 000 litres

Address: Muir of Ord, Ross-shire IV6 7UJ

Tel: **website:**
01463 872004 (vc)   www.malts.com

History:

1838 – Thomas Mackenzie founds the distillery and licenses it to Ord Distillery Co. (Robert Johnstone and Donald MacLennan).

1847 – Robert Johnstone, by now single owner of Ord Distillery Co., becomes bankrupt and the distillery is put up for sale.

1855 – Alexander MacLennan and Thomas McGregor buy the distillery.

1870 – Alexander MacLennan dies and the distillery is taken over by his widow who eventually marries the banker Alexander Mackenzie.

1877 – Alexander Mackenzie leases the distillery.

1878 – Alexander Mackenzie builds a new still house and barely manages to start production before a fire destroys it.

1882 – Mackenzie registers the name Glenoran to be used for whisky from Glen Ord.

1896 – Alexander Mackenzie dies and the distillery is sold to the blending company James Watson & Co. for £15,800.

1923 – John Jabez Watson, James Watson's son, dies and the distillery is sold to John Dewar & Sons. The name is changed from Glen Oran to Glen Ord.

1925 – Dewar's joins Distillers Company Limited.

1930 – Glen Ord is transferred to Scottish Malt Distillers (SMD).

1961 – Floor maltings is abandoned in favour of a Saladin box.

1966 – The two stills are increased to six.

1968 – To augment the Saladin box a drum maltings is built.

1983 – Malting in the Saladin box ceases.

1988 – A visitor centre is opened.

2002 – A 12 year old is launched.

2003 – A limited-edition cask strength, 28 years, is launched.

2004 – A 25 year old is launched.

2005 – A 30 year old is launched as a Special Release from Diageo.

2006 – A 12 year old Singleton of Glen Ord is launched.

Singleton of Glen Ord

DR – Red fruits and blackcurrant, mince pies, red apple and sherry on the nose, enjoyable taste of apple, prune and cinnamon, and a delightful and more-ish finish.

DS – Sweet pine and resin with eucalyptus on the nose. Sweet in the mouth with some fruitiness and lots of oak especially in the long, sherried finish.

Glen Ord is situated 15 miles west of Inverness in the fertile Black Isle. This is a veritable giant in the Diageo family of distilleries and in terms of capacity it shares second place with Dufftown, behind the new distillery in Roseisle. The buildings are a mix of modern and old with a new still house with glazed curtain walls built in 1966, to accommodate another four stills. The equipment currently consists of a cast iron lauter mash tun, eight washbacks made of Oregon pine (75 hours of fermentation) and three pairs of stills. There are five dunnage warehouses with a capacity of 15,000 casks. Since autumn 2007 the distillery is working a seven-day week with 17 mashes which means 4.4 million litres per year.

A major part of the site is occupied by the Glen Ord Maltings. This is one of four maltings owned by Diageo (the others are Roseisle, Burghead and Port Ellen) and with a capacity of 36,000 tonnes per year it produces malt for several other Diageo distilleries. The distillery used floor maltings until 1961 when it was replaced by Saladin boxes. The Saladin boxes supplied malt for the distillery until 1984 but already in 1968 the large drum malting with 18 drums was built. Neighbours had been complaining for years about the odour coming from the maltings, especially when peated malt was made, and in December 2008 Diageo had to build a 45 metre high chimney at a cost of £900,000 to deal with the problem.

The *12 year old Flora & Fauna* has now been discontinued in favour of *Singleton of Glen Ord*, also 12 years but with a 50/50 mix of sherry and bourbon casks. The Singleton 12 year old was released already in 2006 together with an *18 year old* as an exclusive to Asia but also sold at the distillery. The range was expanded with a *32 year old* (only 1,300 bottles) in March 2008 and in 2009 came an even more exclusive expression (just 100 cases) - *Singleton of Glen Ord 35 years*, launched in Asian markets.

The Singleton of Glen Ord

Glenrothes

Owner:
The Edrington Group

Region/district:
Speyside

Founded: 1878
Status: Active
Capacity: 5 600 000 litres

Address: Rothes, Morayshire AB38 7AA

Tel: 01340 872300
website: www.glenrotheswhisky.com

History:
1878 – James Stuart & Co., licensees of Macallan since 1868, begins planning a new distillery in Rothes. Robert Dick and William Grant, both from Caledonian Bank, and the lawyer John Cruickshank are partners in the company. Stuart has financial problems so Dick, Grant and Cruickshank terminate the partnership and form William Grant & Co. while James Stuart focuses on Macallan. William Grant & Co. takes over the building of the distillery in Rothes.

1879 – Production starts in May.

1884 – The distillery changes name to Glenrothes-Glenlivet.

1887 – William Grant & Co. joins forces with Islay Distillery Co. (owners of Bunnahabhain Distillery) and forms Highland Distillers Company.

1897 – A fire ravages the distillery in December.

1898 – Capacity doubles.

1903 – An explosion causes substantial damage.

1922 – A fire breaks out in one of the warehouses.

1963 – Expansion from four to six stills.

1980 – Expansion from six to eight stills.

1989 – Expansion from eight to ten stills.

1999 – Edrington and William Grant & Sons buy Highland Distillers.

2002 – Four single cask malts from 1966 and 1967 are launched.

2005 – A 30 year old is launched together with Select Reserve and Vintage 1985.

2006 – 1994 and 1975 Vintage are launched.

2007 – A 25 year old is released as a duty free item.

2008 – 1978 Vintage and Robur Reserve are launched.

2009 – The Glenrothes John Ramsay, two vintages (1988 and 1998) and Alba Reserve are released.

Glenrothes Select Reserve

DR – On the nose, oranges dominating a fruit bowl of flavours that includes berries among the citrus. The palate is wonderfully rounded and complete, a masterclass in fruit, wood and spice balance, and the finish is a total joy, perfectly weighted and balanced.

DS – Rich malt and ripe fruit flavours on the nose. The palate is again rich with added spice and orange peel in syrup. A warming finish with subtle spices.

Glenrothes has become known as a vintage-based distillery but this has not always been the case. In 1987, Christopher Berry Green, chairman of Berry Bros & Rudd (BBR) who owned the Cutty Sark blend, suggested to Highland Distilleries that Glenrothes, the signature malt of Cutty Sark, should be launched as a single malt. A 12 year old appeared but soon vanished amongst all other 12 year olds. BBR, having experience in working with vintages from the wine trade, proposed that the same should be done with the single malt, and in 1993 the first vintage Glenrothes was released.

Glenrothes is currently producing at 90% of its capacity which translates into 5 million litres a year. The distillery is equipped with a stainless steel semi-lauter mash tun. Ten washbacks made of Oregon pine are in one room whilst an adjacent modern tun room houses eight new stainless steel washbacks. The still house has five pairs of stills and the spirit is stored in twelve dunnage and four racked warehouses on site.

The core expression of Glenrothes is the *Select Reserve* without age statement. In 2007 and 2008 two expressions were launched for the Duty Free market - a *25 year old* and *The Glenrothes Robur Reserve*. As previously mentioned, it is the vintages which have brought fame to Glenrothes. Two new vintages were released in 2009 - a *1988* destined for Taiwan but that will find its way to other markets eventually, and a *1998* which will be the core vintage in Taiwan, Singapore and China. But the biggest thrill was a new bottling released in September, *The Glenrothes John Ramsay*. Ramsay has been the Master Blender of Glenrothes since the early nineties and in the summer of 2009 he retired after 43 years in the business. As part of his legacy he has vatted together a selection of ex-sherry casks from 1973 to 1987. In August, *Alba Reserve*, matured solely in American oak refill bourbon casks, was released as an exclusive for the American market. Recent independent bottlings include a 14 year old Signatory and an 18 year old Single Malts of Scotland.

1988 Vintage

Glen Scotia

Owner: **Region/district:**
Loch Lomond Distillery Co Campbeltown

Founded: **Status:**   **Capacity:**
1832   Active   750 000 litres

Address: High Street, Campbeltown,
Argyll PA28 6DS

Tel: **website:**
01586 552288   www.lochlomonddistillery.com

History:
1832 – The family Galbraith founds Scotia Distillery (the year 1835 is mentioned by the distillery itself on labels).

1895 – The distillery is sold to Stewart Galbraith.

1919 – Sold to West Highland Malt Distillers.

1924 – West Highland Malt Distillers goes bankrupt and one of its directors, Duncan MacCallum, buys the distillery.

1928 – The distillery closes.

1930 – Duncan MacCallum commits suicide and the Bloch brothers take over.

1933 – Production restarts.

1954 – Hiram Walker takes over.

1955 – A. Gillies & Co. becomes new owner.

1970 – A. Gillies & Co. becomes part of Amalgated Distillers Products.

1979–82 – Reconstruction takes place.

1984 – The distillery closes.

1989 – Amalgated Distillers Products is taken over by Gibson International and production restarts.

1994 – Glen Catrine Bonded Warehouse Ltd takes over and the distillery is mothballed.

1999 – Production restarts 5th May through J. A. Mitchell & Co., owner of Springbank.

2000 – Loch Lomond Distillers runs operations with its own staff from May onwards.

2005 – A 12 year old is released.

2006 – A peated version from 1999 is released.

Glen Scotia 12 year old

DR – The nose is of rich fudge and butter, the palate sliced apricot, walnut and fudge, with a medium finish touched with sweet spice.

DS – An oily nose with some fruitiness and malt. Mild sweetness with a big hit of maltiness – spiky mouthfeel. A warming, if lacklustre, finish.

Glen Scotia, one of only three distilleries left in Campbeltown, lies hidden away between modern high-rise buildings and is nowadays rather run-down and in need of investment. The latest major reconstruction was in the early eighties before the current owner took over.

One of many owners throughout the years was Jimmy Gulliver, one of the most gifted Scottish businessmen of his time. Born and raised in Campbeltown he and two partners founded Argyll Foods specialising in food retailing. In 1979 they took control of Amalgamated Distillers, who had bought Glen Scotia in 1970, as he wished to enter the drinks business too. But Gulliver's and Argyll Group's biggest moment came when they challenged the gigantic Guinness Plc in the battle to buy Distillers Company Limited in 1985, the former drinks giant and owner of, among others, Johnnie Walker. Eventually Guinness won when DCL accepted a possibly illegal bid in an affair which is still viewed as one of the biggest financial scandals of the 1980s in Britain. With the merger of GrandMet and DCL a few years later Diageo, the world's biggest drinks company, was born. Jimmy Gulliver died in 1996 at the age of 66.

The distillery's equipment consists of a traditional cast iron mash tun, six washbacks and one pair of stills. The washbacks are special in that they are made of Corten steel and Glen Scotia is probably the last distillery in Scotland to use this material. Currently the distillery is running at 15% of the capacity which translates into 100,000 litres per year. Glen Scotia single malt is usually unpeated but peated spirit (30 ppm) has been produced since 1999. The core range consists of a *12 year old* which replaced the 8 and 14 year olds in 2005. Peated expressions (*6* and *7 year old*) were released in 2006 and 2007 and some *single casks* of the unpeated version have also been bottled.

A handful of independent bottlings have appeared lately: a 17 year old port finish and a 16 year old Sauternes finish, both by Murray McDavid and a 1991 from Blackadder.

12 years old

Glen Spey

Owner: Diageo

Region/district: Speyside

Founded: 1878

Status: Active

Capacity: 1 390 000 litres

Address: Rothes, Morayshire AB38 7AU

Tel: 01340 831215

website: www.malts.com

History:
1878 – James Stuart & Co. founds the distillery which becomes known by the name Mill of Rothes.

1886 – James Stuart buys Macallan.

1887 – W. & A. Gilbey buys the distillery for £11,000 thus becoming the first English company to buy a Scottish malt distillery.

1920 – A fire breaks out.

1962 – W. & A. Gilbey combines forces with United Wine Traders and forms International Distillers & Vintners (IDV).

1970 – The stills are increased from two to four.

1972 – IDV is bought by Watney Mann who is then acquired by Grand Metropolitan.

1997 – Guiness and Grand Metropolitan merge to form Diageo.

2001 – A 12 year old is launched in the Flora & Fauna series.

Glen Spey 12 year old

DR – Delicate and floral on the nose, a complex mix of flavours on the palate with orange, citrus fruits, honey, vanilla and cinnamon in the mix.

DS – A fresh, minty and herbal nose – icing sugar. The palate is malty with lots of heathery sweetness. A tongue tingling finish with a fennel aftertaste.

There are four active distilleries in the town of Rothes, and Glen Spey is definitely the least known among them. From the very beginning it has been a distillery producing malt whisky destined to become a part of blended Scotch, in particular J&B which currently is the third best selling blend in the world after Johnnie Walker and Ballantines. J&B has sold around 6 million cases a year since 2002 and despite losing ground in strongholds such as Spain, recent marketing campaigns have attracted new customers in for example Mexico, Turkey and Argentina. Glen Spey became the first Scottish distillery to have an English owner when W. & A. Gilbey bought it in 1887. At that time the Gilbey brothers were not known for their gin as the gin production did not start until 1895. They actually started as wine traders but the plague of wine lice in France in the 1860s led them to enter the whisky business. Another two distilleries, Strathmill and Knockando, were acquired during the following years.

Those with a technical interest in whisky distilling should take note of some features. First, the distillery has two pairs of stills where the spirit stills are equipped with purifiers. The stills are also operated at a lower pressure than usual (4 pounds per square inch instead of 8psi) so there is no need to ever use the release valves on the stills. Second, a special type of semi-lauter mash tun was installed in the renovation of 1970. When it was used in other distilleries it was known as the Glen Spey mash tun.

Glen Spey is mainly found as a component in J & B. There are no other official bottlings apart from the *12 year old Flora & Fauna*.

Independent bottlings are quite rare. Recently a 30 year old Single Malts of Scotland and a 16 year old matured in German oak from Ian MacLeod were released.

Flora & Fauna 12 years old

Glentauchers

Owner:
Chivas Brothers
(Pernod Ricard)

Region/district:
Speyside

Founded: **Status:**
1897 Active

Capacity:
4 500 000 litres

Address: Glentauchers, Keith,
Banffshire AB55 6YL

Tel: **website:**
01542 860272 -

History:

1897 – James Buchanan and W. P. Lowrie, a whisky merchant from Glasgow, found the distillery. A company named Glentauchers Distillery Co. is also formed at the same time.

1898 – Production starts.

1902 – Buchanan offers to buy out Lowrie who is in financial difficulties.

1906 – James Buchanan & Co. takes over the whole distillery and acquires an 80% share in W. P. Lowrie & Co.

1915 – James Buchanan & Co. merges with Dewars.

1923-25 – Mashing house and maltings are rebuilt.

1925 – Buchanan-Dewars joins Distillers Company Limited (DCL).

1930 – Glentauchers is transferred to Scottish Malt Distillers (SMD).

1965 – The number of stills is increased from two to six.

1969 – Floor maltings is decommissioned.

1985 – DCL mothballs the distillery.

1989 – United Distillers (formerly DCL) sells the distillery to Caledonian Malt Whisky Distillers, a subsidiary of Allied Distillers.

1992 – Production recommences in August.

2000 – A 15 year old Glentauchers is released.

2005 – Chivas Brothers (Pernod Ricard) become the new owner through the acquisition of Allied Domecq.

Glentauchers 1990 Gordon & MacPhail

DR – Deep plum and sherry on the nose, then cocoa and blackcurrant. The palate is soft, with plum, raisin and green banana, and the finish is banana and date cake.

DS – Malt and sherry dominate the nose with burnt sugar. Sweet and fruity at first (plums) followed by strong sherry flavours – balanced. Sweet, elegant finish.

Glentauchers Distillery has always been the faithful provider of malt whisky for blending purposes rather than being a brand of its own. Two famous blends have relied on the single malt produced here. From its foundation until its closure in 1985 it was Buchanan´s Black & White; James Buchanan was also one of the founders back in 1897. After Allied Distillers took over it was made an important part of Ballantines instead.

The owner has recently invested a substantial amount of money in the distillery which was closed during part of 2006 for an upgrade of the still house, and then, in summer 2007, the old cast iron mash tun was replaced. Today the distillery is equipped with a stainless steel semi-lauter mash tun with the copperdome from the old mash tun fitted on top. There are six washbacks made of European larch and three pairs of stills. Since 2006 each pair of stills has its own designated low wines & feints receiver (previously shared). The spirit is filled in bourbon casks and part of them mature in the two racked warehouses on site holding a total of 6,000 casks while the rest is taken to Chivas' central warehouses in Keith by road tanker.

The capacity of Glentauchers is generally considered to be 3.4 million litres but that is with a six-day production cycle. With 19 mashes the full capacity is more in the range of 4.5 million litres. Already in 1910 trials with continuous distillation of malt whisky using column stills were carried out at Glentauchers, similar to the ones that caused a debate between Loch Lomond Distillery and Scotch Whisky Association (SWA) last year.

An official *15 year old* was released by Allied Domecq some years ago but has recently been difficult to obtain. Independent bottlings, though, are more available. The most recent ones were released in 2007: an 18 year old from 1989 by Blackadder, a 15 year old from 1992 by Ian MacLeod and a 1990 released by Duncan Taylor.

Gordon & MacPhail
Glentauchers 1990

Glenturret

Owner:
The Edrington Group

Region/district:
Eastern Highlands

Founded: **Status:**
1775 Active (vc)

Capacity:
340 000 litres

Address: The Hosh, Crieff, Perthshire PH7 4HA

Tel:
01764 656565

website:
www.thefamousgrouse.com

History:
1775 – Whisky smugglers establish a small illicit farm distillery named Hosh Distillery.

1818 – John Drummond is licensee until 1837.

1826 – A distillery in the vicinity is named Glenturret, but is decommissioned before 1852.

1852 – John McCallum is licensee until 1874.

1875 – Hosh Distillery takes over the name Glenturret Distillery and is managed by Thomas Stewart.

1903 – Mitchell Bros Ltd takes over.

1921 – Production ceases and the buildings are used for whisky storage only.

1929 – Mitchell Bros Ltd is liquidated, the distillery dismantled and the facilities are used as storage for agricultural needs.

1957 – James Fairlie buys the distillery and re-equips it.

1959 – Production restarts.

1981 – Remy-Cointreau buys the distillery and invests in a visitor centre.

1990 – Highland Distillers takes over.

1999 – Edrington and William Grant & Sons buy Highland Distillers for £601 million. The purchasing company, 1887 Company, is a joint venture between Edrington (70%) and William Grant (30%).

2002 – The Famous Grouse Experience, a visitor centre costing £2.5 million, is inaugurated.

2003 – A 10 year old Glenturret replaces the 12 year old as the distillery's standard release.

2007 – Three new single casks are released.

Glenturret 10 year old

DR – Full and rich honeyed nose, oily and fruity palate with some appealing rootsy savouriness. Something of the farmyard about it. Charming finish.

DS – An oily and malty nose with herbal notes. The palate is gentle but sweet and fruity and this continues into the aftertaste which is short but delicate.

Glenturret is a nice little distillery and some even say it is the oldest still active distillery in Scotland. But coming here is not so much about the single malt. The owner has branded Glenturret the spiritual home of The Famous Grouse blend which is substantiated by the most visited of all visitor centres among Scottish distilleries, "The Famous Grouse Experience". It was opened in 2002 and has been continuously expanded since. In 2007, for example, a purpose-built sample room was constructed within Warehouse No. 9 where groups can take part in exclusive, tutored, nosing and tasting sessions of The Famous Grouse malt range. In the beginning of July 2009 the next attraction was established - an interactive 3-D show using cutting edge technology to the tune of £500,000.

The Famous Grouse is one of the most sold blended whiskies in the world and 3 million cases were already sold in 2006, counting in Famous Grouse vatted malts. The latter is a brand extension which was introduced as late as 2000 but is already showing impressive sales figures.

Glenturret Distillery is equipped with an open stainless steel mash tun dressed in wood and it is perhaps the only one in Scotland where the mash is still turned manually by large wooden spades. There are also eight Douglas Fir washbacks, one pair of stills and 10,500 casks maturing in six warehouses on site. Eight mashes a week result in 156,000 litres of spirit per year. There is only one official bottling in the core range, the 10 year old. An 8 year old that used to be produced has now been discontinued. A limited edition of three single casks was released in spring 2007: a 14 year old from 1991, a 15 year old from 1992 and a 29 year old from 1977. Independent bottlings have become scarce but an 18 year old matured in German Oak was released by Ian MacLeod in 2009.

10 years old

The Tun Room

Highland Park

Owner:
The Edrington Group

Region/district:
Highlands (Orkney)

Founded: 1798

Status: Active (vc)

Capacity: 2 500 000 litres

Address: Holm Road, Kirkwall, Orkney KW15 1SU

Tel: 01856 874619

website: www.highlandpark.co.uk

History:

1798 – David Robertson founds the distillery. The local smuggler and businessman Magnus Eunson previously operated an illicit whisky production on the site.

1816 – John Robertson, an Excise Officer who arrested Magnus Eunson, takes over production.

1826 – Highland Park obtains a license and the distillery is taken over by Robert Borwick.

1840 – Robert´s son George Borwick takes over but the distillery deteriorates.

1869 – The younger brother James Borwick inherits Highland Park and attempts to sell it as he does not consider the distillation of spirits as compatible with his priesthood.

1876 – Stuart & Mackay becomes involved and improves the business by exporting to Norway and India.

1895 – James Grant (of Glenlivet Distillery) buys Highland Park.

1898 – James Grant expands capacity from two to four stills.

1937 – Highland Distilleries buys Highland Park.

1979 – Highland Distilleries invests considerably in marketing Highland Park as single malt which increases sales markedly.

There have been a total of eight legal distilleries on Orkney but now only two remain - the youngest (Scapa) and the oldest (Highland Park). The last one to close was Man O´Hoy in Stromness in 1928.

In 2006 a goal was set that Highland Park (at that time in place 13) should enter the top 10 single malts on the sales list before 2011. It is still possible to reach but can prove tougher than originally thought. Fast-rising brands such as Talisker for example have to be beaten. Still, an increase of 175% in ten years is impressive and now 1.3 million bottles per year are sold.

The equipment consists of one full lauter mash tun, twelve Oregon pine washbacks and two pairs of stills. The whisky matures in 19 dunnage and four racked warehouses holding a total of 44,000 casks. Highland Park is one of few distilleries malting part (20%) of their barley themselves, with the balance coming from Edrington´s maltings at Tamdhu and Simpson´s in Berwick-upon-Tweed. There are five malting floors with a capacity of almost 36 tonnes of barley. The malt is dried for 18 hours using peat and the final 12-18 hours using coke.

The distillery was working at full capacity in the beginning of 2009 with 25 mashes per week. After a couple of months production went down to a five-day week (16 mashes). 60% of production is destined for the core range while the remaining 40% is earmarked for single casks and blended whisky.

The core range of Highland Park consists of *12, 15, 18, 25, 30* and *40 years old*. Travel retail exclusives are *16* and *21 year old*. The last one was released in late 2007 with a strength of 47.5% and instantly became very popular. In spring 2009 however it has been reduced, at least temporarily, to 40%, the reason being that the casks in stock from mid to late 1980s (key components of the expression) have a lower strength. The same reduction may be applied to the 25 and the 30 year old but not for at least two years.

Recent limited editions include the fifth (and last) of *Ambassador's Cask*. In July 2009 came *Hjärta*, a 12 year old cask strength limited to the Scandinavian market, in September two *Vintages, 1964* and *1968*, and finally in October the *12 year old Earl Magnus*.

From independent bottlers a Cadenhead 17 year old, a Single Malts of Scotland 13 year old and a 1968 Duncan Taylor were released in 2008/2009.

History (continued):

1986 – A visitor centre, considered one of Scotland's finest, is opened.

1997 – Two new Highland Park are launched, an 18 year old and a 25 year old.

1999 – Highland Distillers are acquired by Edrington Group and William Grant & Sons.

2000 – Visit Scotland awards Highland Park "Five Star Visitor Attraction". The distillery has spent over £2 million on the visitor centre and distillery.

2005 – Highland Park 30 years old is released, first in the US and in the autumn in the UK. A 16 year old for the Duty Free market and Ambassador's Cask 1984 are released.

2006 – The second edition of Ambassador's Cask, a 10 year old from 1996, is released. New packaging is introduced.

2007 – The Rebus 20, a 21 year old duty free exclusive, a 38 year old and a 39 year old are released.

2008 – A 40 year old and the third and fourth editions of Ambassador's Cask are released.

2009 – Two vintages and two 12 year old limited editions are released.

Highland Park 12 year old

DR – Honey, peat and marmalade fruit in balance on the nose, then on the palate a big mouth feel with dark chocolate, chilli, sharp barley and honey, concluding with a monster pot pouri of a finish.

DS – A sweet and smoky nose with wafts of sherry and malt. The palate is luxuriously full of sherry and delicate smoky flavours that settle into the long finish.

40 years old

16 years old

Hjärta 12 years old

12 years old

18 years old

25 years old

Imperial

Owner:
Chivas Brothers
(Pernod Ricard)

Region/district:
Speyside

Founded: 1897

Status: Mothballed

Capacity: 1 600 000 litres

Address: Carron, Morayshire AB38 7QP

Tel: -

website: -

History:
1897 – Thomas Mackenzie, who already owns Dailuaine and Talisker, founds the distillery helped by architect Charles Doig. The distillery's name hints at Queen Victoria's Diamond Jubilee this year.

1898 – The distillery is inaugurated in the summer and is administered by Thomas Mackenzie's company Dailuaine-Talisker Distilleries Limited.

1899 – The Pattison whisky crash forces the distillery to close.

1916 – Imperial is bought by Distillers Company Limited (DCL), Dewar's, Johnnie Walker and W. P. Lowrie.

1919 – Production restarts.

1925 – The distillery becomes fully owned by DCL and closes again although the maltings remains active.

1955 – Imperial, now administered by Scottish Malt Distillers (SMD), reopens.

1965 – The number of stills is doubled from two to four and a Saladin box is installed for malting.

1985 – The distillery closes.

1989 – Allied Distillers buys Imperial from United Distillers and starts refurbishing.

1991 – Once again in operation.

1998 – Imperial is mothballed.

2005 – Chivas Brothers (Pernod Ricard) becomes the new owner through the acquisition of Allied Domecq.

Imperial 1991 Gordon & MacPhail

DR – Lime starburst and honey on the nose, melon and lemon on the palate, and drying, long and salty finish.

DS – A malty, fruity, earthy nose with hints of honey and pastry. Mild and malty at first with a flood of fruit flavours. Long, fruity finish.

Closed or mothballed distilleries, sometimes situated in remote areas, are occasionally subjected to the risks of looting. This is exactly what happened to Rosebank distillery where equipment worth a six-figure sum in sterling was stolen in the beginning of 2009 to be sold as scrap. In spring 2009 another attempt was made at Imperial distillery near Carron in Speyside but this time the owner's (Chivas Brothers) staff unexpectedly turned up and scared away the intruders.

One would hope for a much better destiny for this distillery which opened its doors in 1897. In the last two years, Chivas Brothers has reopened two closed distilleries and it now has three to go (Imperial, Glen Keith and Caperdonich). Still, bearing the current recession in mind, it is perhaps doubtful if it actually will happen.

The history of Imperial has always been dramatic and has taken many twists. In over a century it has been out of production for 60% of the time. The last time it came out of hibernation was in 1989 when Allied Distillers acquired Imperial and Glentauchers from United Distillers (Diageo) for £10m. Allied managed to reopen not just these two but also Ardbeg within a few years. The heyday for Imperial lasted only seven years and it closed again in 1998. Virtually all the distilling equipment is still in place which means one stainless steel mash tun with traditional mixing gear, six washbacks made of larch and two pairs of stills. When it was still producing it had a capacity of 1.6 million litres of alcohol. All the dunnage warehouses are now empty.

An official *15 year old* was released several years ago but has recently been difficult to obtain.

Independent bottlers have begun picking up on Imperial more recently. The past two years Duncan Taylor for instance, has released at least five different bottlings from 1990-1998 and from Dewar Rattray came an older one from 1983.

*Gordon & MacPhail
Imperial 1991*

The part of the whisky production when sugar is transformed into alcohol is called the fermentation. From the mash tun, where the enzyme *amylase* breaks down the starch into *maltose sugar* (almost 50% of the wort), the wort is pumped through a heat exchanger to the washbacks. Reducing the heat of the wort to around 20 degrees is essential. If the wort is too hot, the yeast will be destroyed in the next step.

The washbacks, where the fermentation takes place, are large vats, traditionally made of wood but nowadays often of stainless steel. Wooden washbacks, usually made of larch or Oregon pine, are more difficult to clean but supporters claim that the wood has a positive effect on the wash. Others say that the material of the washbacks is irrelevant and prefer the efficiency of the stainless steel washbacks. One thing is true though: few distilleries today dare change the material of their washbacks for fear of changing the established character of their whisky. The size of the washbacks can vary between 1,000 and 70,000 litres and they are usually filled two-thirds full.

Now the yeast goes into the wort to start transforming the sugar into alcohol. The process is often described as yeast cells feeding frantically on sugar which is not entirely correct. During the first (aerobic) phase, the yeast cells reproduce and in order to do so, they assimilate free, dissolved oxygen from the wort. As the oxygen is reduced and the carbon dioxide increased, the environment becomes anaerobic and hostile to the yeast cells. They need more oxygen and now get this from the sugar molecules. The resultant byproducts contains even more carbon dioxide, alcohol and various congeners.

Unlike beer production, this is not a sterile process so various wild yeast fungi contribute to the picture and are essential for producing flavours. All sugar has been utilised after roughly 48 hours and the yeast cells sink to the bottom. The third fermentation then takes place caused by the different bacteria, mainly lactic acid ones, in the wort which no longer face competition from the yeast. The pH decreases and many new congeners are created and the ones present are enhanced. This is called a *malolactic fermentation*. If allowed to ferment for too long, the pH can become too low and the wash destroyed.

So the final result after 48 to 120 hours of fermentation is actually an ale without hops and with an alcohol content between 5 and 8%. Approximately 85% of the solids in the wash have been converted into alcohol and the remaining 15% goes with the wash to the *wash still* for the first distillation.

Until the early seventies, there was only one type of yeast available, namely *Brewer's Yeast*. Not only did this yeast transform sugar into alcohol but by being less efficient than modern yeast strains, it also left some sugar and esters in the wash thus contributing to the flavour of the whisky.

In search of a more efficient yeast strain which could give a higher alcohol content, some producers came up with the cultivated *Distiller's Yeast*. It gave a better financial yield, but there were worries that it would affect the taste of the whisky too much. Since 2005, Brewer's Yeast has not been available outside the brewing industry so even if the distilling industry would have wanted to, there was no turning back. This is the reason why a lot of research has gone into finding a substitute for Brewer's Yeast that can be used, if not by itself, then in combination with Distiller's Yeast. Yeast is used either in a dried or compressed state or as a liquid (slurry) and the major part of yeast for distilling today comes from two large food companies, Kerry Group and AB Mauri (affiliate of Associated British Foods).

A great deal of the final character of the whisky is determined during fermentation and the person responsible for this is the Brewer. Factors to take into consideration are fermentation time, temperature and alcohol strength of the finished wash. Some distilleries have practised short fermentation times for years, but to suddenly cut down on the fermentation time in order to produce more spirit could easily backfire. The malolactic fermentation, important to create certain congeners, will be shorter and this could also have an impact on the character of the spirit. Some advocates are of the opinion that a fermentation time of at least 60 hours is necessary in order to achieve complexity.

Inchgower

Owner:
Diageo

Region/district:
Speyside

Founded: 1871
Status: Active
Capacity: 1 990 000 litres

Address: Buckie, Banffshire AB56 5AB

Tel: 01542 836700
website: www.malts.com

History:
1871 – Alexander Wilson & Co. founds the distillery. Equipment from the disused Tochieneal Distillery, also owned by Alexander Wilson, is installed.

1936 – Alexander Wilson & Co. becomes bankrupt and Buckie Town Council buys the distillery and the family's home for £1,600.

1938 – The distillery is sold on to Arthur Bell & Sons for £3,000.

1966 – Capacity doubles to four stills.

1985 – Guinness acquires Arthur Bell & Sons.

1987 – United Distillers is formed by a merger between Arthur Bell & Sons and DCL.

1997 – Inchgower 1974 (22 years) is released as a Rare Malt.

2004 – Inchgower 1976 (27 years) is released as a Rare Malt.

Inchgower 14 year old
DS – Grassy and sweet at first on the nose with vanilla and cream. Soft and sweet on the palate and again creamy – quite mellow. Vanilla lingers for an age on the finish.

Inchgower is difficult to miss as it is situated just by the A98 only 10 miles west of Glenglassaugh distillery near the small fishing port of Buckie. If one is driving from Elgin towards Banff it is even easier to spot as the name appears on the roof. Both Glenglassaugh and Inchgower were built in the first years of the 1870s but their destinies differed from then on. While Glenglassaugh was closed during long periods, often extending upwards of 20 years at a time, Inchgower has been producing uninterruptedly except for during World War II.

The distillery is equipped with a stainless steel semi-lauter mash tun, six washbacks made from Oregon Pine and two pairs of stills. Most of the production is matured elsewhere, but there are also 13 warehouses on site with room for 60,000 casks, a large part of which come from other distilleries within the Diageo group. This is common practice nowadays within the major whisky companies; all eggs should not be in one basket with the risk of loosing the entire stock from one distillery in the event of a fire. There are only a few miles from the distillery to the Greencore Maltings in Buckie but that is not from where the malt is acquired. Diageo is self-sustaining when it comes to malted barley through its facilities in Port Ellen, Glen Ord, Roseisle and Burghead where the malt for Inchgower comes from.

The absolutely greater part of production is used for Bell´s blended whisky. Aside from the official *Flora & Fauna 14 years old* there have been two *Rare Malt* bottlings: *1974* (22 years) and *1976* (27 years).

Independent bottlings are not so common. One of the most recent is a 1974 from Dewar Rattray.

Flora & Fauna
14 years old

Jura

Owner:
Whyte & Mackay
(United Spirits)

Region/district:
Highlands (Jura)

Founded: **Status:** **Capacity:**
1810　　 Active (vc)　 2 200 000 litres

Address: Craighouse, Isle of Jura PA60 7XT

Tel:
01496 820240

website:
www.isleofjura.com

History:

1810 – Archibald Campbell founds a distillery named Small Isles Distillery.

1831 – William Abercombie obtains the first licence for Isle of Jura Distillery.

1853 – Richard Campbell leases the distillery to Norman Buchanan from Glasgow.

1867 – Buchanan files for bankruptcy and J. & K. Orr takes over the distillery.

1876 – The licence is transferred to James Ferguson & Sons.

1901 – The distillery closes and Ferguson dismantles the distillery.

1960 – Charles Mackinlay & Co. embarks on reconstruction and extension of the distillery. Newly formed Scottish & Newcastle Breweries acquires Charles Mackinlay & Co.

1962 – Scottish & Newcastle forms Mackinlay-McPherson for the operation of Isle of Jura.

1963 – The first distilling takes place.

1978 – Stills are doubled from two to four.

1985 – Invergordon Distilleries acquires Charles Mackinlay & Co., Isle of Jura and Glenallachie from Scottish & Newcastle Breweries.

1993 – Whyte & Mackay (Fortune Brands) buys Invergordon Distillers.

1996 – Whyte & Mackay changes name to JBB (Greater Europe).

2001 – The management of JBB (Greater Europe) buys out the company from the owners Fortune Brands and changes the name to Kyndal.

2002 – Isle of Jura Superstition is launched.

2003 – Kyndal reverts back to its old name, Whyte & Mackay. Isle of Jura 1984 is launched.

2004 – Two cask strengths (15 and 30 years old) are released in limited numbers.

2006 – The 40 year old Jura is released.

2007 – United Spirits buys Whyte & Mackay. The 18 year old Delmé-Evans and an 8 year old heavily peated expression are released.

2008 – A series of four different vintages, called Elements, is released.

2009 – Three new vintages called Paps of Jura are released.

Jura 10 year old

DR – The nose is sweet condensed milk, the palate an intriguing mix of earthy malt and tangy spice, with a medium sweet and spice finish.

DS – Green vegetables and malty on the nose. The palate is sweet at first followed by sour dough bread flavours which continue into the lingering finish.

Most of us lifted more than just an eyebrow when Glenglassaugh was resurrected as a working distillery last year after 22 years of silence. It pales in significance, however, when comparing with Isle of Jura distillery that was reconstructed in 1963 after having been closed since 1901. This was thanks to landowners Tony Riley-Smith, Lord Astor and Robin Fletcher who had seen the island's population decrease to 150 and wanted to give the community a new lease on life. The architect William Delmé-Evans did not just draw the new buildings but also designed the tall stills which reminded of the ones he had done for Tullibardine some 15 years earlier.

Jura has one semi-lauter mash tun, six stainless steel washbacks and two pairs of stills. The stills are extremely high - 25 ¼ feet - compared to the ones at Glenmorangie which are Scotland's tallest at over 26 feet. There is capacity for 30 mashes per week but for 2009 Jura has settled on 24 which gives 1.7 million litres of alcohol. The spirit is matured in bourbon casks mainly from Heaven Hill and Jim Beam and with 5% maturing in sherry casks. There are five racked warehouses with a total of 28,000 casks in maturation.

The core range consists of *10, 16, 18, 21 years old* and *Superstition*. Jura single malt from the sixties and onwards has been unpeated but since 1999 a heavily peated Jura has also been distilled. The majority of it goes into Superstition which consists of 13% peated Jura and various casks from 13 to 21 years of age. Limited releases last year included a *1974 Vintage* and the Elements series of four different vintages named *Earth, Fire, Air* and *Water*. In connection with Feis Isle 2009 a limited release of three different 15 year olds with different finishes called *Paps of Jura* appeared: *Mountain of the Sound* (Cabernet Sauvignon), *Mountain of Gold* (Pinot Noir) and *Sacred Mountain* (Barolo).

One of the most recent independent bottlings is a 12 year old distilled in 1997 from Ian MacLeod.

10 years old

Kilchoman

Owner:
Kilchoman Distillery Co.

Region/district:
Islay

Founded: 2005
Status: Active (vc)
Capacity: 100 000 litres

Address: Rockside farm, Bruichladdich,
Islay PA49 7UT

Tel: 01496 850011
website: www.kilchomandistillery.com

History:
2002 – Plans are formed for a new distillery at Rockside Farm on western Islay.

2005 – Production starts in June.

2006 – A fire breaks out in the kiln causing a few weeks' production stop but malting has to cease for the rest of the year.

2007 – The distillery is expanded with two new washbacks.

2009 – The first single malt, a 3 year old, is released on 9th September. The very first bottle, filled in December 2005 is sold already in May at a charity auction for £5,400.

Kilchoman Inaugural Release 3 yo

DR – Strong peat and wood smoke with some fresh green fruit on the nose, intense peat, citrus fruits and chocolate on the palate, and a clean and intense smoke and peat finish.

In 2005 Kilchoman opened as the first distillery on Islay since Malt Mill (on Lagavulin Distillery's premises) in 1908. Anthony Wills, with a background in the wine industry, is the main owner. This farm distillery lies a few miles northwest of Bruich-laddich just a stone's throw from the Atlantic. Kilchoman is one of few distilleries in Scotland with own floor maltings. What makes it even more special is the fact that as much as a third of barley requirements come from fields surrounding the distillery. The malt is peated for 10 hours to a peating level of 20 to 25 ppm and then dried using warm air for 30 to 60 hours depending on the season. The remaining malt, with the same specification as for Ardbeg (50 ppm), is bought from Port Ellen. Other equipment include a stainless steel semi-lauter mashtun, four stainless steel washbacks (two of them installed in 2007), a wash still (2,700 litres charge) and a spirit still (1,500 litres charge). The average fermentation time is 100 hours and the average spirit yield for Ardbeg specification malt is 385 litres per tonne and for their own malted barley 365 litres. The spirit is filled into fresh and refill bourbon casks (80%) and fresh oloroso sherry butts (20%). Maturation takes place in a dunnage warehouse with a capacity of 600 casks. The first full year 50,000 litres were produced and in 2008 Kilchoman came close to full capacity at 91,000 litres.

The first expression was released on 9th September 2009. It was a bourbon matured 3 year old with a finish for six months in Oloroso sherry butts. The next expression will probably be released in November or in spring 2010 and in the future the bottles based on Port Ellen malt will have the name Kilchoman on the label whereas the bottles containing whisky made from own malted barley will be called Kilchoman 100% Islay.
There is also a visitor centre with a café and a shop and 10,000 visitors a year are already attracted to the distillery.

Inaugural Release

Kininvie

Owner:
William Grant & Sons

Region/district:
Speyside

Founded: 1990
Status: Active
Capacity: 4 800 000 litres

Address: Dufftown, Keith, Banffshire AB55 4DH

Tel:
01340 820373

website:
-

History:
1990 – Kininvie distillery is inaugurated on 26th June and the first distillation takes place 18th July.

2006 – The first expression of a single malt Kininvie is released as a 15 year old limited edition under the name Hazelwood.

2008 – In February a 17 year old Hazelwood Reserve is launched at Heathrow's Terminal 5.

Family-owned whisky companies rarely delve into deeper detail on the secrets of their production. This also applies to William Grant & Sons which owns four malt whisky distilleries (Glenfiddich, Balvenie, Kininvie and Ailsa Bay) and one grain distillery (Girvan). Sometimes it can be quite relieving when a producer does not beat the drum as soon as something happens, such as with Ailsa Bay. Just six months after a minor press release, the huge, five million litres capacity distillery was up and running. In other cases it may be more difficult to understand the secrecy such as with Kininvie distillery. Kininvie was built in 1990 for the purpose of producing malt for Grant's blended whiskies. A still house, visible from the Balvenie tun room, was erected on the back side of Balvenie and the stills came on stream in July 1990.

Kininvie is equipped with a stainless steel full lauter mash tun which is placed next to Balvenie's. The tun is filled with 10.8 tonnes of malted barley and can run 28 mashes per week.

Ten Douglas fir washbacks (six large and four small) can be found in two separate rooms next to the Balvenie washbacks. Three wash stills and six spirit stills are all heated by steam coils. The only piece of equipment that Kininvie shares with Balvenie is the mill. Kininvie malt whisky is frequently sold to other companies for blending purposes under the name Aldundee. To protect it from being sold as Kininvie single malt, the whisky is always "teaspooned", i. e. a small percentage of Balvenie whisky is blended with the make.

Kininvie is mainly used for the Grant's blend but is also a major part of the blended malt Monkey Shoulder.

The first time Kininvie appeared as an official single malt bottling was in August 2006 when a *15 year old* was launched to celebrate the 105th birthday of Janet Sheed Roberts, the last surviving grandchild of the founder of the company, William Grant. A two year older version of this was released in February 2008 as *Hazelwood Reserve* and was sold at Heathrow's Terminal 5. No other bottlings are planned.

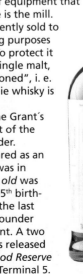

*Hazelwood Reserve
17 years old*

Knockando

Owner:
Diageo.

Region/district:
Speyside

Founded: 1898

Status: Active

Capacity: 1 500 000 litres

Address: Knockando, Morayshire AB38 7RT

Tel: 01340 882000

website: www.malts.com

History:

1898 – John Thompson founds the distillery which is administered by Knockando-Glenlivet Distillery Company. The architect is Charles Doig.

1899 – Production starts in May.

1900 – The distillery closes in March and J. Thompson & Co. takes over administration.

1904 – W. & A. Gilbey purchases the distillery for £3,500 and production restarts in October.

1962 – W. & A. Gilbey merges with United Wine Traders (including Justerini & Brooks) and forms International Distillers & Vintners (IDV).

1968 – Floor maltings is decommissioned.

1969 – The number of stills is increased from two to four.

1972 – IDV is acquired by Watney Mann who, in its turn, is taken over by Grand Metropolitan.

1978 – Justerini & Brooks launches a 12 year old Knockando.

1997 – Grand Metropolitan and Guinness merge and form Diageo; simultaneously IDV and United Distillers merge to United Distillers & Vintners.

Knockando 12 year old

DR – Beeswax, honey and gentle peat on the nose, the palate is altogether bolder, with pepper and earthy peat in evidence mixing it with very sweet crystallised barley and a sweet and rounded finish.

DS – A spirity, grassy nose which is slightly earthy. The palate is malty with date and walnut cake flavours and a hint of ginger in the spicy finish.

In the same way that Royal Lochnagar is seen as a spiritual centre for the Diageo malt whiskies, Knockando is the spiritual centre for the company's blended whiskies. There used to be a visitor centre but it closed for the public ten years ago and is now exclusively used for trade visitors and people working within Diageo. Knockando has been the signature malt for the J&B blend for many years but it is also sells almost 700,000 bottles per year on its own merits which puts it at number five, shared with Oban, on the internal Diageo sales list. Spain and especially France are the two biggest markets.

Knockando is equipped with a semi-lauter mash tun, eight Douglas fir washbacks and two pairs of stills. Knockando's heavy, nutty character, a result of the cloudy worts coming from the mash tun, has given it its fame. However, in order to balance the taste, the distillers also wish to produce the typical Speyside floral notes by using boiling balls on the spirit stills in order to increase reflux. On site filling stopped six years ago and, in common with most Diageo distilleries in Speyside, the spirit is tankered to either Glenlossie or Auchroisk.

Knockando has always worked a five-day week with 16 mashes per week. The spirit is filled mainly into bourbon barrels, although sherry butts are also used, and matures in two dunnage and two racked warehouses. The fifth warehouse is called Ultima after the legendary blend J&B Ultima, released in 1994 to celebrate the 500th anniversary of Scotch whisky.

Since the 1970s, Knockando has bottled its whisky according to vintage and without any age statement, but lately bottles on all markets show both vintage and age on the label. The core range consists of a *12 year old* (90% bourbon and 10% sherry), an *18 year old Slow Matured* (20% sherry), mainly reserved for the French market and a *21 year old Master Reserve* (30% sherry casks). Independent bottlings are virtually impossible to find.

1991 12 years old

Meet the Manager

DUNCAN TAIT
DISTILLERY MANAGER, KNOCKANDO DISTILLERY

When did you start working in the whisky business and when did you start at Knockando?

I started working with United Distillers (as it was then) in 1990, and moved into my current role at Knockando in July 2008.

Have you been working in other lines of business before whisky?

I had previously worked in the production of carbon fibre and bricks.

What kind of education or training do you have?

I left school after sitting my O Grades and all further education has been vocational, although I have stated my Diploma in Distilling through the Institute of Brewing & Distilling.

Describe your career in the whisky business.

The only drinks company I have worked for is Diageo, but in my 19 years I have worked at a large number of distilleries. I started out as a Dark Grains Plant Operator at Teaninich before moving into the role of Stillman / Mashman and transferring to Linkwood & Glen Elgin Distilleries. In 1999, I was accepted onto our Malt Distilling Management Training Course and moved to Cardhu Group as acting Site Operations Manager (SOM). When I finished my training I was appointed as SOM at Glenkinchie Distillery. 4 years later I moved back to Speyside to take up the SOM role at Glendullan & Mortlach Distilleries. My role then developed into a Risk / Compliance role for the Speyside Group of distilleries. In 2006 I was appointed to the role of SOM at Oban Distillery before returning to Speyside (yet again) to take up my current role at Knockando in July 2008.

What are your main tasks as a manager?

My main duties are ensuring that Knockando Distillery produces New Make Spirit to the same quality every week, regardless of weather conditions and any other variables.

What are the biggest challenges of being a distillery manager?

The challenges can be different from day to day and I have to be able to react to any situation at any time, but I would say that the biggest challenge I have is keeping up to date with changing Environmental and Health & Safety legislation, whilst continuing to maintain the operational side of the Distillery and the overall product quality.

What would be the worst that could go wrong in the production process?

The worst thing that could go wrong would be to run out of process water, but as Knockando has been using the Cardnach Spring for more than 110 years without any interruptions, this does seem highly unlikely.

How would you describe the character of Knockando single malt?

Nose – Nutty with fragrant fruity notes
Palate – Light, delicate and fruity with a hint of marzipan
Finish – Smooth and creamy with toffee notes drying slowly

What are the main features in the distillation/maturation process at Knockando, contributing to this character?

Knockando operates a Semi-Lauter Mashtun, which produces cloudy Worts. We operate a 50/50 ratio of long to short fermentations and a perfectly balanced distillation. Our 12-year-old Single Malt is bottled from 90% ex Bourbon American Oak and 10% ex Sherry European Oak casks.

What is your favourite expression of Knockando and why?

My favourite expression of Knockando is the 12 year old. I like the balance between the distillery character and the wood influence, which bring out the nutty, fruity fragrant notes.

If it were your decision alone – what new expression of Knockando would you like to see released?

My personal wish would be to see a slightly younger expression of Knockando (around 8 years old) fully matured in ex Bourbon refill American Oak.

If you had to choose a favourite dram other than Knockando, what would that be?

I have a wide range of favourites, but I do like to sit down on a cold winter's night (after a long day) and relax at the fireside with a nice warming Lagavulin 16 year old.

What are the biggest changes you have seen the past 10-15 years in your profession?

I think that the biggest change within that time is the emphasis placed on quality and not just quantity. There has been a lot of research into Spirit Character and wood management and this can only benefit the industry going forward.

Do you see any major changes in the next 10 years to come?

There will always be changes and while there is the need to continue doing what we have always done we have to be able to adapt to the changing need of the consumer / markets.

Do you have any special interests or hobbies that you pursue?

I am a supporter of Inverness Caledonian Thistle Football Club and I enjoy outdoor activities such as hill walking and mountain biking and these activities allow me to pursue my interest in photography. I also like to travel and I keep Tropical Fish.

You have some extensive space behind the office. How is this space being used?

The Knockando Distillery Brand Home is used mainly as a staff training, social venue and meeting facility. Recently, during the 'Spirit of Speyside Whisky Festival', the venue was used as a Whisky Academy.

The Brand Home was used for training sales & marketing teams in J&B. This was the venue for the J&B 1779 Society and had been used for the 'J&B Of Course' training, but this has not been the case for a few years. The venue is still available if / when any marketing teams require it.

One of your warehouses is called the Ultima Warehouse. Please tell me a little more about that.

The 'J&B Ultima' display forms a part of No.1 Duty Free Warehouse. The first record of whisky distilling in Scotland is considered to be the industry's 'founding document', and the 1494 Exchequer Rolls show Friar John Cor of Lindores Abbey being granted 'eight bolls of malt wherewith to make acqua vitae' by King James IV.

The Ultima blend was brought together by the J&B Master Blender Jim Milne to celebrate the 500th Anniversary of this event in 1994. He brought together 128 different whiskies (116 Malts and 12 Grains) in the ultimate blended Scotch Whisky. One single cask of each was kept to commemorate this momentous achievement and they still lie maturing with this Warehouse. Some of the casks are from (now) closed distilleries and are very rare.

Knockdhu

Owner:
Inver House Distillers
(Thai Beverages plc)

Region/district:
Speyside

Founded: **Status:**
1893 Active

Capacity:
1 500 000 litres

Address: Knock, By Huntly,
Aberdeenshire AB54 7LJ

Tel:
01466 771223

website:
www.ancnoc.com

History:
1893 – Distillers Company Limited (DCL) starts construction of the distillery.

1894 – Production starts in October.

1924 – Distillery management is transferred to Distillers Agency.

1930 – Scottish Malt Distillers (SMD) takes over production.

1931 – The distillery closes.

1933 – The distillery opens up again.

1983 – The distillery closes in March.

1988 – Inver House buys the distillery from United Distillers.

1989 – Production restarts on 6th February.

1990 – First official bottling of Knockdhu.

1993 – First official bottling of An Cnoc, the new name to avoid confusion with Knockando.

2001 – Pacific Spirits (Great Oriole Group) purchases Inver House Distillers at a price of $85 million.

2003 – Reintroduction of An Cnoc 12 years, with new, contemporary packaging.

2004 – A 14 year old from 1990 is launched.

2005 – Two limited editions, a 30 year old from 1975 and a 14 year old from 1991 are launched.

2006 – International Beverage Holdings acquires Pacific Spirits UK.

2007 – anCnoc 1993 is released.

2008 – anCnoc 16 year old is released.

An Cnoc 12 year old

DR – Complex and layered nose, with delicate peat, green fruits and pear. On the palate there's a full savoury peatiness then tingling yellow fruity follow through and fairydust finale.

DS – Grassy with a sweet toasted caramel nose. The predominant flavours are caramel sweetness and malt. A quick, sweet finish.

Knockdhu distillery lies in the fertile part of the Highlands, a few miles east of Keith. The distillery can be seen from the A95 to Banff but is easily missed if coming from the south. It is a beautiful distillery and one that the owner, Inver House, is investing in. Equipment upgrades have been made the last couple of years and some exciting new releases have seen the light of day. Together with Speyburn, Knockdhu is the only Inver House distillery working a seven-day week this year (the rest are down to five days) and 15% of production (around 200,000 litres) is destined to be used for single malts. These are filled on site while the rest is tankered away to Airdrie. Knockdhu used to have a cast iron mash tun which was replaced in summer 2009 with a modern lauter type made of stainless steel. To achieve the light and fresh character of anCnoc, the aim is for a clear wort which goes into six washbacks made of Oregon pine. The distillery is equipped with one pair of stills and the spirit vapours are condensed in a classic cast iron worm tub. Both the wash worm and the spirit worm are in the same tub and are each 60 metres long. One racked and four dunnage warehouses can hold approximately 8,600 casks. In general, a mix of bourbon and sherry casks are used but some interesting experiments with rum casks have been made, the results yet to be seen.

anCnoc is traditionally an unpeated malt but for the last few years Knockdhu has also produced a more peated variety (22ppm) each year. During 2009, 700 tonnes of peated malt were bought which means almost 20% of the production is peated. It has until now been destined for use in Inver House's blended whiskies but the first single malt expressions may be released soon.

The core range consists of a *12 year old* since 2004, but the owner has also launched some limited editions: a *14 year old* (the latest version from 1993 and bottled in 2007) and a *30 year old* from 1975. The latest addition was a *16 year old* launched in January 2008.

16 years old

Meet the Manager

GORDON BRUCE
DISTILLERY MANAGER, KNOCKDHU DISTILLERY

When did you start working in the whisky business and when did you start at Knockdhu?

As a mash man at Pulteney in 1988. Came to the Knock' as manager in August 2006.

Have you been working in other lines of business before whisky?

Time served plumbing/ heating engineer, could this be where my fascination with copper began?

What kind of education or training do you have?

Left school and (briefly) studied computers. Relevant industry education; Institute of Brewing & Distilling GCD and Diploma (distilling).

Describe your career in the whisky business.

Have been lucky enough to work at three cracking distilleries. As a shift operator, brewer and assistant manager at both Pulteney and Balblair. As manager at Knockdhu.

What are your main tasks as a manager?

It's a long list, but basically to manage all day to day operations of a very traditional wee malt distillery. A rare mixture of production, meeting and greeting trade and public visitors, administration, engineering, barrel pushing. We are also required to develop our sites potential, both personnel and plant. Our owners are very supportive of these improvements. One of the delights of this job is that no two days are ever the same.

What are the biggest challenges of being a distillery manager?

We prefer to call them opportunities! We work in a constantly changing environment. Malt by it's very nature of being produced from living material can change from load to load, the weather affects how the place runs as well. It's very much a case of constantly adapting to these and other changes, the work force are absolute masters at it.

What would be the worst that could go wrong (your worst nightmare) in the production process?

Anything that involved someone being hurt. From a production point of view tun room hygiene is critical, if neglected both quality and yield will suffer. Regular servicing and inspections of equipment eliminates things that could become nasty surprises, it's better to avoid plant failures than have to deal with them.

How would you describe the character of anCnoc single malt?

New make is citrusy, zesty, fresh and fragrant with a touch of green apples. The 12 year old has these characteristics but with a gentle honey sweetness and vanilla. The annual vintage develops on this with more evidence of tannins. The 16 year old has a wonderful peppery bite, with a superb toffee sweetness. The 30 year old has so much happening, the sherry influence is far more pronounced. Critically despite cask influence they are all still recognisable as anCnoc.

What are the main features in the distillation/maturation process at Knock Dhu, contributing to this character?

I'd honestly have to say the most important bit is the people. A lot of distilleries make a claim of some sort, be it biggest, oldest, smallest, etc. The Knock' is none of these, but I'm proud to work with the most dedicated, fun filled, enthusiastic and knowledgeable team you are likely to find in any Scottish distillery. The other obvious factors are water source/ type, mashing/ fermentation process, size and shape of the stills and how they are used, cask type and warehouse conditions.

What is your favourite expression of anCnoc and why?

Currently enjoy the 30 year old as my winter dram, a real wind down, sniff and sip whisky. The 16 year old really comes in to it's own in the lighter spring/ summer days, it's my wind up whisky (also the most popular expression for the guys who make it).

If it were your decision – what new expression of anCnoc would you like to see released?

Probably something that would let the character of the whisky shine through without too much cask influence, perhaps a younger first fill bourbon.

If you had to choose a favourite dram other than anCnoc, what would that be?

Tough question, really enjoy the aromatic properties of Balblair.

What are the biggest changes you have seen the past 10-15 years in your profession?

The Knock' used to be run by 19 people,

we now have 6 operators (plus me to add a touch of glamour). Everyone needs to multi-task and be very adaptable to the needs of the operation. Selective barley breeding has increased yields over the last 15 years (very much ongoing).

Do you see any major changes in the next 10 years to come?

Quite rightly there will be more emphasis on the industries green credentials.

Do you have any special interests or hobbies that you pursue?

My long suffering family is very important, they are really understanding about the unusual hours that the job requires - thanks.

What are the implications of distilling both peated and unpeated spirit at the same distillery?

Separation, separation, separation, when we are running peated malt you go home at night smelling like a kipper! Absolutely wonderful! We have malt storage bins dedicated to peated malt. No peated new make spirit comes into contact with the wooden spirit receiver. The phenols stick to everything, all plant needs to be steam cleaned once our annual run of peated malt is used. A lot of hassle, but well worth it.

You are used to distillery cats but at Knock Dhu you are greeted by two dogs. Please tell me more.

The dogs are very much part of the team, we get people coming to visit them rather than the distillery. To be honest they are far more photogenic than anyone who works here.

Lagavulin

Owner: **Region/district:**
Diageo   Islay

Founded: **Status:**   **Capacity:**
1816   Active (vc)   2 250 000 litres

Address: Port Ellen, Islay, Argyll PA42 7DZ

Tel: **website:**
01496 302749 (vc)   www.malts.com

History:
1816 – John Johnston founds the distillery.

1825 – John Johnston takes over the adjacent distillery Ardmore founded in 1817 by Archibald Campbell and closed in 1821.

1835 – Production at Ardmore ceases.

1837 – Both distilleries are merged and operated under the name Lagavulin by Donald Johnston.

1852 – The brother of the wine and spirits dealer Alexander Graham, John Crawford Graham, purchases the distillery.

1867 – The distillery is acquired by James Logan Mackie & Co. and refurbishment starts.

1878 – Peter Mackie is employed.

1889 – James Logan Mackie passes away and nephew Peter Mackie inherits the distillery.

1890 – J. L. Mackie & Co. changes name to Mackie & Co. Peter Mackie launches White Horse onto the export market with Lagavulin included in the blend. White Horse blended is not available on the domestic market until 1901.

Lagavulin experienced some difficult years in terms of sales in the beginning of the new millenium. It used to be the undisputable number one among Islay malt, but sales decreased. This was not caused by a reduction in interest but due rather to limited supplies. This has now been rectified and sales have increased by 40% in the recent five years, but despite this the brand has slipped down to third place on the list of Islay malts. For some time now, operations have been running 24 hours a day, seven days a week, which means 28 mashes per week and 2.25 million litres of spirit. The distillery is equipped with a stainless steel full lauter mash tun, ten washbacks made of larch and two pairs of stills. Unusually, the spirit stills are slightly larger than the wash stills. The former are filled to 95% of capacity during distillation which is very unconventional. The result is that the spirit vapour's diminished contact with the copper produces a more robust spirit. The tough production scheme causes wear and tear on the stills and the replacements that started already in 2005 continued during 2008 when the spirit stills were partially replaced. In summer 2009 it was the wash stills' turn. Bourbon hogsheads are used almost without exception for maturation and all of the new production is stored on the mainland. There are only around 16,000 casks on Islay split between warehouses at Lagavulin, Port Ellen and Caol Ila.

Lagavulin has a new distillery manager since autumn 2008. Graham Logie resigned but only had to relocate a mile to the west for his new job as Manager of Port Ellen Maltings. Lagavulin's new Manager Peter Campbell was recruited from Port Ellen Maltings. He led the work there for eight years and has previously been at Glenlossie and Mannochmore in Speyside as well.

Lagavulin was bottled at 12 years until 1989; thereafter the classic 16 year old was introduced. Today, the core range of Lagavulin consists of *12 years old cask strength*, *16 years* and the *Distiller's Edition 1993*, a Pedro Ximenez sherry finish. As in recent years, a new *12 year old*, matured on refill American Oak casks, was released in autumn 2009 as a Special Release. A couple of months earlier the traditional limited bottling for the Feis Isle (Islay Festival) was launched, this year a *14 year old*. Independent bottlings are almost impossible to find. One of the latest was a 21 year old released by Murray McDavid three years ago.

History (continued):

1908 – Peter Mackie uses the old distillery buildings to build a new distillery, Malt Mill, on the site. Mackie had previously been agent for Laphroaig but the owners were not content and terminated the contract. Malt Mill was an attempt by Mackie to compete and force Laphroaig out of the market.

1924 – Peter Mackie passes away and Mackie & Co. changes name to White Horse Distillers.

1927 – White Horse Distillers becomes part of Distillers Company Limited (DCL).

1930 – The distillery is administered under Scottish Malt Distillers (SMD).

1952 – An explosive fire breaks out and causes considerable damage.

1960 – Malt Mills distillery closes and today it houses Lagavulin's visitor centre.

1974 – Floor maltings are decommisioned and malt is bought from Port Ellen instead.

1988 – Lagavulin 16 years becomes one of six Classic Malts.

1998 – A Pedro Ximenez sherry finish is launched as a Distillers Edition.

2002 – Two cask strengths (12 years and 25 years) are launched.

2006 – A 30 year old is released.

2007 – A 21 year old from 1985 and the sixth edition of the 12 year old are released.

2008 – A new 12 year old is released.

2009 – A new 12 year old appears as a Special Release.

Lagavulin 12 year old

DR – A monster truck nose with rich smoke, lychee and unripe pear, with prickly smoke and banana skin notes on the palate, and a superb long dark chocolate and smoky finish.

DS – Peaty fudge and oil on the nose. Licorice root flavours flood through with hot pepper and spice. Long bitter finish with a licorice aftertaste.

30 years old *Distiller's Edition*

12 years old (8ᵗʰ edition) *16 years old* *21 years old*

x

Laphroaig

Owner:
Beam Global
Spirits & Wine

Region/district:
Islay

Founded: 1810

Status: Active (vc)

Capacity: 2 900 000 litres

Address: Port Ellen, Islay, Argyll PA42 7DU

Tel: 01496 302418

website: www.laphroaig.com

History:

1810 – Brothers Alexander and Donald Johnston found Laphroaig.

1815 – Official year of starting.

1836 – Donald buys out Alexander and takes over operations.

1837 – James and Andrew Gairdner found Ardenistiel a stone's throw from Laphroaig.

1847 – Donald Johnston is killed in an accident in the distillery when he falls into a kettle of boiling hot burnt ale. The Manager of neighbouring Lagavulin, Walter Graham, takes over.

1857 – Operation is back in the hands of the Johnston family when Donald's son Dugald takes over.

circa 1860 – Ardenistiel Distillery merges with Laphroaig.

1877 – Dugald, being without heirs, passes away and his sister Isabella, married to their cousin Alexander takes over.

1907 – Alexander Johnston dies and the distillery is inherited by his two sisters Catherine Johnston and Mrs. William Hunter (Isabella Johnston).

1908 – Ian Hunter arrives in Islay to assist his mother and aunt with the distillery.

Saleswise, Laphroaig showed strength last year with an increase of 6% to a total of 2.2 million bottles. It is still the best-selling of all Islay single malts (with Bowmore second) and has further enforced its right to be among the top ten single malts. Laphroaig is one of very few distilleries with their own maltings. Four malting floors hold 7 tonnes each and together account for 15% of requirements, another 70% comes from Port Ellen maltings on Islay while 15% are imported from the mainland. The malt is dried for 18 hours over a peat fire followed by 15 hours using warm air. It gives a malt with a phenol content of 50-55 ppm. The malt specification from Port Ellen is set to 40 ppm and the final result is 25 ppm in the finished spirit. There is a stainless steel full lauter mash tun and six washbacks also made of stainless steel. The distillery uses an unusual combination of three wash stills and four spirit stills. The last one which was installed in 1972 is twice the size of the others. In order to increase flexibility and capacity, the mash tun is now filled with 5.5 tonnes of grist instead of 8.5 tonnes. With two of these new mashes the washbacks can be filled fuller (52,750 litres instead of 42,000 litres). There will be 28 of these smaller mashes per week in 2009 resulting in 2.6 million litres of alcohol. 56,000 casks are maturing in three dunnage and five racked ware-houses and a further 10 000 casks at Ardbeg. Some significant changes have been made to the range since last year. The *10 year old* and *Quarter Cask* are still two of the core expressions but the 15 year old had to give room for an *18 year old* in April 2009. The popular *10 year old cask strength* has also changed in that it is now bottled in two batches per year (the first bottled in March 2009). To quote Distillery Manager John Campbell, "Rather than trying to match each batch that is bottled we are going to let each bottling 'live' as an individual in its own right." Limited releases include *Cairdeas 30 year old* from last year and during Feis Isle 2009 a *Cairdeas 12 year old* (5,000 bottles) was released. In September 2008 a *25 year old cask strength* was launched, which will phase out the previous *25 year old* from 2007. Finally, *Laphroaig Triple Wood* with maturation first in ex-bourbon barrels, then in Quarter Casks and finally in European Oak, was released into Duty Free in autumn 2008. In September 2009 more bottles were released and this time also for Friends of Laphroaig. Independent bottlings are common. Recent releases include a 13 year old Single Malts of Scotland from 1996, an 18 year old Signatory, a 12 year old Ian MacLeod and a 1998 Blackadder.

History (continued):

1923 – The two stills are increased to four.

1927 – Catherine Johnston dies and Ian Hunter takes over.

1928 – Isabella Johnston dies and Ian Hunter becomes sole owner.

1950 – Ian Hunter forms D. Johnston & Company

1954 – Ian Hunter passes away and management of the distillery is taken over by Elisabeth "Bessie" Williamson, who was previously Ian Hunters PA and secretary. She becomes Director of the Board and Managing Director.

1967 – Seager Evans & Company buys the distillery through Long John Distillery, having already acquired part of Laphroaig in 1962.

1968 – The number of stills is increased from four to six.

1972 – Bessie Williamson retires. Another spirit still is installed bringing the total to seven.

1975 – Whitbread & Co. buys Seager Evans (now renamed Long John International) from Schenley International.

1989 – The spirits division of Whitbread is sold to Allied Distillers.

1991 – Allied Distillers launches Caledonian Malts. Laphroaig is one of the four malts included.

1993 – A severe gale blows the pagoda roof off the kilns, but it is repaired.

1994 – HRH Prince Charles gives his Royal Warrant to Laphroaig. Friends of Laphroaig is founded.

1995 – A 10 year old cask strength is launched.

2001 – 4,000 bottles of a 40 year old, the oldest-ever Laphroaig, are released.

2002 – The legendary distillery manager Iain Henderson retires.

2004 – Quarter Cask, a 5 year old Laphroaig matured for 7 months in a quarter cask (i. e. 105 litres) is launched in a limited edition.

2005 – Fortune Brands becomes new owner.

2007 – A vintage 1980 (27 years old) and a 25 year old are released.

2008 – Cairdeas, Cairdeas 30 year old and Triple Wood are released.

2009 – An 18 year old is released.

Laphroaig 10 year old

DR – Salt, peat, seawood and tar in a glorious and absorbing nose, then structured and rock like barley with waves of tarry peat washing over them, then a long phenolic and peaty finish.

DS – Pungent peat, oats and seaweed on the nose. Salty and earthy on the palate with a heavy thud of medicinal flavours (muscle rub) and a long peppery finish.

18 years old   *Triple Wood*

10 years old   *10 years old cask strength*   *Quarter Cask*

Linkwood

Owner:
Diageo

Region/district:
Speyside

Founded: 1821

Status: Active

Capacity: 3 500 000 litres

Address: Elgin, Morayshire IV30 3RD

Tel: 01343 862000

website: www.malts.com

History:

1821 – Peter Brown founds the distillery.

1825 – Linkwood comes on stream.

1868 – Peter Brown passes away and his son William inherits the distillery.

1872 – William demolishes the distillery and builds a new one.

1874 – The new distillery is inaugurated.

1897 – Linkwood Glenlivet Distillery Company Ltd takes over operations.

1902 – Innes Cameron, a whisky trader from Elgin, joins the Board and eventually becomes the major shareholder and Director.

1932 – Innes Cameron dies and Scottish Malt Distillers takes over in 1933.

1962 – Major refurbishment takes place.

1971 – The two stills are increased by four. Technically, the four new stills belong to a new distillery sometimes referred to as Linkwood B.

1982 – Distillers Company Limited (DCL) launches its series The Ascot Malt Cellar which includes Linkwood 12 years.

1985 – Linkwood A (the two original stills) closes.

1990 – Linkwood A is in production again for a few months each year.

2002 – A 26 year old from 1975 is launched as a Rare Malt.

2005 – A 30 year old from 1974 is launched as a Rare Malt.

2008 – Three different wood finishes (all 26 year old) are released.

Linkwood 12 year old

DS – Sour fruits dominate the nose which is also buttery. The palate is cerealy and similar to new oak. The finish is short but warming.

Just a couple of miles south of Elgin lies Linkwood distillery. Built already in 1821, it has been renovated and expanded several times. The only buildings remaining from the original days are the kiln and the malt barn. The latest major refurbishment was in 1971 when the new still house was built. The old one, with one pair of stills, lies next to the road but has not been in use since 1996 even though the stills remain. The old mash house has also been closed and sealed off and the six old washbacks, which were not used after 2000 but were refurbished in 2008, are once again a part of the production. When the old stills were used the spirit vapours were cooled in a cast iron worm tub which is still there but probably cannot be used in the future even if a need should arise.

This means that all the production (except for part of the fermentation) now takes place in the new still house with its large glass curtains. There is a traditional cast iron mash tun (due for replacement in two years), five wooden washbacks with a fermentation time of 75 hours, and two pairs of stills. The lye pipes of both wash stills and the bottom of spirit still number 1 were replaced in summer 2009 and the distillery is running at full capacity. Linkwood, together with Glen Spey, Benrinnes, Dailuaine, Glenlossie, Mannochmore and Glen Elgin belongs to the Diageo group of distilleries called "Speyside West". The site managers hold an unofficial competition every year to determine which distillery that is the most efficient in terms of spirit yield. Recently Linkwood and Glen Elgin have been at the very top of that league with a yield of 416 litres of spirit per tonne of malt.

Most of the production goes into Johnnie Walker and White Horse but around a million litres are sold to other companies each year. The core expression is a *12 year old Flora & Fauna* but in autumn 2008, Diageo came up with a real surprise; three new *26 year old* Linkwood bottlings were released but perhaps the biggest thrill was that they had all been finished for the last 14 years in three different types of casks - port, rum and sweet red wine.

12 years old

Loch Lomond

Owner:
Loch Lomond
Distillery Co.

Region/district:
Western Highlands

Founded: **Status:** **Capacity:**
1965 Active 4 000 000 litres

Address: Lomond Estate, Alexandria G83 0TL

Tel:
01389 752781

website:
www.lochlomonddistillery.com

History:
1965 – The distillery is built by Littlemill Distillery Company Ltd owned by Duncan Thomas and American Barton Brands.

1966 – Production commences.

1971 – Duncan Thomas is bought out and Barton Brands reforms as Barton Distilling (Scotland) Ltd.

1984 – The distillery closes.

1985 – Glen Catrine Bonded Warehouse Ltd with Alexander Bulloch at the helm buys Loch Lomond Distillery.

1987 – The distillery resumes production.

1993 – Grain spirits are also distilled.

1997 – A fire destroys 300,000 litres of maturing whisky.

1999 – Two more stills are installed.

2005 – Inchmoan and Craiglodge are officially launched for the first time. Both are 4 years old from 2001. Inchmurrin 12 years is launched.

2006 – Inchmurrin 4 years, Croftengea 1996 (9 years), Glen Douglas 2001 (4 years) and Inchfad 2002 (5 years) are launched.

Loch Lomond

DS – Malt and honey on the oily nose with a whiff of mussels. The palate is briny and spicy with malty flavours – light and dry. Short finish with a seafood aftertaste.

Loch Lomond Distillery, situated at the southern end of the Loch bearing the same name, has always taken its own path which can also be said about its owner, Alexander "Sandy" Bulloch, who is now in his late seventies and living on an estate at Tighnabruaich in Argyll. Apart from Loch Lomond Distillery, Glen Catrine Bonded Warehouse, which is the largest independent bottler of spirit in Scotland today, is included in his holding company A Bulloch (Agencies) Ltd, where also wholesaler and wine merchant William Morton and Gibson Scotch Whisky Distilleries are found. More than 37 million bottles of whisky, gin, vodka, rum and brandy are bottled each year and two of their big sellers are Glen´s Vodka and High Commissioner. The former was born when a name change was forced as a result of losing a legal battle with William Grant & Sons over the rights of the name Grants and the second is the fastest growing whisky in England.

Loch Lomond is a virtually self-sufficient distillery. It has its own malt distillery, grain distillery and cooperage and only lacks own maltings. The distillery has two normal stills with traditional swan necks and four stills with adjustable rectifying columns. The Coffey Still installed in 1993 contributes to Loch Lomond's uniqueness of being the only Scottish distillery producing both malt and grain whisky at the same site. Annual production at Loch Lomond is 10 million litres of grain alcohol and 2.5 million litres of malt alcohol.

Loch Lomond produces a broad range of whiskies. While there were three different single malt brands in the range previously, another five surfaced in 2005/2006. There are now eight, from unpeated Glen Douglas to heavily peated (40ppm) Croftengea.

Single malt: Loch Lomond no age, Loch Lomond 18 and 21 years, Old Rhosdhu 5 years, Old Rhosdhu 1967 32 years, Inchmurrin 4 and 12 years, Inchmoan 2001 4 years, Craiglodge 2001 4 years, Croftengea 2003 4 years, Glen Douglas 2002 5 years, Inchfad 2002 5 years.

Single blended: Loch Lomond

Blended: Scots Earl **Single grain:** Loch Lomond

Inchmurrin 12 years old

Longmorn

Owner:
Chivas Brothers
(Pernod Ricard)

Region/district:
Speyside

Founded: **Status:** **Capacity:**
1894 Active 3 500 000 litres

Address: Longmorn, Morayshire IV30 8SJ

Tel: **website:**
01343 554139 -

History:
1893 – John Duff & Company, which founded Glenlossie already in 1876, starts construction. John Duff, George Thomson and Charles Shirres are involved in the company. The total cost amounts to £20,000.

1894 – First production in December.

1897 – John Duff buys out the others and founds Longmorn Distillery.

1898 – John Duff builds another distillery next to Longmorn which is called Benriach (at times aka Longmorn no. 2). Duff declares bankruptcy and the shares are sold by the bank to James R. Grant.

1970 – The distillery company is merged with The Glenlivet & Glen Grant Distilleries and Hill Thomson & Co. Ltd. Own floor maltings ceases.

1972 – The number of stills is increased from four to six.

1974 – Another two stills are added.

1978 – Seagrams takes over through The Chivas & Glenlivet Group.

1994 – Seagrams introduces The Heritage Selection. Apart from Longmorn, Glen Keith, Benriach and Strathisla are included.

2001 – Pernod Ricard buys Seagram Spirits & Wine together with Diageo and Pernod Ricard takes over the Chivas group.

2004 – A 17 year old cask strength is released.

2007 – A 16 year old is released replacing the 15 year old.

Longmorn 16 year old

DR – Cut flowers and mixed fruit on the nose, rounded and full fruit and honey with some wood and spice adding complexity, long and rich finish.

DS – Soft hints of tropical fruits and malt on the nose. Strong sherry flavours mingle with sharp fruit and malt. A long, tingling finish.

Longmorn is a top quality malt and enjoys a solid reputation amongst blenders. It is also the most important ingredient in Chivas Regal 18 years old and in the Royal Salute.
The distillery is equipped with a stainless steel traditional mash tun with rakes and the wooden washbacks were replaced some years ago by eight stainless steel ones. The four wash stills and the four spirit stills are separated in their own still houses, actually the same building but with a sliding door inbetween. The number 1 and 2 wash stills were replaced in 2007 as were the necks of number 3 and 4. On two of the spirit stills the furnace is still visible in the bottom, a remainder from the time when the stills were coal fired (this procedure was abandoned in 1994). The spirit safe is probably the most eye-catching in the industry and each spirit still has its own receiver which means that technically four different kinds of malt could be made if desired. On site there are six dunnage and six palletised warehouses, of which three are placed with neighbouring BenRiach Distillery. The ties between the two distilleries have always been close and even today Longmorn supplies water from its boreholes to BenRiach and also takes care of its effluents.
The distillery has been working at full capacity since Pernod Ricard took over in 2002 but from April 2009 it is down to a five-day week producing 2.65 million litres of alcohol. The efficiency in terms of spirit yield is very good as 416 litres of alcohol is acquired from one tonne of malted barley.
Pernod Ricard owns 12 active distilleries but only four of them are really promoted as brands in their own right. Glenlivet and Aberlour are the big ones with Longmorn and Scapa being the other two.
The *16 year old* was released in 2007 and there is also a *17 year old cask strength* for sale at Chivas´s visitor centres.
One of the few recent independent bottlings is a 12 year old Ian MacLeod distilled in 1996.

16 years old

Barley | Malting | Mashing | Fermentation | Wash still | Spirit still | Maturation | Oak & Casks

With the exception of Auchentoshan and Hazelburn which are both triple distilled and Springbank, Benrinnes and Mortlach, all of which are partially triple distilled, Scottish malt distilleries all practise double distillation. This means there are two stills usually working in pairs: a wash still and a spirit still.

The stills are made of copper which is of the utmost importance. The reaction between the copper and the spirit will reduce any unwanted impurities in the spirit and the more copper contact there is the cleaner the spirit will be. Therefore one could argue that distillers always aim for as much copper contact as possible in order to get as pure spirit as possible. This is not true however. In these impurities are also congeners that give each whisky its distinctive taste, so if you are known to produce a full-bodied, powerful spirit you will want to keep more congeners as opposed to a distillery known for its light and clean whisky.

From the washbacks, where the fermentation has taken place, the (often pre-heated) wash is pumped into the wash still. Thereafter the wash starts to warm up and the first of two distillations commences.

There are different ways of heating the still. The commonest method today is through indirect heating by steam. The steam, which has been heated by either oil or gas, is transported into the bottom of the still by steam coils. The steam coils are, in their turn, connected to round steam kettles, rectangular steam pans or steam plates which heat the wash.

A few distilleries still use the old way of heating the stills by burning an open flame under the still. Glenfiddich has 28 stills, all direct-fired by a gas flame, at Macallan some of the wash stills are directly fired by gas while the spirit stills have steam coils, at Glenfarclas all six stills are directly fired by gas and, finally, at Springbank, the wash still is directly fired using oil but also has steam coils installed. One disadvantage with direct firing is that solids will have a tendency to stick to the bottom and burn, thus affecting the taste of the spirit. To deal with that, a *rummager* is installed at the inside bottom of the kettle. Basically it is a copper chain that revolves, scraping off solids before they burn.

When the temperature in the still has reached 95 degrees, the alcohol will rise as vapours to the top of the still, but before we go into what happens next, let´s have a look at the different shapes of the pot stills.

There are three main types:

Onion still (traditional still) - as the name indicates, shaped like an onion

Boiling ball still (reflux bulge still) - with a bulb fitted between the pot and the neck

Lantern still - with a narrow "waist" between pot and neck

Within these three groups there is a plethora of variations with wide or narrow necks, long or short necks and with the *lyne arm* (the copper pipe leading from the top of the neck to the condenser) inclined at various angles.

The reason for having different shapes as well as sizes is that the shape decides how much copper contact the spirit will have and also how much *reflux* that is obtained when distilling. Reflux is the term used for re-distillation of the spirit vapours. If there are tall or narrow necks or a lyne arm that is angled upwards, the result will be that a large portion of the heavier spirit vapours will not make it to the condenser in the first try but will instead go down to the bottom of the still to be distilled once more. This process will give a lighter spirit. The boiling ball still will add more copper contact to the spirit and often results in a less heavy spirit than the onion still. The lantern still also adds more copper contact due to its often wide neck and the narrow waist also reduces the risk of the wash frothing and rising up the neck. If the wash cannot be stopped from frothing (or "boiling over") and reaches the condenser, the distillation will

be wasted. To avoid frothing (which only appears in the wash still during the first distillation) anywhere between 60 and 80% of the full capacity of the still should be charged. There is a sight glass on the side of the neck to monitor if the level is rising and the temperature has to be lowered.

Once the spirit vapours have made their way through the neck and down the lyne arm, they are condensed into liquid och gathered in the low wines receiver. The strength is now 20-25% as it is charged into the second still, the spirit still, for a second distillation. More about that on page 175.

163

Macallan

Owner:
Edrington Group

Region/district:
Speyside

Founded: **Status:** **Capacity:**
1824 Active (vc) 8 000 000 litres

Address: Easter Elchies, Craigellachie,
Morayshire AB38 9RX

Tel: **website:**
01340 871471 www.themacallan.com

History:
1824 – The distillery is licensed to Alexander
Reid under the name Elchies Distillery.

1847 – Alexander Reid passes away and James
Shearer Priest and James Davidson take over.

1868 – James Stuart takes over the licence. He
founds Glen Spey distillery a decade later.

1886 – James Stuart buys the distillery.

1892 – Stuart sells the distillery to Roderick
Kemp from Elgin. Kemp expands the distillery
and names it Macallan-Glenlivet.

1909 – Roderick Kemp passes away and the
Roderick Kemp Trust is established to secure the
family's future ownership.

1965 – The number of stills is increased from six
to twelve.

1966 – The trust is reformed as a private limited
company.

1968 – The company is introduced on the
London Stock Exchange.

1974 – The number of stills is increased to 18.

1975 – Another three stills are added, now
making the total 21.

1979 – Allan Schiach, descendant of Roderick
Kemp, becomes the new chairman of the board
after Peter Schiach.

1984 – The first official 18 year old single malt is
launched.

1986 – Japanese Suntory buys 25% of Macallan-
Glenlivet plc stocks.

The struggle between Macallan and Glenlivet over second place
on the sales list, after the outstanding Glenfiddich, has been
tough since 2004. That year Macallan surpassed its rival for the
first time after having introduced the highly successful Fine Oak
range. Glenlivet has since taken over once again but, despite an
unassuming increase from 570,000 cases sold in 2007 to 584,000
cases in 2008, Macallan is still in a strong third place.
In September 2008 Macallan went from a capacity of producing
six million litres to eight million. That was when the old still
room with another six stills was recommissioned and therefore
the production is now taking place in two separate plants. The
number one plant holds one full lauter mash tun, 16 stainless
steel washbacks, five wash stills and ten spirit stills. The recommissioned number two plant is comprised of one semi-lauter
mash tun, six new wooden washbacks, two wash stills and four
spirit stills. Macallan has for a long time been among the few
distilleries still heating some of their stills by direct fire (using
gas). At the moment only four wash stills are heated that way
and from next year it will only be three. The production is at
full capacity since the number two plant began operations but
starting in August 2009 the working week was reduced from
seven to five days. Warehouse capacity has also expanded with
the two newest (each holding 20,000 casks) located to the right
of the road leading to the distillery. There are now 16 dunnage
and 21 racked warehouses holding the equivalent of 62 million
litres of spirit. The reopening of the still house and the two
new warehouses required an investment of £17.7 million.
Starting in April 2009 a new range of four, non-aged Duty Free
bottlings were launched under the name *The Macallan 1824
Collection - The Macallan Select Oak, The Macallan Whisky
Maker's Edition, The Macallan Estate Reserve* and *The Macal-
lan 1824 Limited Release*. The latter was not released until
October 2009. In autumn 2008 another addition to the Fine &
Rare Collection was launched, a *Vintage 1947* bottled in 1962.
September 2009 saw the release of the third in the *Lalique*
decanter collection. It is a *57 year old* including one cask going
back to 1949.
The current range can be divided into:
Sherry Oak: 10 and 12 years, Cask Strength (US only), 18, 25 and 30 years
Fine Oak: 8, 10, 12, 15, 17, 18, 21, 25 and 30 years old.
Travel retail: Elegancia 12 years, Cask Strength 10 years, 1824 Collec-
tion (Select Oak, Whisky Maker's Edition, Estate Reserve, 1824 Limited
Reserve), 40 years
Distillery exclusives: Woodland Estate, Estate Oak
Fine and Rare: A range of vintages from 1926 to 1976.

History (continued):

1996 – Highland Distilleries buys the remaining stocks and terminate the Kemp family's influence on Macallan. 1874 Replica is launched.

1999 – Edrington and William Grant & Sons buys Highland Distilleries (where Edrington, Suntory and Remy-Cointreau already are shareholders) for £601 million. They form the 1887 Company which owns Highland Distilleries with 70% held by Edrington and 30% by William Grant & Sons (excepting the 25% share held by Suntory).

2000 – The first single cask from Macallan (1981) is named Exceptional 1.

2001 – A new visitor centre is opened and 1861 Replica (17,400 bottles) are introduced.

2002 – Elegancia replaces 12 year old in the duty-free range. 1841 Replica, Exceptional II and Exceptional III, from 1980, are also launched.

2003 – 1876 Replica (19,800 bottles) and Exceptional IV, single cask from 1990 (864 bottles) are launched.

2004 – Exceptional V, single cask from 1989 (858 bottles) is launched as well as Exceptional VI, single cask from 1990 (816 bottles). The Fine Oak series is launched.

2005 – New expressions are Macallan Woodland Estate, Winter Edition and the 50 year old.

2006 – Fine Oak 17 years old and Vintage 1975 are launched.

2007 – 1851 Inspiration and Whisky Maker's Selection are released as a part of the Travel Retail range. 12 year old Gran Reserva is launched in Taiwan and Japan.

2008 – Estate Oak and 55 year old Lalique are released.

2009 – Capacity increased by another six stills. The Macallan 1824 Collection, a range of four duty free expressions, is launched. A 57 year old Lalique bottling is released.

Estate Reserve

Whisky Maker´s Edition

Select Oak

Macallan 12 year old Sherry Oak

DR – Unmistakenly the sherried version of The Macallan, with a classic red berry and orange mix. The palate is plummy, with intense sherry and some toffee and cocoa notes. The finish is medium long sweet and fruity.

DS – Spicy sherry notes with rich fruit in syrup. Syrupy-sweet at first before some sherry and oak flavours. Oily and dry in the finish with some earthiness.

Macallan 12 year old Fine Oak

DR – Vanilla, butterscotch, satsumas and orange candy on the nose, mixed grapefruit, orange and other fruits on the palate and then a big dash of spice, and a reasonably long and balanced mix of fruit and spice in the finish.

DS – Barley water and cinnamon rolls with rasins on the nose. Pastry (sweet) with more barley flavours and a sweetish, slightly floral finish and aftertaste.

Fine Oak 17 yo

1949 vintage

Cask Strength

10 years old

18 years old

25 years old

Elegancia

Mannochmore

Owner:
Diageo

Region/district:
Speyside

Founded: 1971

Status: Active

Capacity: 3 220 000 litres

Address: Elgin, Morayshire IV30 8SS

Tel: 01343 862000

website: www.malts.com

History:
1971 – Scottish Malt Distillers (SMD) founds the distillery on the site of their sister distillery Glenlossie. It is managed by John Haig & Co. Ltd.

1985 – The distillery is mothballed.

1989 – In production again.

1992 – A Flora & Fauna series 12 years old becomes the first official bottling.

1997 – United Distillers launches Loch Dhu – The Black Whisky which is a 10 year old Mannochmore. A 22 year old Rare Malt from 1974 and a sherry-matured Manager's Dram 18 years are also launched.

Mannochmore 12 year old

DS – Fresh and minty with malty notes on the nose. Sweet and again minty on the palate with fresh baked bread flavours. A hint of oak in the finish with a bready sweetness in the aftertaste.

Some distilleries in Scotland require careful attention to find while others can be spotted from miles away. Mannochmore definitely belongs to the first category. It lies just a few miles off the A941 between Elgin and Rothes on the same site as Glenlossie. Mannochmore, built 95 years later, is obscured from view by the old kiln house and stillhouse of Glenlossie as well as the joint offices. If entering the area (do ask the staff first because this is primarily a working distillery and not a showpiece) you see Mannochmore stillhouse, and behind the huge dark grains plant and on the left hand side, the ten warehouses. The workforce used to alternate between Glenlossie and its sister distillery Mannochmore with each of them being in production for half a year at a time. In 2007 this changed and now both distilleries produce simultaneoulsy. During 2009 they are working a five-day week doing 12 mashes.

Mannochmore is equipped with a cast iron lauter mashtun with a copper dome, eight washbacks made of larch and three pairs of stills. Both distilleries share the cask warehouses which hold 250,000 casks in total, a large part coming from other distilleries within Diageo. There is also a huge dark grains plant on site which processes draff and pot ale from 21 different distilleries. It produces no less than 1,000 tonnes of dark grains used for feeding livestock per week, from 2,600 tonnes of draff and 8 million litres of pot ale.

Aside from the *12 year old Flora & Fauna* a special, dark-coloured Mannochmore named Loch Dhu was launched in 1996 and quickly became a cult whisky. In 2009, Mannochmore appeared for the first time as a Special Release from Diageo. The limited (2,604 bottles) *18 year old* from 1990 is an exciting combination of re-charred sherry casks, bourbon casks and new American Oak casks.

Independent bottlings are not very common. Recent ones include a 16 year old sherry matured from Cadenhead and a Signatory 1991.

18 years old

Meet the Manager

POLLY MACDONALD
SITE OPERATIONS MANAGER, MANNOCHMORE DISTILLERY

When did you start working in the whisky business and when did you start at Mannochmore?

I started with Tomatin November 2004 and joined Diageo in January 2008 at Mannochmore.

Have you been working in other lines of business before whisky?

Not really, I started off in whisky and I have full intentions of staying.

What kind of education or training do you have?

I left school in 2000 for Heriot Watt University where I graduated in 2004 with a B Sc (HONS) in Brewing and Distilling.

Describe your career in the whisky business.

My first experience with the whisky industry was with Diageo in 2002 at Clynelish Distillery and Glen Ord Maltings on a student summer placement. In the summer of 2003, I worked at Invergordon grain distillery in the lab for Whyte & Mackay, again on placement. I then graduated and started with Tomatin Distillery in November 2004 as Production Manager where I remained until I joined Diageo in my current role as Site Operations Manager in January 2008.

What are your main tasks as a manager?

Among other things, setting and controlling budgets, control of contractors, dealing with legislative requirements with HMRC, SEPA etc. Hitting KPI's and of course safe day-to-day running of the distillery.

What are the biggest challenges of being a distillery manager?

All the challenges associated with maintaining a consistently quality spirit, which can include all manner of things! My current role is varied and no two days are the same, which naturally keeps you on your toes!

What would be the worst that could go wrong (your worst nightmare) in the production process?

My personal worst nightmare is someone being hurt in the distillery. Production wise, breakdowns are a part of life, but thankfully we have a very good team behind us to get us up and going again and keep us going.

How would you describe the character of Mannochmore single malt?

Mannochmore 12 years Flora and Fauna is light with delicate citrus fruity notes, a touch of sweet honeysuckle and a crisp, light but sweet citrus finish. A very pleasant light dram.

What are the main features in the distillation/maturation process at Mannochmore, contributing to this character?

At Mannochmore, we operate to maximise our fruity character, so long fermentations and slow distillation in our big wash and spirit stills. Mannochmore is unique in that our spirit stills are larger than our wash stills. Mannochmore is then filled into a wide range of casks including rejuvenated hogsheads and bourbon barrels.

What is your favourite expression of Mannochmore and why?

There are a few independent bottlings available, but I would remain loyal to the Flora and Fauna version, for me personally it captures the delicacy of Mannochmore.

If it were your decision alone – what new expression of Mannochmore would you like to see released?

My own opinion would maybe be something younger perhaps eight or ten year old filled into a Bourbon barrel, or possibly filled into a Fino sherry cask, now that might be interesting!

If you had to choose a favourite dram other than Mannochmore, what would that be?

Tough question, I could certainly narrow it down to maybe ten or so! Staying in Speyside, I would have to pick a Dailuaine, its rich spicy fruitcake note is cracking. I am also getting quite partial to a Caol Ila Cask Strength now and again, with a wee drop water its salty peatiness makes it my favourite Islay dram.

What are the biggest changes you have seen the past 10-15 years in your profession?

Well, as I have only been in the industry for 5 years, I couldn't possibly say! Though looking from the outside, I would say the emphasis on maturation and the introduction of cask finishes must be one of the most marketed changes.

Do you see any major changes in the next 10 years to come?

I expect that like all industries, we must maintain delivering what the market demands and to do this, certain changes and updates shall always be a necessity.

Do you have any special interests or hobbies that you pursue?

Yes indeed, we have recently started competing in Motorsport, I have a race car for the sprint circuits and we also have a historic Alfa Romeo for Vintage rallies and we have been known to take it into the sprints too!

I have a keen interest in photography and living in Speyside has encouraged this, with all the wonderful scenery and wildlife around us.

Are you still a member of the management committee of Malt Distillers Association of Scotland? If so, please tell me a little more.

The Management Committee of the MDA is made up of representatives from distilling companies. I was Tomatin's representative and when I left Tomatin to move to Diageo, I also left that position. Being a part of the committee was an excellent opportunity for me and brilliant insight into a lot of the common issues facing the industry not to mention an unforgettable introduction to many of the characters within the industry.

In the past, Mannochmore and Glenlossie have enjoyed a kind of symbiotic relationship when it comes to distillation and sharing workforce. How does it look today?

As the distilleries are barely 100 yards away from one another, and worked only one distillery at a time, it was a logical arrangement to use the same workforce to cover both sites. Nowadays, the two distilleries are running all year round and yes, they still share the same water sources, boilers and there are several operators who maintain the ability to operate both sites, though both have their own operator populations.

Has being one of the few female distillery managers in the business, had any implications on your work?

I don't believe so, I think that nowadays women are just as capable as doing some jobs as well as men and increasingly so this is becoming the case. Women are becoming more prevalent all through the industry in a range of levels from operator to Director and are doing great jobs all round.

Macduff

Owner:
John Dewar & Sons Ltd
(Bacardi)

Region/district:
Highlands

Founded: 1962
Status: Active
Capacity: 3 200 000 litres

Address: Banff, Aberdeenshire AB45 3JT

Tel: 01261 812612
website: -

History:
1962 – The distillery is founded by Marty Dyke, George Crawford and Brodie Hepburn (who is also involved in Tullibardine and Deanston). Macduff Distillers Ltd is the name of the company.

1963 – Production starts.

1965 – The number of stills is increased from two to three.

1967 – Stills now total four.

1972 – William Lawson Distillers buys the distillery from Glendeveron Distilleries.

1980 – William Lawson is bought by Martini Rossi through the subsidiary General Beverage Corporation.

1990 – A fifth still is installed.

1992 – Bacardi buys Martini Rossi (including William Lawson) and transfers Macduff to the subsidiary John Dewar & Sons.

Glen Deveron 10 year old

DR – The nose is a mix of crisp barley, orange, hay and a trace of smoke, and on the palate an oily and fruity combination beautifully coats the mouth before giving way to a pepper, savoury and astringent finish.

DS – A malty, heathery nose with some earthy, peaty notes. Some peatiness at first, again quite earthy with rich spice. A medium, peaty finish.

Among the five Dewar's distilleries, Macduff is the one that sells most single malts. Around 325,000 bottles a year are sold more or less exclusively abroad, mainly in France but also in Italy. The strong position in southern Europe goes back to the early eighties when the then owner was acquired by Martini Rossi. Saleswise though, the distillery has seen better days. Ten years ago it occupied 14th place on the sales list but has now slid down to 30th. Macduff is an important ingredient in William Lawson's blend which sells 15 million bottles annually. Bacardi, the owners of Macduff (and Dewar's), is the largest privately held spirits company in the world but is, despite its size, considerably smaller than Diageo, Pernod Ricard and United Spirits. The current economic climate may force Bacardi to team up with another company to retain its position. Brown Forman, another family-owned company based in Kentucky and owners of brands like Jack Daniel's, Canadian Mist and Woodford Reserve, would be a good bet. The two companies have a joint distribution agreement since many years and in 2000 they teamed up to bid for Seagram's liquor business which they lost to Diageo and Pernod Ricard. The distillery is equipped with a stainless steel semi-lauter mash tun, nine washbacks made of stainless steel and five stills (two wash stills and three spirit stills). For maturation, a mix of sherry and bourbon casks is used. Parts of the distillery were rebuilt in 1990 and 2000 and new boilers were installed in 2007.

A bottle of single malt bearing the name Glen Deveron is an official bottling from Macduff Distillery. If the name on the label is Macduff, it is an independent bottling. The most common Glen Deveron today is a *10 year old* but there is also a *15 year old*. Older versions of *8* and *12 year olds* are also available. Recent independent bottlings include a couple of old ones from Duncan Taylor (1968 and 1969) and a 17 year old from 1991 from Single Malts of Scotland.

10 years old

Miltonduff

Owner:
Chivas Brothers
(Pernod Ricard)

Region/district:
Speyside

Founded: **Status:** **Capacity:**
1824 Active 5 500 000 litres

Address: Miltonduff, Elgin,
Morayshire IV30 8TQ

Tel: **website:**
01343 547433 -

History:
1824 – Andrew Peary and Robert Bain obtain a licence for Miltonduff Distillery. It has previously operated as an illicit farm distillery called Milton Distillery but changes name when the Duff family buys the site it is operating on.

1866 – William Stuart buys the distillery.

1895 – Thomas Yool & Co. becomes new part-owner.

1936 – Thomas Yool & Co. sells the distillery to Hiram Walker Gooderham & Worts. The latter transfers administration to the newly acquired subsidiary George Ballantine & Son.

1964 – A pair of Lomond stills is installed to produce the rare Mosstowie.

1974-75 – Major reconstruction of the distillery.

1981 – The Lomond stills are decommissioned and replaced by two ordinary pot stills, the number of stills now totalling six.

1986 – Allied Lyons buys 51% of Hiram Walker.

1987 – Allied Lyons acquires the rest of Hiram Walker.

1991 – Allied Distillers follow United Distillers´ example and introduce Caledonian Malts in which Tormore, Glendronach and Laphroaig are included in addition to Miltonduff. Tormore is later replaced by Scapa.

2005 – Chivas Brothers (Pernod Ricard) becomes the new owner through the acquisition of Allied Domecq.

Miltonduff 10 year old (Gordon & MacPhail)

DR – Clean, honeyed and deceptively gentle on the nose, chunky malt and clean vanilla on the plate, pleasant and warming finish

DS – Sweet biscuit and pine nuts on the nose. Mildly sweet with some maltiness and again pine nuts on the palate. Sweet-ish finish with a malty aftertaste.

Together with Glenburgie, Miltonduff is considered the most important malt whisky in the Ballantine´s blended whisky. This brand itself had a troublesome year in 2008 and early 2009 with sales volumes dropping 4% and the position of the core expression, Ballantine´s Finest, as the second most sold Scotch blend now being threatened by Johnnie Walker Black Label. Miltonduff is a high-capacity distillery, in fact one of the ten biggest in Scotland in this respect. It is equipped with a full lauter mash tun and, when producing at full capacity, performs 40 mashes a week. There are no less than 16 stainless steel washbacks and three pairs of stills. A balanced distillation similar to that of, for example, Glenburgie incorporating one wash and one spirit still working in tandem and served by a designated feints and low wines receiver was introduced in autumn 2009.

Several racked warehouses on the site hold 54,000 casks. Evidence of this distillery's strong position with Pernod Ricard is that the company recently moved its headquarters for Northern Division from Strathisla to Miltonduff.

Miltonduff used to have equipment to convert residues from the distilling into cattle feed, so called dark grains, but that has now gone. Several distilleries built their own dark grains plants in the seventies but the process has now been concentrated to a few bigger facilities, for example Glenlossie and Dialuaine owned by Diageo and the big plant in Rothes, operated by Combination of Rothes Distillers.

From 1964 to 1981 Lomond stills were also used at Miltonduff. The malt from these stills was named Mosstowie and is still available. An official Miltonduff *15 year old* was released some years ago but it has now been discontinued. Otherwise Gordon & MacPhail are more or less responsible for "official" bottlings from Miltonduff. A 10 year old and a cask strength from 1996 are the current ones. Another recent bottling is a Duncan Taylor 1999.

*Gordon & MacPhail
1993 Cask Strength*

Mortlach

Owner:
Diageo

Region/district:
Speyside

Founded: 1823
Status: Active
Capacity: 2 910 000 litres

Address: Dufftown, Keith, Banffshire AB55 4AQ

Tel: 01340 822100
website: www.malts.com

History:
1823 – The distillery is founded by James Findlater.

1824 – Donald Macintosh and Alexander Gordon become part-owners.

1831 – The distillery is sold to John Robertson for £270.

1832 – A. & T. Gregory buys Mortlach.

1837 – James and John Grant of Aberlour become part-owners. No production takes place at Mortlach as the equipment is probably dismantled and used in building Glen Grant Distillery.

1842 – The distillery is now owned by John Alexander Gordon and the Grant brothers.

1851 – Mortlach is producing again after having been used as a church and a brewery for some years.

1853 – George Cowie joins and becomes part-owner.

1867 – John Alexander Gordon dies and Cowie becomes sole owner.

1895 – George Cowie Jr. joins the company.

1897 – The number of stills is increased from three to six.

1923 – Alexander Cowie sells the distillery to John Walker & Sons.

1925 – John Walker becomes part of Distillers Company Limited (DCL).

1930 – The administration is transferred to Scottish Malt Distillers (SMD).

1964 – Major refurbishment.

1968 – Floor maltings ceases.

1996 – Mortlach 1972 (23 years) is released as a Rare Malt. The distillery is renovated at a cost of £1.5 million.

1998 – Mortlach 1978 (20 years) is released as a Rare Malt.

2004 – Mortlach 1971, a 32 year old cask strength is released.

2009 – Mortlach 1997, a single cask in the new Manager's Choice range is released.

Mortlach 16 year old

DR – Christmas cask and rich sherry nose, and a rich full plum-fruit and soft summer fruit palate. The finish is rich, full and long, with the wood making its presence felt.

DS – Heavily sherried and fruity on the nose – floral and spicy. The palate is also floral and heavy with stewed fruit flavours – visocus. Dried fruits dominate the finish.

Unlike Dewar's or The Famous Grouse, Johnnie Walker has not had a visible spiritual home. In order to link a visitor centre to a specific blend, it requires at least two things; the malt whisky from that distillery should be a vital part of the blend and, preferably, that the blending company has owned the distillery for some time. In the case of Johnnie Walker, that leaves us just two possibilities – either Cardhu (since 1893) or Mortlach (since 1923). Both were fully owned by John Walker & Co, whereas Dailuaine and Talisker were jointly owned by others as well. Mortlach is the greater of the two and the impact of the powerful and sherried Mortlach malt is probably bigger on Johnnie Walker than that of Cardhu. Despite that it is the more picturesque Cardhu that houses a visitor centre while signs at Mortlach say "Sorry - no visitors".

The distillation process at Mortlach, sometimes called partial triple distillation, is unique in Scotland. There are three wash stills and three spirit stills where the No. 3 pair act as a traditional double distillation. The stronger parts (some 80%) of the low wines from wash stills No. 1 and 2 go into spirit still No. 2 while the weaker parts go into the smallest spirit still, No. 1, also known as "Wee Witchie". Before the final spirit run in the "Wee Witchie", some of the spirit has already been distilled both once or even twice resulting in a fraction being quadruple distilled. The spirit vapours are cooled using wooden worm tubs on the outside.

Apart from the six stills, the distillery is equipped with a semi-lauter mash tun and six washbacks made of larch. There are also five dunnage warehouses with a total of 21,000 casks maturing.

Mortlach is important to the Johnnie Walker blends and the only official bottling used to be the *16 year old Flora & Fauna*. In autumn 2009, however, a *Mortlach 1997* single cask was released in the new range Manager's Choice. Recent independent bottlings include a 16 year old from Cadenhead, a 17 year old from Adelphi Distillery and a 19 year Amarone finish from Murray McDavid.

Manager's Choice 1997

Oban

Owner:
Diageo

Region/district:
Western Highlands

Founded: **Status:** **Capacity:**
1794 Active (vc) 670 000 litres

Address: Stafford Street, Oban, Argyll PA34 5NH

Tel: **website:**
01631 572004 (vc) www.malts.com

History:
1793 – John and Hugh Stevenson found the distillery on premises previously used for brewing.

1794 – Start of operations.

1820 – Hugh Stevenson dies.

1821 – Hugh Stevenson's son Thomas, having recently returned from Buenos Aires, takes over.

1822 – Thomas Stevenson acquires the remaining shares in Oban Brewery Company.

1829 – A series of unsuccessful business investments force Thomas Stevenson into bankruptcy with debts of over £8,000. His eldest son John takes over operations at the distillery.

1830 – John buys the distillery from his father's creditors for £1,500.

1866 – Peter Cumstie buys the distillery.

1883 – Cumstie sells Oban to James Walter Higgins who refurbishes and modernizes it.

1898 – The Oban & Aultmore-Glenlivet Co. takes over with Alexander Edwards at the helm.

1923 – The Oban Distillery Co. owned by Buchanan-Dewar takes over.

1925 – Buchanan-Dewar becomes part of Distillers Company Limited (DCL).

1930 – Administration is transferred to Scottish Malt Distillers (SMD).

1931 – Production ceases.

1937 – In production again.

1968 – Floor maltings ceases and the distillery closes for reconstruction.

1972 – Reopening of the distillery.

1979 – Oban 12 years is on sale.

1988 – United Distillers launches Classic Malts. Oban 14 year is selected to represent Western Highlands.

1989 – A visitor centre is built.

1998 – A Distillers' Edition is launched.

2002– The oldest Oban (32 years) so far is launched in a limited edition of 6,000 bottles.

2004 – A 20 year old cask strength from 1984 (1,260 bottles) is released.

2009 – Oban 2000, a single cask in the new Manager's Choice range is released.

Oban 14 year old

DR – A mixed nose of heather, honey, pineapple and nuts, a perfectly balanced mix of grapey fruit, pineapple chunks, roast nuts and smoky undertow, and a rounded and fruity finish, drying and more-ish.

DS – A heavily perfumed nose with honey and malt notes. Soft, fruity and mildly spicy. A dry finish with a honey after-taste.

Oban distillery, which is situated in the middle of the city with the same name, is the second smallest in the Diageo group (Royal Lochnagar is the smallest). In summer 2009 the youngest distillery manager in the history of the distillery took up his post; at the tender age of 28, Brendan McCarron replaced Kenny Gray who had retired earlier that year after 40 years in the company, the last seven as manager for Oban.

The distillery is equipped with a stainless steel mash tun, four washbacks made of European Larch and one pair of stills. There is also a rectangular, double worm tub built into the roof. This was the traditional way of condensing the spirit vapours, allowing the spirit to run through long, spiralling copper pipes submerged in water. The more modern way consists in using a condenser connected directly to the spirit where the spirit flows in a copper tube with a number of pipes into which cooling water flows. Tube condensers tend to deliver a lighter spirit due to the massive copper contact while the spirit from a worm tub cooled distillation hints at ruggedness. However, it is important to understand that other parts of the process can both compensate and enforce this. Five of the original six Classic Malts still use worm tubs, Lagavulin being the odd one out.

Strangely enough, all of the production at Oban goes to single malt which might not be so unusual after all considering the small capacity and Oban's great popularity as one of the original six Classic Malts chosen to represent the Western Highlands. Just over 700,000 bottles are sold annually which makes it Diageo's fifth best sold single malt.

Official bottlings are a *14 year old*, a *Distiller's Edition* with a montilla fino finish and some limited editions, among them a *32 year old*, a *20 year old* and an *18 year old* limited to the American market. In autumn 2009 an *Oban 2000* single cask was released in the new range Manager's Choice. It is virtually impossible to find independent bottlings. The latest from Cadenhead appeared in the early nineties.

14 years old

Pulteney

Owner:
Inver House Distillers
(Thai Beverages plc)

Region/district:
Northern Highlands

Founded: 1826
Status: Active (vc)
Capacity: 3 000 000 litres

Address: Huddart St, Wick, Caithness KW1 5BA

Tel: 01955 602371
website: www.oldpulteney.com

History:

1826 – James Henderson founds the distillery.

1920 – The distillery is bought by James Watson.

1923 – Buchanan-Dewar takes over.

1925 – Buchanan-Dewar becomes part of Distillers Company Limited (DCL).

1930 – Production ceases.

1951 – In production again after being acquired by the solicitor Robert Cumming.

1955 – Cumming sells to James & George Stodart Ltd, a subsidiary to Hiram Walker & Sons.

1958 – The distillery is rebuilt.

1959 – The floor maltings close.

1961 – Allied Breweries buys James & George Stodart Ltd.

1981 – Allied Breweries changes name to Allied Lyons after the acquisition of J Lyons in 1978.

1994 – Allied Lyons acquires Pedro Domecq and changes name to Allied Domecq plc.

1995 – Allied Domecq sells Pulteney to Inver House Distillers.

1997 – Old Pulteney 12 years is launched.

2001 – Pacific Spirits (Great Oriole Group) buys Inver House at a price of $85 million.

2004 – A 17 year old is launched (4,200 bottles).

2005 – A 21 year old is launched (3,000 bottles).

2006 – International Beverage Holdings acquires Pacific Spirits UK.

2009 – A 30 year old is released.

Old Pulteney 12 year old

DR – Honey and lemon lozenges on the nose, sweet citrus fruits, chunky malt and some traces of sea brine on the palate, an amusing sweet and sour two step at the finish.

DS – A hint of peat with some sugary sweetness. The palate is sweet caramel and again just the slightest touch of peat smoke which eases into the gentle finish.

In the Inver House group of brands it may be Balblair and anCnoc which have stolen the show recently, but it is Old Pulteney (as the whisky produced at Pulteney Distillery is called) and Speyburn which are responsible for volumes among single malts. Sales of Old Pulteney grew by 16% in 2008 (with a 24% increase in the UK alone) which means that more than 600,000 bottles are sold annually and almost half of them are exported. Pulteney is equipped with one pair of stills. The wash still is large (21,700 litres) with a huge ball creating added reflux. Its top is quaintly chopped off as the still was apparently too tall for the stillroom when it was installed. The spirit still (17,300 litres) is equipped with a purifier and both stills use stainless steel worm tubs for condensing the spirit.

The semi-lauter mash tun is made of cast iron and for the six washbacks, rather unusually, Corten steel has been used. Few distilleries (Glen Scotia is one) still use this type of washbacks. The capacity is 3 million litres but for 2009 there will be 15 mashes per week which is the equivalent of 1.2 million litres of spirit. New roofs were laid in 2008/2009 on the five warehouses which can hold 24,000 casks.

The distillery joined the local community a few years ago engaging in a project whereby excess heat from the distillery is being used to heat 270 houses. A plant has also been built on the distillery premises where 30,000 tonnes of wood chip will annually be turned into gas to make environmentally-friendly electricity. Due to technical difficulties, though, the plant has not been commissioned yet.

The core range is a *12 year old* with limited editions of a *17 year old* and a *21 year old*. In July 2009 a *30 year old*, the oldest Old Pulteney ever, was released. Matured in ex-bourbon casks, it is non-chill filtered and without colouring.

An 18 year old from 1990 by Cadenheads, a 1982 from Dewar Rattray and a 1990 released by Blackadder are among the most recent independent releases.

1991 15 years old

Royal Brackla

Owner:
John Dewar & Sons
(Bacardi)

Region/district:
Highlands

Founded: 1812
Status: Active
Capacity: 3 900 000 litres

Address: Cawdor, Nairn, Nairnshire IV12 5QY

Tel: 01667 402002
website: -

History:

1812 – The distillery is founded by Captain William Fraser.

1835 – Brackla becomes the first of three distilleries allowed to use 'Royal' in the name.

1852 – Robert Fraser & Co. takes over the distillery.

1898 – The distillery is rebuilt and Royal Brackla Distillery Company Limited is founded.

1919 – John Mitchell and James Leict from Aberdeen purchase Royal Brackla.

1926 – John Bisset & Company Ltd takes over.

1943 – Scottish Malt Distillers (SMD) buys John Bisset & Company Ltd and thereby acquires Royal Brackla.

1966 – The maltings closes.

1970 – Two stills are increased to four.

1985 – The distillery is mothballed.

1991 – Production resumes.

1993 – A 10 year old Royal Brackla is launched in United Distillers' Flora & Fauna series.

1997 – UDV spends more than £2 million on improvements and refurbishing.

1998 – Bacardi–Martini buys Dewar´s from Diageo.

2004 – A new 10 year old is launched.

Royal Brackla 10 year old

DR – Pineapple and citrus fruits on the nose, candy barley, melon and pleasant sweet spice on the palate, medium sweet finish with a trace of green melon.

DS – A honey-sweet nose which is sligthly scented. The palate is earthy and quite lively – slightly bitter. The finish is long and malty with a yeasty aftertaste.

Dewar & Sons owns five distilleries in Scotland but only two of them are promoted as brands - Aberfeldy and Glen Deveron (Macduff distillery). There are official bottlings from the remaining three but only a few thousand bottles are sold every year. Still, the owner would probably be interested in marketing Royal Brackla on a larger scale. The distillery is beautiful, has an interesting story (one of just three ever allowed to use the prefix Royal) and the whisky is excellent. The only problem is that stock has to be built up first. When Bacardi bought Dewar´s (and the distillery) from Diageo ten years ago not a single cask was included in the deal. That is why the oldest Brackla cask in the central warehouses in Glasgow is from as recently as 1998. On a few occasions older casks have been bought back, such as when the 25 year old was released a few years ago.

The distillery, beautifully situated just south of Nairn and Moray Firth, is equipped with a big (12 tonnes) full lauter mash tun from 1997. There are six wooden washbacks (but with stainless steel tops!) and another two made of stainless steel and insulated because they are placed outside and the fermentation time is quite long (72 hours). Finally, there are two pairs of stills. At the moment the distillery is running at full capacity which means 17 mashes per week and 3.9 million litres of alcohol per year. This makes it the biggest distillery in the Dewar´s group.

All of the production is filled onto tankers and matured elsewhere as the huge racked warehouses on the right hand side of the road leading down to the distillery are on a long-term lease to Diageo.

Today's core range consists of a *10 year old* and a limited edition of a *25 year old*. Several independent bottlers have shown interest in Royal Brackla. Recent examples include a 14 year old with a finish in a Jurancon wine barrel by Murray McDavid and a 16 year old distilled in 1992 and released by Cadenheads.

10 years old

Royal Lochnagar

Owner:		Region/district:
Diageo		Eastern Highlands

Founded:	Status:	Capacity:
1845	Active (vc)	450 000 litres

Address: Crathie, Ballater,
Aberdeenshire AB35 5TB

Tel:	website:
01339 742700	www.malts.com

History:

1823 – James Robertson founds a distillery in Glen Feardan on the north bank of River Dee.

1826 – The distillery is burnt down by competitors but Robertson decides to establish a new distillery near the mountain Lochnagar.

1841 – This distillery is also burnt down.

1845 – A new distillery is built by John Begg, this time on the south bank of River Dee. It is named New Lochnagar. This is today considered as the official opening year of Royal Lochnagar.

1848 – Lochnagar obtains a Royal Warrant.

1882 – John Begg passes away and his son Henry Farquharson Begg inherits the distillery.

1896 – Henry Farquharson Begg dies.

1906 – The children of Henry Begg rebuild the distillery.

1916 – When Henry Begg's only son Albert dies, the distillery is sold to John Dewar & Sons.

1925 – John Dewar & Sons becomes part of Distillers Company Limited (DCL).

1930 – Administration of the distillery is transferred to Scottish Malt Distillers (SMD).

1963 – A major reconstruction takes place.

2004 – A 30 year old cask strength from 1974 is launched in the Rare Malts series (6,000 bottles).

2008 – A Distiller's Edition with a Moscatel finish is released.

Royal Lochnagar 12 year old

DR – Rich fruit and honey on the nose, sophisticated mix of crystal barley, chunky fruit and delicious peat base and a warming and rounded finish.

DS – Grassy, slightly minty, with a mild spiciness on the nose. Mint is also in the mouth with more mild spices on the medium body and short finish.

Situated just a mile from Balmoral, Royal Lochnagar looks like a reincarnation of how a typical Highland distillery should be with its well maintained granite houses. The pretty visitor centre attracts 10,000 visitors a year, a figure that could easily be quadrupled if it had been more accessible by way of one of the main roads.

The distillery is equipped with a traditional cast iron mash tun and three wooden washbacks. The fermentation time is quite long, from 75 up to 126 hours. The two stills are small - the wash still holds 7,400 litres and the spirit still 5,450 litres - and the lyne arms lead to the two cast iron worm tubs outside. The whole production is filled on site with around 1,000 casks stored in the only warehouse (the former maltings) and the rest sent to Glenlossie for maturation.

This is Diageo's smallest operating distillery with only 4 mashes per week which gives an annual production of 450,000 litres. Royal Lochnagar is also used for education and runs the Malt Advocate Courses for personnel working for Diageo. As a result of this, casks from all of Diageo's distilleries, including some rarities from closed ones, are in place. The manager of Royal Lochnagar is the experienced Donald Renwick who has been with the company for almost 30 years. His previous position was manager at Lagavulin. The founder of the new distillery in 1845, John Begg, was a close friend of the creator of VAT 69 blended whisky, William Sanderson, and for many years Lochnagar made up an important part of it. Today, however, it is reserved for more exclusive Johnnie Walker expressions like Blue Label.

The core range consists of the *12 year old* which sells around 60,000 bottles a year and the more unusual expression *Selected Reserve*. The latter is a vatting of selected casks (half sherry and half bourbon, usually around 18-20 years of age). This expression is not produced every year but a release of 4,700 bottles appeared in 2008. Another new release was the first *Distiller's Edition* of Royal Lochnagar with a finish in Moscatel casks. Independent bottlings are rare. Two recent ones came from Douglas Laing, 21 and 23 years old.

Selected Reserve

In Focus...

Barley | Malting | Mashing | Fermentation | Wash still | **Spirit still** | Maturation | Oak & Casks

The first distillation takes part in the *wash still* and once the spirit from that distillation has been collected in the low wines & feints receiver, it is pumped through the low wines charger into the *spirit still*.

At the beginning of the second distillation, the strength of the spirit is around 20%. After a while, when the temperature of the still has increased, the strength will have reached 82%. The risk of frothing that prevails during the first distillation is minimal during the second due to the fact that no carbon dioxide is left in the low wines. On the other hand, it is more important during the second distillation to keep a close watch on the temperature. A high temperature will lessen the reflux and bring heavy congeners through the neck and the lyne arm to the condenser. Depending on the desired character of the spirit, this can result in an unwanted taste.

Traditionally the spirit vapours were condensed using a *worm tub*. This is a large tub, 3 to 5 metres deep, made of wood or cast iron and placed outside the still house. Inside the tub, which is filled with water, is a copper spiral which sometimes measures up to 120 metres long. The spirit flows through it and is cooled by the surrounding water. Worm tubs are still in use at 13 distilleries. A more modern cooling device, placed at the end of the lyne arm, is called a *shell and tube condenser*. This is a wide copper tube with a number of smaller copper pipes inside through which cold water flows condensing the surrounding vapours.

The *spirit safe* is divided into two parts - the wash safe and the spirit safe. All of the low wines, distilled in the wash still, are collected into one glass bowl with a hole in the bottom. The spirit from the spirit still, on the other hand, is divided into three fractions - *foreshot, middle cut* and *feints*. The stream of these three parts of the spirit run is directed by a pipe that can be moved to any of three glass containers with openings at the bottom. Traditionally it was the stillman's job to switch the handle but nowadays it is often done by computers.

The first part of the run, called the *foreshots* and which takes 15-30 minutes, has a high percentage of impurities and unwanted congeners and would have damaged the final spirit if collected. So this part, with an alcoholic strength of 75-80% goes back to the low wines & feints receiver to be re-distilled.

The next fraction, the *middle cut*, is the part which will be saved for maturation. This part of the run, which goes into the intermediate spirit receiver, contains up to 100 different aromatic esters that will give the spirit its fruity and fragrant character. After a while the esters start to decrease and the feints to increase.

The *feints* are pleasant to start with and necessary in the spirit. After a while, though, the feints change into a variety of unpleasant aromas and this is where the stillman (or the computer) stops the middle cut and turns the pipe to the third glass container in the spirit safe. Just like the foreshots, the feints are directed to the low wines & feints receiver to become a part of the next distillation.

So, it is obvious that determining the start and end of the middle cut is crucial. To ascertain this hydrometers are used to measure alcohol strength. Depending on what character one is aiming for in the final whisky, the length of the middle cut differs from distillery to distillery. If a fruity and flowery whisky is desired, the stillman will start collecting the middle cut at around 75% and stop at perhaps 68%. Others, looking for a heavier, more pungent spirit, will start at 70% and will not stop until 60% or even lower.

During the middle cut, it is important to run the still as slowly as possible in order to increase the reflux and this will typically take somewhere between two and three hours.

The middle cut is often called the *new make* (the proper term is BPS British Plain Spirit) and has an alcohol strength of around 70%. The new make is finally pumped from the intermediate spirit receiver to the spirit vat where the spirit from several distillations is mixed to even out the differences. The spirit vat is placed in the filling store which is the last step before the spirit goes into casks (read more on page 179).

Scapa

Owner:
Chivas Brothers
(Pernod Ricard)

Region/district:
Highlands (Orkney)

Founded: **Status:**   **Capacity:**
1885   Active   1 500 000 litres

Address: Scapa, St Ola, Kirkwall,
Orkney KA15 1SE

Tel: **website:**
01856 876585   www.scapamalt.com

History:

1885 – Macfarlane & Townsend founds the distillery with John Townsend at the helm.

1919 – Scapa Distillery Company Ltd takes over.

1934 – Scapa Distillery Company goes into voluntary liquidation and production ceases.

1936 – Production resumes.

1936 – Bloch Brothers Ltd (John and Sir Maurice) takes over.

1954 – Hiram Walker & Sons takes over.

1959 – A Lomond still is installed.

1978 – The distillery is modernized.

1994 – The distillery is mothballed.

1997 – Production takes place a few months each year using staff from Highland Park.

2004 – Extensive refurbishing takes place at a cost of £2.1 million. Scapa 14 years is launched.

2005 – Production ceases in April and phase two of the refurbishment programme starts. Chivas Brothers (Pernod Ricard) becomes the new owner.

2006 – Scapa 1992 (14 years) is launched.

2008 – Scapa 16 years is launched.

Scapa 14 year old

DR – The nose is relatively gentle, with grapefruit and melon and a slight sea saltiness while the palate starts with soft yellow fruit, peaks with clean barley and then finishes with a salt and sweet interplay.

DS – Icing sugar and peach skin on the nose with rosewater and cream coming through on the palate. Hints of vanilla and spice in the finish.

For many years the core expression of Scapa was a 12 year old. In 2004 this was changed to a 14 year old and at the end of 2008 it was time again - a 16 year old was released. The reason for all this is that production has been more or less intermittent (at best) for several years when Scapa was either mothballed or staff came from Highland Park to fire up the stills. Consequently, the small stock of older Scapa is not a blender's dream. Still, Chivas Brothers has expressed a desire to spend effort on the brand and production increases every year. The ultimate capacity is 1.5 million litres per year. At the moment 8 mashes in a three-day week are acheived which corresponds to around 550,000 litres of alcohol.

The equipment consists of a semi-lauter mash tun and eight washbacks. Four of them (installed in 1968) are made of stainless steel while the old ones (1955) are made of the cheaper Corten steel. Scapa probably has the longest fermentation time of any distillery in Scotland with its 160 hours. The feature that distinguishes Scapa from all other distilleries is the still set-up. The wash still is of type Lomond, although with the rectifying plates removed so it works like an ordinary still. This is the only distillery in Scotland left with a Lomond still. However, it remains to be seen if the old Lomond-type stills from closed Inverleven and which were brought to Islay will be used in the future Port Charlotte Distillery. Scapa´s spirit still is equipped with a purifier. There are three dunnage and three racked warehouses.

Rumour even has it that there could be plans to build a visitor centre at the distillery.

The Scapa range is fairly small with the new *16 year old* replacing the *14 year old*. Recent limited editions include a *25 year old* from 1980 and a *Vintage 1992*. Douglas Laing has released a couple of bottlings in recent years - a 12 year old from 1995 and a 16 year old from 1991.

16 years old

Speyburn

Owner:
Inver House Distillers
(Thai Beverages plc)

Region/district:
Speyside

Founded: 1897
Status: Active
Capacity: 2 000 000 litres

Address: Rothes, Aberlour,
Morayshire AB38 7AG

Tel: 01340 831213
website: www.inverhouse.com

History:

1897 – Brothers John and Edward Hopkin and their cousin Edward Broughton found the distillery through John Hopkin & Co. They already own Tobermory. The architect is Charles Doig. Building the distillery costs £17,000 and the distillery is transferred to Speyburn-Glenlivet Distillery Company.

1916 – Distillers Company Limited (DCL) acquires John Hopkin & Co. and the distillery.

1930 – Production stops.

1934 – Productions restarts.

1962 – Speyburn is transferred to Scottish Malt Distillers (SMD).

1968 – Drum maltings closes.

1991 – Inver House Distillers buys Speyburn.

1992 – A 10 year old is launched as a replacement for the 12 year old in the Flora & Fauna series.

2001 – Pacific Spirits (Great Oriole Group) buys Inver House for $85 million.

2005 – A 25 year old Solera is released.

2006 – Inver House changes owner when International Beverage Holdings acquires Pacific Spirits UK.

2009 – The un-aged Bradan Orach is introduced for the American market.

Speyburn 10 year old

DR – Sweet malt nose, then one of the sweetest and most easy-drinking of all malts, with the faintest touch of smoke in the mix. Like eating a bag of sugar.

DS – A real malt fest on the nose with grassy notes. The palate is also very malty and slightly chalky which continues onto the tingly, warming finish.

For the first 24 years Inver House had an American owner, the following 13 years it was Scottish-owned and since 2001 it has been controlled from Asia. Perhaps therein lies a part of the explanation for the company's ability to adapt to new possibilities and new markets. The Speyburn brand has succeeded very well with that. The American connections led to an agreement with Barton Brands in 1993 to distribute Speyburn single malt on the American market. It was a success and sent the brand to sixth place on the US sales lists. The agreement with Barton expired in 2009 and from 1st August the brand is represented by the American branch of InterBev, a subsidiary of Thai Beverages. The aim is not only to promote Speyburn but also other brands from Inver House and from the Thai owner.

The distillery is equipped with a stainless steel mash tun which replaced the old cast iron tun in 2008. There are six washbacks made of larch and one pair of stills using stainless steel worm tubs with 104 metre long copper tubes for cooling. There are three dunnage warehouses with 5,000 casks where the spirit intended for bottling as single malt is maturing mainly in bourbon casks. The rest of the spirit is tankered away to the company's central warehouses in Airdrie. The distillery is doing 18 mashes per week in 2009, i. e. 85% of the capacity.

In 1900, Speyburn was the first distillery to abandon floor malting in favour of a new method - drum malting. In the late sixties the maltings closed and ready malt was bought instead but the drum maltings are still there to see, protected by Historic Scotland.

For a long time now, Speyburn single malt has been known by its *10 year old* apart from a few limited expressions (*21, 25* and *25 year old Solera*). In late 2008 a decision was made to introduce yet another expression in the core range of the American market. This is *Bradan Orach* (golden salmon in Gaelic) without an age statement. The goal is to have an entry level single malt priced under $20 and to be able to move the 10 year old higher up the price range.

10 years old

Speyside

Owner:
Speyside Distillers Co.

Region/district:
Speyside

Founded: 1976

Status: Active

Capacity: 600 000 litres

Address: Glen Tromie, Kingussie
Inverness-shire PH21 1NS

Tel: 01540 661060

website: www.speysidedistillery.co.uk

History:

1956 – George Christie buys a piece of land at Drumguish near Kingussie.

1957 – George Christie starts a grain distillery near Alloa.

1962 – George Christie (founder of Speyside Distillery Group in the fifties) commissions the drystone dyker Alex Fairlie to build a distillery in Drumguish.

1986 – Scowis assumes ownership.

1987 – The distillery is completed.

1990 – The distillery is on stream in December.

1993 – The first single malt, Drumguish, is launched.

1999 – Speyside 8 years is launched.

2000 – Speyside Distilleries is sold to a group of private investors including Ricky Christie, Ian Jerman and Sir James Ackroyd.

2001 – Speyside 10 years is launched.

Speyside 12 year old

DR – Rootsy damp straw nose, a sharp and clean barley delivery on the palate with an earthy, peaty undertow, and a willowy, nutty savoury finish.

DS – Dried wheat with spoonfuls of honey and oatmeal on the nose. A biscuity and slightly sweet palate leading to the medium finish with honey on the aftertaste.

In 2010 it is time for Speyside distillery, just south of Kingussie, to celebrate its 20th anniversary. The strange thing is that it took 25 years to build from when the first stone was laid. The whisky blender and most likely the last true whisky baron, George Christie, asked a drystone dyker, Alex Fairlie, to build the distillery which he did by hand, brick by brick, which could explain the long time it took. The result is amazing - a beautiful farm distillery set in stunning surroundings. George Christie's ownership ceased years ago but as he lives next door he was often found on the premises trying out the new make. He is now well into his nineties and has unfortunately had to stop this habit.

The distillery is equipped with a semi-lauter mash tun, four stainless steel washbacks and one pair of stills. At the moment, annual production is 500,000 litres per year in five or six-day weeks. Since December 2006 a peated spirit is produced one week per year. The first of the peated production will legally become whisky at the end of 2009 but according to Distillery Manager Andrew Shand, Speyside will probably wait another couple of years before releasing it. Speyside produces three brands of single malt: Speyside (360,000 bottles) where one can still find the 8 and 10 year olds even though the core range is 12 and 15 year old, Drumguish (600,000) and the quaint and almost black Cu Dubh (60,000 bottles). The release of a special bottling of the first batch of distillation from 1990 is planned for 2010. A vatted malt named Glentromie is also produced and. In addition, the company owns some 20 brands of blended whiskies and two ranges of single malts from other distilleries - Scott's Selection and Private Cellar. The distillery can also boast of a couple of oddities - the number one Scotch blend in Mongolia, the Yokozuna, and the first Kosher-certified Scotch back in 2006.

12 years old

In Focus...

The average strength of new make spirit is around 70%, sometimes a little more. Prior to being filled into the casks (more about oak and different casks on page 187) for maturation, the new make is diluted to 63.5%. The reason for diluting the spirit has been under debate but one argument is that at a high alcohol strength, maturation takes longer and the formation of certain congeners which will give the final whisky its character, is made difficult. On the other hand, diluting the spirit increases warehousing costs as more casks are needed as well as more space. There is a risk that after many years of maturation the alcohol strength due to evaporation has sunk below 40%, the legal requirement for whisky.

The majority of the industry has decided that 63.5% is the optimal strength. However, this routine is not acknowledged by everyone and at least the people at Bruichladdich fill their casks without diluting. Also, many producers have not followed this routine for all of their production during the years. That is why one can sometimes find cask strength bottlings that are more than 20 years old but still have an alcohol strength of more than 60%. If it had been filled at 63.5%, two decades of evaporation would have brought the strength

down to somewhere below 50% at the least.

The evaporation we are talking about here is what is generally called *the angel's share*. Oak is a semi-porous material and alcohol as well as water will evaporate during maturation. The rate depends very much on the temperature of the warehouse. Higher temperature means a higher degree of evaporation. The air humidity also plays an important role. High humidity surrounding the cask means that water evaporation is less, which in its turn means that the alcohol is reduced in relation to amount of water, thus creating a lower alcohol content from year to year. This is the case in Scotland with its high humidity, especially in the winter. In other places, for example southern USA, temperature is high and humidity low so more water than alcohol will be lost from evaporation and this may result in the alcohol strength growing higher during maturation.

After diluting, the spirit is filled into wooden casks and, according to law, it has to be oak to be allowed to be called Scotch whisky. Sometimes different types of wood are used in other parts of the world and there have been occasional experiments in Scotland in the old days with casks made of for example chestnut, but without success. With very few exceptions, second-hand casks are used in Scotland and they have usually held either sherry or bourbon.

The oak's importance for the maturation of whisky can be divided into

three parts: *subtractive, additive* and *interactive*.

The *subtractive* part is about breaking down and removing especially sulphury compounds in the spirit. Actually it is not the oak itself doing this job but rather carbon derived from the toasting or charring of the inside of the cask. In order to put the cask together, the oak staves are heated to the point where they obtain a toasted character. For a bourbon cask, however, that is not enough. After the cask has been put together, the inside is exposed to an open flame and the walls are charred to a depth of about one millimetre. An American bourbon cask will therefore be more efficient in reducing the sulphur in the spirit.

The *additive* mechanism is about lending the spirit both flavour and colour. Depending on how many times a cask has been used, the effect on the colour will differ. A whisky from a first-fill sherry cask will therefore be darker than one deriving from a third-fill cask. The tannin in the wood also influences the colour and European Oak, being more tannic than American Oak, results in a darker colour. Furthermore, the tannin adds to the taste of the whisky as does lignin which when heated, adds vanilla and coconut notes to the spirit. An obvious addition to the flavour comes not from the oak itself but from whichever wine or spirit was in the cask previously (sherry, bourbon, Port etc).

The *interactive* process is yet the least understood of the three maturation elements. Evaporation and oxidation (when oxygen replaces the evaporated water and alcohol) is one part and this eliminates harshness and adds complexity to the spirit. But interaction also means oak and spirit together creating compounds that were not present from the beginning. While the first of the two maturation processes are active during the first couple of years, the interactive part will continue during the entire time of maturation and is also very dependent on how the cask is stored (temperature, humidity, atmospheric pressure).

Springbank

Owner:
Springbank Distillers
(J & A Mitchell)

Region/district:
Campbeltown

Founded: 1828 **Status:** Active **Capacity:** 750 000 litres

Address: Well Close, Campbeltown,
Argyll PA28 6ET

Tel: 01586 552085 **website:** www.springbankdistillers.com

History:

1828 – The Reid family, in-laws of the Mitchells (see below), founds the distillery as the fourteenth in Campbelltown.

1837 – The Reid family encounters financial difficulties and John and William Mitchell buy the distillery.

1897 – J. & A. Mitchell Company Ltd is founded. William Mitchell founded Glengyle in 1872 and when he and John parted ways, John Mitchell continued operating Springbank first alone and then with his son Archibald.

1926 – The depression forces the distillery to close.

1933 – The distillery is back in production.

1960 – Own maltings ceases.

1969 – J. & A. Mitchell buys the independent bottler Cadenhead.

1979 – The distillery closes.

1985 – A 10 year old Longrow is launched as an experiment.

1987 – Limited production restarts.

1989 – Production restarts.

1990 – Longrow becomes a standard label.

1992 – Springbank takes up its own maltings again.

1997 – First distillation of Hazelburn.

1998 – Springbank 12 years is launched.

1999 – Dha Mhile (7 years) is the world's first organic single malt and is released as a limited expression of 1,000 bottles.

2000 – A 10 year old is launched.

A handful of malts have achieved something of a cult status with a devoted following and favourable reviews when new bottlings appear. Family-owned Springbank Distillery certainly belongs to them. Its status is further enhanced by the fact that it has always gone its own way, such as it boldly did when, in early summer 2008, it announced a temporary closure. The announcement was made a few months before the global recession set in and while most in the business still believed in a continued whisky boom.

Springbank was heavily criticized but defended itself with the argument that it wanted to strike a balance between what the distillery produces and what the future sales of this maturing stock will be. Plans were for yearly growths in sales but Springbank was producing more whisky than it could comfortably sell in future years.

Malting started again in late 2008 and on 25th February 2009 distilling resumed. However, the owner still has a careful approach to the current climate on the market and once again stopped production for the rest of the year after the summer. Malting will commence again in October/November 2009 and the plans are to distill during May and early June in 2010. Local barley is malted using peat from a bog at the nearby Machrihanish and from Tomintoul in the Highlands. Springbank produces three distinctive single malts with different phenol contents in the malted barley; Springbank is distilled two and a half times (12-15ppm), Longrow is distilled twice (50-55 ppm) and Hazelburn is distilled three times (unpeated). Currently, Springbank makes up 60% of production while the remaining part is split between Longrow and Hazelburn.

All whisky is matured on site in nine dunnage and two racked warehouses. There are six washbacks made of Scandinavian larch, one wash still and two spirit stills. The wash still is unique in Scotland as it is fired by both an open oil-fire and internal steam coils. The spirit stills are heated using steam coils. Ordinary condensers are used to cool the spirit vapours except in the first of the two spirit stills where a worm tub is used.

The core range of Springbank distillery is *Springbank 10* and *15 years, Springbank 10 years 100 proof, Longrow 10 and 14 years, Longrow 10 years 100 proof, Longrow CV* and *Hazelburn 12 years old*. The latter was released in summer 2009. Limited releases of Springbank this past year were the *11 year old Madeira*, the *18 year old* which will become a part of the core range and the *Springbank Vintage 2001*. In 2008 a *7 year old Longrow* with the last 18 months in Gaja Barolo casks was released.

History (continued):

2001 – Springbank 1965 'Local barley' (36 years), 741 bottles, is launched. .

2002 – Number one in the series Wood Expressions is a 12 year old with five years on Demerara rum casks. Next is a Longrow sherry cask (13 years). A relaunch of the 15 year old replaces the 21 year old.

2004 – J. & A. Mitchell's main owner, Hedley Wright, reopens Glengyle Distillery. Springbank 10 years 100 proof is launched as well as Springbank Wood Expression bourbon, Longrow 14 years old, Springbank 32 years old and Springbank 14 years Port Wood.

2005 – 2 400 bottles of Springbank 21 years old take the market by surprise when they are released in March. The first version of Hazelburn (8 years old) is released. Longrow Tokaji Wood Expression is launched.

2006 – Longrow 10 years 100 proof, Springbank 25 years (1,200 bottles), Springbank 9 years Marsala finish, Springbank 11 years Madeira finish and a new Hazelburn 8 year old are released.

2007 – Springbank Vintage 1997 and a 16 year old rum wood are released.

2008 – The distillery closes temporarily. Three new releases of Longrow - CV, 18 year old and 7 year old Gaja Barolo.

2009 – Springbank Madeira 11 year old, Springbank 18 year old, Springbank Vintage 2001 and Hazelburn 12 year old are released.

Springbank Vintage 2001   Hazelburn 12 years old   Springbank Madeira 11 years old

---

Springbank 10 year old 100 proof

DR – Biscuit, toffee crisp, almonds and dried fruits on the nose, intense oily and complex taste with some oak, honey and spice notes, and a rich full finish.

DS – Oily and earthy on the nose with heavy malt notes and rich shortbread. Again very oily with pronounced peat and malt flavours. A super-hot, cayenne, finish with pepperiness galore.

Longrow 10 year old 100 proof

DR – Subtle lemon and daffodil nose with traces of phenols, sweet, fruity and oily palate covered in a smattering of charcoal dust, lengthy, subtle and fragrant finish.

DS – Lemon sherbets, sweet peat, pear drops. Again lots of sweet and citrus flavours mixed with zesty peat - like a peated 'real' lemonade. Fizzy and citrus finish with a jellied lemon peel aftertaste.

Hazelburn 12 year old

DR – Rich and fruity nose of nectarine, peach, plums and some nuttiness. On the palate rich plums, red berries, dry sherry and drying tannins, with an intense rich and fruity finish.

DS – Burnt oak, soft sherry (amoroso?), marzipan and mulled wine. Loads of delicious sherry flavours, so well balanced with deep, rich fruit flavours and powerful woody flavours. A gem of an aftertaste with lots of little sherry notes rising to the surface.

Springbank 10 years old 100 proof   Longrow 10 years old 100 proof

181

Strathisla

Owner: Chivas Brothers (Pernod Ricard)

Region/district: Speyside

Founded: 1786

Status: Active (vc)

Capacity: 2 400 000 litres

Address: Seafield Avenue, Keith, Banffshire AB55 5BS

Tel: 01542 783044

website: www.maltwhiskydistilleries.com

History:

1786 – Alexander Milne and George Taylor found the distillery under the name Milltown, but soon change it to Milton.

1825 – MacDonald Ingram & Co. purchases the distillery.

1830 – William Longmore acquires the distillery.

1870 – The distillery name changes to Strathisla.

1876 – The distillery is badly damaged by fire.

1879 – Another accident strikes - a dust explosion in the malt mill.

1880 – William Longmore retires and hands operations to his son-in-law John Geddes-Brown. William Longmore & Co. is formed.

1890 – The distillery changes name to Milton.

1940 – Jay (George) Pomeroy acquires majority shares in William Longmore & Co. Pomeroy is jailed as a result of dubious business transactions and the distillery goes bankrupt in 1949.

1950 – Chivas Brothers buys the run-down distillery at a compulsory auction for £71,000 and starts restoration.

1951 – The name reverts to Strathisla.

1965 – The number of stills is increased from two to four.

1970 – A heavily peated whisky, Craigduff, is produced but production stops later.

2001 – The Chivas Group is acquired by Pernod Ricard.

Strathisla 12 year old

DR – Rich full and fruity nose with lots of barley, then barley, currants and a touch of oak, peat and pepper, concluding with a complex and intriguing finish.

DS – Fennel and cream on the nose. The palate is medium bodied with a taste of brown bread. The finish is quite long and warming.

Two distilleries are situated within a few hundred metres from each other in Keith - Strathisla and Glen Keith. The former is up and running while the latter has been dormant since 2000. Despite this Glen Keith is an integrated part of Strathisla's production. First of all, the steam for Strathisla comes from the boiler at Glen Keith. Secondly, the spirit produced at Strathisla is piped to Glen Keith for filling or to be tankered away. Finally, effluent from Strathisla is stored at Glen Keith and from there transferred to the Keith Water Treatment Works.

Strathisla Distillery is one of the most picturesque distilleries in Scotland and has an excellent visitor centre that recently was awarded Five Star status by Visit Scotland. The centre, however, is more focussed on the blend Chivas Regal than the single malt Strathisla. This is the spiritual home of the famous Scotch blend of which the single malt produced here plays an increasingly important role.

Strathisla is one of the oldest distilleries in Scotland, equipped with a traditional stainless steel mash tun with a raised copper dome, ten (formerly eleven, but one has been remade into a pot ale tank) washbacks of Oregon pine and two pairs of stills. A small amount is stored on site in two racked and one dunnage warehouse. The rest is sent to different facilities in Scotland.

Strathisla and Glen Keith are not the only facilities in Keith owned by Pernod Ricard. The town is also the home to Keith Bond 1 (KB1), a 34 acre warehousing complex and Keith Bond 2 (KB2) a blending and filling facility with 35 staff. Pernod Ricard has only released two official bottlings - the *12 year old* and a *15 year old cask strength*. Recent independent bottlings include a 10 year old from Ian Macleod and a 1967 from Duncan Taylor.

12 years old

Strathmill

Owner:		Region/district:
Diageo		Speyside
Founded:	**Status:**	**Capacity:**
1891	Active	2 300 000 litres

Address: Keith, Banffshire AB55 5DQ

Tel:	website:
01542 883000	www.malts.com

History:

1891 – The distillery is founded in an old mill from 1823 and is named Glenisla-Glenlivet Distillery.

1892 – The inauguration takes place in June.

1895 – The gin company W. & A. Gilbey buys the distillery for £9,500 and names it Strathmill.

1962 – W. & A. Gilbey merges with United Wine Traders (including Justerini & Brooks) and forms International Distillers & Vintners (IDV).

1968 – The number of stills is increased from two to four and purifiers are added.

1972 – IDV is bought by Watney Mann which later the same year is acquired by Grand Metropolitan.

1993 – Strathmill becomes available as a single malt for the first time since 1909 as a result of a bottling (1980) from Oddbins.

1997 – Guinness and Grand Metropolitan merge and form Diageo.

2001 – The first official bottling is a 12 year old in the Flora & Fauna series.

Strathmill 12 year old

DS – A hint of strawberries and vanilla on the sweet nose. Complex and heathery on the palate with a touch of oakiness which continues onto the finish.

Strathmill, beautifully embedded in the greenery along the river Isla on the outskirts of Keith, is not among the most well-known distilleries. Despite that, many have probably sampled its produce as it is since long ago an important ingredient of J&B blended whisky.

Scotch whisky history has its share of mergers and acquisitions but few have been of such a magnitude as when Grand Metropolitan Plc and Arthur Guinness, Son & Co merged in 1997 to form Diageo. The value of the deal was a staggering £24 billion. Of the 28 Scottish malt distilleries owned and operated by Diageo today, only four came from Grand Met in that deal, namely Strathmill, Auchroisk, Knockando and Glen Spey. The rest (with the obvious exception of newly built Roseisle) came from Guinness which acquired them when it bought Distillers Company Limited (DCL) a decade earlier.

Strathmill distillery is equipped with a stainless steel semi-lauter mash tun, six stainless steel washbacks and two pairs of stills. Strathmill is one of a few select distilleries using a facility called purifier on the spirit stills. This device is mounted between the lyne arm and the condenser and acts as a mini-condenser allowing the lighter alcohols to travel towards the condenser and forcing the heavier alcohols to go back into the still for another distillation. The result is a lighter and more fruity spirit.

The spirit is tankered away to Auhcroisk for filling and some of the casks find their way back for storage in six on site warehouses.

The only official bottling is a *12 year old* in the Flora & Fauna series. Except for the two butts (25 years old) that were bottled in 1992 to celebrate the centenary of the distillery, there are no other bottlings from the owner. Recent independent bottlings of Strathmill have also been scarce, but 2007 treated us to the ancient Douglas Laing - 45 years old, from 1962!

Flora & Fauna 12 years

Talisker

Owner: Diageo

Region/district: Highlands (Skye)

Founded: 1830

Status: Active (vc)

Visitor centre: 1 940 000 litres

Address: Carbost, Isle of Skye, Inverness-shire IV47 8SR

Tel: 01478 614308 (vc)

website: www.taliskerwhisky.com

History:

1830 – Hugh and Kenneth MacAskill, sons of the local doctor, found the distillery.

1848 – The brothers transfer the lease to North of Scotland Bank and Jack Westland from the bank runs the operations.

1854 – Kenneth MacAskill dies.

1857 – North of Scotland Bank sells the distillery to Donald MacLennan for £500.

1863 – MacLennan experiences difficulties in making operations viable and puts the distillery up for sale.

1865 – MacLennan, still working at the distillery, nominates John Anderson as agent in Glasgow.

1867 – Anderson & Co. from Glasgow takes over.

1879 – John Anderson is imprisoned after having sold non-existing casks of whisky.

1880 – New owners are now Alexander Grigor Allan and Roderick Kemp.

1892 – Kemp sells his share and buys Macallan Distillery instead.

1894 – The Talisker Distillery Ltd is founded.

1895 – Allan dies and Thomas Mackenzie, who has been his partner, takes over.

1898 – Talisker Distillery merges with Dailuaine-Glenlivet Distillers and Imperial Distillers to form Dailuaine-Talisker Distillers Company.

Among the Diageo single malts, Talisker has become the great success story showing a remarkable growth of 100% over the past five years. It is mainly Europe that has seen this increase but the USA and Asia (in particular India) have also shown their interest for this Skye whisky. It is now the best selling of all Diageo single malts after Cardhu.

The distillery is equipped with a stainless steel lauter mash tun, which not long ago replaced the old one made of cast iron. Two new washbacks were recently installed in order to increase capacity which means that eight washbacks now serve the unusual combination of two wash stills and three spirit stills. This is a leftover from the time when Talisker was triple distilled. Some of the stills at Talisker, in common with a handful of the other Diageo distilleries (Strathmill and Glenspey), are equipped with purifiers, a device between the still and the lyne arm which is intended to increase the reflux during distillation. At Talisker there is an old style purification using the colder outside air and a u-bend in the lyne arm instead of a water jacket. Also, the purifiers are attached to the wash stills instead of the spirit stills. Another peculiarity these days is that cooling is performed with the aid of five worm tubs instead of the more common shell/tube variety. Only a small part of the produce is matured on the island (the warehouses can store 6,000 casks) while the rest is tankered and taken to the mainland for storage.

A new manager took up his position at the distillery in summer 2008 when Willie McDougall left and was replaced by Mark Lochhead who has been in the business for more than 20 years. The success of the brand has also inspired the owner to recently launch a new website - *www.taliskerwhisky.com*.

Talisker's core range consists of a *10 year old*, an *18 year old* and a *Distiller's Edition* with an Amoroso sherry finish.

In January 2008 *Talisker 57° North* was released. The name alludes to both the latitude of the distillery and its alcohol content. It was initially launched as a duty-free item but is now available across the UK. Additionally, the seventh version of *25 year old cask strength* and the fourth of the *30 year old* were released as part of Special Releases in autumn 2009.

Independent bottlings of Talisker are rare and when they do occur the names do not reveal their origin. One of the most recent is Tactical from Douglas Laing, an 18 years old from 1988.

History (continued):

1916 – Thomas Mackenzie dies and the distillery is taken over by a consortium consisting of, among others, John Walker, John Dewar, W. P. Lowrie and Distillers Company Limited (DCL).

1928 – The distillery abandons triple distillation.

1930 – Administration of the distillery is transferred to Scottish Malt Distillers (SMD).

1960 – On 22nd November the distillery catches fire and substantial damage occurs.

1962 – The distillery reopens after the fire with five new identical copies of the destroyed stills.

1972 – Malting ceases and malt is now purchased from Glen Ord Central Maltings.

1988 – United Distillers introduce Classic Malts, Talisker 10 years included. A visitor centre is opened.

1998 – A new stainless steel/copper mash tun and five new worm tubs are installed. Talisker is launched as a Distillers Edition with an amoroso sherry finish.

2004 – Two new bottlings appear, an 18 year old and a 25 year old.

2005 – To celebrate the 175th birthday of the distillery, Talisker 175th Anniversary is released (60 000 bottles). The third edition of the 25 year old cask strength is released (15 600 bottles).

2006 – A 30 year old and the fourth edition of the 25 year old are released.

2007 – The second edition of the 30 year old and the fifth edition of the 25 year old are released.

2008 – Talisker 57° North, sixth edition of the 25 year old and third edition of the 30 year old are launched.

2009 – New editions of the 25 and 30 year old are released.

Talisker 10 year old

DR – Grilled oily fish in lemon oil, on the nose, dry salt and pepper on the palate, peat and pepper in a tastebud treat of a finish.

DS –Immediate sea-weed – peppery with a hint of sherry and citrus. Much more peat on the palate which is full bodied. Peppery finish – warming.

57° North

*25 years old
7th edition*

*30 years old
4th edition*

10 years old

18 years old

Distiller's Edition 1992

Tamdhu

Owner:		Region/district:
Edrington Group		Speyside

Founded:	Status:	Capacity:
1896	Active	4 000 000 litres

Address: Knockando, Aberlour, Morayshire AB38 7RP

Tel:	website:
01340 872200	-

History:
1896 – The distillery is founded by Tamdhu Distillery Company, a consortium of whisky blenders with William Grant as the main promoter. Charles Doig is the architect.

1897 – The first casks are filled in July.

1898 – Highland Distillers Company, which has several of the 1896 consortium members in managerial positions, buys Tamdhu Distillery Company.

1911 – The distillery closes.

1913 –The distillery reopens.

1928 – The distillery is mothballed.

1948 – The distillery is in full production again in July.

1950 – The floor maltings is replaced by Saladin boxes when the distillery is rebuilt.

1972 – The number of stills is increased from two to four.

1975 – Two stills augment the previous four.

1976 – Tamdhu 8 years is launched as single malt.

2005 – An 18 year old and a 25 year old are released.

Tamdhu (no age statement)
DR – Something of a rollercoaster ride. Ripe fruit salad in juice and syrup on the nose, crystallised barley, fruit flavoured sherbet, sharp pepper, nuts and peat on the palate and a spicy finish.

One of the reasons for Tamdhu ending up with Highland Distillers and eventually Edrington as owner, was a fire at Glenrothes Distillery in 1897 which destroyed most of the whisky in stock. This distillery was also owned by Highland Distillers and, in search for another source of whisky nearby, Tamdhu was acquired.

Tamdhu may be comparatively unknown as a single malt but has an important role as producer of malt whisky for e. g. The Famous Grouse. But there are also other activities on-going which are important for owner Edrington; the maltings contribute 30% of the malt requirement of the other distilleries in the group. 16,000 tonnes of barley are refined into 14,000 tonnes of malted barley each year. This is done in so-called Saladin boxes (installed in 1950), a technique which is only in use at Tamdhu among the Scottish distilleries but occurs with some of the commercial maltsters. A Saladin box is a long concrete box with revolving rakes. The barley is steeped and turned by the rakes and air circulates through perforated floors to keep the temperature under control. To dry, the green malt is transferred into a kiln very different from traditional ones. It is simply a large, self-filling and self-emptying box with air blowing through it.

Tamdhu is a distillery with a large capacity but currently works a five-day week producing 1.9 million litres of alcohol, a decrease of 1 million litres compared to 2008. There is one semi-lauter mash tun and nine Oregon pine washbacks serving three pairs of stills and there are four dunnage and one racked warehouse on site holding 18,000 casks.

Around 8,000 cases of Tamdhu were sold in 2008. The official range only consists of a *non-aged version*. In 2005 an *18* and a *25 year old* were introduced but, according to the owner, they are not being bottled anymore. The same applies for a *10 year old*. Recent independent bottlings include a 15 year old from 1994 by Ian MacLeod and an 18 year old from 1991 released by Cadenhead.

Gordon & MacPhail
Tamdhu 8 years old

On page 179 we discussed what actually happens inside the cask during the maturation period. However, different types of casks and the oak itself is such a broad subject and needs further refinement. In fact, many claim that up to 60-80% of the whisky's final character depends on the maturation and, most importantly, on the cask.

Until the Scotch Whisky Act of 1988 whisky was allowed to mature in casks made from wood other than oak. Even so, for at least 100 years oak has been the choice of all the producers in Scotland.

There are more than 400 different kinds of oak in the genus *Quercus* (200 in the USA alone) but only three that are of major interest to the distilleries, all of them belonging to the category white oak:

Pedunculate Oak or English Oak
(*Quercus robur*)

Sessile Oak or Durmast Oak
(*Quercus petraea*)

American White Oak
(*Quercus alba*)

The first two grow in Europe and the last, obviously, in North America, particularly in Arkansas, Kentucky, Missouri and Tennessee.

American White Oak is often preferred because it brings in better revenue. The trees grow faster and it is tighter grained which means it can be sawn rather than split by an axe. This also results in less wasted wood.

The European Oak on the other hand, is more porous which means that whisky is lost at a higher speed, but the increased oxidization can often be of benefit during the maturation. European Oak also contains more tannin whereas American Oak has a higher content of vanillin, both of them contributing to the flavour of the whisky.

A fourth variety of oak which has become increasingly interesting is Japanese Oak (*Quercus mongolica*) or Mizunara Oak as it is also known as. Sherry casks were difficult to get hold of just after the second World War and several Japanese distilleries filled whisky into casks of this indigenous oak. They were not fully satisfied with the wood's ability to hold the spirit so when sherry casks once again became available, these were preferred. Decades later, however, it was discovered that the whisky that had matured in Japanese Oak had a unique sandal or cedar flavour to it and now most of the distilleries in Japan have started using Japanese Oak again, at least to some extent.

In the old days, the distilleries would fill their spirit into any wooden cask they could find because the cask was merely seen as a transport vessel. In the late 1800s, a new regime

came into being when distillers started using empty sherry casks from Spain. Huge amounts of sherry were imported to England and casks were cheap. In the mid 1900s, though, the demand for sherry, at least in the UK, had diminished substantially and the producers had to look for other solutions. One was to make their own casks in Spain and lend them to the sherry bodegas for a few years and then bring them to Scotland. The other alternative was to import empty bourbon barrels from the USA. By law, bourbon has to be matured in new, charred oak casks so there was always a good supply to be had from across the Atlantic.

There are about 18 million casks of whisky maturing in Scotland and 95% of these are made of American Oak with 300,000 new casks being shipped every year from the USA to Scotland.

In the last two decades new types of casks have entered the scene. Today it is quite common to find whisky that has matured in Port pipes, Madeira casks, rum casks or casks that have held different kinds of wine. In some cases the spirit has been in the same cask for the whole period of maturation but more frequent is that the whisky is re-racked from a bourbon or sherry cask to obtain a final maturation of a few months or a couple of years in a second cask. There are different terms for this procedure - finishing, enhancing, acing - which aims to give the whisky an added flavour profile.

With just a few exceptions, the spirit destined to become whisky is always filled into a cask that has once held spirit or wine. That filling is called *first-fill*, then comes *second-fill* and from the third filling it is often simply called *refill*. A first-fill cask has to be handled with great care when blending the whisky as the previous spirit or wine will sometimes dominate the whisky character. Second-fill and third-fill contribute less and are therefore easier to use in a blend or to sell as a single cask whisky (with no blending). After each filling, most bourbon casks are rejuvenated which means that a thin layer is shaved off on the inside and then the wood re-charred, i. e. burnt with a flame to create a carbon surface. Sherry casks are often toasted and sometimes seasoned with new sherry.

Tamnavulin

Owner:
Whyte & Mackay
(United Spirits)

Region/district:
Speyside

Founded: 1966 **Status:** Active **Capacity:** 4 000 000 litres

Address: Tomnavoulin, Ballindalloch,
Banffshire AB3 9JA

Tel: 01807 590285

website: -

History:
1966 – Tamnavulin-Glenlivet Distillery Company, a subsidiary of Invergordon Distillers Ltd, founds Tamnavulin.

1993 – Whyte & Mackay buys Invergordon Distillers.

1995 – The distillery closes in May.

1996 – Whyte & Mackay changes name to JBB (Greater Europe).

2001 – Company management buy out operations for £208 million and rename the company Kyndal.

2003 – Kyndal changes name to Whyte & Mackay.

2007 – United Spirits buys Whyte & Mackay. Tamnavulin is opened again in July after having been mothballed for 12 years.

Tamnavulin 12 year old

DR – Wet hay, celery and cucumber on the nose and a delightful exotic fruit and citrus taste and a satisfying and pleasant finish.

DS – A honey-pot nose with nutmeg. The palate is buttery and overflowing with honey flavours. It is quite light and has a floral, honeyed after-taste.

For ten years, from 1978 to 1988, Tamnavulin had the most unlikely owner in the modern history of Scotch whisky – the Hawker Siddeley Group. This was an engineering group established in 1935 which quickly became one of the pioneers of the aviation industry. Its founder, Tommy Sopwith, had previously manufactured the famous Sopwith Camel that shot down Germany´s World War I flying ace, The Red Baron. In World War II the company produced the Hawker Hurricane, which played a crucial role in the Battle of Britain in 1940. In 1988, Invergordon was sold through a management buyout and several owners later Tamnavulin is now a part of Indian United Spirits.

Tamnavulin reopened in 2007 after having been mothballed for 12 years. It had only been distilling for six weeks in 2000 in order to maintain the stock of whisky when people came from the nearby Tomintoul distillery to produce some 400,000 litres of spirit.

The distillery is equipped with a full lauter mash tun, eight washbacks (four of them made of stainless steel and the rest of Corten steel) and three pairs of stills. The wash stills were all replaced in summer 2008 but a planned replacement of the spirit stills has been put on hold. Around 3.5 million litres were produced in 2008 but for 2009 the goal is 2.8 million.

Two racked warehouses (10 casks high) on site have a capacity of 34,250 casks with the oldest ones dating back to 1967. Two hundred casks are filled every week on site while the rest of the production is tankered to Invergordon for filling.

There used to be a visitor centre run by the local community, but it closed at the end of the nineties.

The only standard release of Tamnavulin for quite some time now has been a *12 year old*. A number of aged *Stillman's Dram* have also been launched, the most recent a 30 year old.

Independent bottlings occur now and then. A 40 year old Single Malts of Scotland was recently released as well as a 1993 by Blackadder.

12 years old

Teaninich

Owner:
Diageo

Region/district:
Northern Highlands

Founded: **Status:** **Capacity:**
1817   Active   4 000 000 litres

Address: Alness, Ross-shire IV17 0XB

Tel:
01349 885001

website:
www.malts.com

History:

1817 – Captain Hugh Monro, owner of the estate Teaninich, founds the distillery.

1831 – Captain Munro sells the estate to his younger brother John.

1850 – John Munro, who spends most of his time in India, leases Teaninich to the infamous Robert Pattison from Leith.

1869 – John McGilchrist Ross takes over the licence.

1895 – Munro & Cameron takes over the licence.

1898 – Munro & Cameron buys the distillery.

1904 – Robert Innes Cameron becomes sole owner of Teaninich. He has had interests in Linkwood Distillery since 1902.

1932 – Robert Innes Cameron dies.

1933 – The estate of Robert Innes Cameron sells the distillery to Distillers Company Limited.

1970 – A new distillation unit with six stills is commissioned and becomes known as the A side.

1975 – A dark grains plant is built.

1984 – The B side of the distillery is mothballed.

1985 – The A side is also mothballed.

1991 – The A side is in production again.

1992 – United Distillers launches a 10 year old Teaninich in the Flora & Fauna series.

1999 – The B side is decommissioned.

2000 – A mash filter is installed.

2009 – Teaninich 1996, a single cask in the new Manager's Choice range is released.

Teaninich 10 year old

DS – A heavy, malty nose with spice and apple skin. The palate is sweet at first with some spice and a hint of smoke. A spicy finish.

The only remaining building from the old distillery

At one time, back in the seventies, Teaninich was one of the largest distilleries in Scotland with a capacity of 6 million litres. This was due to a completely new distillation complex with six stills having been added in 1970, bringing the total number of stills to ten. The old distillery buildings with the first four stills were demolished in 1999, which left a very modern-looking distillery with few visible traces of the 19th century.

One interesting feature distinguishes Teaninich from all other distilleries; in 2000 a Meura 2001 mash filter was installed in place of a traditional mash tun. Many breweries already use a mash filter and the advantages are that a mash can be made in half the time and a more efficient extraction of sugars is obtained which results in a higher spirit yield. During trials at the International Centre for Brewing and Distilling in autumn 2008, a sensory analysis was made comparing the new make from a traditional mashing and that from a mash filter. The lauter tun spirit appeared cleaner with more floral and fresh fruit aromas whereas the mash filter new make was more sulfury and meaty. In order to operate the mash filter the malt needs to be ground into a very fine flour without husks, so an Asnong hammer mill capable of this was installed at Teaninich instead of a traditional roller mill. The mash filter itself required a staggering £3m investment.

Besides the six stills the distillery is equipped with 10 washbacks - eight made of larch and two of stainless steel. There are no warehouses on site; instead 4-5 tankers leave the distillery each week for filling elsewhere. 19 mashes are done per week corresponding to 4 million litres which is more or less at capacity.

Teaninich is mainly produced to be a component of Johnnie Walker blended whiskies. The only official bottling was a *10 year old* in the Flora & Fauna series until autumn 2009 when a *Teaninich 1996* single cask was released in the new range Manager's Choice.

Independent bottlings are not that common. The most recent one is a 1971 from Douglas Laing which was released in 2008 and a 1996 from Duncan Taylor.

Manager's Choice 1996

Tobermory

Owner: Burn Stewart Distillers (C L Financial)

Region/district: Highland (Mull)

Founded: 1798
Status: Active (vc)
Capacity: 1 000 000 litres

Address: Tobermory, Isle of Mull, Argyllshire PA75 6NR

Tel: 01688 302647
website: www.burnstewartdistillers.com

History:

1798 – John Sinclair founds the distillery.

1837 – The distillery closes.

1878 – The distillery reopens.

1890 – John Hopkins & Company buys the distillery.

1916 – Distillers Company Limited (DCL) takes over John Hopkins & Company.

1930 – The distillery closes and is used as both a canteen and a power station

1972 – A shipping company in Liverpool and the sherrymaker Domecq buy the buildings and embark on refurbishment. When work is completed it is named Ledaig Distillery Ltd.

1975 – Ledaig Distillery Ltd files for bankruptcy and the distillery closes again.

1979 – The estate agent Kirkleavington Property Company of Cleckheaton buys the distillery, forms a new company, Tobermory Distillers Ltd and starts production.

1982 – No production. Some of the buildings are converted into flats and some are rented to a dairy company for cheese storage.

1989 – Production resumes.

1993 – Burn Stewart Distillers buys Tobermory for £600,000 and pays an additional £200,000 for the whisky supply.

2002 – Trinidad-based venture capitalists CL Financial buys Burn Stewart Distillers for £50m.

2005 – A 32 year old from 1972 is launched.

2007 – A Ledaig 10 year old is released.

2008 – A limited edition Tobermory 15 year old is released.

Tobermory 10 year old

DR – Barley and crystal ginger on the nose, but the palate carries this, with a nice oily mouth feel, and creamed fruits giving way to a sharper spicier conclusion.

DS – Immediately malty on the nose with a hint of brine. The palate is sweet with some honey and peppery smoke. Lavender in the long finish.

Ledaig 10 year old

DR – Peat and smoke on the nose, more fruity and malty on the palate but with a definite tarry heart, and then gristly smoke in the finish.

DS – Grass and sweet liqueur with a hint of honey on the nose. Sweet and malt and grass on the palate with a delicious waft of smoke in the finish.

From the time the first distillery was built back in 1798 until its closure in 1930, it was called Tobermory. When a new owner re-opened the distillery in 1972 it decided to call it Ledaig after the area where the distillery is built. Production from 1972 until 1989 was very intermittent and with mixed results and at least three different owners were involved during those years. When Burn Stewart bought Tobermory in 1993, the first thing they did was to revert to the old name Tobermory. A couple of years later, Master Blender Ian MacMillan came up with the idea of recreating how the original Tobermory would have tasted prior to prohibition. Production with peated malt (35ppm) brought in from Islay started in 1996 and the new whisky was called Ledaig to differentiate it from the unpeated Tobermory. Today production runs in a six day week producing 800,000 litres of alcohol with a 50/50 split between Tobermory and Ledaig.

To ensure there is no cross contamination of distillates, additional feints vessels were installed. Mashing and fermentation is similar to Tobermory's but the spirit run has a much lower cut off point for Ledaig in order to collect the rich, peaty flavours. The distillery has a cast iron mash tun, four washbacks made of Oregon pine and two pairs of stills. Storage space is small and most produce is sent to Deanston distillery on the mainland for filling and then to Bunnahabhain on Islay for maturation. However, in 2007 a part of the old tun room was converted into a small warehouse where Ian MacMillan is laying down new fill Ledaig casks in order to compare with casks being matured on Islay.

Ledaig has been launched in many different versions. The current expression of Ledaig is a *10 year old* but earlier releases included a *7 year old*, a *15 year old*, a *20 year old* and several *vintages*. For many years the only official version of Tobermory was the *10 year old* but it was supplemented in 2008 by a *15 year old* limited edition. A couple of Tobermorys from 1994 have been released by Murray McDavid lately (one with a Haut Brion finish) and there is also a 1995 by Blackadder.

10 years old

Tomatin

Owner:
Tomatin Distillery Co
(Marubeni Europe plc)

Region/district:
Highland

Founded: 1897

Status: Active (vc)

Capacity: 5 000 000 litres

Address: Tomatin, Inverness-shire IV13 7YT

Tel: 01463 248144 (vc)

website: www.tomatin.com

History:

1897 – The Inverness businessmen behind Tomatin Spey Distillery Company found Tomatin.

1906 – Production ceases.

1909 – Production resumes through Tomatin Distillers Co. Ltd.

1956 – Stills are increased from two to four.

1958 – Another two stills are added.

1961 – The six stills are increased to ten.

1964 – One more still is installed.

1974 – The stills now total 23 and the maltings closes.

1985 – The distillery company goes into liquidation.

1986 – Two long-time customers, Takara Shuzo Co. and Okara & Co., buy Tomatin through Tomatin Distillery Co. Tomatin thus becomes the first distillery to be acquired by Japanese interests.

1997 – Tomatin Distillery Co buys J. W. Hardie and the brand Antiquary.

1998 – Okara & Co, owners of 20% of Tomatin Distillery, is forced to sell its share to Takara Shuzo Co. which now is part of the Marubeni group.

2004 – Tomatin 12 years is launched.

2005 – A 25 year old and a 1973 Vintage are released.

2006 – An 18 year old and a 1962 Vintage are launched.

2008 – A 30 and a 40 year old as well as several vintages from 1975 and 1995 are released.

2009 – A 15 year old, a 21 year old and four single casks (1973, 1982, 1997 and 1999) are released.

Tomatin 12 year old

DR – Strawberry cream and raspberry ripple ice cream and pecan on the nose, delicate zesty barley on the palate, with a sweet citrus and powdery spice mix contributing to a very welcoming finish. More-ish.

DS – A rich malty, if slightly green, nose. The palate is sherried and creamy, rather like a trifle. The finish is quick but is sweet and warming.

It feels good to see a brand like Tomatin suddenly bursting into a variety of different expressions with new vintages and single cask bottlings being launched every year. Only a 10 year old existed some five years ago. It was then replaced by a 12 year old which was followed by a plethora of expressions. The brand is selling close to 200,000 bottles per year and is the sixth best selling Scotch single malt in Japan.

The distillery was founded at the end of the 19th century but it was from 1956 and the following 20 years that saw its most rapid expansion. The number of stills increased and had reached 23 by 1974. By then it was Scotland's largest distillery with a production of 12 million litres of alcohol (cf Glenfiddich which makes 10 million litres today). However it only ran at full capacity between 1975 and 1980 when it encountered financial trouble and was liquidated in 1985. Rescue came from Japan when two Japanese companies became the first to own a Scottish distillery. Today the capacity is lower with 5 million litres (actual production in 2009 is 2.6 million) as 11 of the original stills were dismantled in 2002.

The distillery is equipped with two stainless steel mash tuns (one is not being used), 12 stainless steel washbacks and six pairs of stills, all the same size (almost 17,000 litres). There are 12 racked and two dunnage (where single malts are maturing) warehouses holding 170,000 casks. The distillery also has a cooperage with two coopers working. Normally the whisky produced by Tomatin is unpeated but since 2004 a peated spirit (12ppm) has been produced the last week every year.

The larger part of production is either sold to other companies or used for their own blended whiskies but the range of single malts has increased considerably in recent years. The core range of *12 year old* (80% of sales), *18 year old* and *25 year old* was complemented by a *15 year old* in August 2009. Limited editions in 2009 included a *21 year old*, a *1999 single cask* with a *Tempranillo finish* as well as single casks from *1973, 1982* and *1997*.

15 years old

Tomintoul

Owner: **Region/district:**
Angus Dundee Distillers   Speyside

Founded: **Status:**   **Capacity:**
1964   Active   3 300 000 litres

Address: Ballindalloch, Banffshire AB37 9AQ

Tel: **website:**
01807 590274   www.tomintouldistillery.co.uk

History:
1964 –The distillery is founded by Tomintoul Distillery Ltd, which is owned by Hay & MacLeod & Co. and W. & S. Strong & Co.

1965 – On stream in July.

1973 – Scottish & Universal Investment Trust, owned by the Fraser family, buys the distillery. It buys Whyte & Mackay the same year and transfers Tomintoul to that company.

1974 – The two stills are increased to four and Tomintoul 12 years is launched.

1978 – Lonhro buys Scottish & Universal Investment Trust.

1989 – Lonhro sells Whyte & Mackay to Brent Walker.

1990 – American Brands buys Whyte & Mackay.

1996 – Whyte & Mackay changes name to JBB (Greater Europe).

2000 – Angus Dundee plc buys Tomintoul.

2002 – Tomintoul 10 year is launched as the first bottling after the change of ownership.

2003 – Tomintoul 16 years is launched.

2004 – Tomintoul 27 years is launched.

2005 – A young, peated version called Old Ballantruan is launched.

2008 – 1976 Vintage and Peaty Tang are released.

2009 – A 14 year old and a 33 year old are released.

Tomintoul 10 year old

DR – Toffee and fruit on the nose then an easy, pleasant rounded and sweet barley taste before a gently fading finish.

DS – A honeyed, citrus nose with malt and mint. The palate is sweet and earthy and bitter. The finish is oily and surprisingly peppery.

Tomintoul, a typical sixties distillery a few miles south of Glenlivet, lies in some of the most beautiful surroundings in Scotland. It is equipped with one mash tun and six washbacks, all made of stainless steel, and two pairs of stills heated by steam kettles. There are currently 15 mashes per week which means that capacity is used to the full, and the six racked warehouses have a storage capacity of 116,000 casks. The malt used for mashing is slightly peated but two weeks per year heavily peated (55 ppm) malt is used for the peated range. A blend centre was built in 2003 with ten blend vats varying in size from 10,000 bulk litres to 100,000 bulk litres.

Angus Dundee Distillers operates in the same way as several other family-owned whisky companies do, i. e. tending to their business without putting themselves in focus. Originally a whisky broker, Angus Dundee first bought Tomintoul and three years later Glencadam distillery. The company is run by 79 year old Terence "Terry" Hillman, a former Burn Stewart executive, and his two children Aaron and Tania, who are both part-owner and involved in the daily business. The core of the business is still to produce and sell blended Scotch - in fact almost 5% of all Scotch exported comes from Angus Dundee. 2007/2008 was the best year ever with a £8.9m profit on £40m sales.

Almost the whole production is used in different blended whiskies. The core range consists of *10 year old, 14 year old* (released in 2009), *16 year old* and *Old Ballantruan*, a peaty expression distilled in 2001. Limited editions include *1976 Vintage*, the oldest official Tomintoul so far, a *12 year old* with the 18 last months in Oloroso sherry butts, *Peaty Tang*, a vatting of 4-5 year old peated Tomintoul and 8 year old unpeated Tomintoul and finally, a *33 year old* released in August 2009 and replacing the 27 year old.

Independent bottlings are unusual and with the new owner being an independent itself it seems unlikely that they will become commonplace.

14 years old

Meet the Distiller

ROBERT FLEMING
DISTILLERIES DIRECTOR, TOMINTOUL AND GLENCADAM DISTILLERIES

When did you start working in the whisky business and when did you start at Tomintoul?

I started working full time in the industry in 1974 at The Glenlivet Distillery. I was a fourth generation at The Glenlivet as my father, grandfather and great-grandfather had all worked there as well as my uncle and great-uncle. I commenced at Tomintoul in 1990.

Have you been working in other lines of business before whisky?

I had a short spell in Government employment but knew early on this was not going to be my career path and that my heart was in the whisky industry.

Describe your career in the whisky business.

Started working at The Glenlivet Distillery in warehousing before covering all aspects of production. I was selected to join the Chivas' management training scheme and appointed Trainee Brewer at Benriach and Longmorn Distilleries. After a year at Benriach I was posted back to The Glenlivet as Assistant Brewer, then spent a year at the Dark Grains Plant before returning to Glenlivet as Brewer. After nearly 3 years at Glenlivet I was appointed Brewer covering Glen Keith and Strathisla distilleries. In 1990 I left Chivas to join Whyte & Mackay as Manager of Tomintoul Distillery taking on the additional role as Manager of Tamnavulin Distillery. In 2000 Angus Dundee Distillers, owned by the Hillman family, purchased Tomintoul and in 2003 purchased Glencadam Distillery from Allied Distillers. I was appointed a Director of Angus Dundee Distillers in 2003.

What are your main tasks as the Distilleries Director?

I oversee all aspects of production, warehousing and blending for the two distilleries. This includes everything from malted barley arriving to the matured whiskies leaving the sites. I also have overall responsibility for all production and warehousing administration, Health and Safety, Environmental and Revenue and Customs. I am fortunate in that at both distilleries I have a very dedicated team around me who have the same values as myself.

What are the biggest challenges of being the Distilleries Director?

There are many as new challenges occur every day. There are challenges to ensure production, warehousing and blending runs efficiently and that product quality remains a high priority. There are challenges to ensure we are compliant with all the relative legislation. There are challenges to remain within budgets.

What would be the worst that could go wrong (your worst nightmare) in the production process?

Obviously the fear of any distiller is a major incident on site which results in injury or loss of life or a major fire occurs but we have procedures in place to minimise the likelihood of such an incident. Within production any incident which results in production downtime or a loss of alcohol are never good experiences.

How would you describe the character of Tomintoul single malt?

Tomintoul range of whiskies (except our Old Ballantruan) are light and mellow and rightly identified on the bottles as 'The Gentle Dram'.

What are the main features in the distillation/maturation process at Tomintoul, contributing to this character?

The lightness mainly comes from the size / height of the copper stills and the rate of distillation. The more contact with copper the lighter the spirit.

What is your favourite expression of Tomintoul and why?

My favourite is the 16 year old as on the nose it has a honey sweetness which is combined with the delicate floral aroma plus it has a mellow taste.

If it were your decision alone – what new expression of Tomintoul would you like to see released?

Within the Tomintoul family of whiskies we have covered most ages and styles and therefore it is difficult to select an additional bottling. However during my visits to Jerez selecting sherry casks for the company I have sampled many different sherry styles and the one which stood out for me was the Pedro Ximenez which has a nose of raisins therefore a 10 year old or 16 year old finished in a PX cask would be interesting.

If you had to choose a favourite dram other than Tomintoul or Glencadam, what would that be?

Drinking whisky is all about sharing the experience with others and I could mention a few of many memories where the ambience and the company make it special and where at that moment in time I am drinking the best dram in the world. My memories include celebrating when my two children were born by sharing a Glenlivet 12yo with my Dad, watching a sunset during an evening drive in Londolozi Game Reserve in Kruger National Park in South Africa drinking 16yo Tomintoul, enjoying the sunset on the pier at Bruichladdich with their old style 15yo, in Orkney with friends overlooking Scapa Distillery enjoying a Scapa 14yo, sitting in a leather Chesterfield suite in office at Laphroaig overlooking the bay drinking their 15yo, sharing a 1983 Convalmore single cask bottling with family and friends in remembrance of my father in law who had worked there at that time.

What are the biggest changes you have seen the past 10-15 years in your profession?

The biggest changes within the industry have been the many takeovers and changes of ownership of distilleries and the merging of companies. At operational level there is more legislation in respect of health and safety and environmental issues to address and comply with.

Do you see any major changes in the next 10 years to come?

It is important to have a positive outlook because in our favour scotch whisky is renowned the world over and there will always be existing and emerging markets whether in the luxury, premium or own label sector. Therefore once the world come out of this recession we should be prepared and in a position to take advantage of those markets.

Angus Dundee is one of the big blenders as well. How does that affect your work?

Building the Blend Centres at Tomintoul and Glencadam has been one of our success stories and has added a new dimension to my work. Previously our whiskies were sent out in casks to be blended and exported by third parties but from the outset after purchasing Tomintoul in 2000 our Chairman, Mr Hillman, wanted to be more self sufficient and had the idea of building a blending facility. It was an exciting challenge transforming his vision into reality. The quality of the new spirit and the selection of casks for maturation has always been an important part of the job but now ensuring the mature whiskies are chosen and blended to the correct recipes and that the quality of the blends are to the customers satisfaction has added another layer of responsibility.

Tormore

Owner: Chivas Brothers (Pernod Ricard)

Region/district: Speyside

Founded: 1958   **Status:** Active   **Capacity:** 4 100 000 litres

Address: Tormore, Advie, Grantown-on-Spey, Morayshire PH26 3LR

Tel: 01807 510244   **website:** www.tormore.com

History:
1958 – Schenley International, owners of Long John, founds the distillery.

1960 – The distillery is ready for production.

1972 – The number of stills is increased from four to eight.

1975 – Schenley sells Long John and its distilleries (including Tormore) to Whitbread.

1989 – Allied Lyons (to become Allied Domecq) buys the spirits division of Whitbread.

1991 – Allied Distillers introduce Caledonian Malts where Miltonduff, Glendronach and Laphroaig are represented besides Tormore. Tormore is later replaced by Scapa.

2004 – Tormore 12 year old is launched as an official bottling.

2005 – Chivas Brothers (Pernod Ricard) becomes new owners through the acquisition of Allied Domecq.

Tormore 12 year old

DR – A perfumey and delicate smell on the nose and soft but pleasant palate with macaroni cake and toasted almond in the mix, and a soft fading finish.

DS – Heather and vanilla with some fruitiness and raisins on the nose. Sweet at first on the palate with soft, round flavours and shortbread. A light finish with some spiciness on the finish.

When Tormore distillery was built in the late fifties it marked the beginning of a new era in the Scotch whisky industry. The aftermath of WWII had fizzled out and while Scotch whisky production only had increased by 13% in the period from 1938 to 1955 the increase between 1955 and 1965 was as much as 230%. Optimism was high and for a newcomer to the Scottish market such as American Schenley it was important to reflect this in the establishment of their first distillery. Tormore therefore became a showpiece distillery, not the least because of its exterior which is still today unique among Scottish distilleries. The famous architect Sir Albert Richardson was contracted and the distillery cost £600,000 in total to build, which in today's currency would correspond to £10m. Tormore became the first distillery in the 20th century to be constructed from scratch (Tullibardine and Glen Keith both made use of existing buildings). Another 16 distilleries were erected during the sixties and seventies before times changed and en masse closures were a reality.

The equipment at Tormore is made up of one stainless steel lauter mash tun from Newmill Ironworks in Elgin and eight stainless steel washbacks serving four pairs of stills. All the stills are fitted with purifiers resulting in a lighter spirit. The spirit is tankered away to Keith Bonds or another Chivas Bros facilities for filling in ex-bourbon casks and part of it returns to the distillery for maturation in a combination of six palletised and racked warehouses. Tormore's role within the Chivas Brothers group of distilleries is to produce whisky for blends and there is only one official bottling, a *12 year old* introduced in 2004/05. A *15 year old* was released several years ago but has been difficult to obtain lately.

Independent bottlings of Tormore are rare and the most recent is a 12 year old distilled in 1996 and released by Douglas Laing.

12 years old

Tullibardine

Owner:
Tullibardine Distillery Ltd

Region/district:
Highlands

Founded: 1949
Status: Active (vc)
Capacity: 2 700 000 litres

Address: Blackford, Perthshire PH4 1QG

Tel: 01764 682252
website: www.tullibardine.com

History:

1949 – The architect William Delmé-Evans founds the distillery.

1953 – The distillery is sold to Brodie Hepburn.

1971 – Invergordon Distillers buys Brodie Hepburn Ltd.

1973 – The number of stills doubles from two to four.

1993 – Whyte & Mackay (owned by Fortune Brands) buys Invergordon Distillers.

1994 – Tullibardine is mothballed.

1996 – Whyte & Mackay changes name to JBB (Greater Europe).

2001 – JBB (Greater Europe) is bought out from Fortune Brands by management and changes name to Kyndal (Whyte & Mackay from 2003).

2003 – A consortium including Michael Beamish buys Tullibardine in June for £1.1 million. The distillery is in production again by December. The first official bottling from the new owner is a 10 year old from 1993.

2004 – Three new vintage malts, from 1964, 1973 and 1988 respectively, are launched. Tullibardine 1488 Shop and 1488 Café open.

2005 – Three wood finishes from 1993, Port, Moscatel and Marsala, are launched together with a 1986 John Black selection.

2006 – Vintage 1966 (plus a special World Cup version), Sherry Wood 1993 and a new John Black selection are launched.

2007 – Five different wood finishes are released as well as a couple of single cask vintages.

2008 – A Vintage 1968 40 year old is released.

Tullibardine 1993

DR – The nose is restrained with floral, almost perfumed notes, on the palate soft and gentle malt is decorated with the most delicate spice, a bit like scented talcum powder. The finish is ordered and polite, with a peaty note right at the finish.

DS – Spicy and earthy with honey and oak on the nose. More oak and honey on the palate with a long and dry finish.

Tullibardine was rescued from oblivion in 2003 when a consortium headed by former directors of DCL and United Spirits (predecessors of Diageo) Michael Beamish and Doug Ross bought the distillery and started up production after a ten year long standstill. They have since made an impressive journey and demonstrated black figures in the balance sheets already in 2007. Despite this they confirmed in summer 2008 that contacts had been made with Swiss investment bank UBS to assess various offers to buy the distillery. Since then nothing has been heard about a possible sale of the distillery which at that time was deemed worth £15m.

The distillery is equipped with a stainless steel mash tun, nine stainless steel washbacks and two pairs of stills. In the first year of operation 100,000 litres of alcohol were produced. Last year (2008) full capacity, i. e. 2.7 million litres, was reached but for 2009 the plans are to produce 1.7 million in a five-day week. Adjacent to the distillery is a huge shopping complex and more than 100,000 visitors find their way there each year.

The current range of malts from Tullibardine builds on produce from the previous owner. Included in the deal when the distillery was bought were 3,000 casks of mature whisky. It is difficult to identify a core range of bottlings from Tullibardine. The general idea is to bottle vintages and various wood finishes. Many expressions are limited editions but vintages from 1988, 1992 and 1993 have been released in larger quantities.

A series of *wood finishes* from *1993* have included bottlings of *port, marsala, sherry, moscatel, sauternes* and *rum*. Single cask *vintages* from *1973* and *1975* and a *vatted vintage* from *1988* are also a part of the special range. In 2008 the only remaining cask from 1968 was bottled as a *40 year old* (252 bottles) and in 2009 a sherry hogshead from *1988* was selected by Distillery Manager John Black to celebrate the 250th Anniversary of Robert Burns. An unexpected move was the release of *Pure Pot Spirit*, new spirit distilled in 2008.

1988 vintage

The really new ones!

Daftmill

Owner:	Region/district:	
Cuthbert family	Lowlands	
Founded:	**Status:**	**Capacity:**
2005	Active	c 65 000 litres
Address:	**Tel:**	**website:**
By Cupar, Fife KY15 5RF	01337 830303	www.daftmill.com

Permission was granted in 2003 for a steading at Daftmill Farmhouse in Fife to be converted into a distillery. Contrary to most other new distilleries selling shares in their enterprise, Hazel and Francis Cuthbert together with Francis´ brother Ian, have quietly established the distillery. The distilling license was granted on St Andrews Day 2005 and the first distillation was on 16th December that same year. It is run as a typical farmhouse distillery. The barley is grown on the farm and malted without peat at commercial maltsters. The equipment consists of a one tonne semi-lauter mash tun, two stainless steel washbacks with a 90 hour fermentation and one pair of stills with slightly ascending lyne arms. The wash still has a capacity of 3,000 litres and the spirit still 1,600 litres. The owner fill the spirit into ex-bourbon casks from Heaven Hill but also uses casks from Makers Mark and Jack Daniels. There are also a few sherry butts in the warehouse.

The establishment of Daftmill increased the number of Lowland distilleries from three to four, and with Ailsa Bay there are now five. It could have been possible to launch a 3 year old whisky already in December 2008 but the owner has not decided a launch year yet, preferring to make the launch when the whisky is considered mature enough. Daftmill Farm is not just about whisky. Besides distilling, the Cuthberts also grow potatoes and have a fine herd of beef cattle. Distilling has been irregular recently as taking care of the rest of the business on the farm (which is what is bringing in the money at the moment) takes its time.

Abhainn Dearg

Owner:	Region/district:	
Mark Tayburn	Islands (Isle of Lewis)	
Founded:	**Status:**	**Capacity:**
2008	Active	c 20 000 litres
Address:		
Carnish, Isle of Lewis, Outer Hebrides HS2 9EX		
Tel:	**website:**	
01851 672429	www.abhainndearg.co.uk	

When Kilchoman Distillery opened on Islay in 2005 it became the westernmost distillery in Scotland. This did not last for long though three years later, in September 2008, spirit flowed from a newly constructed distillery in Uig on the island of Lewis in the Outer Hebrides. The Gaelic name of this distillery is Abhainn Dearg which means Red River, and the founder and owner is Mark "Marko" Tayburn who was born and raised on the island. Very little was known about Abhain Dearg until it was suddenly ready and producing. Part of the distillery was converted from an old fish farm while some of the buildings are new. There are two 500 kg mash tuns made of stainless steel and two 7,500 litre washbacks made of Douglas fir. The two stills are modelled after an old, illicit still which is now on display at the distillery. The wash still has a capacity of 2,112 litres and the spirit still 2,057 litres. Both have very long necks and steeply descending lye pipes leading out into two wooden worm tubs. To start with Marko is using ex-bourbon barrels for maturation but

is planning for ex-sherry butts as well. The malted barley is imported from North of Scotland but he plans on using local barley in the future. This year over ten acres of the Golden Promise variety were planted.

According to plans the first whisky will be called The Spirit of Lewis with a limited launch in 2011. We will probably have to wait a couple of years more after that for a general release but Marko has decided to release a limited amount of new spirit (500 half-litre bottles) already in late 2009.

Roseisle

Owner:	Region/district:	
Diageo	Highlands	
Founded:	**Status:**	**Capacity:**
2009	Active	10 000 000 litres
Address:	**Tel:**	
Roseisle, Morayshire IV30 5YP	01343 832100	

The planning for a new mega distillery at Roseisle, a few miles west of Elgin, commenced in early 2006, and in October 2007 it was approved by Moray Council. Commissioning was planned in early 2009 with production starting in spring. The work was slightly delayed, however, and the distillery was commissioned first in spring 2009 with production commencing in early autumn. The location makes sense as the distil-

lery was built on the same grounds as the already existing Roseisle maltings. The cost was £40m and the size is huge. The equipment consists of two mash tuns, 14 stainless steel washbacks and 14 stills. The stills were manufactured by Diageo´s own coppersmiths at Abercrombies, Alloa.

But Roseisle will not only be state of the art when it comes to distilling. Green technology has been in the focus and it only emits 15% of the carbon dioxide an ordinary, same-sized distillery does. The pot ale from the distillation will be piped into anaerobic fermenters to be transformed into biogas and the dried solids will act as a biomass fuel source. Furthermore, the waste water from the distillery will be re-used in the adjacent maltings. Around 25 people work at the distillery and the output will increase Diageo´s whisky production by 10-12%.

Ailsa Bay

Owner:	Region/district:	
William Grant & Sons	Lowlands	
Founded:	**Status:**	**Capacity:**
2007	Active	6 000 000 litres
Address:	**Tel:**	
Girvan, Ayrshire KA26 9PT	01465 713091	

It was not haphazardly that William Grant constructed its new, large malt distillery at Girvan near Ayr on Scotland´s west coast. Girvan Distillery, one of seven Scottish grain distilleries with a capacity of 75 million litres, was already located there and the site also holds a giant warehousing (39 warehouses to be exact) and blending complex. It was the perfect place bearing in mind that the produce from Ailsa Bay is destined for blended whisky. There has been malt whisky distillation at Girvan before by the much smaller Ladyburn Distillery (from 1968 to 1975).

It only took nine months to build the distillery which was commissioned in September 2007. It is equipped with a 15 tonne full lauter mash tun and the eight stills are made according to the same standards as Balvenie's. A unique feature is the octangular spirit safe which sits between the two rows of stills. Each side corresponds to one specific still. Another feature is the preheater for the wash. This is in common use in Cognac where wine heaters let steam pass through the wine tank for the next distillation in order to save heat and speed up the distillation.

Using this technique at Ailsa Bay the wash enters the still preheated at 60° C.

There will be three different kinds of whisky made: a light, a more heavy and oilier and one heavily peated (responsible for circa 2% of the production).

Closed distilleries

*The following distilleries are either demolished,
closed or dismantled and the chances of any of them
producing whisky again are slim to say the least. Even so,
new bottlings are regularly released from these silent distilleries.
Most of these releases stem from independent bottlers
whom have come across casks, but some are also
bottled by the owners themselves.*

Banff

Owner:	Region:	Founded:
Diageo	Speyside	1824

Status:
Closed in 1983, partly demolished in 1985, destroyed in a fire 1991.

Bottlings:
Banff has only occurred once as an official bottling in the *Rare Malts* series when a *21 year old* from 1982 was released in 2004. Several casks have found their way to independent bottlers, among them Gordon & MacPhail, Douglas Laing, Signatory and Cadenhead. Three of the most recent are a 1976 (32 years) from Cadenhead, a 1980 (28 years) from Signatory and a 32 year old from 1975 released by Douglas Laing.

Brora

Owner:	Region:	Founded:
Diageo	N Highlands	1819

Status:
Closed in 1983.

Bottlings:
A *30 year old* was released by Diageo for the first time in 2002 and a new variety has appeared annually since then. In autumn 2008 a 25 year old was released by Diageo. Douglas Laing is known among the independents for some exceptional Broras. In autumn 2008 they released one distilled in 1981. Other recent independent bottlings include a Signatory, a Duncan Taylor and one from Ian MacLeod - all distilled in 1981.

Coleburn

Owner:	Region:	Founded:
Diageo	Speyside	1897

Status:
Closed in 1985, dismantled in 1996.

Bottlings:
Coleburn has appeared in the *Rare Malts* series once, a *21 year old* from 1979 released in 2000. This is the only existing official bottling available. Independent bottlings have also become extremely rare; a 34 year old from Douglas Laing and a 20 year old from Gordon & MacPhail appeared in 2002. After that it took until 2006 when Signatory released a 36 year old from 1970, matured in a wine treated puncheon.

Convalmore

Owner: Diageo
Region: Speyside
Founded: 1894

Status:
Closed in 1985, dismantled and buildings sold to William Grant in 1990.

Bottlings:
Diageo kept the rights to issue bottlings of Convalmore when the distillery was sold but have not taken advantage of this to a great extent. The first bottling was a *Rare Malts 24 years* from 1978 that appeared in 2003 and the second, a *28 year old Special Release*, that was launched in 2005. Independent bottlings are rare. Among the latest are a 23 year old from 1984 by Gordon & MacPhail and a 32 year old from 1975 by Douglas Laing.

Dallas Dhu

Owner: Diageo
Region: Speyside
Founded: 1898

Status:
Closed in 1983, sold to Historic Scotland in 1986 who now runs it as a museum.

Bottlings:
Apart from two releases in the *Rare Malts* series, the owners have released three bottlings for Historic Scotland in recent years. The first one was in 1998, followed by Centenerary 15 years old (1999) to commemorate the 100th anniversary of the first distilling and Millenium 25 years old (1999). Independent bottlings include Duncan Taylor 1981, Douglas Laing 1970 (37 years) and Signatory 1975 (32 years).

Glen Albyn

Owner: Diageo
Region: N Highlands
Founded: 1844

Status:
Closed in 1983, demolished in 1986.

Bottlings:
With the exception of a 10 year old from the 1970s which is reported to have been sold in Italy, there are no official bottlings except a *Rare Malt 1975* (26 years) which turned up in 2002. Independent bottlings are definitely rare. Gordon & MacPhail has released two, 1966 and 1975, both bottled in 2005. There is also a Duncan Taylor 1979, a Douglas Laing 30 year old and quite recently a Blackadder 1974 (33 years).

Glen Esk

Owner: Diageo
Region: E Highlands
Founded: 1897

Status:
Closed in 1985, dismantled in 1996, now used as maltings.

Bottlings:
It is extremely difficult to find official bottlings. Diageo has released *Hillside* as a *Rare Malt* on three occasions, the last one in 1997. There has also been a *24 year old Glenesk*. It was released in 1993 to celebrate the 25th anniversary of Glenesk maltings.
Independent bottlings have become rare. Among the more recent ones is a 26 year old Duncan Taylor from 1981.

Glenlochy

Owner: Diageo
Region: W Highlands
Founded: 1898

Status:
Closed in 1983, demolished in 1992 except for the kiln and the malt barn.

Bottlings:
Official bottlings have occurred twice in the *Rare Malts* series (released *1995* and *1996*). Douglas Laing (Old Malt Cask) released a 49 year old in 2003 and that same year Gordon & McPhail (Rare Old) released a 37 year old. More recent independents come from Signatory and Duncan Taylor, both 24 years old and bottled in 2005.

Glen Mhor

Owner: Diageo
Region: N Highlands
Founded: 1892

Status:
Closed in 1983, demolished in 1986.

Bottlings:
The only official bottlings of Glen Mhor are a couple of *Rare Malts, 22 years old* from *1979* and *28 years old* from *1976*.
Independent bottlings have become increasingly rare. Among the more recent are a 32 year old from 1975 released by Douglas Laing , Duncan Taylor 1975 (released 2009) and a 1982 by Dewar Rattray.

Glenury Royal

Owner: Diageo
Region: E Highlands
Founded: 1825

Status:
Closed in 1983 and later demolished.

Bottlings:
A couple of spectacular official bottlings have been released in recent years - a *50 year old* in 2003, a *36 year old* in 2005 and again in 2007, a *36 year old* distilled in 1970. In addition to them, Glenury Royal occurred three times in the *Rare Malts* series. Independent bottlings are few. Among recent ones are a 32 year old from 1976 by Douglas Laing, a 34 year old from 1973 by Blackadder and, from Duncan Taylor, a 1984 bottled in 2005, 2006 and 2007.

Littlemill

Owner: Loch Lomond Distillery Co.
Region: Lowlands
Founded: 1772

Status:
Closed in 1992, dismantled in 1996, later demolished.

Bottlings:
The owner is still bottling a 12 year old (used to be a 10 year old). Recent independent bottlings include a 17 year old from 1992 and a 19 year old from 1990, both released by Douglas Laing. An odd variety was also produced at Littlemill. Dunglas, distilled in 1967, was released by The Whisky Exchange in 2003.

Lochside

Owner: Chivas Brothers **Region:** E Highlands **Founded:** 1957

Status:
Closed in 1992, demolished in 2005.

Bottlings:
Official bottlings of Lochside have occurred but they are virtually impossible to get hold of.
Independent bottlings are also rare. A couple of the more recent are a Blackadder from 1981 and a 1987 released by Dewar Rattray. Douglas Laing has also released an unusual version of Lochside - a single grain from 1963 (42 years).

Millburn

Owner: Diageo **Region:** N Highlands **Founded:** 1807

Status:
Closed in 1985, dismantled in 1988.

Bottlings:
A couple of *Rare Malts* have been released by Diageo (the most recent and last in 2005, *35 years old*).
Independent bottlings are increasingly rare to encounter. Some of the most recent ones are Cadenhead 1974 (31 years), Douglas Laing 1969 (36 years), Signatory 1979 (26 years) and Blackadder 1974 (33 years).

North Port

Owner: Diageo **Region:** E Highlands **Founded:** 1820

Status:
Closed in 1983, demolished in 1993.

Bottlings:
The names North Port and Brechin are used interchange-ably on the whisky labels.
The first two official bottlings of North Port were released as *Rare Malts; 1971* (*23 years old*) and *1979* (*20 years old*). In 2005 a *28 year old* Brechin appeared as a part of Diageo's Special Release.
Independent bottlings include Signatory 1975 (29 years) and Duncan Taylor (Rarest of the Rare) 1981 (24 and 25 years respectively).

Pittyvaich

Owner: Diageo **Region:** Speyside **Founded:** 1974

Status:
Closed in 1993, demolished in 2002.

Bottlings:
The only official bottling of Pittyvaich used to be the *12 year old Flora & Fauna*. In autumn 2009 however, Pittyvaich surprisingly appeared as a 20 year old in the Special Releases. A total of 6,000 bottles were released Independent bottlings are becoming rarer. Example of recent ones are Gordon & MacPhail 1993, Duncan Taylor 1979, an 18 year old from 1990 released by Douglas Laing and a 23 year old rum finish from Cadenhead.

Port Ellen

Owner: Diageo
Region: Islay
Founded: 1825

Status:
Closed in 1983, dismantled in the 1990's.

Bottlings:
In 2001, Diageo began releasing one official bottling a year when a *22 year old cask strength* was launched. This years release (the ninth) was a 30 year old distilled in 1979.
Port Ellen is a favourite with independent bottlers. Recent ones include Douglas Laing 1983 (24 years), Signatory 1982 (25 years), Ian MacLeod 1982 (27 years) and a 27 year old from 1982 by Signatory.

Rosebank

Owner: Diageo
Region: Lowlands
Founded: 1798

Status:
Closed in 1993. Buildings sold to British Waterways and Westpoint Homes.

Bottlings:
There have been a number of official bottlings in the *Rare Malts* series and a *Flora & Fauna 12 years* can still be found. In 2007 a *25 year old*, distilled in 1981, appeared in the Special Release series. Several independent bottlers have also shown their interest in Rosebank. The most recent is a 19 year old from 1990 by Douglas Laing. Others include Gordon & MacPhail, Blackadder and Cadenheads - all from 1991 and 16 years old.

St Magdalene

Owner: Diageo
Region: Lowlands
Founded: 1795

Status:
Closed in 1983, most of the buildings converted into flats in the mid 1990's

Bottlings:
Diageo have released four bottlings the last couple of years, three as *Rare Malts* and a *30 year old Linlithgow* from 1973.
The whisky can be difficult to obtain but a 26 year old from 1982 by Douglas Laing, a 1982 Linlithgow from Single Malts of Scotland and a 26 year old distilled in 1982 from Ian MacLeod were recently released.

—————The extremely rare ones—————

Ben Wyvis - opened in 1965 and closed in 1977
Ben Wyvis is highly sought after among collectors of rare single malts. The latest release was an official bottling of a 37 year old in 2002.

Glen Flagler - opened in 1964 and closed in 1985
A major rarity. Signatory launched two Glen Flagler in the mid 1990s and Inver House released a Glen Flagler 1973 in 2003.

Glenugie - opened in 1831 and closed in 1983
No official bottling of Glenugie exists but independent bottlings occur. Among recent ones are a Duncan Taylor from 1981 and a 1982 (26 years) by Douglas Laing.

Inverleven - opened in 1938 and closed in 1991
There are no official bottlings, but recent releases from

independent bottlers include a Duncan Taylor 1979 and a 30 year old from 1977 by Signatory.

Killyloch - opened in 1964 and closed in 1975
Extremely rare. In 2003 InverHouse released a bottling from 1967.

Kinclaith - opened in 1957 and closed in 1975
There are no official bottlings. Two of the most recent and perhaps final bottlings were distilled in 1969 and released by Signatory and Duncan Taylor.

Ladyburn - opened in 1966 and closed in 1975
Two official and a couple of independent bottlings have been released since 2000, the most recent one being a Signatory 1975 and a Duncan Taylor 1973.

Distilleries per owner

c = closed, d = demolished, mb = mothballed, dm = dismantled

Diageo
Auchroisk
Banff (d)
Benrinnes
Blair Athol
Brora (c)
Bushmills
Caol Ila
Cardhu
Clynelish
Coleburn (dm)
Convalmore (dm)
Cragganmore
Dailuaine
Dallas Dhu (c)
Dalwhinnie
Dufftown
Glen Albyn (d)
Glendullan
Glen Elgin
Glenesk (dm)
Glenkinchie
Glenlochy (d)
Glenlossie
Glen Mhor (d)
Glen Ord
Glen Spey
Glenury Royal (d)
Inchgower
Knockando
Lagavulin
Linkwood
Mannochmore
Millburn (dm)
Mortlach
North Port (d)
Oban
Pittyvaich (d)
Port Ellen (dm)
Rosebank (c)
Roseisle
Royal Lochnagar
St Magdalene (dm)
Strathmill
Talisker
Teaninich

Pernod Ricard
Aberlour
Allt-a-Bhainne
Braeval
Caperdonich (mb)
Glenallachie
Glenburgie
Glen Keith (mb)
Glenlivet
Glentauchers
Imperial (c)
Inverleven (d)
Lochside (d)
Longmorn
Miltonduff
Scapa

Strathisla
Tormore

Edrington Group
Glenrothes
Glenturret
Highland Park
Macallan
Tamdhu

Inver House (Thai Beverage)
Balblair
Balmenach
Glen Flagler (d)
Knockdhu
Pulteney
Speyburn

John Dewar & Sons (Bacardi)
Aberfeldy
Aultmore
Craigellachie
Macduff
Royal Brackla

Whyte & Mackay (United Spirits)
Dalmore
Fettercairn
Jura
Tamnavulin

William Grant & Sons
Ailsa Bay
Balvenie
Glenfiddich
Kininvie
Ladyburn (dm)

Glenmorangie Co. (Moët Hennessy)
Ardbeg
Glenmorangie

Morrison Bowmore (Suntory)
Auchentoshan
Bowmore
Glen Garioch

Burn Stewart Distillers (CL Financial)
Bunnahabhain
Deanston
Tobermory

Loch Lomond Distillers
Glen Scotia
Littlemill (d)
Loch Lomond

Angus Dundee Distillers
Glencadam
Tomintoul

Long John Whitbread
Glenugie (dm)
Kinclaith (d)

J & A Mitchell
Glengyle
Springbank

Beam Global Spirits & Wine
Ardmore
Laphroaig

Benriach Distillery Co.
Benriach
Glendronach

Campari Group
Glen Grant

Isle of Arran Distillers
Arran

Signatory Vintage Scotch Whisky Co.
Edradour

Ian Macleod Distillers
Glengoyne

Tomatin Distillery Co. (Marubeni Europe plc)
Tomatin

J & G Grant
Glenfarclas

Bruichladdich Distillery Co. (Murray McDavid)
Bruichladdich

Co-ordinated Development Services
Bladnoch

Gordon & MacPhail
Benromach

Glenglassaugh Distillery Co Ltd (Scaent Group)
Glenglassaugh

La Martiniquaise
Glen Moray

Ben Nevis Distillery Ltd (Nikka)
Ben Nevis

Tullibardine Distillery Ltd
Tullibardine

Speyside Distillers Co.
Speyside

Cooley Distillery plc
Cooley
Kilbeggan

Kilchoman Distillery Co.
Kilchoman

Cuthbert family
Daftmill

Mark Tayburn
Abhainn Dearg

Single malts from Japan

Hakushu Distillery

Two events were indicative of different scenarios on the Japanese whisky market in 2009. On the positive side was the release of Suntory´s Hibiki 12 year old blended whisky. The Hibiki brand was first introduced 20 years ago and has been available as 17, 21 and 30 year olds. So why the fuzz over another Hibiki? Well, the interesting thing this time is that it was released first in Europe in May while the Japanese had to wait until autumn to get their hands on it. This shows the commitment from Japanese whisky producers, also confirmed by Suntory officials, to increase the export market. So good news for all lovers of Japanese malts living outside Japan.

On the negative side was the news that Suntory and Kirin Brewery were negotiating a possible merger of the companies before the end of 2009. Suntory has 13% of the domestic market for beer and Kirin 37%. If we look at the whisky segment it gets even scarier with Suntory holding 70% and Kirin 10%.

The uncertainty of how a possible merger would affect the Japanese whisky industry is huge but it is sure that one dominant player would control most of the market if it took place. Fingers crossed that the second scenario will not result in closed distilleries or a reduction of new, exciting bottlings being released.

The contents in the following pages is based on Hideo Yamaoka´s texts from previous editions of Malt Whisky Yearbook with additional updates where relevant. We would like to recommend two sources for a deeper insight. First of all a book devoted solely to Japanese whisky, *Japanese Whisky - facts, figures and taste* by Ulf Buxrud (ISBN 978-91-633-2093-4). In order to be updated on the most recent developments we can recommend Chris Bunting´s blog *www.nonjatta.blogspot.com*. A new book by Chris to be published in 2010 should also be consulted. The working title is Drinking Japan and it will cover all the main types of alcohol in Japan, not least whisky.

Chichibu

Owner:	Founded:	Capacity:
Ichiro Akuto	2008	90 000 litres

Malt whisky range:
none

Eight years after the first Chichibu distillery or Hanyu as it is often called, had to close, the grandson of the founder, Ichiro Akuto, opened the first new whisky distillery in Japan since 1973. In spring 2008 he started distilling at his Chichibu distillery two hours northwest of Tokyo. According to tradition and in order to bring fortune to the future distillery, before building started two years ago, a local Shinto priest visited the site in order to conduct a Jichinsau ground breaking ceremony.

Ichiro Akuto uses two types of malt for the production, one imported from Germany and one from England but his goal is to become self-sustaining in the future and he has even found a source for peat in the vicinity. The distillery is equipped with a mash tun, five washbacks made of Japanese Oak and one pair of stills made by Forsyth´s in Scotland. Until the whisky is ready to sell, Akuto has released new make spirit which is only a few months old. The first releases, which appeared in 2008, had been maturing in ex-bourbon barrels and new American Oak and were bottled at 62-64%.

Eigashima

Owner:	Founded:	Capacity:
Eigashima Shuzo	1919	60 000

Malt whisky range:
White Oak Single Malt 8 years old

Eigashima Shuzo is primarily a maker of sake and shochu and full-scale whisky production did not commence until 1984 when they built the current distillery located in Akashi near Kobe in Hyogo Prefecture.

Japanese microdistillery whiskies were very popular in Japan in the early 1980s, keeping the Eigashima Distillery in operation around the clock. However, the shochu boom of the mid 1980s, the revision of Japan's Liquor Tax Law in 1989 and the decline in prices of imports took their toll and demand dropped and continues at a low level. It now produces malt whisky only once a year.

The distillery is equipped with a semi-lauter mash tun, four stainless steel washbacks, one wash still (5,000 litres) and one spirit still (2,500 litres).

Most of the malt whisky is matured in sherry hogsheads which previously held Scotch malt whisky, but they also have peated malt whisky which has been maturing in sherry butts for over 10 years. The average length of maturation is 4 years. The maturation warehouses are beside the sea and it is very hot in the summer. Annual loss to the angels' share is between 7% and 8 %.

All the malt whisky produced goes to the blend, "White Oak", in which it is mixed with no age grain spirit from the USA or their own shochu. An exception was made in 2007 when 4,500 bottles of an 8 year old single malt were released.

Fuji-Gotemba

Owner:	Founded:	Capacity:
Kirin Holdings	1973	12 000 000 litres (incl grain whisky)

Malt whisky range:
Fuji-Gotemba Single Malt 18 year old, Fuji-Sanroku Single Malt 18 year old, Fuji-Gotemba Single Cask 10 year old.

The location of Fuji-Gotemba Distillery is unrivalled by the foot of Mount Fuji. In 2002, Kirin Brewery became the sole owner of the distillery, and in 2007 they also acquired Mercian including its Karuizawa Distillery. However, Kirin currently has no plans to release a blend using malt whisky from both Fuji-Gotemba and Karuizawa.

The distillery is equipped with one stainless steel semi-lauter mash tun, six stainless steel washbacks and two pairs of pot stills. There is also a continuous still for grain whisky production, a bottling plant and a cooperage. It was founded by Kirin-Seagram in 1973. Kirin-Seagram was a joint venture of Kirin Brewery (Japan), Seagram´s (USA) and Chivas Brothers (UK). The premium blend "Evermore", versions of which had been released every year from 1999 to 2005, used to contain the same vatted malt as that used in Chivas Regal, but matured in Japan and blended with malt and grain whisky produced at Fuji-Gotemba.

The whisky is marketed under two names: Fuji-Gotemba and Fuji-Sanroku (the latter meaning "At the feet of Fuji"). Both brands are represented by 18 year olds but Fuji-Sanroku is twice the price as it also contains 24 year old whisky. In 2007 the first six single casks were released by the distillery. The ABVs were around 43-46% but they are all cask strength. The cask filling strength was around 50.5%.

Hakushu

Owner:	Founded:	Capacity:
Suntory	1973	3 000 000 litres

Malt whisky range:
Hakushu Single Malt 10, 12, 18 and 25 year old.

The second distillery, Hakushu, was built by Suntory fifty years after their first, Yamazaki. The distillery is known as the "Forest Distillery" because it was constructed within a dense green forest covering the foothills of Mount Kaikomagatake in Yamanashi Prefecture.

In 1981 on the same grounds, a new distillery, Hakushu East, was built. The old distillery, Hakushu West was mothballed in 2006 but for a period in the eighties both complexes with 36 stills in total were producing and at that time it was the largest distillery in the world.

Although the original lantern-shaped pot stills of Hakushu East were smaller than those of Hakushu West, some have been replaced with even smaller pot stills. Hakushu East has a wide variety of pot stills enabling it to produce many different styles of spirit. There are pot stills with different sizes and shapes, different lyne arm configurations and both direct-fired (using natural gas) and indirect-heated stills. The No.3 wash still has a cast iron worm tub while all the other stills have shell-and-tube condensers. The

distillery is also equipped with a full lauter mash tun and ten washbacks made of Oregon pine.

Some of Hakushu's malt whiskies are filtered after maturation using bamboo charcoal giving it a rounded character. These are used in the blended whisky, "Zen". Recently Hakushu has started releasing heavily peated versions, both bottled at 48% and single casks at cask strength.

Hanyu

Owner:	Founded:	Capacity:
Toa Shuzo	1941	Dismantled

Malt whisky range:
Ichiro´s Malt 15 and 20 year old, Ichiro´s Malt Vintage 1988, Ichiro´s Malt Card Series (single casks distilled from 1985 to 2000), Hanyu 1990 17yo (Japanese oak Cask)

Toa Shuzo, a maker of sake and shochu, built Hanyu distillery in Saitama Prefecture in 1946 and began full-scale whisky distillation in 1983. However, the company was sold and the new owner demolished the distillery in 2004. They also planned to discard about 400 casks of malt whisky left in storage but Ichiro Akuto, the grandson of the original founder of Toa Shuzo, arranged to have the casks transferred to Sasanokawa Shuzo, a sake maker in Fukushima Prefecture which once had made whisky and which had an empty warehouse.

Akuto established "Venture Whisky" in 2004 and began to release Hanyu single cask bottlings under the name Ichiro's Malt in 2005. Ichiro's Malt 1988 with the "King of Diamonds" label won top honors in the Japanese whisky tasting in "Whisky Magazine" in 2006. In the same tasting in 2007, the "King of Spades" label bottling was awarded top honors and the "Ace of Hearts" and "Two of Clubs" (finished in Japanese oak) were runners up. A couple of Akuto´s

most recent bottlings are "Ace of Diamonds" 1986, "Ten of Clubs" 1990, "Eight of Hearts" 1991 and "Five of Spades" 2000.

During spring 2008 Akuto started distilling at his new distillery at Chichibu Midori-gaoka in Saitama Prefecture. Read more under Chichibu on page 205.

Karuizawa

Owner:	Founded:	Capacity:
Kirin Holdings	1955	150 000 litres

Malt whisky range:
Karuizawa 15 and 17 year old, Karuizawa Wine Cask 12 year old, Karuizawa Vintage (1982, 1988, 1986, 1973 and 1972).

Karuizawa Distillery, located in the mountain resort town of Karuizawa, and its parent company, Mercian, were acquired by Kirin Holdings in September 2007. Going forward, cooperation between Kirin's Fuji-Gotemba Distillery and Karuizawa Distillery is expected.

The distillery is equipped with two mash tuns, eight washbaks (five wooden and three made of stainless steel) and two pairs of stills. The capacity of each pot still is only 4,000 litres. The malt whisky is matured mainly in sherry casks. All the casks are stored in racked warehouses. There is also one new racked warehouse which is unique because the movement of casks on the racks is automated. The distillery has a capacity of 150,000 litres but has been mothballed since 2001. Occasional production has occured since then, for example Ichiro Akuto´s Peated Golden Promise, released in 2006. The owner, Kirin Holdings, is the largest beer producer in Japan and during summer 2009 it has been in negotiations

with Suntory on a possible merger of the two companies.

In 2007, Karuizawa Wine Cask 12 years old was released to commemorate the 12th anniversary of the museum which is on the site of the distillery. It was sold in the distillery shop and sold out quickly.

In 2008, Karuizawa 1973 was released and in 2009, the English importer Number One Drinks' own bottling, Karuizawa No 1 1972 with a maturation in American White Oak.

Miyagikyo

Owner: Nikka
Founded: 1969
Capacity: 5 000 000 litres

Malt whisky range:
Miyagikyo Single Malt 10, 12 and 15 year old, Miyagikyo Single Cask 1987.

Miyagikyo Distillery, also known as Sendai Distillery, is one of three active whisky distilleries belonging to Nikka. The others are Yoichi malt whisky distillery and Tochigi grain distillery.

When the distillery was built in 1969, two pairs of pot stills were installed. The capacity of the wash stills is 15,500 litres and that of the spirit stills is 12,500 litres. In 1976, two more pairs of stills were installed with the capacity of the wash stills being 25,500 litres and that of the spirit stills 18,500 litres. The malt is flowery and fruity. This is said to be due partly to the fact that the pot stills have boil balls and the lyne arms are slanted slightly upwards. All the stills are steam-heated and use shell-and-tube condensers. There are also two full lauter mash tuns and 22 stainless steel washbacks

Miyagikyo also has Coffey stills, which are now rare even in Scotland. They were moved from the Nishinomiya distillery in 1999. Sometimes they are used to distill wash which is made using only malted barley. This resulted in an exciting bottling a couple of years

ago called Nikka Coffey Malt 12 years old. The whisky for this release was actually made at Nishinomiya before the stills were moved to Miyagikyo. Single malt from Miyagikyo has become known in Europe not least for its single cask vintages. The most recent was a 1986, bottled in 2008.

Shinshu

Owner: Hombo Shuzo
Founded: 1960
Capacity: Mothballed in 1994

Malt whisky range:
Komogatake 10 year old, Komogatake Single Cask 1986 and 1989, Mars Singe Cask 1985, 1986, 1988, 1989, 1991.

Hombo Shuzo, a maker of shochu, built the Yamanashi Distillery in 1960, moved it to Miyata in 1980 and renamed it Shinshu. The brand name of the whisky is Mars. The whisky part of the production at Shinshu stopped in 1994 and there are currently no plans to restart production. Only some 100 casks of malt whisky are still left. There is a distillery tour and a few limited single cask bottlings are available only at the distillery shop.

Hombo Shuzo also has a shochu distillery, Kagoshima Distillery, where they did trial production of peated malt whisky from 1982 to 1984. The capacity of the pot stills was only 500 litres each. Maltage 8 year old is pure malt whisky whose components are this peated malt and the malt from Shinshu Distillery.

Shinshu distillery is equipped with one full lauter mash tun, five cast iron washbacks and one pair of stills. Kiichiro Iwai, who designed the stills, was at one time the boss of Masataka Taketsuru, the founder of Nikka, when they worked at the Japanese sake maker, Settsu Shuzo. This was before Taketsuru

went to Scotland to study whisky production. When Taketsuru returned to Japan, he showed Iwai his "Taketsuru Report" about whisky production in Scotland. The neck shape of the pot still is a straight head like that of Yoichi, which Taketsuru started. The capacity of the distillery is 95,000 litres per year.

Yoichi

Owner:	Founded:	Capacity:
Nikka	1934	5 000 000 litres

Malt whisky range:
Single Malt Yoichi 10, 12, 15 and 20 year old, Nikka Single Cask 1987, 1988.

Yoichi, (also known as Hokkaido Distillery) is the only distillery on the island of Hokkaido and is also the most northern of Japan's distilleries. It was founded in 1934 by Masataka Taketsuru, father of whisky making in Japan, who had previously studied whisky production in Scotland.

Yoichi has developed its own production technique by using first fill and refill new wood American oak casks (i.e. not previously seasoned with other spirits or wines). Yoichi chars the new casks to lower the amount of the woody pencil-shavingslike flavour that is imparted to the whisky by the new wood.

The distillery is equipped with one semi-lauter mash tun, ten stainless steel washbacks, four wash stills (directly fired using coal) and two spirit stills (indirectly heated). All stills but one use cast iron worm tubs for cooling the spirit vapours. Yoichi is the only malt whisky distillery in the world to have direct coal-fired stills. The last distillery in Scotland to have coal-fired stills, Glendronach, switched to steam heating in 2005.

First fill new wood casks have been used for several notable single cask bottlings of Yoichi, including the bottling that received the highest rating in Whisky Magazine's 2001 "Best of the Best" blind tasting.

There are other exciting ranges connected with Nikka and Yoichi. Taketsuru blended malts (12, 17, 21 and the recently released 35 year old) and Nikka All Malt which is a blend of malt whisky from Yoichi and Miyagikyo distilled in pot stills and malt whisky from Miyagikyo distilled in a Coffey still.

Yamazaki

Owner:	Founded:	Capacity:
Suntory	1923	3 500 000 litres

Malt whisky range:
Yamazaki 10, 12, 18, 25, 35 and 50 year old., various vintages.

Yamazaki is the oldest working distillery in Japan and is owned by the huge Suntory Corporation which is responsible for 70% of domestic whisky sales and is also a large beer producer. Negotiations are taking place over a merger with Kirin Brewery (Japan´s biggest brewing company which also owns Karuizawa and Fuji-Gotemba distilleries) which could lead to a group that would control half of the Japanese beer market and 80% of the whisky market. Yamazaki is the most sold Japanese single malt brand and was ranked number 13 in the world in terms of sold cases in 2008 .

The distillery is equipped with two wooden mash tuns, 18 wooden washbacks and six pairs of stills. Three of the wash stills are directly fired using gas while all the others are indirectly heated with steam pans and steam coils.

New releases in Europe in autumn 2008 were Cask of Yamazaki 1993, a heavily peated single cask and Cask of Yamazaki 1990, sherry-matured. The most interesting release in 2009 was the Yamazaki 1984

to celebrate the 25th anniversary of the first Yamazaki Single Malt. Part of the whisky has been maturing in Japanese "mizunara"oak (see page 187). This vintage is limited to 2,000 bottles in Japan, 300 in the USA and 200 in Europe.

Another new release was Suntory´s blend, Hibiki 12 years old, launched in Europe in May, actually ahead of the Japanese launch.

Distilleries
around the globe

Malt whisky distilling has long since stopped being just a Scottish concern. Follow us on an exciting journey to distilleries from all corners of the world.

The Kavalan Distillery, Taiwan

The harsh, global financial climate has affected the start-up of new distilleries. Several projects have been delayed but the ability to find risk capital still impresses and a number of new distilleries have actually come to light since 2008.

A couple of these can be found in the USA where *New Holland Brewing* released a single malt just before the New Year while *Ellensburg Distillery* will release its first whiskey in November. In the meantime there are a number of exciting ventures where we can expect malt whiskey within the near future. One of these is *Balcones Distillery* in Waco, Texas which was commissioned as recently as early 2009. In July the owner, Chip Tate, released his first spirit, a rum-based liqueur, but he has already started to distil a whiskey using peated malt. In Maine, *Penobscot Distillery* is teaming up with Winterport Winery and, having already opened up the Penobscot Brewery in spring 2009, the distillery is expected to come on stream in autumn 2009. Single malt whiskey will be one of its products. Bryan and Kari Schultz of *RoughStock Distillery* in Bozeman, Montana have managed to go one step further; the release of their

first single malt whiskey seems imminent as they have been producing for some time now.

Back in Europe, the Swedes are eagerly waiting for their third whisky distillery to come on stream. The question is which one it will be? *BOX Distillery* and *Grythyttan Whisky* both made successful issues of new shares during spring 2009 to obtain funds and each calculate starting up in 2010.

In neighbouring Denmark the first purpose-built whisky distillery, *Stauning*, started producing in May. There are already plans for another distillery in Farre on Jutland where Jens Erik Jørgensen hopes to commence sometime in 2009.

In England, *The English Whisky Company* in Norfolk released its first whisky after having tempted potential customers for some time with releases of young spirit from the distillery. A couple of new distilleries in Germany also launched their first products, for example *Gerhard Liebl Jr.* with his 3 year old *Collimor*, and in France, *Jean Donnay* of *Glann ar Mor Distillery* in Brittany released his first single malt in autumn 2008.

We can announce a Malt Whisky Yearbook first in a distillery from Taiwan. *Kavalan Distillery* is, admittedly, not completely new as it started producing already in 2006, but in the end of 2008 and during 2009 the first bottlings found their way onto the markets. It is far from a micro distillery as it has capacity of producing over 2 million litres per year. An even larger distillery and also new in this year's edition is *DYC* in Spain. Although established back in the fifties it was not until this year that it released its first single malt which is why we afford DYC a more detailed presentation here.

The developments in Australia continue to impress. In Tasmania the omnipresent Bill Lark has taken part in forming the Tasmanian Distillers Group which consists of the state's six distilleries (the latest is *Mackey's Distillery* at New Town). Lark is also co-owner of the newest distillery to come on stream, this time on the mainland - *Victoria Valley* in Melbourne.

So, it is quite obvious that the family of malt whisky distillers around the world is growing every year, some of which swear by the old Scottish methods while others see no limits for how a whisky could be produced.

*Ian Chang, Chief Blender
Kavalan Distillery, Taiwan*

EUROPE

Austria

DISTILLERY: Waldviertler Roggenhof,
Roggenreith
FOUNDED: 1995
OWNER/MANAGER: Johann & Monika Haider
www.roggenhof.at

In the small village of Roggenreith in northern Austria, Johann and Monika Haider have been distilling whisky since 1995. In 2005 they opened up a Whisky Experience World with guided tours, a video show, whisky tasting and exhibitions. Roggenhof was the first whisky distillery in Austria and the in the first year 1,000 litres were distilled. The quantity increased every year and reached 30,000 litres in 2006.

The wash is allowed to ferment for 72 hours before it reaches either of the two 450 litre Christian Carl copper stills. The desired strength is reached in one single distillation thanks to an attached column.

The new make is filled in casks made of the local Manhartsberger Oak adding a slight vanilla flavour and left to mature for three years. When the casks are used a second time, the whisky matures for five years. The casks are used a third time, but only after dismantling, shaving and charring before filling. Spirit on third fill casks is expected to mature for 12-18 years. A new warehouse was commissioned in June 2009 so there is now storage capacity for almost 3,000 barrels which the owners believe will fill the requirements of the next ten years. Two single malts made of barley are available: Gersten Malzwhisky J. H. (light malt) and Gersten Malzwhisky J. H. Karamell (dark, roasted malt). There are also three different rye whiskies. New expressions are planned for 2011 when two peated, dark roasted varieties (one rye and one single malt) will be launched.

DISTILLERY: Destillerie Weutz,
St. Nikolai im Sausal
FOUNDED: 2002
OWNER/MANAGER: Michael & Brigitte Weutz
www.weutz.at

This family distillery, initially producing schnapps and liqueur from fruits and berries, is situated in Steiermark in the south of Austria. In 2004 Michael Weutz started cooperation with the brewer Michael Löscher and since then Weutz has added whisky to its produce based on the wash from the brewery. The business grew quickly and in 2006 the distillery moved to a bigger location. Since 2004, 14 different malt whiskies have been produced. Some of them are produced in the traditional Scottish style: Hot Stone, St.Nikolaus and the peated Black Peat. Others are more unorthodox, for example Green Panther, in which 5% pumpkin seeds are added to the mash,

and Franziska based on elderflower. Apart from barley wheat, corn and spelt are also used for some expressions.

Annual production is currently at approximately 14,000 litres and for maturation casks made of French Limousin and Alliere oak are used. So far the whisky is only available for purchase in Austria.

DISTILLERY: Wolfram Ortner Destillerie,
Bad Kleinkirchheim
FOUNDED: 1990
OWNER/MANAGER: Wolfram Ortner
www.wob.at

Fruit brandies of all kinds are Wolfram Ortner´s main produce as well as cigars, coffee and other luxuries. For the last few years he has also been producing malt whisky. New oak of different kinds (Limousin, Alolier, Nevers, Vosges and American) is used for the maturation process. His first single malt, WOB DÖ MALT Vergin, began selling in 2001 and an additional product line, in which Ortner mixes his whisky with other distillates such as orange/moscatel, is called WOB Marriage.

DISTILLERY: Reisetbauer, Kirchberg-Thening
FOUNDED: 1994 (whisky since 1995)
OWNER/MANAGER: Julia & Hans Resisetbauer
www.reisetbauer.at

This is a family-owned farm distillery near Linz in northern Austria. It specialises in brandies and fruit schnapps but has included single malt whisky in its range since 1995. The distillery is equipped with five 350 litre stills. All stills are heated using hot water rather than steam which, according to Hans Reisetbauer, allows for a more delicate and gentle distillation. Approximately 20,000 litres of pure alcohol destined for whisky making are produced annually, using local barley to make the malt. The malt is dried without the use of peat due to Austrian health regulations as phenols are believed to be carcinogenic. Casks are sourced locally from the best Austrian wine producers. The whisky is filled the same day the wine casks have been emptied

Reisetbauer 12 year old

in order to save aromas from oxidation and to avoid the use of SO$_2$.

In 2002, the first 6 year old was released. The current range includes a 7 year old single malt which consists of a vatting of whiskies aged in casks that have previously contained Chardonnay and Trockenbeerenauslese. There is also a 10 year old cask strength aged exclusively in Trockenbeerenauslese. In September 2008, the range was expanded with the first ever Austrian 12 year old single malt which has also undergone maturation in Trockenbeerenauslese barrels.

Belgium

DISTILLERY: The Owl Distillery, Grâce Hollogne
FOUNDED: 1997
OWNER/MANAGER: Etienne Bouillon (manager),
Luc Foubert and Pierre Roberti
www.belgianwhisky.com
www.thebelgianowl.com

In 2007, Belgium's first single malt was finally bottled. The casks were filled on 29th October 2004 and in late October 2007 Etienne Bouillon released his first 400 bottles of 'The Belgian Owl' as the whisky was named. The next bottling came in June 2008 but was exclusively reserved for customers. The first commercial bottling to be available in shops was the third, made in November 2008, and in February 2009 another 2,766 bottles were released. Bouillon expects to produce around 24,000 bottles annually with five releases per year. A special cask strength expression will also be launched the end of 2009.

The distillery is equipped with a mash tun holding 4.1 tonnes per mash, one washback where the wash is fermented for 60-100 hours and finally one wash still (550 litres) and one spirit still (450 litres).

Every step of production (including malting) is carried out at the distillery near Liege and maturation takes place in first fill bourbon casks from Kentucky. The whisky is neither coloured nor chill-filtered. At the moment, The Belgian Owl is sold in Belgium, The Netherlands, France, Germany and from this autumn also in Sweden.

DISTILLERY: Het Anker Distillery, Blaasfeld
FOUNDED: 1369 (whisky since 2003)
OWNER/MANAGER: Charles Leclef (owner),
Ali Bosmans (distillery manager)
www.hetanker.be

It all started with the producer of the quality beer Gouden Carolus, Brouwerij Het Anker, and its owner Charles Leclef wanting to have a malt whisky made of the wash from the brewery. The result was Gouden Carolus Single Malt which is the third Belgian malt whisky to reach the market after Belgian Owl and Goldlys. The release of the first 2,000 bottles was in January 2008. Late 2008 saw the release of a Connoiseur´s Pack with 5 cl new make, 20 cl 1 year old spirit and 35 cl 3 year old whisky. The next release will probably take place at the end of 2010.

Inspired by the success, Leclef decided to build a brand new whisky distillery with pot stills. The location chosen was not by the brewery in Mechelen but at Leclef´s family estate Molenberg at Blaasfeld. Leclef is the fifth generation of a family that long since has been involved in jenever distilling and beer brewing. The distillery will be built during 2009, the stills from Forsyth´s will arrive in October and Distillery Manager Ali Bosmans hopes to distil the first spirit at midnight on 31st December. The wash still will have a size of 3,000 litres and the spirit still 2,000 litres with the capacity of making 100,000 litres of alcohol per year. A museum, park and visitor centre will be built adjoining the distillery.

Etienne Bouillon of The Owl Distillery with his first release

Ali Bosmans, manager of Het Anker nosing his Carolus Single Malt

Czech Rebulic

DISTILLERY: Gold Cock Distillery
FOUNDED: 1877
OWNER/MANAGER: Rudolf Jelinek a.s
www.rjelinek.cz

The distilling of Gold Cock whisky started already in 1877. Gold Cock was originally a malt whisky made from abundunt local barley. Now it is produced in two versions – a 3 year old blended whisky and a 12 year old malt. Production was stopped for a while but after the brand and distillery were acquired by R. Jelinek a.s, the leading Czech producer of plum brandy, the whisky began life anew. The malt whisky is double distilled in 500 litre traditional pot stills. The new owner has created a small whisky museum which is also home to the club Friends of Gold Cock Whisky with private vaults, where any enthusiast can store his bottlings of Gold Cock.

Denmark

DISTILLERY: Stauning Whisky, Stauning
FOUNDED: 2006
OWNER/MANAGER:
www.stauningwhisky.dk

The first true malt whisky distillery in Denmark has now entered a more adolescent phase after having experimented with two small pilot stills bought from Spain. In May 2009 two new, Portugal-made stills of 1,000 and 600 litres respectively were in place and the fledging phase of the distillery could start.

The aim has always been to be self-sustaining and Danish barley is bought and turned into malt on an own malting floor. The germinating barley usually has to be turned 6-8 times a day but Stauning has constructed an automatic "grain turner" to do the job. Two core expressions were decided on - Peated Reserve and Traditional Reserve - and the peat for the first one is acquired from one of few remaining peat bogs in Denmark. Most of production is stored in first fill ex-bourbon barrels from Makers Mark. There is also opportunity for some experimenting with sherry butts, Port pipes and casks made of new French oak.

A first, limited editions of 750 bottles each of the two expressions will be released in May 2012. The annual production is roughly 7,000 litres, which will subsequently be expanded.

DISTILLERY: Braunstein, Køge
FOUNDED: 2005 (whisky since 2007)
OWNER/MANAGER: Michael & Claus Braunstein
www.braunstein.dk

Denmark's first micro distillery was built in an already existing brewery in Køge, just south of Copenhagen. The distillation process is special as the spirit is distilled only once and a column still is used. The purpose of this, according to the owners Michael and Claus Braunstein, is to produce an extremely clean spirit. The Braunstein brothers filled their first spirit in a 225 litre ex-Oloroso sherry cask in March 2007 and for the second edition in December 2007 they used a 190-litre ex-bourbon cask.

The first bottling, Edition No. 1, will be released 22nd March 2010 and is already sold out. Edition No. 2 (peated) is due for release in December 2010. Beer and different kinds of schnapps are also produced at Braunstein.

DISTILLERY: Ørbæk Bryggeri, Ørbæk
FOUNDED: 1997 (whisky since 2007)
OWNER/MANAGER: Niels and Nicolai Rømer
www.oerbaek-bryggeri.nu

The combination of microbrewery and microdistillery is apparently a fruitful one and not that surprising

Floor maltings at Stauning Distillery with the clever, automatic grain-turner

as an existing brewery can easily produce the wash which is required in the distillation process to make whisky. This was also the idea of Niels Rømer and his son Nicolai who have run Ørbæk Brewery since 1997 on the Danish island of Fyn. The whisky, in common with their beer, will be ecological and two different expressions are planned for release in 2010 - Isle of Fionia and the peated Fionia Smoked Whisky. It is matured on ex-bourbon barrels from Jack Daniels and ex-sherry casks. Within five years the estimated yearly production will amount to 10-20,000 bottles.

England

DISTILLERY: St. George´s Distillery,
Roudham, Norfolk
FOUNDED: 2006
OWNER/MANAGER: The English Whisky Co.
www.englishwhisky.co.uk

St. George´s Distillery near Thetford in Norfolk was started by father and son, James and Andrew Nelstrop, and came on stream on 12th December 2006. This made them the first English malt whisky distillery for over a hundred years. The legendary Iain Henderson, formerly of Laphroaig and Edradour, joined in for the start-up but was succeeded as distillery manager in July 2007 by ex-brewer David Fitt. Customers, both in the UK and abroad, have had the opportunity to follow the development of the whisky via releases of new make as well as 18 months old spirit, both peated and unpeated. These have been called Chapters 1 to 4. Finally, in December 2009, it was time for the release of the first whisky - unpeated and without chill filtering or colouring. Finding the bottles in the local whisky shop may prove quite difficult though, as only 349 cases with 6 bottles each were released and most of them were destined for pre-orders. Next release will be in May 2010 when 390 cases of the peated version enter the market.

Production has increased to 150,000 bottles this year and important markets are Benelux, France, Scotland, Japan, Singapore and England.

The distillery is equipped with a stainless steel semi-lauter mash tun with a copper top and three stainless steel washbacks with a fermentation of 85 hours. There is one pair of stills, the wash still with a capacity of 2,800 litres and the spirit still of 1,800 litre capacity. First fill bourbon barrels are mainly used for maturation but the odd sherry, Madeira and Port casks have also filled. The casks are stored in a dunnage warehouse on site and a second warehouse will be constructed in late 2009. Non-peated malt is bought from Crisp Malting Group and peated malt from Simpson´s Malt in Berwick-upon-Tweed. Around 60% of production is unpeated and the rest is peated. Recently a bottling line was installed giving St. George's the possibility to bottle with its own water source. The capacity is 800 bottles per day.

A visitor centre opened in the summer of 2007 and already receives 25,000 visitors a year.

DISTILLERY: The Cornish Cyder Farm,
Penhallow, Cornwall
FOUNDED: 2003 (whisky production)
OWNER/MANAGER: David Healy
www.thecornishcyderfarm.co.uk

At the Cornish Cyder Farm 80,000 gallons of apple juice is pressed each year. Most of it becomes cider but c 10,000 gallons are made into wine and fruit juices. A distillery was opened quite recently in 2000 in which cider is distilled to apple brandy in a pot still. It then became the first distillery in Cornwall for

Stillroom at St George´s Distillery and a bottle of the Third Chapter of single malt spirit

300 years. There is only one small still (1,200 litres) in use although the brandy is double distilled and then matured in oak casks.

Five years ago Cornish Cyder Farm together with St Austell Brewery attempted to produce whisky. Wash from the brewery was distilled on the farm resulting in 400 litres of spirit. This seemingly one-off attempt has become an annual occurence. There are no plans for bottling in the next few years but those who have tested the latest new make claim it is much improved compared to the first trials. The first release is expected in 2011.

Finland

DISTILLERY: Teerenpeli, Lahti
FOUNDED: 2002
OWNER/MANAGER: Anssi Pyysing
www.teerenpeli.com

The first Teerenpeli Single Malt was sold as a 3 year old in late 2005, though solely at the owner's restaurant in Lahti. Now, four years later, the first bottles of a 6 year old are sold in the Teerenpeli Restaurants and later in 2009 also in the state owned ALKO-shops. Anssi Pyysing is also negotiating over sales at Helsinki Airport and on board the ferries to Sweden.

Teerenpeli is equipped with one wash still (1,500 litres) and one spirit still (900 litres) and the average fermentation time in the washback is 70 hours. Lightly peated malt obtained locally is used and the whisky matures in ex-sherry and ex-bourbon casks. 7,500 bottles are produced annually.

France

DISTILLERY: Glann ar Mor, Pleubian, Bretagne
FOUNDED: 1999
OWNER/MANAGER: Jean Donnay
www.glannarmor.com

Glann ar Mor Distillery in Brittany ("Glann ar Mor" literally means "By the Sea" in Breton language) reached one of its goals in 2008: the first official bottling was launched - a 3 year old unpeated version - and it sold out in a fortnight! Those readers not having the opportunity to obtain it have a new chance in November 2009 when the second edition, this time of a peated variety, is launched.

The owner, Jean Donnay, started his first trials already back in 1999 and he did release an experimental version (of 99 bottles) in 2004 called Taol Esa. He then made some

changes to the distillery and the process and regular production commenced 12th June 2005. The distillery is very much about celebrating the traditional way of distilling malt whisky. The two small stills are directly fired and Donnay uses worm tubs for condensing the spirit. He practises a long fermentation in wooden washbacks and the distillation is very slow. For maturation, first fill bourbon barrels and ex-Sauternes casks are used and when the whisky is bottled there is neither chill filtration nor caramel colouring. The full capacity will be 50,000 bottles per year.

Two expressions are distilled, a peated (35-40 ppm) and an unpeated, and the first bottling was made available in France, Germany, the Netherlands, the UK, Sweden and Switzerland. The second release will also be extended to Japan and Canada.

Apart from the Glann ar Mor venture, Jean Donnay has also specialised in double maturation Single Malts. The "Celtique Connexion" range includes whiskies originally distilled and matured in Scotland, then further matured at the company's seaside warehouse. The casks used for this are from Sauternes, Vin de Paille du Jura, Armagnac, Champagne and Coteau du Layon amongst others.

The company has opened its new premises, including a larger warehouse and a visitor centre, a couple of miles away from the distillery's location, still by the seaside. The whiskies can be found at www.tregorwhisky.com

Martine and Jean Donnay with the first release from Glann ar Mor

DISTILLERY: Distillerie Guillon,
Louvois, Champagne
FOUNDED: 1997
OWNER/MANAGER: Thierry Guillon
www.whisky-guillon.com

Thierry Guillon, originally a wine man, decided in 1997 to begin distilling whisky. Not perhaps a novel idea if it was not for the fact that the distillery is located in the heart of the Champagne district. But besides champagne this area is also known as a major barley producer in France. In fact several Scotch maltsters buy barley from this region. Guillon distills some 80,000 bottles per year and often uses slightly peated malt in production. The range of single malts is quite large and one in particular, Guillon No. 1, has a rather interesting maturation process. It is a 5 year old matured in a new oak cask the first year, a whisky barrel the second year, then white wine, red wine and finally the last year in a Port pipe. Apart from single malts there is also a blend in the range, Le Premium Blend, consisting of 50% malt and 50% grain whisky and a whisky liqueur.

DISTILLERY: Distillerie Bertrand,
Uberach, Alsace
FOUNDED: 1874 (whisky since 2002)
OWNER/MANAGER: Affiliate of Wolfberger
www.distillerie-bertrand.com

Distillerie Bertrand is an independent affiliate of Wolfberger, the large wine and eaux-de-vie producer. The manager, Jean Metzger, gets his malt from a local brewer and then distils it in Holstein type stills. Two different types of whisky are produced. One is a single malt at 42.2%, non-chill filtered and with maturation in both new barrels and barrels which have previously contained the fortified wine Banyuls. The other is a single cask at 43.8% matured only in Banyuls barrels. The first bottles, aged 4 years, were released in late 2006 and whilst the annual production is 20,000 bottles, currently 5,000 bottles are sold per year. In late 2008 Jean Metzger released a limited Single Cask Collection from six different Banyuls barrels. In June 2009 the next expression came - a double matured whisky with a 12 months finish in a Vin Jaune barrel. There are also plans for future releases of whisky matured in cognac and champagne barrels.

At the moment the whisky is only sold in France but American importers have already shown an interest. The whisky, Uberach Single Malt Alsace, gets its name from the village.

DISTILLERY: Distillerie Warenghem,
Lannion, Bretagne
FOUNDED: 1900 (whisky since 1994)
OWNER/MANAGER: Warenghem
www.distillerie-warenghem.com

Leon Warenghem founded the distillery already at the beginning of the 20th century but Armorik, the first malt whisky, was not distilled until 1994 and released in 1999. A 3 year old blended whisky with 25% share of malt, Whisky Breton W. B. is also produced at Warenghem. Armorik is available in several European countries and is also exported to Japan.

Germany

DISTILLERY: Slyrs Destillerie, Schliersee
FOUNDED: 1928 (whisky since 1999)
OWNER/MANAGER: Florian Stetter
www.slyrs.de

The whole of the bottled production from Slyrs Destillerie, amounting to 30,000 bottles, was already sold out in May 2008. It does therefore not come as a surprise that the owner decided to double the capacity. Investments in three new fermentation tanks (washbacks) and a malt silo during 2009/2010 will increase the capacity to 60,000 bottles in 2011.

Lantenhammer Destillerie in Schliersee, Bavaria was founded in 1928 and was producing mainly brandy until 1999 when whisky came into the picture, and in 2003 Slyrs Destillerie was founded. The malt, smoked with beech, comes from locally grown grain, and the spirit is distilled twice at low temperatures in the 1,500 litre stills. Maturation takes place in charred 225-litre casks of new American White Oak from Missouri.

The non chill-filtered whisky is called Slyrs after the original name of the surrounding area, Schliers. Around 30,000 bottles were released in 2008 and every year 3,000-5,000 bottles are kept for later release. Florian Stetter has plans for releasing a cask strength in 2010 and a 12 year old in 2015. In autumn 2008 a special blended whisky called Raritas Diaboli was launched. This is the result of cooperation between Slyrs and two other partners and is a blend of whiskies from different parts of the world including Slyrs. A new edition was

Armorik, Slyrs and Blaue Maus Old Fahr

released in September 2009. Slyrs whisky is available in several European countries and is also exported to the USA and Australia.

DISTILLERY: Whisky-Destillerie Blaue Maus, Eggolsheim-Neuses
FOUNDED: 1980
OWNER/MANAGER: Robert Fleischmann
www.fleischmann-whisky.de

This is the oldest single malt whisky distillery in Germany and it celebrated its 25th anniversary in February 2008. The first distillate, never released on the market, was made in 1983. It took 15 years until the first whisky, Glen Mouse 1986, appeared. Fleischmann uses unpeated malt and the whisky matures for approximately eight years in casks of fresh German Oak. All whisky from Blaue Maus are single cask and with the release of a new expression in 2009, Old Fahr, there are currently six single malts, the others being Blaue Maus, Spinnaker, Krottentaler, Schwarzer Pirat and Grüner Hund. Some of them are released at cask strength while others are reduced to 40%. According to Mr. Fleischmann the difference between them is in the malt mixture variation which he uses. A new expression was introduced quite recently; Austrasier is the first grain whisky from the distillery. In 2006 a new distillery was built solely for whisky production while mostly new types of malt will be produced in the older distillery.

DISTILLERY: Bayerwald-Bärwurzerei und Spezialitäten-Brennerei Liebl, Kötzting
FOUNDED: 1970 (whisky since 2006)
OWNER/MANAGER: Gerhard Liebl Jr.
www.bayerischer-whisky.de

In 1970 Gerhard Liebl started spirit distillation from fruits and berries. The distillery was rebuilt and expanded on several occasions until 2006 when his son Gerhard Liebl Jr. built a completely new whisky distillery nearby. He uses 100% Bavarian malt from barley and the wash is left to ferment for 3-5 days. It is then double distilled in Holstein stills (wash still 400 litres and spirit still 150 litres). Maturation takes place in first or second fill ex-bourbon barrels except for whisky destined to be bottled as single casks. Sherry, Port, Bordeaux and Cognac casks are used here. About 10,000 litres of whisky are produced per year and in spring and summer 2009 the first 1,500 bottles bearing the name Coillmór were released in three different expressions - American White Oak, Sherry single cask and Bordeaux single cask. A peated version has already been made and is maturing in the warehouse. The whisky is non chill-filtered and non-coloured.

DISTILLERY: Hammerschmiede, Zorge
FOUNDED: 1984 (whisky since 2002)
OWNER/MANAGER: Karl-Theodor and Alexander Buchholz
www.hammerschmiede.de

In common with many other small whisky producers on mainland Europe, Hammerschmiede´s main products are liqueurs, bitters and spirits from fruit, berries and herbs. But whisky distilling was embarked on in 2002 and production has now increased to 15%. They buy their unpeated malt in Germany and mature the spirit in a variety of casks - German Oak, sherry, cognac, port, bordeaux, bergerac, marsala, malaga and madeira casks and also Dornfelder barriques (German red wine).

The first 278 bottles were released in early 2006 under the name Glan Iarran. A month later a bourbon-matured malt called Glan Taint was launched. Since the release in summer 2007 all whisky is named Glen Els after the small river Elsbach which flows past the premises. The most recent bottlings are Single Cask Sherry and Single Cask Madeira, both distilled in 2006 and released in summer 2009.

So far the whisky has been matured for 3-4 years but older expressions can be expected in the future. In 2007 a new warehouse was opened in a nearby

The first range of Coillmór single malts

Hammerschmiede still room

village. The building, constructed between 1250 and 1270, used to harbour a blacksmith. More than 180 casks are maturing there, and in 2010 the first bottlings from this site will be released. Recently experiments with distillation of rye whisky have also commenced.

DISTILLERY: Spreewälder Feinbrand- & Likörfabrik, Schlepzig
FOUNDED: 2004 (whisky production)
OWNER/MANAGER: Torsten Römer
www.spreewaldbrennerei.de

This distillery with attached brewery lies in Spreewald, circa 100 km southeast of Berlin. The main product range consists of different kinds of beers, eau-de-vie and rum, and since 2004 also malt whisky. The spirit is distilled once in a 100 litre still with an attached column still. The yearly production of whisky is 1,500 litres and French Oak casks, that have previously contained wine made of Sylvaner and Riesling grapes, have been acquired from a winery in Franconia. For part of the production new medium toasted Spessart Oak casks are also used. Before filling into casks the spirit is left for six months in stainless steel tanks.

The whisky, which was first released in December 2007 as a 3 year old, is called Sloupisti which is the ancient Sorbic name of the village Schlepzig.

DISTILLERY: Brennerei Höhler, Aarbergen
FOUNDED: 1895 (whisky since 2001)
OWNER/MANAGER: Holger Höhler
www.brennerei-hoehler.de

The main produce from this distillery in Hessen consists of different distillates from fruit and berries. The first whisky, a bourbon variety, was distilled in 2001 and released in 2004. Since then Holger Höhler has experimented with different types of grain (rye, barley, spelt and oat). There was a limited release of a single malt in July 2007. Until recently all casks were made from Sessart oak with a storage capacity of between 30 and 75 litre. In spring 2007 Höhler started filling 225 litres barriques. He aims to increase production and eventually launch older whisky.

The Netherlands

DISTILLERY: Us Heit Distillery, Bolsward
FOUNDED: 2002
OWNER/MANAGER: Aart van der Linde
www.usheitdistillery.nl

This is one of many examples where a beer brewery also contains a whisky distillery. Frysk Hynder, as the whisky is called, was the first Dutch whisky and made its debut in 2005 at 3 years of age. The barley is grown in surrounding Friesland and malted at the distillery. The owner of the brewery and distillery,

Aart van der Lindehar, has even developed a malting technique which he describes on a separate website - *www.mouteryfryslan.nl*. Some 10,000 bottles are produced annually and the whisky is matured in various casks - sherry, bourbon, red wine, port and cognac.

DISTILLERY: Vallei Distilleerderij, Leusden
FOUNDED: 2002 (officially opened 2004)
OWNER/MANAGER: Bert Burger
www.valleibieren.nl

This is the latest addition to Dutch whisky distilleries. Bert Burger buys barley from a local farmer but apart from that he is very much in control of the whole process from malting to bottling. The whisky is double distilled in pot stills and he produces some 2,500 litres per year. The first trials were in 2002 but in 2004 the distillery was officially opened. After a while Burger started bottling his 2 year old spirit as Valley single malt spirit in 40 ml bottles for customers to try. Finally on 1st December 2007 the first bottles of single malt whisky reached the market as a 3 year old. Other products include whisky liqueur and two kinds of beer.

DISTILLERY: Zuidam Distillers, Baarle Nassau
FOUNDED: 1974 (whisky since 1998)
OWNER/MANAGER: Zuidam family
www.zuidam-distillers.com

Zuidam Distillers was started in 1974 as a traditional family distillery producing liqueurs, genever, gin and vodka. The first attempts to distil malt whisky took place in 1998 but according to one of the owners, Patrick van Zuidam, the result is not fit for bottling. Instead the first release was from the 2002 production and it was bottled in February 2007 as a 5 year old.

In 2009 there were no less than three new expressions of the single malt. Limited editions of two 8 year olds, one matured in new American Oak and one in new French Oak, were supplemented with a heavily peated variety. This year also saw the first bottling of a 5 year old 100% potstill rye whisky. The whisky is double distilled in pot stills made by Kothe & Holstein in Germany. At the moment 20,000 litres per year are produced.

Millstone 8 year old American Oak

Russia

DISTILLERY: Kizlyarskoye, Mirny, Kizlyar,
Republic of Dagestan
FOUNDED: 2003
OWNER/MANAGER: Nauchno-Proizvodstvenoye
Predpriyatie Whisky Rossii

In 1948 a winery called Kizlyarski was founded on the outskirts of Kizlyar in Dagestan. Most of the wines are sold locally but some brandy is produced which has become fairly well-known in other parts of Russia.

In 2003 a group of enthusiasts led by Alibek Irazi-hanov, current CEO and distillery manager, ventured into an experiment in the field of whisky. After visiting Inverhouse operations in Scotland and studying the scientific side and economics of the situation they were ready to start pilot samples. Today the equipment consists of four copper pot stills (5000 litres each) and a stainless steel column still. Capacity is 3000 litres of malt whisky per day and 6000 litres of grain whisky. The spirit is matured on American oak as well as Russian oak from Maikop. The first sample of the whisky, a 3 year old malt, was presented at a conference in Krasnodar in 2007. The company's product has not yet been certified, so it is not available for sale but limited sales of Kizkyarskoye malt whisky, Kizlyarskoye grain whisky and Kizlyarsoye blended whisky were planned for the end of 2008.

So far production has been very scarce – not more than one month in 2007. Most of the time the stills are used for distillation of brandy. No official volumes of maturing whiskies are disclosed, nor is it clear when the company will start a consistent regular whisky distillation. But the company receives state support and is listed in prospective Dagestan state plan of Wine and Vineyards development, so it should be just a matter of time for all bureaucratic issues to be resolved.

Span

DISTILLERY: Distilerio Molino del Arco, Segovia
FOUNDED: 1959
OWNER/MANAGER: Distilerias y Crianza
del Whisky (DYC)

www.dyc.es

Spain´s first whisky distillery is definitely not a small artisan distillery like so many others on these pages. Established by Nicomedes Garcia Lopez already in 1959 (with whisky distilling commencing three years later), this is a distillery with capacity for producing eight million litres of grain whisky and two million litres of malt whisky per year. In addition to that vodka and rum are produced and there are in-house maltings which safeguard malted barley for the full production. The distillery is equipped with six copper pot stills and there are about 250,000 casks maturing on site. The blending and bottling plant which used to sit beside the distillery is now relocated to the Anis Castellana plant at Valverde del Majano.

The big seller when it comes to whiskies is a blend simply called DYC which is around 4 years old. It is currently the third most sold whisky in Spain and is supplemented by an 8 year old blend and, since 2007, also by DYC Pure Malt, i. e. a vatted malt consisting of malt from the distillery and from selected Scottish distilleries. It can safely be assumed that two of these Scottish single malts come from Laphroaig and Ardmore as Beam Global owns both as well as DYC. A brand new expression was also launched in 2009 to commemorate the distillery's 50th anniversary - a 30 year old single malt, the first single malt from the distillery. In 2006, Beam Global introduced DYC blended whisky on the Indian market. It was launched as an IMFL brand (Indian Made Foreign Liquor) which means that the variety of DYC sold in India is produced from imported malt and grain whisky produced in India.

DYC has an interesting liaison with a Scottish distillery which dates back to the early seventies. DYC bought Lochside Distillery north of Dundee in 1973 to safeguard malt whisky requirements and retained it until it stopped production in 1992. During that time DYC was acquired by Pedro Domecq, which in its turn was acquired by Allied Lyons, which eventually changed its name to Allied Domecq. When the latter was bought by Pernod Ricard in 2005, a small share, including DYC, went to Beam Global.

30 year old single malt from DYC to celebrate the distillery's 50th anniversary

Sweden_____

DISTILLERY: Mackmyra Svensk Whisky, Valbo
FOUNDED: 1999
OWNER/MANAGER: Mackmyra Svensk Whisky AB
www.mackmyra.se

The first single malt from Sweden has already during its short lifetime been praised both in Sweden and abroad. Inspired by this positive feed-back, the company in March 2009 revealed plans to build a brand new facility in Gävle, a few miles from the present distillery at Mackmyra. It will become a tourist attraction to experience, with its theme on whisky and where the visitors will not just be able to follow the production but also take part in it.

The first stage, estimated at almost £5 million, consists of a visitor distillery and storage and should according to plans be ready by 2010. Thereafter 'Mackmyra Whiskyby' (Mackmyra Whisky Village) will expand in different phases over the next ten years. The total investments are expected to amount to approximately £50 million and the capacity of the different distilleries will be approximately 6 million bottles per year, which is ten times that of today.

Mackmyra whisky is based on two basic recipes, one resulting in fruity and elegant whisky, the other being more peaty. The peatiness does not stem from peat, but from juniper wood and bog moss. The first release in 2006/2007 was a series of six called Preludium. These expressions, all released in volumes between 4,000 and 12,000 bottles, used casks both from the pilot distillery, which operated 1999-2002, and from the current distillery which started in 2002. The first "real" launch was in June 2008 – 'Den Första Utgåvan' (The First Edition). It is still a fairly young whisky and 95% bourbon casks and 5% casks made from Swedish Oak have been used. Circa 45% of the mix is stored in 100 litre casks. A second release of First Edition was made in October. In May 2009, Special:02 - Jubileumsutgåvan (Jubilee Edition) was launched, the second in a new series of limited editions.

The casks for The First Edition have all matured at a depth of 50 metres in the Archean rock in an abandoned mine in northern Sweden. Mackmyra has another three storage sites: an island in the archipelago of Stockholm, on the west coast and at a castle in the southernmost part of Sweden.

About 10% of Mackmyra's production was exported in 2008 and the goal is to increase that to 50%. An introduction of the whisky in the USA is next on the agenda.

DISTILLERY: Spirit of Hven, Ven
FOUNDED: 2007
OWNER/MANAGER: Backafallsbyn AB
www.hven.com

The second Swedish distillery to come on stream after Mackmyra was Spirit of Hven, a distillery situated on the island of Ven right between Sweden and Denmark. The first distillation took place on 7th May 2008.

Henric Molin, founder and owner, is a trained

Special:02 from Mackmyra, released in May 2009

The still room at Spirit of Hven

chemist but this is not the only similarity with Bill Lumsden, Head of Whisky Creation at Glenmorangie. Henric is equally concerned about choosing the right oak for his casks, and like Lumsden he sources his oak mainly in Missouri. The oak is left to air dry for a minimum of two years before the casks are lended to, especially, wine producers in both the USA and Europe. It is mostly sweet wines that are filled in the casks but dry white wines and bourbon could also occur. Around 80% of the casks are made of American White Oak while 18% are of the rarer Spanish Red Oak (*Quercus falcata*) and a few percent are Japanese Mizunara Oak (*Quercus mongolica*).

Henric's initial objective was to keep the whole process of whisky-making on the distillery premises. Starting in autumn 2009 some of the barley is malted on site but more and more will come from own maltings as time passes. For the peated varieties, peat is brought in from Scotland but spiced up with local seaweed and sea-grass. The distillery is equipped with a 500 kilo mash tun, six washbacks made of stainless steel and one pair of stills - wash still 2,000 litres and spirit still 1,500 litres. There is also one very small still known as the Essence Still. Here, experiments can be made with small batches and essences to be used in the gins and vodkas that are produced can be created.

A long fermentation time of 90-120 hours is used in order to achieve a more fully flavoured product with high citric notes and a nutty character. The spirit yield at the distillery, 410-420 litres per tonne of malted barley, is quite impressive given the fact that the distillery is small and part of the production is peated whisky.

Henric Molin - founder and owner of Spirit of Hven

Henric is (to use his own words) obsessed with being able to trace the exact origin of every bottle of whisky down to the field of barley and the specific oak used for the cask. One batch from the spirit still fills exactly one cask and only one cask is made from each oak tree. The plans are to produce four different types of malt whisky - organic, unpeated, lightly peated (22ppm) and heavily peated (90ppm) - with the first bottlings to be available around 2012. Somewhere between 30-50,000 litres of whisky are hoped to be produced during 2009, but also 12,000 litres of rum made from sugar beets and 50,000 litres of vodka, gin and aquavit are expected to be distilled.

Apart from being a distiller, Henric and his wife Anja also run a hotel and restaurant with a very impressive whisky bar.

Switzerland

DISTILLERY: Whisky Brennerei Holle,
Lauwil, Baselland
FOUNDED: 1999 (for whisky distillation)
OWNER/MANAGER: The Bader family.
www.swiss-whisky.ch, www.single-malt.ch

Since WW1 Switzerland has had a law forbidding the use of staple foods such as potatoes and grain for making alcohol. On 1st July 1999 this was abolished and the spirit streamed through the stills of Holle the very same day making it the first Swiss producer of malt whisky. The whisky is stored on French oak casks, which have been used for white wine (Chardonnay) or red wine (Pinot Noir). There are currently circa 100 casks in the warehouse. Most bottlings are 4 years old and contain 42% alcohol. A 5 year old has also been released, which has had three years on Pinot Noir casks followed by two years on Chardonnay casks. Other expressions include a peated version and a cask strength Chardonnay-matured.

In Spring 2008, an Easter bottling having had six years on two different casks - American Oak bourbon and French Oak which previously had contained Chardonnay - was released. Bader also recently launched what he calls a dessert whisky from a white wine cask as well as his first single grain whisky, and late 2008 saw the release of a 9 year old. Annual production amounts to roughly 30,000 bottles. The main production of the distillery consists of schnapps distilled from a variety of fruit.

DISTILLERY: Spezialitätenbrennerei Zürcher,
Port, Bern
FOUNDED: 1954 (whisky from 2000)
OWNER/MANAGER: Daniel & Ursula Zürcher

This distillery was founded already in 1954 by Willi Zürcher. However, the first in the family to distil whisky was Heinz Zürcher in 2000 who released the first 1,000 bottles of Lakeland single malt in 2003.

It was time for the third generation, Daniel and Ursula Zürcher, to take over in 2004. They continued their uncle's work with whisky and launched a second release in 2006. The main focus of the distillery is specialising in various distillates of fruit, absinth and liqueur. Whisky will always be a sideline according to Daniel Zürcher but the good news is that new bottlings will take place annually in the future. The latest barrel of Lakeland single malt was released in 2009 as a 3 year old but the Zürchers are working on the release of older whiskies in the future. The wash for the whisky is bought from a brewery in Interlaken and maturation takes place in Oloroso sherry casks.

Cooperation with the Rugenbräu brewery has developed in recent years in that Zürcher sometimes distils the wash and then sends back the new make to the brewery for it to be filled into casks to mature. Two expressions from Rugenbräu were released in March 2008 - Swiss Highland Single Malt Interlaken (46% and released for the first time in 2007) and brand new Swiss Highland Single Malt Ice Label (58.8%). The latter was an interesting novelty; it was filled in an Oloroso sherry cask and then matured for almost 4 years at 3,454 metres altitude in the ice of Jungfraujoch with a constant temperature of minus 4 degrees Celsius. In April 2009 new editions of both expressions were released.

DISTILLERY: Bauernhofbrennerei Lüthy,
                Muhen, Aargau
FOUNDED: 1997 (whisky since 2005)
OWNER/MANAGER: Urs Lüthy
www.swiss-single-malt.ch

The farm distillery Lüthy in the north of Switzerland started in 1997 by producing distillates from fruit as well as grappa, absinth and schnapps. The range was expanded to include whisky in 2005 which was distilled in a mobile pot still distillery. Since 2006 Lüthy has only been using Swiss barley and in autumn 2009 he will start his own maltings.

The first single malt expression to be launched was Original No.1 in December 2008 and the 567 bottles sold out in two weeks. The spirit matures in casks that have previously held chardonnay, pinot noir and sherry. The selection is so far limited as only 500 bottles are filled per year.

DISTILLERY: Whisky Castle, Elfingen, Aargau
FOUNDED: 2002
OWNER/MANAGER: Ruedi Käser
www.whisky-castle.com

The first whisky from this distillery in Elfingen in the north of Switzerland reached the market in 2004. It was a single malt under the name Castle Hill. Recent new bottlings include a cask strength (71%) called Castle One Käser Edition. A new distillery was built in 2005 and commissioned in 2006, hence the annual production has increased from 5,000 to 25,000 bottles. The whisky is matured in Hungarian and American ex-bourbon and ex-sherry casks and can be bought in Germany, The Netherlands and Austria apart from Switzerland. The whisky production is centred around several different expressions based on barley, rye and spelt while the Käser's main production comprises some 70 different kinds of schnapps based on fruit and berries. Ruedi Käser has constructed a complete visitor's experience including a restaurant and a shop. Recently the whisky has also been exported to China.

DISTILLERY: Brennerei Hagen,
                Hüttwilen, Thurgau
FOUNDED: 1999
OWNER/MANAGER: Ueli Hagen

A triple distilled malt whisky is since a few years produced by Ueli Hagen in the small village of Hüttwilen in the northernmost part of Switzerland. The spirit is matured in bourbon barrels and the

Urs Lüthy's mobile distillery

Whisky Castle single malt

first produce was sold in 2002 as a 3 year old. Ueli Hagen produces mainly schnapps and absinth and distills around 300 bottles of malt whisky a year, a number he expects to double. He has recently been experimenting; four years ago when he was building a new cow shed, he found a 1700 year old oak tree in the ground so he put pieces of the oak into a maturing barrel of spirit and he says it gives the whisky a slightly peated touch. Ueli has plans for expansion and in 2010 a new still room will be built.

DISTILLERY: Burgdorfer Gasthausbrauerei, Burgdorf, Bern
FOUNDED: 1999
OWNER/MANAGER: Thomas Gerber
www.burgdorferbier.ch

The Burgdorfer Single Malt Whisky is an excellent example of the kind of cross-fertilization that more and more breweries are choosing. When a wash is made for beer brewing, it is an excellent opportunity to use the batch (without adding hops) to distil spirit which can be made into whisky. The first whisky from Burgdorfer was released as a five year old in 2006 and it is sold using a kind of subscription system. The customer pays 50 swiss francs for a 50 cl bottle and receives it 5 years later. They produce around 300 bottles annually and will start taking orders this year for a 10 year old.

DISTILLERY: Maison Les Vignettes - Swhisky, Ardon, Tessin
FOUNDED: 2000
OWNER/MANAGER: Alex Delaloye
www.swhisky.ch

The first malt distillation by this distillery in Ardon took place in 2001 and 4,000 bottles are produced annually. There have been four different single malts

in the range since the beginning of production: Annouim, Gwenwed (matured in Syrah casks), Abred (a peaty variety) and Keugant (cask strength 56%). Another four expressions were added in 2006: Challenge, Celtica, Skipper (a peated version) and finally Triad, older than the others and finished in a Vosne Romanée cask. New bottlings for 2007 were Swhisky Must 1825 (six years old and the oldest version so far) and Swhisky Must Grand Cru, matured in a Red Meursault cask.

Wales _____

DISTILLERY: Penderyn Distillery, Penderyn
FOUNDED: 2000
OWNER/MANAGER: Welsh Whisky Company Ltd
www.welsh-whisky.co.uk

In 1998 four private individuals started The Welsh Whisky Company and two years later the first Welsh distillery in more than a hundred years started distilling.

A new type of still, developed by David Faraday for Penderyn Distillery, differs from the Scottish and Irish procedures in that the whole process from wash to new make takes place in one single still. But that is not the sole difference. Every distillery in Scotland is required by law to do the mashing and fermenting on site. At Penderyn, though, the wash is bought from a regional beer brewer and transported to the distillery on a weekly basis. The normal procedure at a brewery is to boil the wash to clear it from any lactic acid which can make it appear cloudy. This was a problem for Penderyn as lactic acid creates a second fermentation which is beneficial in a whisky context and adds more taste. Penderyn has solved this by pumping the wash to a heated tank where lactic acid is added before distillation is commenced.

Penderyn Sherrywood and Distiller Gillian Howells inspecting casks

The first single malt was launched on St. David's Day 1st March 2004. 60,000 bottles were produced the first year and now production has increased to 100,000 bottles. The core range consists of Penderyn Madeira Finish, Penderyn Sherrywood and Penderyn Peated. A limited release was made in summer 2009 - a Portwood Single Cask. Around 95,000 bottles were sold last year in Europe, North America, Japan and Australia. A visitor centre was officially opened by HRH The Prince of Wales in June 2008 at a total cost of £850,000 and in the first year it welcomed 15,000 visitors.

One of the founders, Brian Morgan, stepped down as chairman of the company in 2008 and was succeeded by Nigel Short. Morgan has in parallel with his whisky engagements held a position as Professor of Entrepreneurship at the University of Wales with Nigel Short becoming a partner already in 2003 and helping with funding by investing over £1m.

NORTH AMERICA

USA

DISTILLERY: Clear Creek Distillery,
Portland, Oregon
FOUNDED: 1985
OWNER/MANAGER: Stephen McCarthy
www.clearcreekdistillery.com

Steve McCarthy in Oregon was one of the first to produce malt whiskey in the USA and his 3 year old single malt has earned a reputation as a high-quality whiskey fully comparable to the best Scotch whiskies. Like many other small distilleries, Clear Creek started by distilling eau-de-vie from fruit, especially pears, and then expanded the product line into whiskey. It began making whiskey in 1996 and the first bottles were on the market three years later.

There is only one expression at the moment, McCarthy's Oregon Single Malt 3 years old. Steve has for a long time hoped to launch an 8 year old, but so far it has simply not been possible to save adequate quantities due to high demand.

The whiskey is reminiscent of Islay and, in fact, the malt is purchased directly from Islay with a phenol specification of 30-40 ppm. It is then made into wash at the Widmer Brothers Brewery in Portland and distilled in Holstein pot stills. Steve expanded the number of pot stills to four last year to try and catch up with demand. Maturation takes place in ex-sherry butts with a finish in new Oregon White Oak hogsheads.

Steve has doubled the production of whiskey every year since 2004 which does not, however, seem to be enough to satisfy demand. The procedure used to be one release in March and one in August with both of them selling out quickly and 2008 was no

exception. In 2009 he changed it to one release per year, with the August one being the biggest ever - 700 cases. The next release will be sometime in mid 2010. Unlike many of the single malts from the USA, McCarthy's Oregon Single Malt is available in several European countries. Steve has recently strengthened his cooperation with Maison du Whisky in Paris, and this will be the centre for expansion in Europe.

DISTILLERY: Stranahans Whiskey Distillery,
Denver, Colorado
FOUNDED: 2003
OWNER/MANAGER: Jess Graber,
George Stranahan et al.
www.stranahans.com

The first whiskey distillery in Colorado has entered a new and exciting phase. A continuing rising demand forced the owner to figure out how to cleverly expand to sell more. Wash has been purchased from a couple of local breweries since the distillery's inception back in 2003, but now he wanted to bring it up one step by producing wash in-house. The equipment required was found in the closed Heavenly Daze Brewery in Denver but instead of just buying the mash tun and fermenters, he ended up buying the entire 60,000 square foot building. During spring and summer of 2009 all equipment was moved to the new location and Stranahans is now ready to increase production.

The plan is to make five mashes a day and the six-day fermentation will occur in three closed fermenters. The first distillation takes place in a 2,800 litre Vendome combinated pot still/column still while the second distillation is in a 950 litre pot still.

McCarthy's Oregon Single Malt   Stranahan's Colorado Whiskey

The whisky is filled into heavily charred barrels of new American White Oak from Independent Stave in Lebanon, Missouri and is left to mature for a minimum of two years. Up to 20 barrels with ages between 2 and 5 years are married together when bottling.

The first three barrels were bottled in April 2006 and 40 different batches had been produced until summer 2009. In spring 2009 three different wood finishes called Snowflakes were released. These have all been sold by the barrel and include port, cabernet franc and Hungarian White Oak finish.

In April 2009 the 100,000th bottle was bottled, thus making Stranahans one of the American micro distilleries achieving the most successful sales. From exclusively selling locally in Colorado, the whiskey can now be found in 34 states as well as in Japan and Europe.

DISTILLERY: Tuthilltown Spirits,
Gardiner, New York
FOUNDED: 2003
OWNER/MANAGER: Ralph Erenzo & Brian Lee
www.tuthilltown.com

This is the first whiskey distillery in the State of New York since Prohibition. Just 80 miles north of New York City, Ralph Erenzo and Brian Lee with the help of six employees produce bourbon, single malt whiskey, rye whiskey, rum and Heart and Spirit of the Hudson vodkas, the latter two both distilled from local apples. Erenzo bought the 18th century property in 2002 with the intention of turning it into a camping ground, but neighbours objected. A change in the law in New York State made it possible to start a micro-distillery; paying $1,450 for a license Erenzo changed direction and started distilling instead. Erenzo and Lee built the distillery, acquired licenses and learned the basic craft over the following two years.

The first grain spirits launched were unaged corn whiskey and various expressions of bourbon. The Hudson Baby Bourbon is produced with 100% NY corn while Hudson Four Grain Bourbon uses corn, rye, wheat and malted barley. The same malted barley is now also used for the Hudson Single Malt Whiskey. It is aged in new, charred American Oak and the casks are very small – 3-14 gallons per cask.

The first products came onto the shelves in 2006 in New York and are currently selling in Hudson Valley, New York City and twelve other States. The European distributor is La Maison du Whisky in Paris. On 5th July 2009 the distillery crew hand-harvested the first crop of rye grown at the distillery, and opened for its first public tours. Tuthilltown´s new whiskey tasting room and shop are in the barrel room and are the first at a distillery in New York since 1919. Private single cask bottling of whiskey is also available to consumers at the distillery.

DISTILLERY: Eades Distillery,
Lovingston, Virginia
FOUNDED: 2008
OWNER/MANAGER: The Virginia Distillers Co.
(Chris Allwood, Joe Hungate, Brian Gray)
www.eadeswhisky.com

Chris Allwood and his partners have for most of 2009 busied themselves with financing the remaining $2m (of a total of $5m) that was needed to complete their plans for a distillery in Nelson County, Virginia. The plan was originally to start distilling in spring 2009 but the tough financial recession has delayed the project by about a year and they now calculate starting production in summer 2010. All equipment has been made in Scotland by Northern Fabricators and was delivered in November 2008: a 2 tonne mash tun, a 10,000 litre wash still and an 8,000 litre spirit still. The malting of locally grown barley will be done on site and they are cooperating with Virginia Tech

Ralph Erenzo (left) and Brian Lee from Tuthilltown Spirits

Chris Allwood from Eades Distillery

University to test around six strains in order to find the best variety.

Initial production volumes are expected to be around 2,500 barrels of 200 litres each per year and the spirit will mature in bourbon barrels, Port pipes and wine barrels from local wineries. It will take five years before the first bottlings of matured whiskey are for sale. Meanwhile the owners have created a series of vatted malt whiskies called "Eades Anticipation Series". In association with Jim McEwan of Bruichladdich, single malts from various Scottish producers have been selected. The idea was to select two different malts for each bottling, marry them and then let them have a second maturation in wine barrels. The three expressions released so far are Eades Highland, a combination of Ben Nevis and Clynelish, Eades Speyside with Longmorn and Glen Moray and finally Eades Islay where Bowmore and Caol Ila have been married.

DISTILLERY: Triple Eight Distillery, Nantucket, Massachusetts
FOUNDED: 2000
OWNER/MANAGER: Cisco Brewers
www.ciscobrewers.com

This is the first North American distillery situated on an island - Nantucket Island, Massachusetts. In 1995 Cisco Brewers was established and five years later it was expanded with Triple Eight Distillery. The base of the whiskey production is of course wash from the brewery where Maris Otter barley is used. The first distillation took place as as early as nine years ago and the first 888 bottles (5 barrels) were released on 8th August 2008 as an 8 year old. To keep in line, the price of these first bottles was $888. The whiskey is named Notch (as in "not Scotch"). There are currently 115 barrels in their warehouse. Annual production is approximately 5,000 bottles and the storage is on ex-bourbon casks from Brown Forman (Woodford Reserve) and finished in French Oak.

The Nantucket facility consists of a brewery, winery and distillery. The parent company, Cisco Brewers, produces Whales Tale Pale Ale and they use a similar mash for producing the Notch. Triple Eight also produces vodka and rum that is already on the market. Whiskey production was moved to a new distillery in May 2007.

DISTILLERY: Edgefield Distillery, Troutdale, Oregon
FOUNDED: 1998
OWNER/MANAGER: Mike and Brian McMenamin
www.mcmenamins.com

Brothers Mike and Brian McMenamin started their first pub in Portland, Oregon in 1983. It has now expanded to a chain of more than 40 pubs and hotels in Oregon and Washington. Over 20 of the pubs have adjoining micro-breweries (the first opened in 1985). Their first and so far only distillery opened in 1998 at their huge Edgefield property in Troutdale and their first whiskey, Hogshead Whiskey (46%), was bottled in 2002. Annual production used to be 3,000 bottles but a second washback has now been added making it possible to do four mashes a month which has increased yearly outcome to around 10,000 litres. In the past, ex-bourbon casks were used for maturation but now only charred, new American White Oak barrels are used.

Hogshead Whiskey is the top seller (3,600 bottles in 2007) but Head Distiller James Whelan has a goal of producing four to eight barrels of "speciality" whiskies that differ from the Hogshead. To date he has produced one barrel of a lightly-peated variety and also some whiskey from organically grown barley. Recently he has also introduced a programme for making 5-10 barrels per year of a rye whiskey based on a recipe given to him by the legendary Booker Noe of Jim Beam fame.

DISTILLERY: Nashoba Valley Winery, Bolton, Massachusetts
FOUNDED: 1978 (whiskey since 2003)
OWNER/MANAGER: Richard Pelletier
www.nashobawinery.com

Nashoba Valley Winery lies in the heart of Massachusetts' apple country just 40 minutes from Boston. The winery, founded in 1978 by Jack Partridge, has been owned since 1995 by Richard Pelletier who, prior to this, made his living in construction and real estate development. This place is mainly about wines and they have earned a solid reputation for their products made from both fruit and grapes. In recent years the facilities have expanded with a brewery producing ten different kinds of ales and lagers, and Massachusetts' first distillery which holds a farmers-distiller license. Here he produces a wide range of spirits including vodka, brandy and grappa.

Since 2001 malt whiskey is also distilled. The malt is imported from England, France and Canada and the wash is produced in his own brewery. The whiskey is matured in a combination of ex-bourbon barrels and American and French Oak casks which previously have contained wine from the estate. Richard Pelletier produces around 9,000 bottles per year. In August 2009 the first single malt was released (600 bottles).

DISTILLERY: St. George Distillery, Alameda, California
FOUNDED: 1982
OWNER/MANAGER: Jörg Rupf/Lance Winters
www.stgeorgespirits.com

The distillery is situated in a hangar at Alameda Point, the old naval air station on the San Fransisco Bay. It was founded by Jörg Rupf, a German immigrant who came to California in 1979 with a Holstein pot in tow. Several of his ancestors had preceded him in the trade by being distillers of eau-de-vie and Rupf became one of the forerunners when it came to craft distilling in America. In 1996, Lance Winters joined him and today he is Distiller as well as co-owner.

The main produce is based on eau-de-vie from locally grown fruit, and vodka under the brand name Hangar One. Whiskey production was picked up in 1996 and the first single malt appeared on the market in 1999. Like so many other craft distilleries the wash is not produced in-house but acquired instead from Sierra Nevada Brewery in this case. One advantage of cooperating with a brewery is that brewer´s yeast can be used, something Scottish producers had to give up on in 2005 when it became unavailable. Lance Winters, in common with many other distillers, claims that the fruity character of the whiskey is a result of using brewer´s yeast rather than distiller´s yeast. Some of the malt used has been dried with alder and beech but is non-peated. Maturation is in bourbon barrels (80%), French Oak (15%) or port pipes (5%). St. George Single Malt used to be sold as three years old, but nowadays comes to the market as a blend of whiskeys aged from 4 to 12 years. Another spirit was added in 2007 when St. George became the first distillery since the ban in 1912 to legally produce and sell Absinthe in the USA.

DISTILLERY: Woodstone Creek Distillery, Cincinnati, Ohio
FOUNDED: 1999
OWNER/MANAGER: Donald Outterson
www.woodstonecreek.com

Last year, when I spoke to Don and Linda Outterson who are owners of this, the first licensed micro distillery in Ohio, they were hoping for a change in the Ohio State Law which would allow sales of whiskey directly to the public from the distillery premises. It finally came through which practically meant that the distillery was turned into a state liquor store. The "only" remaining barrier now is that tastings are not allowed on the premises of a state-controlled store.

The first whiskey, a five grain bourbon, was released as Barrel #2 on 4th July 2008 to celebrate the change in Ohio´s regulations. The second release, Barrel #1, was launched on 25th November to celebrate Thanksgiving Day. Both bourbons were made of malted grains (no enzymes), 51% corn, sweet mash

and without chill-filtering and colouring. The first single malt, a heavily peated version, will be released as a 10 year old in autumn 2009.

Don Outterson opened a farm winery in Lebanon, Ohio in 1999 and relocated to the present facilities in 2003. The malted barley is imported from Scotland and port and sherry casks of own production are used for maturation. As Don has another full-time job he only distills at weekends and production will not increase until he is able to fully concentrate on the distillery. Apart from wine and whiskey, Woodstone Creek produces bourbon, brandy, rum and vodka. The capacity for single malts in the future is planned to be 10 barrels per year.

DISTILLERY: The Ellensburg Distillery, Ellensburg, Washington
FOUNDED: 2008
OWNER/MANAGER: Berle Wilson Figgins Jr.
www.theellensburgdistillery.com

Former winemaker Berle "Rusty" Figgins Jr. decided to leave the wine making business after 10 years to open a distillery instead. The distilled produce will include malt whiskey, rye whiskey, cream liqueur and brandy. The malt whiskey is made from an all-malt mash, incorporating a proprietary blend of pale ale and crystal malts, and the wort is fermented with native yeast.

The distillation process is a bit unusual. Rusty uses two alambic pot stills of a design which originates in Armagnac. Both stills, which are united with a T-shaped lyne arm, are simultaneously filled with equal volumes and the spirit distilled twice. The character is aromatic and full-flavoured already from the very beginning and according to Rusty this is achieved by the distilling technique where the spirit vapour from each still is manifolded together to afford a degree of back pressure which increases the degree of reflux. The new make is filled into new American Oak barrels of 112.5 litres and after six months it is re-racked to 225 litre ex-sherry casks for another four months. The first malt whiskey (300 bottles) will be bottled at the age of ten months under the name Gold Buckle Club for a release in November 2009.

Don Outterson from Woodstone Creek

The unusual still arrangement at The Ellensburg Distillery

DISTILLERY: Charbay Winery & Distillery,
St. Helena, California
FOUNDED: 1983
OWNER/MANAGER: Miles and Marko Karakasevic
www.charbay.com

Charbay has a wide range of products: vodka, grappa, pastis, rum, port and since 1999 also malt whiskey. That was the year when Miles and Marko decided to take 20,000 gallons of Pilsner and double distil it in their Charentais still, normally used for distilling for example cognac.

From this distillation, a 4 year old called Double-Barrel Release One (two barrels) was launched in 2002. There were 840 bottles at cask strength and non-chill filtered with a price tag of $325. It took six years before the next release appeared (made from the same distillation). This time five barrels were chosen and the whiskey was bottled at 55% but maintaining the same price as before.

Maturation takes place in newly charred American White Oak barrels. A speciality of Charbay is the addition of dried hops to the wash before distillation.

DISTILLERY: Copper Fox Distillery,
Sperryville, Virginia
FOUNDED: 2000
OWNER/MANAGER: Rick Wasmund
www.copperfox.biz

Copper Fox Distillery was founded in 2000 by Rick Wasmund using the premises and license of an old, existing distillery. The first whiskey, Copper Fox Whiskey, was made in cooperation with the distillery which they were about to buy, but after a disagreement over the contract the project came to a halt. In 2005 they moved to another site, built a new distillery and began distilling in January 2006.

Rick Wasmund started by working for six weeks at Bowmore distillery on Islay to learn the trade and he has become one of the most unorthodox producers of single malt. The malted barley is dried using smoke from selected fruitwood but variations of that concept are also used in other places, for example Sweden and New Zeeland. It is the maturation process that Rick takes one step further thereby differing from common practice. In every barrel of new make spirit, he adds plenty of hand chipped and toasted chips of apple and cherry trees and oak wood.

Adding to the flavour, Wasmund also believes that this procedure drastically speeds up the time necessary for maturation. In fact he bottles his Wasmund´s Single Malt after just four months in the barrel. Every batch ranging from 250 to 1,500 bottles tastes a little different and the distillery is now producing around 2,500 bottles every month.

Twenty one different batches have been launched up to the autumn of 2008. At the moment the Wasmund´s Single Malt can be found in Virginia, Washington DC, Maryland, New Jersey, Illinois, Florida and California among others.

DISTILLERY: High Plains Distillery,
Atchison, Kansas
FOUNDED: 2004
OWNER/MANAGER: Seth Fox
www.highplainsinc.com

Former process engineer Seth Fox is mainly known for his Most Wanted Vodka of which he sells over 13,000 cases a year in Kansas, Missouri and Texas. The product range was expanded in late 2006 also to include a Most Wanted Kansas Whiskey (reminiscent of a Canadian whisky) and Kansas bourbon whiskey. Fox continued in 2007 to produce his first single malt whiskey made from malted barley. He also produced both a wheat and a rye whiskey as well as rum and tequila. The two stills were bought second-hand from Surrey in England. When High Plains opened, it was the first legal distillery in Kansas since 1880. Despite its success, Seth Fox and his wife Dorcie run operations with the help of just two part-timers.

DISTILLERY: St. James Spirits,
Irwindale, California
FOUNDED: 1995
OWNER/MANAGER: Jim Busuttil
www.saintjamesspirits.com

Peregrine Rock is the name of the 3 year old single malt Jim Busuttil produces in Irwindale, east of Los Angeles. The malt comes from Baird Malts in the UK and is medium peated. Heavy charred new American oak barrels, but also ex-bourbon barrels from Jim Beam and Jack Daniels are used.

DISTILLERY: Dry Fly Distilling, Spokane,
Washington
FOUNDED: 2007
OWNER/MANAGER: Don Poffenroth
& Kent Fleischmann
www.dryflydistilling.com

Dry Fly Distilling began distilling as late as autumn 2007 and then became the first grain distillery to open in Washington since Prohibition. The two founders share a mutual interest - dry fly fishing - hence the name of the distillery. To ensure a positive cash flow from the start, in common with many other distilleries, vodka and gin were produced and were already on the shelves in October 2007. The first batch of Malt whisky was distilled on 4th January 2008 and the owners expect to make 200-300 cases of malt whisky annually (total production being estimated at 5,000 cases). The original equipment consisted of one still, a Christian Carl manufactured in Germany. In autumn 2008 another still was installed as well as two additional fermenters which will raise capacity to 10,000 cases per annum. Don and Kent are aiming to release a 4 year old for their first single malt which is expected at the beginning of 2012 but they will start analysing it after two years to monitor maturation. August 2009 saw the first release of their Washington Wheat Whiskey.

DISTILLERY: New Holland Brewing Co.,
Holland, Michigan
FOUNDED: 1996 (whiskey since 2005)
OWNER/MANAGER: Brett VanderKamp, David
White, Fred Bueltmann
www.newhollandbrew.com

This company started as a beer brewery but after a decade it opened up a micro-distillery as well. The wash used for the beer is now also used for distilling whiskey. There is a variety of malts for mashing and the house ale yeast is used for fermentation. The spirit is double distilled in a 225 litre pot still. About 4,000 litres of spirit is produced yearly. The first cases of New Holland Artisan Spirits were released in December 2008 and included in them were several varieties of rum with one year maturation, Knicker-bocker Gin and finally Zeppelin Bend, their 3 year old straight-malt whiskey. This was distilled twice and filled into new American Oak with a heavy char.

Canada

DISTILLERY: Glenora Distillery,
Glenville, Nova Scotia
FOUNDED: 1990
OWNER/MANAGER: Lauchie MacLean
www.glenoradistillery.com

Situated in Nova Scotia, Glenora was the first malt whisky distillery in Canada. The first launch of in-house produce came in 2000 but a whisky called Kenloch had been sold before that. This was a 5 year old vatting of some of Glenora's own malt whisky and whisky from Bowmore Distillery on Islay. The first expression, a 10 year old, came in September 2000 and was named Glen Breton. Since then several expressions have been launched, among them single casks and sometimes under the name Glenora. A new expression, Glen Breton Ice (10 years old), the world's first single malt aged in an ice wine barrel, was launched in November 2006. Interest was massive and another release came onto the market in spring 2007. In 2008 a 15 year old version was available from the distillery only.

Glenora's whisky has not been easy to obtain outside Canada, but exports currently go to countries such as the USA, Poland, Sweden, Switzerland, Spain and Singapore.

Since 2001 Glenora has been locked in a legal fight with Scotch Whisky Association over the name of Glen Breton. The opinion of SWA is that the use of the word Glen is misleading and confusing for the customer and will make many believe that they are actually buying a Scotch whisky. The distillery, on the other hand, states that Glen is an established geographical name in this part of Canada. In 2007 the Trademarks Opposition Board in Ottawa ruled in favour of the distillery's right to continue to sell the whisky under the name Glen Breton. SWA appealed and won in April 2008 when a Federal Court reversed the previous ruling. The next step was Glenora's ap-peal to Canada's Federal Court of Appeal in Decem-ber 2008 which ruled in favour of the distillery by January 2009. Five months later SWA decided not to give up but to petition the Supreme Court of Canada to overturn the Court of Appeal's decision.

DISTILLERY: Shelter Point Distillery, Vancouver
Island, British Columbia
FOUNDED: 2009
OWNER/MANAGER: Andrew Currie,
Jay Oddleifson, Patrick Evans
www.shelterpointdistillery.com

When this distillery, just north of Comox on Vancou-ver Island, is on stream it will be the third Canadian distillery producing malt whisky. Andrew Currie, who co-founded Arran Distillery in Scotland 16 years ago, and Jay Oddleifson, a former accountant who was the CFO of Mount Washington Alpine Resort, are behind the project. The recently completed buildings on the 400-acre property will house the stills and spirit safe, made by Forsyth's in Scotland, and are estimated to be in place by September 2009. The original plans included starting production in early 2009 but it is now hoped that commissioning will be in early autumn 2009 and to start distilling before the year's end. The capacity will be 92,000 litres per year, i. e. of the same magnitude as for example Kil-choman and Edradour. Barley is grown on the estate and is expected to be used in the whisky production.

Glenora Distillery

Construction work at Shelter Point Distillery

In common with many other new established whisky distilleries, the first products will consist of spirits not requiring maturation, such as gin and vodka.

DISTILLERY: Winchester Cellars, Vancouver Island, British Columbia
FOUNDED: 2002 (whisky since 2007)
OWNER/MANAGER: Bryan and Valerie Murray
www.winchestercellars.com

Ken Winchester, a winemaker since 1983, started Winchester Vineyards north of Santa Barbara and then moved the operations in 2002 to Vancouver Island in Canada where he has also opened the first licensed distillery on the island. Ken´s plans were to produce a single malt whisky and he was inspired by a visit to Bruichladdich in 2006. The first distillation took place in summer 2007 in a copper still made by Muller in Germany and the wash was bought from a local micro-brewery.

Since autumn 2008 Ken is no longer part of the business. It has instead been taken over by his former business partners Bryan and Valerie Murray. However, Ken took part in introducing Victoria Gin in early summer 2008 which became an instant success. It was, in fact, so successful that for the time being no wines are produced and the whisky production has also been put on hold.

AUSTRALIA & NEW ZEALAND

Australia _____

DISTILLERY: Bakery Hill Distillery, North Balwyn, Victoria
FOUNDED: 1998
OWNER/MANAGER: David Baker
www.bakeryhilldistillery.com.au

In 2008 Bakery Hill completed the installation of a 2,000 litre brewery and now has total control of all the processes from milling the grain to bottling the matured spirit. Production levels have subsequently been increased and David Baker is eagerly awaiting the maturation of the first barrels of Bakery Hill's very own production.

Apart from distillation, environmental adjustments and engineering have been in focus during 2009. The distillery waste, spent grain and pot ale used to be disposed of but are now sent to Yarra Valley to be used as stock feed and fertiliser. The next step on the green agenda will be harvesting rainwater. The distillery was closed for several weeks in order to undergo a complete systems engineering review, and next year the plan is to install a new wash still.

The first spirit at Bakery Hill Distillery was produced in 2000 and the first single malt was launched in

autumn 2003. Three different versions are available - Classic and Peated (both matured in ex-bourbon casks) and Double Wood (ex-bourbon and French Oak). As Classic and Peated are also available as cask strength bottlings, they can be considered two more varieties. The whisky is double-distilled in a copper pot still. All unpeated malt comes from an Australian maltster while the malt for the peated version is imported from the UK.

Sales have picked up momentum and David has now been forced to limit the number of bottles available to each customer. The peated cask strength and the Double Wood are especially popular.

With the Bakery Hill Distillery being situated about 25 km inland in the southern portion of Australia, the climate is very different to that of Scotland. The overall ambient temperatures are much higher while the air mass is much drier. These factors influence the rate of flavour development and ultimate whisky character, and David Baker is constantly experimenting with a wide variety of oak to find the optimal path.

DISTILLERY: Lark Distillery, Hobart, Tasmania
FOUNDED: 1992
OWNER/MANAGER: Bill Lark
www.larkdistillery.com.au

One can consider Bill Lark the father of the modern whisky distilling we see today in Australia. In 1992 he was the first person for 153 years to take out a distillation license in Tasmania. Since then he has not just established himself as a producer of malt whiskies of high quality but has also helped several new distilleries to start up. Recently he co-founded the Tasmanian Distillers Group together with the five other whisky distilleries on the island. But that is not all - in June 2009 he relocated to Scotland to help build the Kingsbarns Distillery in Fife!

Bill Lark´s original establishment in Kingston was

David Baker - Bakery Hill Distillery

moved to Hobart in 2001. In 2006 a new distillery was constructed on a farm at Mt Pleasant, 15 minutes from Hobart. The farm grows barley for Cascade Brewery and at the moment that is where Lark Distillery gets its malt from. However, their intention is to set up their own floor maltings within two years thereby enabling them to produce everything themselves from barley field to bottle at one site. Not only that - in 2004 they secured their own peat bog at Brown Marsh and in January 2007 they also purchased the cooperage that makes the barrels. All in all, they are now very much in control of the whole chain. The "old site" down in Hobart by the waterfront is now a showcase for the Lark whisky with a shop, café and whisky bar with over 100 different single malts.

The core product in the whisky range is the Single Cask Malt Whisky at 43% but Bill Lark has also recently released a Distillers Selection at 46% and a Cask Strength at 58%, both of which are also single cask. The range is completed by a malt whisky liqueur called Slainte and a Pure Malt Spirit at 45%.

The whisky is double-distilled in an 1,800 litre wash still and a 600 litre spirit still and then matured in 100 litre "quarter casks". The current production is 10-12 barrels per month.

Apart from whisky, Lark Distillery also produces Lark Bush (replacing the old Tasmanian Bush Liqueur) based on Tasmanian Pepperberry, Pepperberry Vodka (triple distilled) and Apple Schnapps.

DISTILLERY: Hellyers Road Distillery,
                Burnie, Tasmania
FOUNDED: 1999
OWNER/MANAGER: Betta Milk Co-op/
Laurie House
www.hellyersroaddistillery.com.au

Hellyer´s Road Distillery is the largest single malt whisky distillery in Australia and although it has

Bill Lark - Lark Distillery

been producing since 1999, the whisky has not been on the market for more than two years. The capacity allows for 500 casks per year to be produced but there are also 2,500 200-litre casks in bond. The Tasmanian barley is malted at Cascade Brewery in Hobart and peat from Scotland is used for the peated expressions. Batches of 6.5 tonnes of grist are loaded into the mash tun and then the wash is fermented for 65 hours. There is only one pair of stills but they compensate for numbers by size. The wash still has a capacity of 60,000 litres which is twice that of the largest wash still in Scotland at Glenkinchie Distillery. The spirit still's capacity is 30,000 litres and the interesting part here is the really slow distillation. The foreshots take around 4-5 hours and the middle cut will last for 24 hours, which is six to seven times longer compared to practice in Scotland. Maturation takes place in ex-bourbon casks.

There are three varieties of Hellyers Road Single Malt Whisky in the range: Original, Slightly Peated and Peated. There is also the premium expression Hellyers Road Distillers Choice which is only available to visitors who take the guided tour at the distillery.

This distillery was previously known as Whisky Tasmania but when the first bottles were released the name was changed to Hellyers Road Distillery after Henry Hellyer, one of the first European explorers to set foot in Tasmania.

DISTILLERY: Great Southern Distilling Company,
                Albany, Western Australia
FOUNDED: 2004
OWNER/MANAGER: Great Southern Distilling
Company Pty Ltd/Cameron Syme
www.distillery.com.au

This is the only whisky distillery in the western part of Australia. It was built in Albany on the southwestern tip of Australia in 2004 with whisky production commencing in late 2005. Throughout the initial years production of whisky, brandy, vodka and gin took place in a set of sheds on the outskirts of Albany. A move was made in October 2007 to a new, custom-built distillery with a visitor centre on Princess Royal Harbour.

Production takes place in pot stills (one wash still of 1,900 litres and one spirit still of 580 litres) and a 600 litre copper pot antique gin still has also been installed. For maturation a mix of ex-bourbon, ex-house brandy and ex-sherry barrels are used as well as new and reshaved/charred American Oak and French Oak casks. Great Southern Vodkas and Gin have been available for sale since October 2006. The first expression of the malt whisky, called Limeburners, was released in April 2008 with the second appearing a couple of months later. Both releases were single casks and non-chill filtered. Limeburner single malt whisky releases are named M for malt with a unique barrel number. To date M3, M4, M5, M9, M11, M15, M19 and M24 have been released, either at 43% or 63% barrel strength. There are plans for other varieties including a peated version, using peat from local peat bogs. The first peated expression went into barrel in August 2008.

DISTILLERY: Tasmania Distillery, Cambridge, Tasmania
FOUNDED: 1996
OWNER/MANAGER: Patrick Maguire
www.tasmaniadistillery.com

Three generations of whisky can trace its origin from Tasmania Distillery. The first was distilled between 1996 and 1998 and, according to the current owner Patrick Maguire, the quality is so poor that he does not want to bottle it. Instead it has been sold to bakeries to be used in Christmas cakes and similar pastries and just a few barrels remain. The second generation was distilled from November 1999 to July 2001 and is bottled today under the name Sullivan´s Cove. The third generation is the whisky distilled from 2003, until now under Patrick's and his three partners' ownership, and will not be bottled until it has reached 12 years of age.

Annual production amounts to 120 casks of 200 litres each of non-chill filtered whisky which is matured in American Oak bourbon casks and French Oak port barrels. The range of 7 year old whiskies is made up of Sullivan´s Cove cask strength (60%) matured in either bourbon casks or port casks and Sullivan´s Cove Double Cask (40%) which is a marriage of port and bourbon casks. Following a number of awards, the rest of the world has now started to take an interest in the whisky, which is available in Scandinavia, Holland, Korea, Singapore, Taiwan, Hong-Kong and China.

DISTILLERY: Nant Distillery, Bothwell, Tasmania
FOUNDED: 2007
OWNER/MANAGER: Keith Batt
www.nantdistillery.com.au

Many of the new malt whisky projects popping up all over the world have sprung from already existing brewing and/or distilling facilities. Nant distillery in Bothwell in the Central Highlands of Tasmania is something quite different. Queensland businessman Keith Batt bought the property in 2004 and has since renovated the Historic Sandstone Water Mill on the

Patrick Maguire - Tasmania Distillery

Estate that was built in 1823 and converted it into a whisky distillery. The first distillation took place on 5th April 2008. Keith´s idea is to manage the whole production process on site. Barley has been grown on the estate since 1821 and continues to this day. On the Estate there was also a 180 year old water driven flour mill which is now used for grinding the barley into grist. Peat from the original Nant summer highland grazing property Lake Echo will also be used in the malting process. The distillery is equipped with an 1,800 litre wash still and a 600 litre spirit still and timber washbacks are used for the fermentation. For maturation Keith will be using quarter casks of 100 litres previously used for port, sherry and bourbon. Tasmanian veteran distiller Bill Lark has been consulted to ensure the quality of the production and the first bottling is expected in 2010. The capacity of the distillery will be about 300 100-litres barrels per year.

DISTILLERY: Victoria Valley Distillery, Essendon Fields, Melbourne, Victoria
FOUNDED: 2008
OWNER/MANAGER: David Vitale, Lark Distillery m fl
www.victoriavalley.com.au

This is the very latest distillery to come on stream in Australia. Co-founder, Managing Director and Head Distiller is David Vitale who previously worked with sales and marketing at Lark Distilleries in Tasmania. Bill Lark from the forementioned distillery has also taken part in the start-up of Victoria Valley. The owner is still looking for a final location for the production but settled for an interim site at Essendon Fields, Melbourne´s original airport. The distillery is actually fitted into an old Qantas maintenance hangar. The stills (an 1,800 litre wash still and a 600 litre spirit still) were bought from Joadja Creek Distillery in Mittagong and contribute to an initial capacity of 20,000 cases of whisky in a year. The target is to increase to 50,000 cases in the future.

David is planning to produce three types of whisky - a single malt, an American-style bourbon and an Australian-style whisky that will provide a clear point of difference. Part of the whisky will mature in Pedro Ximinez sherry butts of which David has already ordered 250. The first products will be ready to launch in October 2011.

DISTILLERY: Old Hobart Distillery Blackmans Bay, Tasmania
FOUNDED: 2007
OWNER/MANAGER: Casey Overeem

This distillery in Tasmania (previously known as Overeem Distillery) came on stream in 2007. By summer 2007 four barrels (100 litres) had been produced and the distillery will continue to produce at least two barrels per month. The omnipresent Bill Lark (see Lark distillery) has also assisted here. The two stills (wash still of 1,800 litres and spirit still of 600 litres) were made by the Hobart still maker Knapp-Lewer.

New Zealand _____

DISTILLERY: New Zealand Malt Whisky Co, Oamaru, South Island
FOUNDED: 2000
OWNER/MANAGER: Warren Preston
www.nzmaltwhisky.co.nz
www.milfordwhisky.co.nz

In 2001, Warren Preston bought the entire stock of single malt and blended whisky from decommissioned Wilsons Willowbank Distillery in Dunedin. Founded by local businessmen in 1969, it stopped producing in 1997 and was dismantled in 2000. The supplies Preston acquired consisted of, among other things, 400 casks of single malt whisky including production dating back to 1987. Before he bought it, the whisky was sold under the name Lammerlaw but Preston renamed it Milford. There have been 10, 12, 15, 18 and 20 year bottlings. The casks containing Milford whisky are maturing at Preston´s 125 year old grain store located in Oamaru, which is a small town on the East Coast of the South Island.

His long-term objective was to establish a whisky distillery at a highland property near Queenstown at Nevis Bluff on the Kawaru River. He was granted a 5 year consent in 2007 from the local authorities to build a boutique distillery. In August 2009, however, the site was offered for sale at an auction. Preston had decided it would make more sense to build the distillery adjacent to the existing warehouses in Oamaru. This will mean that the start of distilling originally planned for 2009 will be postponed.

ASIA

India _____

DISTILLERY: Amrut Distilleries Ltd., Bangalore
FOUNDED: 1948
OWNER/MANAGER: Jagdale Group
www.amrutdistilleries.com
www.amrutwhisky.co.uk

Amrut was the first (and so far only) Indian distillery with serious aspirations of establishing itself on the European market. Its first single malt (matured 3-4 years) became available in the UK at the end of 2004 and can now be found in, among other countries, the Netherlands, Sweden, France, Germany and Italy.

The main part of its malt production, commenced in the mid-eighties, is used for Amrut's blended whiskies. The malt is produced in Jaipur and Delhi from grain grown in Punjab and Rajasthan. Distilling takes place at Amrut in Bangalore and the water is brought by lorry from a well 15 miles outside the town. The casks are mainly ex-bourbon of American Oak. The rather harsh climate during maturation gives an Angel's share of between 12 and 15%. This means that a storage period of longer than four years is practically impossible.

The Amrut family of single malts has grown and except for the unpeated and peated versions which are bottled at 46%, an Amrut cask strength was released in 2006 and in 2008 it was followed up by a peated cask strength (62.8%). There are also Amrut Fusion which is based on both Scottish and Indian barley and, finally, Amrut Two Continents where maturing casks have been brought from India to Scotland for their final period of maturation.

DISTILLERY: McDowell's, Ponda, Goa
FOUNDED: 1988 (malt whisky)
OWNER/MANAGER: UB Group
www.clubmcdowell.com

McDowell's has been part of the United Breweries Group since 1951 when the company was acquired by Vittal Mallya. UB Group, now owned by the son of the founder, Vijay Mallya, is number three in the world after Diageo and Pernod Ricard.

United Spirits dominates the Indian spirits market of which it has a share of 60%. In the fiscal year ending March 2009, sales of 90 million cases of spirit could be reported compared to 75 million the previous year. Since 2008 another three brands have made it into the so-called Millionaire´s Club to which brands that sell more than 1 million nine-litre cases per year belong. Last year 16 brands from United Spirits were in this club.

The major brands in the group are huge sales-wise. Bagpiper blended whisky is the world's best-selling whisky with almost 14.5 million cases sold in 2008/2009. McDowell´s No 1 is one of the fastest growing whiskies in the world. It sold almost 13 million cases in 2008/2009 compared to 2.5 million 10 years ago and is on the way to becoming the largest selling whisky in India. Single malt sales are of course negligible compared to these figures. McDowell´s Single Malt (3-4 years) is made at the distillery in Ponda (Goa) and sells some 20 000 cases each year.

In 2007 United Spirits Limited acquired the Scottish whiskymaker Whyte & Mackay (with, inter alia, Whyte & Mackay blend and Dalmore, Jura and Fettercairn distilleries) for £595m.

Pakistan _____

DISTILLERY: Murree Brewery Ltd., Rawalpindi
FOUNDED: 1860
OWNER/MANAGER: Bhandara family
www.murreebrewery.com

It may seem an impossible mission to produce alcoholic beverages in a Muslim country where as many as 97% of the population are excluded as consumers due to their religion. This leaves the Christian, Hindu and Parsee communities. However, the ingenuity of many Muslim Pakistanis is great and the company claims that 99% of their customers are Muslim.

The owner of Murree Brewery, Minoo Bhandara died 15th June 2008 in a car crash, barely 70 years old. Minoo Bhandara was succeeded as Chief Executive by his son Isphanyar Bhandara.

Murree Brewery in Rawalpindi started as a beer brewery supplying the British Army. The assortment was completed with whisky, gin, rum, vodka and brandy. Three single malts have been available for some time; 3, 8 and 12 years respectively.

In 2005 an 18 year old single malt was launched and the following year their oldest expression so far, a 20 year old, reached the market. There are also a number of blended whiskies such as Vat No. 1, Lion and Dew of Himalaya.

Company sources mention a supply of half a million litres of whisky in underground storage. The brewery makes their own malt (using both floor maltings and Saladin box).

Murree Brewery consists of three divisions – the liquor division (responsible for 70% of income and almost 100% of the profit), Tops division (mainly fruit juices) and a glass division (which manufactures glass containers for the company and other customers).

Taiwan

DISTILLERY: The Kavalan Distillery, Yuanshan, Ilan County
FOUNDED: 2005
OWNER/MANAGER: King Car Food Industrial Co.
www.kingcar.com.tw

The first whisky distillery in Taiwan was built in record time and construction lasted just eight months. The first distillation took place on 11th March 2006. King Car is a leading manufacturer of canned coffee and has 2,000 employees of which 20 are involved with the distillery.

The distillery is equipped with a traditional stainless steel mash tun with copper top and closed stainless steel washbacks. The interesting features are the stills as they have two different production lines. One has two pairs of copper pot stills made by Forsyths; the wash stills have a capacity of 10,500 litres and the spirit stills 6,000 litres. The second line consists of three pairs of Holstein stills with a capacity of 14,000 litres per pair. The total capacity (and current actual production) is no less than 2.52 million litres of alcohol which is twice that of, for example, Ardbeg. The malted barley is imported with Baird´s of Inverness as the main supplier. The whisky matures mainly in ex bourbon barrels and ex sherry casks with a few others used for experimentation.

The first release of Kavalan was in December 2008. In July 2009 a port finish variety appeared and then in August two different single casks were launched - one ex-bourbon and one ex-sherry, both at cask

strength. The most important market is primarily mainland China but it is possible that the whisky will be exported to further destinations in the near future.

Turkey

DISTILLERY: Tekel (Mey Corporation), Ankara
FOUNDED: 1930 (whisky since 1963)
OWNER/MANAGER: Texas Paficic Group (TPG)
www.mey.com.tr

Both production and sales of tobacco and alcohol in Turkey have been administered by the national company Tekel, which also has a salt division. A change in legislation in 2001 opened a window for privatization and the wine and spirits division was sold to four companies, Nurol, Limak, Özaltin and Tütsab, in 2004 for $292 million. They formed a holding company, Mey Industry & Trade to market and distribute the products but kept the company name Tekel. In 2006 Mey Corporation was sold to the American Texas Pacific Group for $900 million. There is a large range of beverages, mainly consisting of wine and raki, but vodka, gin, 'cognac' and whisky are also included. The company has produced a whisky named Ankara Turk Viskisi since 1963. It can probably not be called a single malt as it is reported to contain a portion of malted rye and rice mixed with malted barley. The whisky is aged for three years on oak casks.

*The first release
from Kavalan Distillery*

AFRICA

South Africa ————————————

DISTILLERY: James Sedgwick Distillery,
Wellington, Western Cape
FOUNDED: 1886 (whisky production 1990)
OWNER/MANAGER: Distell Group Ltd.
www.distell.co.za

The James Sedgwick Distillery was founded in 1886 and has been the home to South African whisky since 1990. The distillery is currently under major expansion in order to enable it to continue meeting the growing demand for whisky in South Africa.

It was responsible for South Africa's very first single malt whisky when, back in the autumn of 2003, a limited number of 6,000 bottles of Three Ships 10 year single malt was released. There are plans to reintroduce the 10 year single malt, probably in early 2011, and Distillery Manager Andy Watts says, "The maturation of the next single malt continues to be carefully monitored and it promises to be well worth the wait."

The distillery's line of blended whiskies is, however, larger: Three Ships Select, Three Ships Premium Select 5 years, Three Ships Bourbon Cask Finish, Harrier and Knights which all together amount to circa 7,000,000 bottles a year.

James Sedgwick distillery has the capability of producing both malt and grain whisky and has this year produced yet another first for South Africa. A "single grain" whisky has been released under the Bain's label. It pays tribute to the pioneering pass builder Andrew Geddes Bain who built and completed the Bainskloof mountain pass in 1853 which then connected the Cape region of South Africa with the interior. Bain's Cape Mountain Whisky is the first South African grain whisky and is double matured in the same style of cask. Although it has no age statement it is matured for a minimum of five years.

The distillery is equipped with one still with two columns for production of grain whisky, two pot stills for malt whisky and

Bain's - the first single grain from South Africa

one still with six columns designated for neutral spirit (re-distillation of feints etc. from other processes). There are also two mash tuns and 23 washbacks. Grain whisky is distilled for nine months of the year, malt whisky for two (always during the winter months July/August) and one month is devoted to maintenance. The barley for the malt whisky is imported from UK maltsters.

The interest in whisky in general continues to grow in South Africa with the sales of Scotch whisky now holding the ninth position in the world market in terms of value and fifth position in terms of volume.

DISTILLERY: Drayman's Distillery,
Silverton, Pretoria
FOUNDED: 2006
OWNER/MANAGER: Moritz Kallmeyer
www.draymans.com

Being a full-time beer brewer since 1997, Moritz Kallmeyer decided it was time to take the next step and began distilling malt whisky in July 2006. Until now production has been small (one cask of 225 litres a month) but operations have currently been expanded to two pot stills.

Kallmeyer calculates a first release in February 2010 of about 4,000 bottles. This version will be unpeated, distilled exclusively from South African dry-land barley malt from the Swartland area. It will be aged in used red wine barrels (Pinotage and Cabernet) of European Oak origin.

Kallmeyer is also planning a peated version but since he has been unable to find a supplier of peated malt in South Africa, he has now decided to build a small kiln of his own and will be using Canadian peat to dry the malt. At the time of writing this project has, however, been put on hold for financial reasons. The biggest obstacle for owners of micro-distilleries is often capital. Creativity and innovation are essential traits to possess, especially when it comes to equipping the distillery.

At Drayman's there is a new wash still (1,500 litres) but the spirit still (800 litres) was cleverly reconstructed from a stainless steel tank in which perfume was imported. Kallmeyer let a local welder rebuild it and then connected it by himself to a column still. He also believes in letting the wash spend a long time in the washback, often up to ten days, to allow the malolactic fermentation to transfer its character to the spirit.

The distillery already sells whisky which is bought from Scotland, blended and solera-matured at Drayman's. In addition to whisky, Drayman's produces a range of seasonal craftbeers, as well as the local and for South Africa very typical brandy made of fruit called Mampoer. The latest project is a honey liqueur which is a woodmatured blend of Draymans Solera blended whisky and organically farmed Bushveld honey.

The Whisky Year That Was

—— the fire is still burning——

Will Scotch whisky beat the recession?

The past couple of years have been the best ever for Scotch whisky and most companies had probably prepared themselves for a slightly slower pace of increase in the near future. Then in early autumn 2008 it seemed like the world was dragged into a black hole of economic recession. Banks were taken over by governments and huge corporations were protected from their creditors. Even small countries like Iceland were on the verge of bankruptcy.

The reaction from the whisky industry was comparatively cool. There were times when it was stated that the spirits industry is recession-proof, that people would continue buying alcohol even if times became worse. That has been modified recently to that the industry is recession resilient, and maybe something lies in that, at least when looking at the figures for Scotch whisky for the full year 2008.

Scotch whisky exports rose by 8% compared to 2007 and reached £3.06bn, breaking the £3 billion barrier for the first time.

The increase in value was not followed by an increase in volume. On the contrary, it sunk with 5%, reaching the equivalent of 1.080 million bottles. This reflects the premiumisation trend which we have seen the last years.

The picture, if broken down into malt and blends, is as follows (note that bulk shipments are not included):

BOTTLED MALT - EXPORT
Value: +9% to £497m
Volume: +0.5% to 72m bottles

BOTTLED BLENDED SCOTCH - EXPORT
Value: +9% to £2.43bn
Volume: -2.9% to 848m bottles

The most important market in terms of value is still the USA but the 5% increase which rejoiced producers last year was now changed to a decrease of 11% to £371m. The other countries on the North American market showed strength though and exports to Canada increased by 11% and to Mexico by 59%. The largest market in South America, Venezuela, has been increasing steadily since 2003 but was hit by a significant decrease of 36% in 2008. Brazil on the other hand has huge potential and also showed a 10% increase.

In Asia, South Korea is the biggest market, at least in terms of value. Singapore most often leads the statistics but the vast majority of the shipments to it are re-exported to China as Diageo in particular has started using Singapore as a hub. There is no doubt however that the countries with the largest potential are China and India. China is often called a white spirits market and 99% of consumption is of domestic spirits. India on the other hand is primarily a whisky market and the challenge there lays in competing with domestically produced whisky on terms that are not equal when it comes to taxes. In 2008, China grew by 4% while India, which has increased steadily the last decade, decreased by as much.

The growth in Africa, generally meaning the growth in South Africa, went up by 12% during 2008. The country has been one of the fastest growing markets for several years now and is responsible for more than 70% of the continent's import of Scotch whisky. An even more dominating position (90% of the total) in the Australasian region is Australia, and the export to it increased by 32% in 2008.

Finally, the biggest market of them all is Europe where sales trends have moved very little from 1995 to 2006 in regards to totals. The fluctuations in single countries have been greater. Something happened in 2007 when the value of exported Scotch increased by 27% and the trend, even if somewhat weakened, sustained during 2008 with an increase of 17% to £1.28bn.

All four key markets increased by value but decreased by volume (except for Germany with a 2% increase). France was up 22%, Germany 14%, Greece 10% and Spain 8%. The French market was worth £359m in 2008 and is closing in on USA, which has been number one for some time, while passing Spain which temporarily overtook France in 2007. Some of the biggest increases during 2008 are found among the smaller Eastern European markets such as Poland, Romania, Hungary and Latvia.

First quarter of 2009
- clouds towering up on the horizon

The first months of 2009 came as a nasty shock after the relief of surviving the last quarter of 2008 comparatively well. The global economic downturn now also made its mark on the drinks companies. Compared to the same period in 2008, exports of blended Scotch decreased by 23% and malt whiskies by 22%. (Figures apply for whiskies bottled in Scotland). Bulk-exported malt whiskies increased by 44%. Despite this the total decrease was 19%. The main cause of that was stock reductions by cautious distributors and it now remains to be seen if the consumers will be as cautious and make changes in their drinking patterns.

Some of the largest reductions during January to March are found in the USA where bottled blends were down 44% and bottled malts down 12%. Spain showed even poorer figures with bottled blends down 48% and malts down by 60%. Other markets with declining figures were South Korea (-40%), China (-27%) and Thailand (-67%), and the home market was also subdued with blended Scotch down 31% in the UK and single malts even worse, a fall of as much as 47%.

But there were examples of markets showing strength. In South America, countries like Mexico, Venezuela, Brazil and Argentina were all up compared to last year and India headed the same way.

The big players

N.B.! It is important to keep in mind that while some producers' annual accounts follow calendar years, others like Diageo and Pernod Ricard close their financial year on 30th June. The impact of the economic downturn did not make its mark on the whisky producers until in January 2009 which means that Diageo and Pernod Ricard show a worse result than if they had followed calendar years.

Diageo

When Diageo presented its report for the year ending June 2009, both sales and profit were up compared to last year. But if one breaks down the figures, they are not that convincing after all. Net sales admittedly increased by 15% from £8,090m to £9,311m but included in this increase is exchange rate movements by £1,095m and sales of £151m of Ketel One vodka, a brand that was acquired during the year. This means that organic movement was actually down by £25m. Operating profit increased by 10% from £2,226m to £2,443m and showed a positive organic growth of £99m (+4%).

It is obvious that among the company's major brands it is the Scotch portfolio with a 3% slip in net sales that is the biggest disappointment. Johnnie Walker lost mainly as it is relatively higher priced and customers moved to the lower priced segments. In J&B's case it was more of a downturn on the Spanish market which is of particular importance for that brand. The only key brand whisky that showed sales growth was Windsor with its very strong performance on the Korean market.

Diageo's CEO Paul Walsh warns that fiscal 2010 will be challenging and says "we expect to deliver low single digit organic operating profit growth."

Pernod Ricard

Just like Diageo, Pernod Ricard showed resilience when it announced its report for the year ending 30 June. Net sales were up 9.3% to €7.2bn but on an organic basis it dropped by 0.4%. Operating profit increased by 21.9% to €1.76bn boosted by good sales of Absolut Vodka. Net profits came in 12.5% up while organic growth was 4%, just like Diageo. If we look at the whisky brands amongst Pernod Ricard's 14 strategic brands, Jameson (+8%) and Glenlivet (+7%) showed strength in terms of organic growth by value. Among the losers are Chivas Regal (-2%) and Ballantine's (-5%). There is also a group called local brands where Clan Campbell in France (+8%) and Royal Stag in India (+22%) showed good results.

Pernod Ricard has been burdened by large loans in connection with the acquisition of V&S and Absolut vodka the previous year. So far it has managed to reduce the debt by selling off brands, two of the biggest being Wild Turkey (to Campari for £391m) and Tia Maria (to Illva Saronno for €125m). A successful capital increase through a rights offering in April 2009 brought in over €1bn. Two months later a €800m bond issue was completed to further strengthen the financial position.

Pierre Pringuet, CEO of Pernod Ricard, predicted a difficult economic environment for 2009/2010 with an overall stagnation of the Wines and Spirits industry.

Christian Porta - CEO of Chivas Brothers, owned by Pernod Ricard

United Spirits

United Spirits Limited, which is part of the Indian UB Group and the third largest drinks producer in the world after Diageo and Pernod Ricard, showed an impressive rise in terms of sold cases for the year ending 31st March 2009. The increase was 20% to 90 million cases which made a rise in turnover of 21.2% to Rs. 39.04 billion.

The net profit on the other hand was not a matter for celebration. The drop was 4.5% to Rs. 2.97 billion. The main reason for this was higher interest costs and, bearing in mind that US borrowed $600m when they bought Whyte & Mackay two years ago and by July 2009 had only paid $110m back, it of course has an impact on the result. That is also why Shaw Wallace, a company within the UB Group, sold a 10.2% stake in United Spirits, and the money from these shares will be used to pay back another $180m.

During the year there have also been persistent rumours that market leader Diageo is negotiating to buy a share in United Spirits. A second rumour indicated that Vijay Mallya, owner of UB Group, was looking at selling a 49% minority stake of Whyte & Mackay. A few months later it was rumoured that the intention was to sell the whole Scottish whisky producer. The problem is that there are few companies today that are either interested in or in a financial state to place a bid. In any case, industry sources claim that UB Group would probably be lucky to get in the vicinity of £200m for Whyte & Mackay which cost them £595m back in 2007.

United Spirits dominates the Indian whisky market controlling approximately 60% of it. The biggest sellers in the whisky segment are Bagpiper (almost 15 million cases per year) and McDowell's No. 1 (close to 13 million cases). During 2008 their Signature Rare Whisky became the company's 19th member of the Spirits Millionaire Club, i. e. brands that annually sell over 1 million 9-litre cases.

Edrington

The Edrington Group, owner of Famous Grouse, Macallan and Highland Park among others, showed strong increase in both sales and profits when they presented the figures for the year ending 31 March. Net sales hit £420m, up by 44%, and pre-tax profits rose by 30% to £94.8m. These figures are of course extraordinary in view of the current global economy but the acquisition of a majority stake of family-owned Brugal Rum in early 2008 helped to keep them up. Brugal is the fastest growing rum brand in Europe and sells more than five million cases globally in a year.

Both of the top single malts showed strength with an increase of 2.5% for Macallan to 584,000 cases and 10% for Highland Park to 110,000 cases. Highland Park, now in 12th place on the sales top list amongst single malts, is aiming for a top ten position which may take longer than has been hoped for. The three leading malts are all peated brands (Lagavulin, Talisker and Bowmore) and they take advantage of the strong, still rising, interest for peated whiskies. Famous Grouse went in the opposite direction in terms of sales with a decrease of 3% to 2.8 million cases.

Morrison Bowmore

Morrison Bowmore (owner of Bowmore, Auchentoshan and Glen Garioch distilleries) had a terrific year in 2007 when sales increased by 22%. A slight drop of 7% to £37m in sales in 2008 did not ruffle the feathers much as Morrison Bowmore is still in the process of withdrawing from the high-volume but less profitable blended Scotch market. The 13%

increase in profits during 2008 (to £3.6m) speaks for itself in support of this decision.

An agreement with Drambuie to take over the production of the famous liqueur from Glenmorangie was a major business milestone during spring 2009. The withdrawal from the blended segment has left Morrison Bowmore with excess capacity at the blending and bottling plant at Springburn near Glasgow. From 2010 Drambuie will lease the facilities for an undisclosed sum in order to produce 4 million bottles of the whisky liqueur per year.

LVMH

LVMH Moët Hennessy Louis Vuitton SA was created through a $4 billion merger in 1987 and is the world's leading luxury goods vendor. It provides products ranging from champagne and perfumes to designer handbags. The Wines & Spirits business group includes brands such as Moët & Chandon Champagne, Hennessy Cognac with Glenmorangie and Ardbeg as representatives of Scotch whisky.

Both turnover and profits increased in 2008 albeit not at the pace of the previous year. The total turnover (for all business groups) increased by 4% to €17.193m with Wines & Spirits decreasing by 3% to €3.126m. Total profits for the whole group rose by 2% to €3.628m. There are big differences between the business groups when the profit is analyzed - Perfumes & Cosmetics increased by 13%, Watches & Jewelry decreased by 16% whereas Wines & Spirits

remained at status quo. Sales of champagne and cognac in particular decreased towards the end of the year while the acquisition of the Spanish wine group Numanthia Termes and the Montaudon champagne house during the year compensated for that as did the fine results from the Scottish operations (see Glenmorangie below).

The first six months of 2009 show considerably lower sales from Wine & Spirits. In spring 2009 there were even rumours of Diageo bidding on LVMH's Wine & Spirits division, but nothing more has happened at the time of writing.

Glenmorangie Co

The owner of Glenmorangie and Ardbeg distilleries can reflect on a very successful year. The turnover increased by no less than 34% to £112.58m. It is also interesting to see that 85% of sales are in Europe and as much as 65% are in the UK. Even if the brand has been growing considerably in Asia the last couple of years, there is obviously much more potential there and especially in the Americas where the brand is still not very well known. If the increase in sales was imposing, what can be said about the profits that soared almost fourfold from £10.58m to £39.33m? Even if one-off income such as the sale of Glen Moray Distillery, brand and stock and the sale of its Broxburn site to Diageo is removed, the profits amount to an impressive £30.51m.

Glenmorangie took a decision to withdraw from

Glenmorangie's fine result in 2008 is partly due to the revamp of the whole range two years ago

the low margin blended whisky market in connection with selling Glen Moray to La Martiniquaise.
The only brands retained in the company are Bailie Nicol Jarvie and Martin´s.

Bacardi Limited
Bacardi is the largest privately-held spirits company in the world with a brand portfolio that includes Bacardi (the world´s second best selling premium spirit after Smirnoff), Bombay Sapphire Gin, Grey Goose Vodka, Dewar´s blended Scotch and Aberfeldy single malt.

Bacardi had a very good year ending March 2009 bearing the present economic circumstances in mind. Even if turnover decreased by 4% to $5.335m, the profits rose by 1% to $805m.

In spring 2009, Brown-Forman Corp. (Jack Daniel´s and Southern Comfort) hired investment bankers Lazard to advise them on either selling off certain brands or to merge with Bacardi. No comments have yet come from Bacardi on the outcome of this.

Ian Macleod Distillers
The latest report from the company concerns the fiscal year ending in September 2008 and showed an impressive rise in pre-tax profits of 53% to £1.5m. The turnover rose by 4%. The company´s profile includes being a distiller and blender as well as independent bottler. It bought Glengoyne Distillery in 2003 together with the Scotch blend brand Langs. There is also King Robert II blend, Smokehad Malt Whisky, Rostov Vodka and London Hill Gin in the portfolio. Combined sales exceed 1 million bottles of which 85% are exported to more than 65 markets.

Inver House
Last year Inver House showed an impressive result when profits grew by no less than 108%.The 2008 results, as seen in the light of global recession, can be said to be at least equally impressive. Turnover did, as a matter of fact, decrease by 10% to £51.5m but can mainly be explained by a reduction in bulk trading. Pre-tax profits on the other hand increased by 96% to reach £7.5m. Single malts Balblair (+23%) and Pulteney (+16%) as well as the blend Hankey Banni-ster (+20%) showed the greatest progress. Other brands in the company include Speyburn and anCnoc single malts.

Fortune Brands
The American company with its headquarter in Deer-field, Illinois is active in three different areas; Home & Hardware, Golf and Spirits. The latter is contained within subsidiary Beam Global Spirits & Wine which has major spirits brands such as Jim Beam, Maker´s Mark, Canadian Club, Courvoisier and, in Scotch, Teacher´s and Laphroaig.

Total sales for the company decreased by 11% to $7.6 billion and net profit went down to $317m (-58%). Like last year, Golf and Home & Hardware marred the results of the company; operating income was down 24% and 42% respectively while Spirits only dropped by 12%. Spirits' share of the company´s total operating income is now 57% and of total

sales, 33%.

Laphroaig continues to signal strength and increased sales by 6%, with 2.2 million bottles sold in 2008. Beam Global´s CEO since 2004, Tom Flocco, resigned in October 2008 and was succeeded in May 2009 by Matt Shattock who came from Cadbury´s.

Gruppo Campari
The owners of Glen Grant, Italian Davide Campari-Milano, saw a year of slightly decreasing sales volumes but a small rise in profits. Annual sales went down by 1.6% to €942m while net profits came in at €126m, an increase of 1.1%. Glen Grant was a disappointment with a decrease of 20% to 3 million bottles. The negative figures can be explained by a decreasing interest in whisky on the Italian home market, but in spite of that Glen Grant is still the market leader in Italy. The (non-whisky) brands that kept sales up were Campari, Skyy Vodka and Cinzano. Looking at the various markets, all grew organically in 2008 except for Italy which accounts for around 40% of the company's sales.

The first half-year of 2009 was negative in terms of sales compared to 2008 which is similar to the pattern of many other large spirits producers. Destocking by the distributors, especially during the first couple of months, was the main reason for this. In the end of May 2009, Gruppo Campari made their largest acquisition ever, when they bought Wild Turkey, the world´s top premium bourbon whiskey, from Pernod Ricard. Wild Turkey sells 800,000 cases a year and the price tag was $581m.

The big brands

Most brands have shown negative growth in terms of volume during 2008 or, in some cases, have increased by very little. In terms of value, on the contrary, more have increased which can be explained by the premiumisation trend with a larger share of more expensive products in the range than previously.

If we look at the single malts first; Glenfiddich is of course the undisputed leader but its goal of selling more than 1 million cases by 2008 was never reached, instead they stopped just below it. The struggle for second place is tough - Glenlivet sold 597,000 cases in 2008 and Macallan 584,000 cases. In the important American market, however, Glenfiddich came third as even Macallan overtook it and came in as number two. Glenmorangie with 315,000 cases is found after the top three while Glen Grant continues its decrease. It is now down to 250,000 sold cases in 2008 and could possibly be surpassed by Cardhu if the trend continues.

The number one in Blended Scotch is unrivalled - Johnnie Walker which, including all brand exten-sions, sold 16.2 million cases during 2008. In similar with the situation for single malts the battle over second place is fierce. J&B lost volumes and sold around 6 million cases while Ballantine´s decreased less and reported sales of 6.2 million cases. The number four spot belongs to Grant´s which sells around 4.6 million cases while the nice increase of

Chivas Regal since 2002 now has been halted and it sold 4.2 million cases during 2008. The owner of *Famous Grouse*, Edrington, claimed that it is now the most sold blended Scotch in the whole of the UK and not just Scotland with *Bell's* following them shortly behind.

Effects of the recession

The first effects of the financial downturn to hit the whisky industry was destocking by retailers in the beginning of 2009. The first six months saw declining sales figures for most of the producers. But there are also other consequences which affected the people working in the industry more directly - closing of plants and job cuts.

Diageo announced on 1st July that as part of a cost saving programme it would close the Kilmarnock packaging plant in Ayrshire as well as Port Dundas Grain Distillery and Dundashill Cooperage in Glasgow. The Kilmarnock plant can trace its roots back to 1820 and this is also where millions of bottles of Johnnie Walker have been bottled during the years, a fact which is also stated on the labels. The plant will shut down over a two-year period with 700 people losing their jobs.

Port Dundas Grain Distillery opened in 1810 and was supposed to celebrate its 200th anniversary next year, but instead the distillery will close leaving 140 people unemployed. Diageo states that the need for grain spirit will be taken care of by their other distillery at Cameronbridge.

Combined ramifications of the closures will be 900 jobs lost. On the other hand Diageo will create 400 new jobs by expanding its packaging plant at Leven, Fife at a cost of £86m. A new cooperage will also be built at Diageo's existing site at Cambus near Alloa by summer 2011 - an investment of £9m. The overall reduction of 500 jobs means that the company is cutting more than 10% of its workforce in Scotland.

The government with First Minister Alex Salmond and Finance Secretary John Swinney reacted strongly and demanded talks with Diageo's management seeking ways to avoid job losses. A group of politicians and trade union representatives was formed and an accountancy firm made an independent business report as underlying material for alternative plans, but by the beginning of September nothing had come to light that might change the decision.

Only a month after Diageo's presentation, Whyte & Mackay announced restructuring of their operations which meant that, although no site will be closed, 100 people out of a workforce of more than 560 in Scotland will be made redundant. This will affect seven locations.

In September, Pernod Ricard UK reported that their sales, marketing and communications functions would be reduced by 36 people. Some of the redundancies would be mitigated by natural attrition.

Changes in ownership - mergers and acquisitions

With the exception of Glenmorangie selling Glen Moray Distillery to La Martiniquaise (which took place in September 2008) no take-overs have occur-

Port Dundas Grain Distillery

243

red since the last edition of Malt Whisky Yearbook was published, at least relating to Scotch whisky. This does not mean, however, that this part of the business has been uneventful. On the contrary, the uncertain times have provided plenty of nourishment for rumours of mergers and acquisitions of distilleries under financial pressure.

United Spirits has repeatedly been named in such discussions at regular intervals during the year. It is no secret that its acquisition of Whyte & Mackay in 2007 entailed a large debt burden with heavy interest to be paid. Initial speculation was that United Spirits was looking to sell 49% of the Scotch whisky group, but in spring 2009 it increasingly seemed as if the owner, Vijay Mallya, wanted to sell the whole company. Those in the know within the industry were of the opinion that a deal in the current economic climate would probably only bring in around £200m compared to the £595m United Spirits paid in 2007.

In November 2008 both United Spirits and Diageo, the biggest drinks company, were involved in another discussion. Both companies confirmed that they were considering a possible collaboration. Spring came and it became obvious that progress in negotiations was slow. There were rife speculations that a possible outcome of the deliberations could be United Spirits selling a 15% stake of the company to Diageo. Then by the end of August, Diageo declared that they withdrew from the discussions. The reason was too big disagreements over the financial bits.

Being among the more solvent companies in the business, Diageo has featured in other scenarios during the year. One was aiming to buy the Spirits divison of LVMH including brands like Moët & Chandon Champagne, Hennessy Cognac and Glenmorangie Scotch. Diageo already has a 34% stake in Moët Hennessy and was apparently willing to pay £8.9bn to obtain the whole division. Sources close to the situation said that LVMH wants £10.6bn but Bernard Arnault, main owner and the richest man in France, kept denying that negotiations were ongoing. If a deal would be put together it would most probably mean that Diageo would have to relinquish Glenmorangie and Ardbeg for antitrust reasons.

Continuing with Diageo, it was reported in July that China Investment Corp., a state-owned wealth fund, had acquired 1.1% of Diageo in a deal valued at $365m. Even if that can be considered a very small stake, it is still interesting to see a Chinese minority owner of the world's biggest drinks company.

Meanwhile, the slightly smaller companies in the industry witnessed with some concern how the big conglomerates gained more and more influence. Therefore reports on a possible merger between Bacardi (owner of Dewars among others) and Brown-Forman (maker of Jack Daniel's and Southern Comfort) came as no surprise although neither of the companies has yet confirmed anything. Both companies are medium-sized and family-owned and they have cooperated in distribution for a couple of years. On the other hand similar rumours about a merger between the two flourished already in 2007.

One company which could be up for sale is Burn Stewart Distillers, owner of Bunnahabhain, Black

Bottle and Scottish Leader among others. While Burn Stewart itself is doing well, its Trinidadian owner, CL Financial, has been facing financial difficulties lately. These were so severe that at least three subsidiaries operating in the financial sector were taken over by the government of Trinidad and Tobago and its central bank in January 2009. A sign against a sale is a statement by the Executive Chairman of CL Financial, Lawrence Dupuy, in which he stated that they would now be devoting their attention to developing the group's drinks business.

Changes have also occurred during the past year with regards to distribution and sales. Maxxium Worldwide has been a distributor jointly owned by Beam Global Spirits & Wine, The Edrington Group, V&S and Rémy-Cointreau for ten years now. Due to the take-over of V&S and Absolut by Pernod Ricard last year, an early termination on behalf of V&S was made in October 2008, and in March 2009 Rémy-Cointreau made a planned exit from the partnership. The two remaining partners will continue to work in an alliance covering 24 of the markets previously managed through Maxxium Worldwide.

Changing of the Guards

John Ramsay, Master Blender for the Edrington Group, retired on 31 July 2009 after 43 years in the whisky business. Ramsay joined Edrington in 1991 and has been responsible for several successes such as Highland Park 18 year old, The Macallan Fine Oak range and the Glenrothes vintages, but also the Cutty Sark and, in particular, The Famous Grouse range of blends and vatted malts.
Ramsay was honoured through a limited release of The Glenrothes John Ramsay. He is succeeded by *Gordon Motion* who has been working side by side with Ramsay the last two and a half years.

On 10th August, a woman entered the male-dominated top level of whisky chief executives. She is *Stella David* and took up the position of CEO of William Grant & Sons. David came from the Bacardi Group where she worked as chief marketing officer and she replaced *Roland van Bommel* who had held the post for five years.

Two managers on Islay swapped jobs between them. *Graham Logie*, manager of Lagavulin Distillery, became manager of Port Ellen maltings and *Peter Campbell*, who had held that position for eight years, moved to Lagavulin. Campbell had previously worked for Diageo in Speyside while Logie was manager, of Talisker before he moved to Lagavulin three years ago.

A new manager for the three W. Grant's distilleries in Dufftown (Glenfiddich, Balvenie and Kininvie) started in June 2009. *Stuart Watts* has been with the company for six years. He joined in 2003 as a chemist within the Technical Support Team at Girvan and is also a researcher with the Scottish Whisky Research Institute. The previous manager was *Richard Cotton* who had held that position since 2006.

The Famous Grouse Master Blender John Ramsay (right) with his successor Gordon Motion

Kenny Gray retired as manager of Oban Distillery where he had been since 2002 and was recently celebrated after having been with Diageo for 40 years. Gray was replaced by 28-year old *Brendan McCarron* who is the youngest manager in the history of the distillery. McCarron has been with Diageo since 2006 and came from New York where he spent a year in Diageo´s North American operations.

The prestigious position as manager of the new giant within Diageo, Roseisle Distillery, went to *Gordon Winton* who was manager of Knockando Distillery until summer 2008. He was replaced there by *Duncan Tait* who previously had worked at Oban Distillery.

Clynelish Distillery got a new manager in September 2008. *Sarah Burgess*, who previously has worked at Dailuaine and Glen Spey Distilleries, succeeded *Mark Lochhead* who had been there since 2005. He moved to Skye to head Talisker since *Willie MacDougall* resigned.

New, revived and planned distilleries

Falkirk Distillery
Plans were made in early 2008 to open up a new distillery just a few miles up the road from the traditional Rosebank distillery in Falkirk, which has been closed since 1993. The initiative came from Fiona and Alan Stewart through their company The Falkirk Distillery Company. The original idea was to use the old Rosebank stills and to sell the whisky under the

name Rosebank but it seems that this will now not take place. Most of Rosebank´s remaining distilling equipment was stolen from the premises in January 2009 and as for the name, Diageo (who owns the trademark) says that it is not for sale. Still the Stewarts went ahead with the £5m plans and they were approved by local authorities in spring 2009. The facilities will hold a visitor centre, restaurant and shops aside from the distillery.

Dingle Distillery
Once there were hundreds of whisky distilleries on Ireland but today only four remain - Bushmills, Midleton, Cooley and the recently restarted Kilbeggan. Perhaps they can soon be five. Planning permission to build a distillery in Dingle, Co Kerry, was applied for in autumn 2008 and in March this year it was granted by Kerry County Council. Jerry O´Sullivan, managing director of Southbound Properties who bought the old creamery which will be converted into a distillery, and Porterhouse Brewing Company are behind it all. The project will cost in the region of £7m and it will be up and running in late 2009 if no major obstacles get in the way. The whiskey will be triple distilled and the first bottlings should be ready by 2013. In common with most other newly started distilleries, gin will be produced to provide income while the whisky matures.

Barra Distillery
The classic film Whisky Galore based on the equally classic novel by Sir Compton Mackenzie was filmed on the island of Barra in the Outer Hebrides. It is a story of the SS Politician which was stranded in 1941

The people behind Kingsbarns Distillery - Bill Lark, Greg Ramsay, Peter Bignell, Doug Clement, James Simpson and Sir Peter Erskine

and 264,000 bottles of whisky among her cargo were lost. The island where the ship went missing was in fact Eriskay, a smaller island to the north of Barra, but that did not deter Peter Brown who moved to Barra from Edinburgh 12 years ago. He wants to build a distillery there and is convinced that the connection with the film location will be favourable for the business. The project will cost more than £1m. Building will commence in autumn 2009 and Brown´s hope is that the distillery will be in production by 2011 with the first bottlings available in 2014. Casks have already been sold for £1,000 with orders coming in from Germany, Japan and Sweden among other countries.

Kingsbarns Distillery
Fife will get its third distillery in 2011 if everything goes as planned. The first two are the huge grain spirit complex Cameronbridge and the small farm distillery Daftmill. Kingsbarns Company of Distillers, spearheaded by Greg Ramsay and Doug Clement, are behind the new plans. Greg, who is from Tasmania, met Doug when they were working with establishing the Nant Distillery in Tasmania. Their idea is to build a distillery in the vicinity of St Andrews, an area with thousands of visitors each year but lacking a whisky distillery. Greg and Doug have consulted Bill Lark as advisor. He is the owner of Lark Distillery in Tasmania, godfather of modern whisky-making in Australia, and advisor to several other whisky companies in his native Australia. The idea is to convert

a farmstead on the Cambo Estate which has been home to the Erskine family since 1688 and is owned today by Sir Peter Erskine. The distillery will have one pair of stills (to be built in Tasmania) and the capacity will be around 100,000 litres per year.

Annandale Distillery
In the last Yearbook we could report on the possible resurrection of Annandale Distillery which closed as early as 1921. David and Teresa Thomson bought the site from a local farmer and in December 2008 they presented their plans to Dumfries & Galloway Council. The distillery site is located in Dumfriesshire and will, once constructed, be the southernmost distillery in Scotland. There is no equipment left and therefore Forsyths of Rothes have become involved in the building of stills and a mash tun. The buildings are listed and the mash house and warehouses will be restored while a new tun room and still house will be built. The specification for the equipment is one semi-lauter mash tun (2.5 tonnes), four wooden washbacks (12,000 litres each), one wash still (12,000 litres) and one intermediate still and one spirit still (4,000 litres each). Planned output is 250,000 litres per annum. There is no fixed date when the distillery will be in production but a decision has been made to primarily produce a peated whisky.

Mothballed distilleries still silent
There is nothing to report this year concerning the resurrection of mothballed or closed distilleries. After

Parkmore Distillery in Dufftown

Glenglassaugh started producing again last year there are not that many left which could be revived. Pernod Ricard owns three but Caperdonich does not have all the equipment left and rumours have it that Forsyths may be interested in buying the plant for other purposes. At Imperial most of the equipment is still intact but there are no signs that the owner will restart production. Glen Keith now serves as a technical centre as well as a filling store for Strathisla. Diageo has but one closed distillery where there could be at least a remote possibility of bringing it back from the dead, namely Brora. However with the building of the giant Roseisle Distillery, focus seems to be more on large scale operations rather than putting money into a small, run-down distillery. Judging from discussions the recent year the odds must be said to be high also on Parkmore Distillery in Dufftown. It was built in 1894, but silent since 1931, and is a beautiful distillery with all the buildings intact, including a pagoda roof, but lacking equipment. Owner Edrington today uses the warehouses for storing casks from Macallan. Rumour has it that William Grant & Sons was interested in acquiring the distillery but nothing more has happened.

Port Dundas grain distillery is closing

We are happy not to have had to report about closures in the first four editions of Malt Whisky Yearbook. But this time we have to report on one: Diageo announced in early July 2009 that Port Dundas grain distillery in Glasgow will close for good during the year. Diageo has embarked on a cost-cutting scheme to meet the current recession in global economy and it considers that the requirement for grain spirit can be fulfilled by expansion of the current plant in Cameronbridge, Fife. The closure will cost 100 jobs. Port Dundas Distillery, which opened back in 1810, produces 39 million litres of grain spirit annually.

Investments

In 2006 and 2007 the booming interest in whisky spurred the companies on to invest in new production facilities as well as in marketing campaigns. Few such plans were announced during 2008. Most of the proposed plans were carried out but there were also those that were put on hold. If we look at the major announcements that were made in 2006 and 2007, we see that *Macallan* revived the old still house and at least two of the planned new warehouses have been built. *Glenlivet* increased capacity by commissioning four new stills even though plans originally called for six. A new mash tun, two new stills and four washbacks were installed at *Glenmorangie*, just as planned, while the big kahuna of the industry, Diageo´s £40m *Roseisle Distillery*, was commissioned albeit slightly later than projected.

Inver House, the Airdrie based company opened up a 1m bottling hall in June 2009 and this was only the latest of several big investments made by its parent company, the Thai drink giant ThaiBev.

The new stills are installed at Glenmorangie

Burn Stewart's expanded bottling plant at East Kilbride and a view of the new Glenlivet stills being made

A similar investment was made by *Burn Stewart* (owner of Bunnahabhain, Tobermory and Deanston distilleries among others). It expanded its bottling plant in East Kilbride to a capacity of 84,000 bottles per day. With eight bottling lines there is an overall capacity of 2 million cases per year. The total investment was for £1m but that also included the replacement of four stills at Deanston.

In 2008, *Baird's Malt* demolished its old plant in Arbroath to give space for a brand new state of the art malting facility. There have been several add-on expansions in the malting business during the years but this is the first completely new plant aimed at the distilling industry that is built since 30 years. The total annual production will be 57,000 tonnes, the total investment is £30m and the new plant is expected to be ready for full production in the beginning of 2010. Baird's Malt operates five malting sites across the UK, located in Inverness, Arbroath and Pencaitland in Scotland and Grantham and Witham in England.

When *Glenmorangie* decided to withdraw from the blended whisky segment, it also decided to move headquarters from Broxburn and to build a new bottling plant. The chosen site comprises 11 acres in Livingston, seven miles away from the present location. The Broxburn facilities have been sold to Diageo and Glenmorangie expects to move to its new premises by the summer of 2010. A total of 120 staff will be employed at the new bottling hall facility. The construction of the bottling hall alone is a £15m investment.

Diageo has made the single largest Scottish whisky industry investment in recent years. A bio-energy facility is under construction at *Cameronbridge Grain Distillery* in Fife which, when ready, will supply 80% of the distillery's electricity needs and 98% of its steam requirements. This will result in carbon emissions being reduced by 56,000 tonnes. The plant will use the spent wash (wheat, malted barley, yeast and water) produced during distillation and separate it into liquid and dried solids. The liquids will then be transformed into biogas while the dried solids become biomass which can be used as fuel. The total cost is £65m and it is hoped the facility will be ready in 2010. Cameronbridge is Scotland's second largest distillery with a capacity of 70 million litres of spirit per annum.

Another step towards a more sustainable production of whisky will be taken in Rothes. *Combination of Rothes Distillers (CORD)* is an association of whisky distillers operating in and around the town of Rothes. A combined heat and power plant fuelled by co-products, mainly draff, from the whisky production is planned to be constructed in cooperation with Helius Energy. The other main residue from the distilleries - pot ale - will at the same plant be turned into animal feed. When first announced in March 2008, the project spokesperson declared a cost of £24m and a reduction of CO_2 emissions by 46,642 tonnes. In August 2009, the figures had been revised to £35m and 20,000 respectively. The power plant will generate 7.2 MW of electricity with the start of construction expected in summer 2010 and completion by 2012.

La Martiniquaise, the new owner of Glen Moray and the second largest spirits group in France, has been established in Scotland since 2004 with a huge bottling plant in Bathgate, West Lothian. In 2008 approval was given to expand with more warehouses and, above all, a grain distillery. The first warehouse was completed already in 2008 and the work on the others started in early 2009. The Glen Turner Grain Distillery will have a capacity of 25 million litres and will produce grain whisky for, especially, Label 5, the most sold blended whisky in France.

Bottling grapevine
(see pp 254-257 for a detailed listing)

The malt whisky community keeps an extra watch on Diageo in the beginning of every autumn. That is when *The Special Releases* are launched. This usually means new expressions of the popular *Brora, Port Ellen* and *Talisker* whiskies and that was the case this year too. But the launch was spiced up by three major surprises from rarely heard of distillieries: *Mannochmore* released an 18 year old, *Benrinnes* a 23 year old and, perhaps the biggest surprise of all, *Pittyvaich* a 20 year old. The latter distillery has been closed since 1993. As this was not enough, Diageo announced that they would for the first time ever release single cask bottlings from all 27 distilleries, a range called *Manager's Choice*. The first six were announced beginning of September 2009 and within 10 months, three new batches will follow. According to Diageo themselves, the bottlings are aimed at connoisseurs and collectors and the pricing (betewen £200 and £300) also hint at that. The first batch consisted of *Cardhu 1997, Glen Elgin 1998, Linkwood*

Glen Elgin 1998 - a Manager's Choice

The launch of the new 50 year old from Glenfiddich was followd by a big gala dinner.
Des, Dennis and Eric also found time to celebrate in the warehouse.

Second release of Octomore
from Bruichladdich

Sonnalta PX - Glenmorangie's
new member in the duty free range

1996, *Mortlach 1997*, *Oban 2000* and *Teaninich 1996*. *Arran* distillery continued to follow their successful path leading towards a 14 and an 18 year old in a couple of years with a new *12 year old* as a temporary expression on the way. On Islay, *Bowmore* finished its fashionable series distilled in 1964 with the very exclusive *Gold Bowmore* but *Laimrig*, a special bottling for the Scandinavians, was also released. Still on Islay, *Ardbeg* released their peatiest expression ever, the *Supernova* and the committee bottling of *Corryvreckan* was given a general release.

Premiumisation has really been the way of *Dalmore* in recent years and 2009 was no exception with a *58 year old* and a *Vintage 1951* launched. After the remake of Bowmore's och Auchentoshan's ranges in 2007 and 2008, time had now come for the third distillery in the group, *Glen Garioch*. Two new core expressions were launched in autumn 2009 - *1797 Founders Reserve* and a *12 year old* as well as two limited *cask strength vintages*. Some distilleries aroused the market with bottlings of rare age like *Pulteney* did with their *30 year old*, *Glengoyne* with a *40 year old* and finally *Glenfiddich*, which launched a *50 year old* at a staggering price of £10,000 per bottle.

The people at Springbank had declared last year as the year of Longrow with several new expressions of the peated brand. In 2009 it was time for *Springbank* to receive attention when a *Madeira-matured 11 year old*, an *18 year old* and a *Vintage 2001* were released. Neither was the third variety in the portfolio, *Hazelburn*, neglected when a *12 year old* bottling turned up. The Master Blender for Glenrothes, John Ramsay retired in 2009 and his legacy to whisky lovers was *The Glenrothes John Ramsay*, a vatting of casks from 1973 to 1987. If we stay among Edrington-owned distilleries, *Macallan* released a very exclusive *Lalique* bottling (the third in the series) as well as a whole new range of bottlings destined for the Duty Free market called *The Macallan 1824 Collection*. The owner of the smallest distillery in Speyside, *Benromach*, released its first *10 year old* since the take-over of the distillery and *Scapa* on Orkney became two years older when the 14 year old was replaced by a *16 year old*.

Three distilleries were proud to release their first official bottlings - in summer 2009 *Glengyle* released *Kilkerran "Work in progress"*, two months later *Kilchoman* launched a 3 year old and in December the first official bottling from the only English whisky distillery, *St. George´s* in Norfolk, was presented.

BenRiach Distillers acquired *Glendronach* Distillery in autumn 2008 but have already managed to launch a core range of *12, 15* and *18 year olds* as well as some *single casks*. *Glenfarclas* continued with new vintages in their acclaimed series *Family Casks* but also presented two new versions of their *Glenfarclas 105* cask strength - a *40 year old* and a *duty free* bottling. The owner of resurrected *Glenglassaugh* struggles with a small stock but decided instead to sell new make spirit under the name *The Spirit Drink that dare not speak its name*. A distillery that never hesitates on speaking of its name is *Bruichladdich* and some ten new expressions were launched as customary. These included the second edition of the heavily peated *Octomore*, an *Organic Bruichladdich* and the sherried 19 year old *Black Art*.

Angus Dundee released new expressions from both of their distilleries; from *Glencadam* a 25 and a 30 year old and from *Tomintoul*, a new member of the core range, 14 years old. *Bunnahabhain* entered a new phase by launching its first duty free exclusive *Darach Ur* and also destined for travel retail was the first in the new series Private Collection by *Glenmorangie - Sonnalta PX*. Finally, in Ireland, *Cooley* distillery repackaged its range of *Connemara* and at the same time introduced a new member, the *Small Batch Sherry Finish*.

Robet Fleming, Director of Angus Dundee Distillers, made succesful launches from both his distilleries - Glencadam and Tomintoul

Independent Bottlers

The independent bottlers play an important role in the whisky business. With their innovative bottlings, they increase the diversity. Single malts from distilleries where the owners' themselves decide not to bottle also get a chance through the independents. The following are a selection of the major companies.

Gordon & MacPhail
www.gordonandmacphail.com
Established in 1895 the company which is owned by the Urquhart family still occupies the same premises in Elgin. Apart from being an independent bottler, there is also a legendary store in Elgin and, since 1993, an own distillery, Benromach.
There is a wide variety of bottlings, for example Connoisseurs Choice, Private Collection, MacPhail´s Collection and Pride of the Regions. Many of the bottlings have been diluted to 40%, 43% or 46% but the series Cask Strength obviously, as the name implies, contains bottlings straight from the cask. Another range called Rare Old consists of unusually old single malts which quite often come from closed distilleries as well.

Berry Bros. & Rudd
www.bbr.com
Britain´s oldest wine and spirit merchant, founded in 1698 has been selling their own world famous blend Cutty Sark since 1923. Berry Brothers had been offering their customers private bottlings of malt whisky for years but it was not until 2002 that they launched Berry´s Own Selection of single malt whiskies. Under the supervision of Spirits Manager Doug McIvor, some 30 expressions are offered every year. Bottling is usually at 46% but expressions bottled at cask strength are also available.

Signatory Vintage Scotch Whisky
Founded in 1998 by Andrew and Brian Symington, Signatory lists at least 50 single malts at any one occasion. The most widely distributed range is Cask Strength Collection which sometimes contains spectacular bottlings from distilleries which have long since disappeared. Another range is The Un-chill Filtered Collection bottled at 46%. Andrew Symington bought Edradour Distillery from Pernod Ricard in 2002.

Ian Macleod Distillers
www.ianmacleod.com
The company was founded in 1933 and is one of the largest independent family-owned companies within the spirits industry. Gins, rums, vodkas and liqueurs are found within the range apart from whisky and they also own Glengoyne Distillery. In total 15 million bottles of spirit are sold per year. Smokehead Islay Single Malt, single malt ranges like The Chieftain´s

and Dun Bheagan and Isle of Skye blended Scotch whisky are examples of brands.

Speciality Drinks
www.thewhiskyexchange.com
Sukhinder Singh, known by most from his two very well-stocked shops in London, The Whisky Exchange, is behind this company. Since 2005 he is also a bottler of malt whiskies operating under the brand name The Single Malts of Scotland. He has around 50 bottlings on offer at any time, either as single casks or as batches bottled at cask strength or at 46%. In 2009 a new range of Islay malts under the name Port Askaig was introduced, starting with a cask strength, a 17 year old and a 25 year old.

*Port Askaig 17 years
from Single Malts of Scotland*

Duncan Taylor
www.dtcscotch.com
Duncan Taylor & Co was founded in Glasgow in 1938 and in 2001 Euan Shand bought the company and operations were moved to Huntly. The company bottles around 200 expressions per year. The range includes Rarest of the Rare (single cask, cask strength whiskies of great age from demolished distilleries), Duncan Taylor Collection (single cask, cask strength malts and grains aged 17-42 years), NC2 (mainly single casks, 12-17 years, non chill-filtered at 46%), Battlehill (younger malts at 43%), Lonach (vattings of two casks from same distillery of the same age to bring them up to a natural strength of over 40%) and Big Smoke (Islay whiskies at 40% and 60%).

Douglas Laing & Co
www.douglaslaing.com
Established in 1948 by Douglas Laing and currently run by his two sons, Fred and Stewart. One of their most talked about ranges is The Old Malt Cask which contains rare and old bottlings. More than 100 different expressions can be found regularly in this range where bottlings are diluted to 50%. Some malts are released in an even more exclusive range - The Old and Rare Selection, offered at cask strength. A third range is called McGibbon´s Provenance, often aged around 10-12 years and almost always diluted to 46%. Sometimes some very old and rare single grains are released in the Clan Denny range.

Blackadder International
www.blackadder.nu
Blackadder is owned by Robin Tucek, together with John Lamond. Apart from the Blackadder and Blackadder Raw cask, there are also a number of other ranges - Aberdeen Distillers, Clydesdale Original and Caledonian Connections. All bottlings are single cask and in the case of Raw Casks they are also completely unfiltered. Most of the bottlings are diluted to 43-45% but there are also cask strength expressions on offer. Around 100 different bottlings are launched each year.

Dewar Rattray
www.adrattray.com
Founded by Andrew Dewar and William Rattray in 1868. In 2004 the company was revived by Tim Morrison, previously of Morrison Bowmore Distillers and fourth generation descendent of Andrew Dewar, with a view to bottling single cask malts from different regions in Scotland. A 12 year old single malt named Stronachie is also found in their portfolio. It is named after a distillery that closed in the 1930s. Tim Morrison bought one of the few remaining bottles of Stronachie and found a Highland distillery that could reproduce its character.

William Cadenhead & Co.
www.wmcadenhead.com
Established in 1842 and owned by J & A Mitchell (who also ows Springbank) since 1972. The single malts from Cadenheads are never chill filtered nor coloured. When it comes to whisky, they work

Adelphi Distillery - Macallan 30 years old

essentially with three different ranges; Authentic Collection (cask strength), Original Collection (diluted to 46%) and Chairman's Stock (older and rarer whiskies).

Adelphi Distillery
www.adelphidistillery.com
The Adelphi Distillery, one of the largest whisky distilleries in Scotland at the time, ceased production in 1902. The name was revived in 1992 by the great-grandson of the last owner, Jamie Walker, who established the company as an independent bottler of single cask single malts. He then sold the company in 2004 to Keith Falconer and Donald Houston who recruited Alex Bruce from the wine trade to act as Marketing Director. The company bottles around 50 casks a year. Unusually for an independent, Adelphi has an on-line shop on their website.

Murray McDavid
www.murray-mcdavid.com
Established in 1995 by Mark Reynier, Gordon Wright and Simon Coughlin. Murray McDavid makes three to four releases a year averaging 25 expressions per time. The range is highly selective and all casks are chosen by Jim McEwan who has more than 40 years experience in the whisky industry. Unlike most independent bottlers, the bottlings are vattings of four or five casks (same age) at 46% without chill filtration or tinting. The range can be divided into three categories: – the Murray McDavid range, the Mission Range (unusual aged stock) and finally the Celtic Heartlands range - exceptionally old or unique casks from the sixties and seventies.

Celtic Heartlands - Banff 1975

New bottlings

It is virtually impossible to list all new bottlings during a year,
there are simply too many and sometimes it is difficult to find information on them.
In this list we have selected 500 that were released from late 2008 until autumn 2009.
All bottlings (except for certain official ones) are listed with year of distillation, age,
finish or special maturation (if applicable), alcohol strength and bottler.
Read more about the major independent bottlers on pages 252-253.

Aberfeldy
1990	Chris Anderson´s		54.8%	OB
1996	13		58,3%	CAD
1997			58,5%	BA
1994	14		50,0%	DL

Aberlour
1995			46,0%	DT
1992			46,0%	DT
1996			57,3%	DR
1990			60,3%	BA

Allt a Bhainne
1995	14	Medoc	43,0%	IM
1992	16		55,9%	CAD
1991	17	Amarone	46,0%	MM
1991	17	Amarone	52,9%	MM
1996	12		46,0%	MM

Ardbeg
Corryvreckan			57.1%	OB
Supernova			58.9%	OB
1998	11	Feis Isle	54.0%	OB
1998	11	Feis Isle	54.7%	OB
1998	11		46,0%	IM
1993			58,9%	DT
1991	17		56,3%	CAD
1994	15		58,1%	CAD
1999	9		58,5%	AD
1998	10		58,8%	AD
1998	11		58,0%	AD
1991	17		50,0%	DL
1991	17	Rum	50,0%	DL
1991	18	Rum	50,0%	DL

Ardmore
1997	11		57,1%	CAD
1996	12		46,0%	DL

Arran
	12		46.0%	OB
		Pinot Noir	50.0%	OB
		Pomerol	50.0%	OB
2004		Peated	60.0%	OB
1996		Peacock	46.0%	OB
1996			46,0%	DT
1996			55,7%	DR
1996	12	Margaux	46,0%	MM

1996	12	Sherry	46,0%	DL
1997	11		46,0%	DL

Auchentoshan
1999			46,0%	DT
1990	19		56,8%	CAD
1999	10	Chen. Blanc	46,0%	MM
1990	18		50,0%	DL
1995	13		50,0%	DL

Auchroisk
1979	29		57,3%	SIG

Aultmore
1997	12	Medoc	46,0%	IM
1997	12	Sherry	50,0%	IM
1997	11	Manzanilla	43,0%	IM
1989			51,3%	BA
1996	13		46,0%	DL

Balblair
1990	Vintage		46.0%	OB
1991	Vintage		43.0%	OB

Balmenach
1990	18		43,1%	DL

Balvenie
1978			53.8%	OB
	17	Madeira	43.0%	OB
	14	Rum	43.0%	OB
Golden Cask 14yo			47.5%	OB

Banff
1976	32		47,1%	CAD
1980	28		54,5%	SIG
1975	32		48,7%	DL

Ben Nevis
1999			46,0%	DT
1999		Port	46,0%	DT
1998			46,0%	DT
1996	12		57,1%	CAD
1999	9	Grenache	46,0%	MM
1996	12		46,0%	DL

Benriach
	18	Moscatel	46.0%	OB
	18	Gaja Barolo	46.0%	OB

1970	38	PX Sherry	49.1%	OB
1975	34	Tawny Port	52.2%	OB
1977	31	Virgin Oak	43.2%	OB
1978	31	Gaja Barolo	51.2%	OB
1978	30	Bourbon	49.2%	OB
1984	24	PX Sherry	49.2%	OB
1988	20	Gaja Barolo	54.3%	OB
1990	19	Bourbon	57.1%	OB
1994	14	Bourbon	59.5%	OB
1996			46,0%	DT
1986	23		53,3%	CAD
1966	42		43,9%	SIG
1990	19		50,0%	DL

Benrinnes
1985	23		58.8%	OB
1994	14		46,0%	IM
1997	11		46,0%	DL
1988	21		43,6%	DL

Benromach
	10		43.0%	OB

Bladnoch
	7	Peated	57.0%	OB
	8			OB
	19		54.5%	OB
1992	16		48,0%	IM
1992	17		55,1%	CAD
1992	16	Amarone	46,0%	MM
1992	16		46,0%	SD

Blair Athol
1989	19		53,7%	CAD
1976	32		55,4%	DL
1999	9		46,0%	DL

Bowmore
1964		Gold Bowmore	42.4%	OB
Maltmen´s Selection			54.6%	OB
Laimrig 15yo			50.3%	OB
	10	Tempest	55.3%	OB
1999	9	Feis Isle	57.1%	OB
1982			53,7%	DT
1998			46,0%	DT
1968			42,3%	DT
1997	11		56,7%	CAD
1991			56,2%	DR

OB = Official bottling from the owner, AD = Adelphi Distillery, BA = Blackadder, BB = Berry Brothers, CAD = Cadenhead, DL = Douglas Laing, DR = Dewar Rattray, DT = Duncan Taylor, GM = Gordon & MacPhail, IM = Ian MacLeod, MM = Murray McDavid, SIG = Signatory, SD = Speciality Drinks

Year	Age	Note	ABV	Bottler
1990			52,6%	DR
2002	6	Margaux	46,0%	MM
1999	9	Syrah	46,0%	MM
1999	10	Syrah	46,0%	MM
1998	10		46,0%	MM
1987			48,7%	BA
1972	36		45,4%	SIG
1999	9		50,0%	DL
1998	10		46,0%	DL

Braeval
Year	Age	Note	ABV	Bottler
1989	19		58,4%	CAD
1998	10		46,0%	DL

Brora
Year	Age	Note	ABV	Bottler
	30		53.2%	OB
1981			53,8%	DT

Bruichladdich
Year	Age	Note	ABV	Bottler
Classic			46.0%	OB
Infinity 3rd edition			50.0%	OB
1989 Black Art			51.1%	OB
Organic 2003			46.0%	OB
DNA	36		41.0%	OB
X4+3	3		63.5%	OB
	17	Rum	46.0%	OB
	17	Fino sherry	46.0%	OB
	17	PX sherry	46.0%	OB
1991	17		54,0%	CAD
1988			54,4%	BA
1989	19		46,0%	SIG
1993	15		50,0%	DL

Bunnahabhain
Year	Age	Note	ABV	Bottler
Toiteach			46.0%	OB
Darach Ur			46.3%	OB
Moine		Feis Isle	58.4%	OB
1979	29		45,5%	IM
1985	24		48,1%	IM
1995	14	Medoc	46,0%	IM
1970			40,2%	DT
1990			51,8%	DR
1997	11		59,9%	AD
1964	35		56,6%	AD
1976	31		51,9%	MM
1997	10	Port	46,0%	MM
1999	9		46,0%	DL
1978	30		50,0%	DL

Caol Ila
Year	Age	Note	ABV	Bottler
1996	12		65.8%	OB
1996	12	Feis Isle	58.0%	OB
1998	10	Unpeated	65.8%	OB
1998	11		43,0%	IM
1999	9	Manzanilla	46,0%	IM
1991	18	German oak	48,0%	IM
1992			46,0%	DT
1982			55,9%	DT
1995	13		60,8%	CAD
1995			60,5%	DR
2001	8		61,3%	AD
1980	28	Sauternes	55,4%	MM
1990	18	Port	53,9%	MM

Year	Age	Note	ABV	Bottler
1990	17		52,5%	MM
2000		Zinfandel	46,0%	MM
1992			55,1%	BA
1982			55,8%	BA
1991	18		54,7%	SD
1979	29		50,0%	DL
1998	10		46,0%	DL
1996	13		46,0%	DL
1984	25		50,0%	DL
1994		Tokaji	45,0%	GM

Caperdonich
Year	Age	Note	ABV	Bottler
1968			42,2%	DT
1970			45,9%	DT
1972			54,4%	DT
1996	12		52,6%	CAD
1970	38		47,1%	AD
1970	38		43,5%	SIG
1996	12		46,0%	DL

Cardhu
Year	Age	Note	ABV	Bottler
1997		Man. Choice	57.3%	OB

Clynelish
Year	Age	Note	ABV	Bottler
	12		46.0%	OB
1982			51,0%	DR
1993	15		58,4%	AD
1987	20		49,2%	MM
1995		Ch Latour	46,0%	MM
1992	16		53,7%	SD
1973	33		54,5%	SIG
1992	15		46,0%	SIG
1995	12		58,4%	SIG
1971	38	Sherry	50,0%	DL

Cragganmore
Year	Age	Note	ABV	Bottler
1993			46,0%	DT
1989			60,4%	BA

Craigellachie
Year	Age	Note	ABV	Bottler
1994	14		56,5%	CAD
1994	15		46,0%	SD
1999	9		46,0%	DL

Dailuaine
Year	Age	Note	ABV	Bottler
1997	11		46,0%	DL

Dallas Dhu
Year	Age	Note	ABV	Bottler
1975	32		48,5%	SIG

Dalmore
Year	Age	Note	ABV	Bottler
	18		43.0%	OB
1981		Matusalem	44.0%	OB
1981		Amoroso	42.0%	OB
1951			45.0%	OB
	58		44.0%	OB
1996	12	Rum	43,0%	IM
1990			56,7%	DT
1992	17	Sauternes	59,1%	CAD
1990	18		60,1%	SIG
1976	32		50,0%	DL

Deanston
Year	Age	Note	ABV	Bottler
	12		46.3%	OB

Year	Age	Note	ABV	Bottler
	17	Marks & Spencer		OB
1995			60,8%	DR
1992	16		50,0%	DL

Dufftown
Year	Age	Note	ABV	Bottler
1978	31		48,6%	CAD
1994	14		50,0%	DL
1980	28		50,0%	DL

Edradour
Year	Age	Note	ABV	Bottler
2003		Port mat.	46.0%	OB
1997		C N de P		OB
Ballechin Oloroso			46.0%	OB

Glenallachie
Year	Age	Note	ABV	Bottler
1995			46,0%	DT
1992	16		60,8%	CAD
1971	38		50,0%	DL

Glenburgie
Year	Age	Note	ABV	Bottler
1993	15	Port	55,8%	CAD
1996	12		46,0%	DL

Glencadam
Year	Age	Note	ABV	Bottler
1983	25		46.0%	OB
1978	30		46.0%	OB
1989	19		57,6%	SIG

Glencraig
Year	Age	Note	ABV	Bottler
1974			42,4%	DT
1975			43,0%	GM

Glendronach
Year	Age	Note	ABV	Bottler
	12		43.0%	OB
	15	Revival	46.0%	OB
	18	Allardice	46.0%	OB
	33		40.0%	OB
1971	38		49.4%	OB
1972	37		54.8%	OB
1992	16		57.2%	OB
1993	16		60.4%	OB
1996	13		59.4%	OB
1975	34		47,8%	IM
1990	18		54,0%	CAD

Glendullan
Year	Age	Note	ABV	Bottler
1996	12		58,2%	CAD
1993	15	Rioja	46,0%	MM

Glen Elgin
Year	Age	Note	ABV	Bottler
1998		Man. Choice	61.1%	OB
1978	30		49,1%	CAD
1978	30		46,9%	AD
1991			57,3%	BA
1991	16		59,8%	SIG
1996	12	Virgin Oak	46,0%	SIG

Glenfarclas
Year	Age	Note	ABV	Bottler
Family Casks,				
14 different vintages				OB
Glenfarclas 105 (40yo)			60.0%	OB
1988	20		51,9%	CAD
1966	42		48,8%	DL

OB = Official bottling from the owner, AD = Adelphi Distillery, BA = Blackadder, BB = Berry Brothers, CAD = Cadenhead, DL = Douglas Laing, DR = Dewar Rattray, DT = Duncan Taylor, GM = Gordon & MacPhail, IM = Ian MacLeod, MM = Murray McDavid, SIG = Signatory, SD = Speciality Drinks

255

Glenfiddich

50		46.1%	OB
1975 Vintage Reserve		53.4%	OB

Glen Garioch

1797 Found. Reserve		48.0%	OB
12		48.0%	OB
1978 Vintage		52.0%	OB
1990 Vintage		52.0%	OB
1988		54,4%	DT
1990	17	52,3%	SIG
1992	16	50,0%	DL

Glenglassaugh

21	46.0%	OB
30	55,1%	OB
40	44,6%	OB

Glengoyne

12		43.0%	OB
1986			OB
1995			OB

Glen Grant

Cellar Reserve 1992		46.0%	OB
1970		49,9%	DT
1972		46,2%	DT
1974		43,4%	DT
1985	23	55,9%	AD
1967	41	46,9%	SIG
1996	12	46,0%	DL
1976	32 Wine	50,0%	DL

Glengyle

Kilkerran Work in Pr.	46.0%	OB

Glen Keith

1995	14 Rum	43,0%	IM
1990	18	50,0%	DL

Glenkinchie

1987	21	51,6%	CAD
1975		60,7%	DR

Glenlivet

1991 Nadurra Triumph		48.0%	OB
1968		42,3%	DT
1970		50,7%	DT
1968	40	51,0%	AD
1994	14	61,0%	AD
1978	30	50,0%	DL
1959		47,5%	GM

Glenlossie

1993	Tokaji	46,0%	DT
1988		52,4%	BA

Glen Mhor

1975		40,6%	DT
1982		55,4%	DR

Glenmorangie

Sonnalta PX	46.0%	OB

Glen Moray

1992	16	Madeira	46,0%	MM

Glen Ord

1998	11	46,0%	DL

Glenrothes

1988			43.0%	OB
1998			43.0%	OB
John Ramsay			46.7%	OB
Alba Reserve			40.0%	OB
1995	14		43,0%	IM
1997	11	Rum	46,0%	IM
1968			50,2%	DT
1970			42,3%	DT
1990	18	Sherry	56,9%	CAD
1990			51,4%	DR
1990	18		46,0%	SD
1995	14		59,6%	SIG
1975	32		50,0%	DL
1996	12		46,0%	DL
1990	18		50,0%	DL

Glen Scotia

1991	17	Port	54,0%	MM
1992	16	Sauternes	46,0%	MM
1991			61,2%	BA
1974	33		44,2%	SIG

Glenspey

1993	16	German oak	46,0%	IM
	30		54,5%	SD

Glentauchers

2000	8	46,0%	DL
1995	13	50,0%	DL

Glenturret

1990	18	German oak	46,0%	IM
1985	22		55,2%	SIG
1989	19	Rum	50,0%	DL

Glenugie

1982	26	50,0%	DL
1982	27	50,0%	DL

Glenury Royal

1976	32	50,0%	DL

Hazelburn

12	46.0%	OB

Highland Park

1964 Vintage		42.2%	OB
1968 Vintage		45.6%	OB
Hjärta		58.1%	OB
Earl Magnus		52.6%	OB
1968		40,9%	DT
1986		55,7%	DT
1991		55,2%	DT
1992	17	64,0%	CAD
1995	13	46,0%	SD
1998	10	46,0%	DL
1996	12	46,0%	DL

Imperial

1995		46,0%	DT
1996		46,0%	DT
1994		46,0%	DT
1990		48,3%	DT
1998		46,0%	DT
1983		46,9%	DR
1996	12	46,0%	DL

Inchgower

1974		61,3%	DR
1974	34	50,0%	DL

Inverleven

1977	31	47,6%	SIG

Jura

Mount. of the Sound			46.0%	OB
Mount. of Gold			46.0%	OB
Sacred Mountain			46.0%	OB
1997	12	Manzanilla	43,0%	IM
1996	12		60,3%	AD
1992	16	Port	46,0%	MM
1992	16		50,0%	DL

Kilchoman

Inaugural Release	46.0%	OB

Knockando

1994	14	50,0%	DL

Lagavulin

	12	59.9%	OB
1995	Feis Isle	54.4%	OB

Laphroaig

	18	48.0%	OB
Cairdeas (12yo)		57.5%	OB
1997	12	46,0%	IM
1996	13	46,0%	SD
1996		60,3%	DR
1990		56,0%	DR
1998		59,0%	BA
1990	18	52,6%	SIG
2001	8	46,0%	SIG
1992	16	50,0%	DL
1987	21	50,0%	DL
1998	10	46,0%	DL
2001	8	46,0%	DL
1988	21	50,0%	DL

Linkwood

1996	Man. Choice	58.2%	OB
1983		53,0%	DR
1990	17	48,0%	AD
1989		53,5%	BA
1983	25	50,0%	DL
1959		45,0%	GM

Littlemill

1990	18	53,5%	MM
1992	17	50,0%	DL
1990	19	47,9%	DL

Lochside
1987		59,8%	DR
1981		56,0%	BA

Longmorn
1996	12	46,0%	IM
1994	14	50,0%	DL
	30	43,0%	GM

Macallan
	57 Lalique	48.5%	OB
Select Oak		40.0%	OB
Whisky Maker´s Ed.		42.8%	OB
Estate Reserve		45.7%	OB
1824 Limited Release		48.0%	OB
1990		55,4%	DT
1991		55,1%	DT
1997		46,0%	DT
1987	20 Sherry	53,2%	CAD
1990	18	52,8%	AD
1991	17 Tempran.	46,0%	MM
1992	15	46,0%	MM
1997	10 Ch Latour	46,0%	MM
1997	9 Zinfandel	46,0%	MM
1993	15	50,0%	DL
1988	20 Wine	50,0%	DL
1985	23 Rum	50,0%	DL
1997	11	46,0%	DL
1989	19 Rum	50,0%	DL
1985	24	50,0%	DL
1978	30	50,0%	DL

Macduff
1969		40,9%	DT
1968		45,5%	DT

Mannochmore
1990	18	54,9%	OB
1992	16 Sherry	55,6%	CAD
1991		57,2%	SIG
1991	18	50,0%	DL

Miltonduff
1999		46,0%	DT
1980	28	50,0%	DL
1998	11	46,0%	DL

Mortlach
1997	Man. Choice	57,1%	OB
1993		46,0%	DT
1992	16	57,2%	CAD
1991	17	57,0%	AD
1986	21	51,1%	MM
1988	20 Amarone	51,9%	MM
1990	19 Amarone	53,2%	MM
1988	19	58,5%	SIG
1996	12	46,0%	DL
1992	16	46,0%	DL

Mosstowie
1975		47,7%	DT
1979		43,0%	GM

Oban
2000	Man. Choice	58.7%	OB

Octomore
	5 2nd edition	62.5%	OB

Pittyvaich
1989	20	57.5%	OB
1985	23 Rum	49,6%	CAD
1990	18	50,0%	DL

Port Charlotte
2001	8	60.5%	OB

Port Ellen
1979	30	57.7%	OB
1982	27	56,8%	IM
1982	26	58,4%	SIG
1982	27	59,0%	SIG
1983	25	46,0%	DL
1982	26	50,0%	DL
1978	30	52,5%	DL

Pulteney
	30	44.0%	OB
1990	18	57,2%	CAD
1982		47,7%	DR
1990		58,9%	BA

Rosdhu
1996	12	46,0%	MM

Rosebank
1989	19	53,4%	CAD
1990	19	50,0%	DL
1991	17	46.0%	SD

Royal Brackla
1992	16	54,7%	CAD
1994	14 Jurancon	46,0%	MM
1999	9	46,0%	DL

Royal Lochnagar
1986		56,4%	DT
1990		54,2%	DT
1996	12	58,5%	CAD
1991	17	57,0%	SIG
1998	10	46,0%	SIG
1977	32	47,7%	DL

St Magdalene
1982	26	50,0%	IM
1982	26	55,0%	IM
1982	26	50,0%	DL

Scapa
	16	40.0%	OB
1993	15	50,0%	DL

Speyburn
Bradan Orach		40.0%	OB
1990	18 Rum	50,0%	DL

Speyside
1994	15	64,6%	CAD

Springbank
	11 Madeira	55.1%	OB
	18	46.0%	OB
2001	Vintage	55.3%	OB
1968	40	54,0%	IM
1996		46,0%	DT
1993	15	50,0%	DL

Strathisla
1967		48,3%	DT
1996	12	46,0%	DL
1991	18	50,0%	DL

Talisker
	25	54.8%	OB
	30	53.1%	OB

Tamdhu
1994	15	53,4%	IM
1991	18	58,5%	CAD
1991	17	50,0%	DL

Tamnavulin
1993		57,6%	BA
	40	40,4%	SD
1968	40	42,2%	DL
1968	40	50,0%	DL

Teaninich
1996	Man. Choice	55.3%	OB
1996		46,0%	DT

Tobermory
1994	15	46,0%	MM
1994	14 Haut Brion	46,0%	MM
1995	12 Ch Latour	46,0%	MM
1995		59,1%	BA

Tomatin
	15	43.0%	OB
	30		OB
	21		OB
1973			OB
1982			OB
1997			OB
1992	16 Medoc	50,0%	IM
1988		55,4%	DR
1990		56,6%	BA

Tomintoul
	14	46.0%	OB
	33	43.0%	OB
1975	33	55,4%	DL

Tormore
1996	12	46,0%	DL

Tullibardine
1988		56.0%	OB
1990		59,1%	DR

Whisky Shops

AUSTRIA

Potstill
Strozzigasse 37
1080 Wien
Phone: +43 (0)676 965 89 36
www.potstill.org
Austria's premier whisky shop with over 1100 kinds of which c 900 are malts, including some real rarities. Arranges tastings and seminars and ships to several European countries. On-line ordering.

BELGIUM

Whiskycorner
Kraaistraat 16
3530 Houthalen
Phone: +32 (0)89 386233
www.whiskycorner.be
A very large selection of single malts, no less than 1100 different! Also other whiskies, calvados and grappas. The site is in both French and English. Mail ordering, but not on-line. Shipping worldwide.

Jurgen´s Whiskyhuis
Gaverland 70
9620 Zottegem
Phone: +32 (0)9 336 51 06
www.whiskyhuis.be
An absolutely huge assortment of more than 2,000 different single malts with 700 in stock and the rest delivered within the week. Also 40 different grain whiskies and 120 bourbons. Online mail order with shipments worldwide.

Huis Crombé
Engelse Wandeling 11
8500 Kortrijk
Phone: +32 56 21 19 87
www.crombewines.com
A wine retailer with a heritage dating back to 1894 and now covers all kinds of spirits. The whisky range is very nice where a large assortment of Scotch is supplemented with whiskies from Japan, the USA and Ireland to mention a few. Regular tastings in the shop.

CANADA

Kensington Wine Market
1257 Kensington Road NW
Calgary
Alberta T2N 3P8
Phone: +1 403 283 8000
www.kensingtonwinemarket.com
With 400 different bottlings this is the largest single malt assortment in Canada. Also 2,500 different wines. Regular tastings in the shop.

DENMARK

Juul´s Vin & Spiritus
Værnedamsvej 15
1819 Frederiksberg
Phone: +45 33 31 13 29
www.juuls.dk
A very large range of wines, fortified wines and spirits. Around 500 single malts. Also a good selection of drinking glasses. On-line ordering. Shipping outside Denmark (except for Scandinavian countries).

Cadenheads Whisky & Lifestyle
Vestergade 21
5000 Odense C
Phone: +45 66 139 505
www.whiskyandlifestyle.com
Whisky specialist with a very good range, not least from Cadenhead's. Nice range of champagne, cognac and rum. Arranges whisky and beer tastings. On-line ordering. Shipping to a few countries outside Denmark.

Whiskyhouse.dk
Peter Bangs Vej 74
2000 Frederiksberg
Phone: +45 38 878 670
www.whiskyhouse.dk
A large range of spirits and beers including c 400 kinds of whisky. Arranges recurrent tastings. On-line ordering.

ENGLAND

The Whisky Exchange (2 shops)
Unit 7, Space Business Park
Abbey Road, Park Royal
London NW10 7SU
Phone: +44 (0)208 838 9388

The Whisky Exchange
Vinopolis, 1 Bank End
London SE1 9BU
Phone: +44 (0)207 403 8688
www.thewhiskyexchange.com
This is a great whisky shop established in 1999 and owned by Sukhinder Singh. Started off as a mail order business which was run from a showroom in Hanwell, but since some years back there is also an excellent shop at Vinopolis in downtown London. The assortment is huge with well over 1000 single malts to choose from. Some rarities which can hardly be found anywhere else are offered much thanks to Singh's great interest for antique whisky. There are also other types of whisky and cognac, calvados, rum etc. On-line ordering and ships all over the world.

The Whisky Shop
(See also Scotland, The Whisky Shop)
Unit 1.09 MetroCentre
Red Mall

Gateshead NE11 9YG
Phone: +44 (0)191 460 3777

11 Coppergate Walk
York YO1 9NT
Phone: +44 (0)1904 640300

510 Brompton Walk
Lakeside Shopping Centre
West Thurrock, Essex RM20 2ZL
Phone: +44 (0)1708 866255

7 Turl Street
Oxford OX1 3DQ
Phone: +44 (0)1865 202279

3 Swan Lane
Norwich NR2 1HZ
Phone: +44 (0)1603 618284

7 Queens Head Passage
Paternoster
London EC4M 7DY
Phone: +44 (0)207 329 5117
www.whiskyshop.com
The first shop opened in 1992 in Edinburgh and this is now the United Kingdom's largest specialist retailer of whiskies with 14 outlets. A large product range with over 700 kinds, including 400 malt whiskies and 140 miniature bottles, as well as accessories and books. The own range 'Glenkeir Treasures' is a special assortment of selected malt whiskies. On-line ordering and shipping all over the world except to the USA.

Royal Mile Whiskies
3 Bloomsbury Street
London WC1B 3QE
Phone: +44 (0)20 7436 4763
www.royalmilewhiskies.com
The London branch of Royal Mile Whiskies. See also Scotland, Royal Mile Whiskies.

Berry Bros. & Rudd
3 St James´ Street
London SW1A 1EG
Phone: +44 (0)870 900 4300
www.bbr.com/whisky
A legendary shop that has been situated in the same place since 1698. One of the world's most reputable wine shops but with an exclusive selection of malt whiskies. There are also shops in Dublin and Hong Kong specialising primarily in fine wines. Mail order for wine only.

The Wright Wine and Whisky Company
The Old Smithy, Raikes Road, Skipton
North Yorkshire BD23 1NP
Phone: +44 (0)1756 700886
www.wineandwhisky.co.uk
A very good selection of over 750 different whiskies to choose from. There is also a nice range of armagnac, rum, calvado etc. 900 different wines are likely to impress the visitor.

Whiskys.co.uk
The Square, Stamford Bridge
York YO4 11AG
Phone: +44 (0)1759 371356
www.whiskys.co.uk
Good assortment with more than 600
different whiskies. Also a nice range of
armagnac, rum, calvados etc. On-line
ordering, ships outside of the UK.
The owners also have another website,
www.whiskymerchants.co.uk with a
huge amount of information on just
about every whisky distillery in the
world and very up to date.

Mainly Malts
3-4 The Courtyard, Bawtry
Doncaster DN10 6JG
Phone: +44 (0)1302 714 700
www.whisky-malts-shop.com
A good range with c 400 different
whiskies of which 300 are single malts.
Arranges tastings and seminars. On-line
ordering with shipping also outside
the UK.

Chester Whisky & Liqueur
59 Bridge Street Row
Chester
Cheshire CH1 1NW
Phone: +44 (0)1244 347806
www.chesterwhisky.com
A newly opened shop that specialises in
single malt Scotch and American, Irish,
Japanese and Welsh whisky.There is
also a good range of calvados, armagnac and rum and the shop has its own
house blend, Chester Cross Blended
Scotch Whisky, as well as three casks
for tasting and bottling in the store.

Master of Malt
2 Leylands Manor
Tubwell Lane
Crowborough
East Sussex TN6 3RH
+44 (0)1892 888 376
www.masterofmalt.com
Independent bottler and online retailer
since 1985. A very impressive range
of more than 1,000 Scotch whiskies of
which 800 are single malts. In addition
to whisky from other continents there
is a wide selection of rum, cognac,
Armagnac and tequila. The website is
redesigned and contains a wealth of
information on the distilleries.

Nickolls & Perks
37 Lower High Street, Stourbridge
West Midlands DY8 1TA
Phone: +44 (0)1384 394518
www.nickollsandperks.co.uk
Mostly known as wine merchants but
also has a good range of whiskies with
c 300 different kinds including 200
single malts. On-line ordering with
shipping also outside of UK

Gauntleys of Nottingham
4 High Street
Exchange Arcade
Nottingham NG1 2ET
Phone: +44 (0)115 9110555
www.gauntley-wine.co.uk
A fine wine merchant established
in 1880. The range of wines (especially Rhone, Alsace and Burgundy) are

among the best in the UK. All kinds
of spirits, not least whisky, are taking
up more and more space and several
rare malts can be found. The monthly
whisky newsletter by Chris Goodrum
makes good reading and there is also a
mail order service available .

The Wine Shop
22 Russell Street, Leek
Staffordshire ST13 5JF
Phone: +44 (0)1538 382408
www.wineandwhisky.com
In addition to wine there is a good
range of c 300 whiskies and also calvados, cognacs, rums etc. They also stock
a range of their own single malt bottlings under the name of 'The Queen
of the Moorlands'. Mailorders by
telephone or email for UK delivery.

The Lincoln Whisky Shop
87 Bailgate
Lincoln LN1 3AR
Phone: +44 (0)1522 537834
www.lincolnwhiskyshop.co.uk
Mainly specialising in whisky with more
than 400 different whiskies but also
500 spirits and liqueurs and some 100
wines. Mailorder only within UK.

Arkwrights
114 The Dormers
Highworth
Wiltshire SN6 7PE
Phone: +44 (0)1793 765071
www.whiskyandwines.com
A good range of whiskies (over 600 in
stock) as well as wine and other spirits.
Regular tastings in the shop. On-line
ordering with shipping all over the
world except USA and Canada.

Milroys of Soho
3 Greek Street
London W1D 4NX
Phone: +44 (0)20 7437 2385
www.milroys.co.uk
A classic whisky shop in Soho now
owned by the retail wine merchant
Jeroboams Group. A very good range
with over 700 malts and a wide
selection of whiskies from around
the world. Tastings are arranged in
the tasting cellar in the shop. On-line
ordering for shipping within the UK.

Cadenhead´s Whisky Shop
26 Chiltern Street
London W1U 7QF
Phone: +44 (0)20 7935 6999
www.whiskytastingroom.com
Used to be in Covent Garden but
moved 2008 and was expanded with
a tasting room. One in a chain of
shops owned by independent bottlers
Cadenhead. Sells Cadenhead's product
range and c 200 other whiskies. Newsletter and regular tastings. On-line
ordering.

The Vintage House
42 Old Compton Street
London W1D 4LR
Phone: +44 (0)20 7437 5112
www.sohowhisky.com
A huge range of 1400 kinds of malt

whisky, many of them rare or unusual.
Supplementing this is also a selection
of fine wines. On-line ordering with
shipping only within the UK.

The Wee Dram
5 Portland Square, Bakewell
Derbyshire DE45 1HA
Phone: +44 (0)1629 812235
www.weedram.co.uk
Large range of Scotch single malts (c
450) with whiskies from other parts of
the world and a good range of whisky
books. Run 'The Wee Drammers Whisky
Club' with tastings and seminars. On-
line ordering.

Whisky On-line
Units 1-3 Concorde House, Charnley
Road, Blackpool, Lancashire FY1 4PE
Phone: +44 (0)1253 620376
www.whisky-online.com
A good selection of whisky and also
cognac, rum, port etc. On-line ordering
with shipping all over the world.

Constantine Stores
30 Fore Street
Constantine, Falmouth
Cornwall TR11 5AB
Phone: +44 (0)1326 340226
www.drinkfinder.co.uk
A full-range wine and spirits dealer
with a good selection of whiskies from
the whole world (around 800 different,
of which 600 are single malts).
Worldwide shipping except for USA
and Canada.

FRANCE

La Maison du Whisky (2 shops)
20 rue d´Anjou
75008 Paris
Phone: +33 (0)1 42 65 03 16

(2 shops outside France)

47 rue Jean Chatel
97400 Saint-Denis, La Réunion
Phone: +33 (0)2 62 21 31 19

The Pier at Robertson Quay
80 Mohamed Sultan Road, #01-10
Singapore 239013
Phone: +65 6733 0059
www.whisky.fr
France's largest whisky specialist with
over 1000 whiskies in stock. Also a
number of own-bottled single malts.
Three shops and on-line ordering. Ships
to some 20 countries.

GERMANY

Celtic Whisk(e)y & Versand
Otto Steudel
Bulmannstrasse 26
90459 Nürnberg
Phone: +49 (0)911 450974-30
www.whisky.de/celtic
A very impressive single malt range
with well over 1000 different single
malts and a good selection from other
parts of the world. On-line ordering
with shipping also outside Germany.

SCOMA - Scotch Malt Whisky GmbH
Am Bullhamm 17
26441 Jever
Phone: +49 (0)4461 912237
www.scoma.de
Very large range of c 750 Scottish malts
and many from other countries. Holds
regular seminars and tastings. The
excellent, monthly whisky newsletter
SCOMA News is produced and can be
downloaded as a pdf-file from the
website. On-line ordering.

The Whisky Store
Am Grundwassersee 4
82402 Seeshaupt
Phone: +49 (0)8801-23 17
www.thewhiskystore.com
A very large range comprising c 700
kinds of whisky of which 550 are malts.
Also sells whisky liqueurs, books and
accessories. The website is a veritable
goldmine of information about the
whisky business and especially so
when it comes to photographs of
distilleries. There are 7500 photos of
168 distilleries. On-line ordering.

Cadenhead's Whisky Market
Luxemburger Strasse 257
50939 Köln
Phone: +49 (0)221-2831835
www.cadenheads.de
This first Cadenhead shop outside of
the UK was established in 2001. Good
range of malt whiskies (c 350 different
kinds) with emphasis on Cadenhead's
own bottlings. Other products include
wine, cognac and rum etc. Arranges
recurring tastings and also has an on-
line shop.

Cadenhead's Whisky Market
Fasanenstrasse 4
10623 Berlin-Charlottenburg
Phone: +49 (0)30-30831444
www.cadenhead-berlin.de
Good product range with c 350
different kinds of malt with emphasis
on Cadenhead's own bottlings as well
as wine, cognac and rum etc. Arranges
recurrent tastings.

Malts and More
Hosegstieg 11
22880 Wedel
Phone: +49 (0)40-23620770
www.maltsandmore.de
Very large assortment with over 800
different single malts from Scotland
as well as whiskies from many other
countries. Also a nice selection of
cognac, rum etc. Orders can be
placed on-line or through Email and
telephone.

Reifferscheid
Mainzer Strasse 186
53179 Bonn / Mehlem
Phone: +49 (0)228 9 53 80 70
www.whisky-bonn.de
A well-stocked shop which has been
listed as one of the best in Germany several times. Aside from a large range of
whiskies (among them a good selection
from Duncan Taylor), wine, spirit, cigars
and a delicatessen can be found. Holds
regular tastings.

Whiskywizard.de
Christian Jaudt
Schulstrasse 57
66540 Neunkirchen
Phone: +49 (0)6858-699507
www.whiskywizard.de
Large assortment of single malt (over
500) and other spirits. Only orders on-
line, shipping also outside Germany.

Whisky-Doris
Germanenstrasse 38
14612 Falkensee
Phone: +49 (0)3322-219784
www.whisky-doris.de
Large range of over 300 whiskies
and also sells own special bottlings.
Orders via email. Shipping also outside
Germany.

Finlays Whisky Shop
Köpperner Strasse 109
61273 Wehrheim-Saalburgsiedlung
Phone: +49 (0)6081 - 58 67 15
www.finlayswhiskyshop.de
Whisky specialists with a large range of
over 700 single malts. Finlays also work
as the importer to Germany of Douglas
laing, James MacArthur and Wilson &
Morgan. There is an impressive listing
of 700 bottlings of Port Ellen on the
website (The Port Ellen Archive). Shop
in Wehrheim as well as on-line orders.

Weinquelle Lühmann
Lübeckerstrasse 145
22087 Hamburg
Phone: +49 (0)40-25 63 91
www.weinquelle.com
An impressive selection of both wines
and spirits with over 1000 different
whiskies of which 850 are malt whiskies. Also an impressive range of rums.
General information about whisky on
the site, part of which is in English.
On-line ordering with shipping also
possible outside Germany.

Liquids
Heerstrasse 350
50169 Kerpen-Brüggen
Phone: +49 (0)2237-975491
www.liquids-and-more.de
A good range (over 200 single malts)
and a fine assortment of whiskies
from other countries. Also books and
accessories. On-line ordering.

The Whisky-Corner
Reichertsfeld 2
92278 Illschwang
Phone: +49 (0)9666-951213
www.whisky-corner.de
A small shop but large on mail order.
A very large assortment of over 1600
whiskies. Also sells blended and
American whiskies. The website is very
informative with features on, among
others, whisky-making, tasting and
independent bottlers. On-line ordering.

World Wide Spirits
Hauptstrasse 12
84576 Teising
Phone: +49 (0)8633 50 87 93
www.worldwidespirits.de
A nice range of c 500 whiskies with
some rarities from the twenties. Also

large selection (c 1000) of other spirits.

Banneke
Kreuzeskirchstr. 37
45127 Essen
Phone: +49 (0)201 247710
www.banneke.de
Very impressive assortment of 4500
different kinds of spirit and wine. Good
range of malt whiskies (c 400) and
rum (c 200). On-line ordering and will
deliver outside of Germany.

WhiskyKoch
Weinbergstrasse 2
64285 Darmstadt
Phone: +49 (0152) 29 51 75 72
www.whiskykoch.de
The English chef, Christopher Pepper,
and his wife Marion opened up this
interesting combination of a whisky
shop and restaurant end of 2007. The
shop has a nice selection of single malts
as well as other Scottish products and
the restaurant has specialised in whisky
dinners and tastings.

Whisk(e)y Shop Tara
Rindermarkt 16
80331 München
Phone: +49 (0)89-26 51 18
www.whiskyversand.de
Whisky specialists with a very broad
range of, for example, 800 different
single malts. On-line ordering.

Mara Malt-Rarities
Roland Puhl & Co. GbR
Cahenslystr. 14
65549 Limburg
Phone: +49 (0)6431-41176
Phone: +49 (0)6432-508690
www.maltwhisky-mara.com
Probably the main experts on rare
whisky offering over 1000 kinds. Also
arranges tastings. Mail orders by fax or
phone. Shipping also outside Germany.

Single Malt Collection
(Glen Fahrn Germany GmbH)
Hauptstraße 38
79801 Hohentengen a. H.
Phone: +49 (0)77 42 -857 222
www.singlemaltcollection.com
A very large range of single malts
(c 600). Newsletter. On-line ordering.
Shipping also outside Germany.

Kierzek
Weitlingstrasse 17
10317 Berlin
Phone: +49 (0)30 525 11 08
www.kierzek-berlin.de
Over 400 different whiskies in stock
(of which 250 are single malts). In the
product range 50 kinds of rum and
450 wines from all over the world are
found among other products. Mail
order is available within Germany.

Whisky & Cigars
Sophienstrasse 8-9
10178 Berlin-Mitte
Phone: +49 (0)30 2820376
www.whisky-cigars.de
Over 1000 kinds of whisky and a large
selection of cigars from all over the
world. Tastings are arranged.

House of Whisky
Ackerbeeke 6
31683 Obernkirchen
Phone: +49 (0)5724-399420
www.houseofwhisky.de
Aside from over 1,200 different malts
also sells a large range of other spirits
(including over 100 kinds of rum).
On-line ordering with shipping also
outside Germany.

Whiskyscheune
Alte Bornstrasse 4
61250 Usingen
Phone: +49 (0)6081-582642
www.whiskyscheune.de
Large selection with c 500 Scottish
malts in addition to whiskies from
other countries. Also mail order.

Whiskyworld
Ziegelfeld 6
94481 Grafenau / Haus i. Wald
Phone: +49 (0)8555-406 320
www.whiskyworld.de
A very good assortment of more than
1,000 malt whiskies. Also has a good
range of wines, other spirits, cigars and
books. Also on-line ordering.

Whisky Spirits
Wallstraße 23
60594 Frankfurt
Phone: +49 (0)69-96 20 06 43

Berlinerstrasse 39
60311 Frankfurt
Phone: +49 (0)69-36 70 33 44
www.whiskyspirits.de
Large assortment of over 500 whiskies.
Tastings with different themes. No
on-line mail order but goods can be
sent home.

Dudelsack (5 shops)
Treibgasse 6
63739 Aschaffenburg
Phone: +49 (0)6021-219654
www.dudelsack.com
One of five in a chain. All shops hold
recurring whisky seminars.

Kirschgarten 4, 55116 Mainz
Phone: +49 (0)6131-3297518
www.whisky-selection.de
Large assortment of more than 300
kinds of Scottish single malts. On-line
ordering.

Bischofsplatz 1, 65549 Limburg
Phone: +49 (0)6431-590388
www.dudelsack-limburg.de
My Whisky Frankfurt
Dreieichstr. 35, 60594 Frankfurt a.M.
Phone: +49 (0)69-60607524

Highlander Whisky & More
Schönborn Str. 9, 76698 Ubstadt-Weiher
Phone: +49 (0)7253 - 6466

Wine, Spirits & Cigars
(Whiskypack Spirituosenhandel)
Schnakenberg 15-19
31608 Marklohe/Lemke
Phone: +49 (0)5021-888150
www.nurvomfeinsten.de
Has a nice selection of cigars in
addition to whisky, wines and spirits.
On-line ordering.

World Wide Whisky (2 shops)
Eisenacher Strasse 64
10823 Berlin-Schöneberg
Phone: +49 (0)30-7845010

Hauptstrasse 58
10823 Berlin-Schöneberg
www.world-wide-whisky.de
Large range of 1,500 different whiskies.
Arranges tastings and seminars. Has a
large number of rarities. Orders can be
made via email.

HUNGARY
Whisky Net / Whisky Shop
Kovács Làszlò Street 21
2000 Szentendre

(shop)
Veres Pálné utca 8.
1053 Budapest
Phone: +36 1 267-1588
www.whiskynet.hu, www.whiskyshop.hu
A whisky trader established in 2007. In
the shop in downtown Budapest one
finds the largest selction of whisky in
Hungary. Agents for Douglas Laing, Cadenhead, Bruichladdich and Glenfarclas
among others. Also mailorder.

IRELAND
Celtic Whiskey Shop
27-28 Dawson Street
Dublin 2
Phone: +353 (0)1 675 9744
www.celticwhiskeyshop.com
More than 70 kinds of Irish whiskeys
but also a good selection of Scotch,
wines and other spirits. On-line ordering with shipping all over the world.

THE NETHERLANDS
Whiskyslijterij De Koning
Hinthamereinde 41
5211 PM 's Hertogenbosch
Phone: +31 (0)73-6143547
www.whiskykoning.nl
An enormous assortment with more
than 1400 kinds of whisky including
c 800 single malts. Also whisky-related
items like decanters, books etc.
Arranges recurring tastings. The site is
in Dutch and English. On-line ordering.
Shipping all over the world.

Whisky- en Wijnhandel Verhaar
Planetenbaan 2a
3721 LA Bilthoven
Phone: +31 (0)30-228 44 18
www.whiskyshop.nl
A wide selection of wines and spirits
with 1300 whiskies of which 1000 come
from Scotland. Email orders.

Wijnhandel van Zuylen
Loosduinse Hoofdplein 201
2553 CP Loosduinen (Den Haag)
Phone: +31 (0)70-397 1400
www.whiskyvanzuylen.nl
Excellent range of whiskies (c 1100)
and wines. Email orders with shipping
to some ten European countries.

Wijnwinkel-Slijterij
Ton Overmars
Hoofddorpplein 11
1059 CV Amsterdam
Phone: +31 (0)20-615 71 42
www.tonovermars.nl
A very large assortment of wines,
spirits and beer which includes more
than 400 single malts. Arranges
recurring tastings. Orders via email.

Van Wees - Whiskyworld.nl
Leusderweg 260
3817 KH Amersfoort
Phone: +31 (0)33-461 53 19
www.whiskyworld.nl
A very large range of 1000 whiskies
including over 500 single malts. On-line
ordering.

NEW ZEALAND
Whisky Galore
797 Colombo Street
Christchurch 8013
Phone: +64 (3) 377 6824
www.whiskygalore.co.nz
The best whisky shop in New Zealand
with 550 different whiskies, approximately 350 which are single malts. The
owner Michael Fraser Milne, has also
founded The Whisky Guild which has,
as one of its aims, to produce exclusive
single cask bottlings for members.
There is also online mail-order shipping
within New Zealand.

POLAND
George Ballantine's
Krucza str 47 A, Warsaw
Phone: +48 22 625 48 32

Pulawska str 22, Warsaw
Phone: +48 22 542 86 22
www.sklep-ballantines.pl
These two shops have the biggest
assortment in Poland with more than
360 different single malts. Apart from
whisky there is a full range of spirits
and wines from all over the world.
Recurrent tastings are arranged and
mail-orders are dispatched.

PORTUGAL
Whisky & Co
Rua Visconde de Seabra 12-A
1700-370 Lisboa
Phone: +351 217 933 314
www.whiskyco.com
Established in 2001 this is the foremost
whisky shop in Portugal with more
than 800 different whiskies and also a
Whisky Museum with more than 10.000
bottles on display.

RUSSIA
Whisky World Shop
9, Tverskoy Boulevard
123104 Moscow
Phone: +7 495 787 9150
www.whiskyworld.ru
Opened in 2003 in the centre of
Moscow. The assortment is huge with
more than 1,000 different single malts,

mainly from independent bottlers. It also stocks a selection of rare and old whiskies and a blended Scotch under their own label, Glen Clyde. The range is supplemented with a nice range of cognac, armagnac, calvados, grappa and wines. Tastings are also arranged.

SCOTLAND

Gordon & MacPhail
58 - 60 South Street, Elgin
Moray IV30 1JY
Phone: +44 (0)1343 545110
www.gordonandmacphail.com
This legendary shop opened already in 1895 in Elgin. The owners are perhaps the most well-known among independent bottlers. The shop stocks more than 800 bottlings of whisky and more than 600 wines and there is also a delicatessen counter with high-quality products. Tastings are arranged in the shop and there are shipping services within the UK and overseas. The shop attracts visitors from all over the world.

Royal Mile Whiskies (2 shops)
379 High Street, The Royal Mile
Edinburgh EH1 1PW
Phone: +44 (0)131 2253383

3 Bloomsbury Street
London WC1B 3QE
Phone: +44 (0)20 7436 4763
www.royalmilewhiskies.com
Royal Mile Whiskies is one of the most well-known whisky retailers in the UK. It was established in Edinburgh in 1991. There is also a shop in London since 2002 and a cigar shop close to the Edinburgh shop. The whisky range is outstanding with many difficult to find elsewhere. They have a comprehensive site regarding information on regions, distilleries, production, tasting etc. Royal Mile Whiskies also arranges 'Whisky Fringe' in Edinburgh, a two-day whisky festival which takes place annually in mid August. On-line ordering with worldwide shipping.

The Whisky Shop
(See also England, The Whisky Shop)
Unit L2-02
Buchanan Galleries
220 Buchanan Street
Glasgow G1 2GF
Phone: +44 (0)141 331 0022

17 Bridge Street
Inverness IV1 1HD
Phone: +44 (0)1463 710525

11 Main Street
Callander FK17 8DU
Phone: +44 (0)1877 331936

93 High Street
Fort William PH33 6DG
Phone: +44 (0)1397 706164

Shop Unit 1
Station Road
Oban PA34 4NU
Phone: +44 (0)1631 564409

Unit RU58B, Ocean Terminal
Edinburgh EH6 6JJ
Phone: +44 (0)131 554 8211

Unit 23
Princes Mall
Edinburgh EH1 1BQ
Phone: +44 (0)131 558 7563

www.whiskyshop.com
The first shop opened in 1992 in Edinburgh and this is now the United Kingdom's largest specialist retailer of whiskies with 14 outlets. A large product range with over 700 kinds, including 400 malt whiskies and 140 miniature bottles, as well as accessories and books. The own range 'Glenkeir Treasures' is a special assortment of selected malt whiskies. On-line ordering and shipping all over the world except to the USA.

Loch Fyne Whiskies
Inveraray
Argyll PA32 8UD
Phone: +44 (0)1499 302 219
www.lfw.co.uk
A legendary shop with an equally legendary owner, Richard Joynson. Joynson is known as a person with a high degree of integrity who does not mince his words on whisky matters. The range of malt whiskies is large and they have their own house blend, the prize-awarded Loch Fyne, as well as their 'The Loch Fyne Whisky Liqueur'. There is also a range of house malts called 'The Inverarity'. Loch Fyne Whiskies also publish the highly readable 'Scotch Whisky Review' which previously was produced by Joynson but now has authorities such as Charles MacLean and Dave Broom on the staff. Also on-line ordering with worldwide shipping.

Duncan Taylor's "Whiskies of Scotland"
Gordon Street, Huntly
Aberdeenshire
Phone: +44 (0)1466 794055
www.dtcscotch.com
Duncan Taylor is one of Scotland's largest independent bottlers and has quite recently opened a new shop in Huntly which sells videos, books and DVDs on whisky as well as the whole Duncan Taylor range.

Parker's Whisky
27 Low Street, Banff AB45 1AU
Phone: +44 (0)1261 812353
www.parkerswhisky.co.uk
Dedicated malt whisky specialist with a very nice range of more than 500 malt whiskies. On-line ordering with worldwide shipping.

The Whisky Shop Dufftown
1 Fife Street, Dufftown, Keith
Moray AB55 4AL
Phone: +44 (0)1340 821097
www.whiskyshopdufftown.co.uk
Whisky specialist in Dufftown in the heart of Speyside, wellknown to many of the Speyside festival visitors. Nearly 500 single malts as well as other whiskies. Arranges tastings as well as special events during the Festivals. On-line ordering with worldwide shipping.

The Scotch Whisky Experience
354 Castlehill, Royal Mile
Edinburgh
Phone: +44 (0)131 220 0441
www.whisky-heritage.co.uk
The Scotch Whisky Heritage Centre is a must for whisky devotees visiting Edinburgh. An interactive visitor centre dedicated to the history of Scotch whisky. This five-star visitor attraction has an excellent whisky shop with almost 300 different whiskies in stock. The shop is open to the general public and not only to those who have taken the whisky tour. Do not miss the award-winning Amber Restaurant where whisky is being used in the cooking.

Cadenhead's Campbeltown Whisky shop (Eaglesome)
7 Bolgam Street
Campbeltown
Argyll PA28 6HZ
Phone: +44 (0)1586 551710
www.wmcadenhead.com
One in a chain of shops owned by independent bottlers Cadenhead. Sells Cadenhead's products and other whiskies with a good range of, for example, Springbank. On-line ordering.

Cadenhead's Whisky Shop
172 Canongate, Royal Mile
Edinburgh EH8 8BN
Phone: +44 (0)131 556 5864
www.wmcadenhead.com
The oldest shop in the chain owned by Cadenhead. Sells Cadenhead's product range and a good selection of other whiskies and spirits. Arranges recurrent tastings. On-line ordering.

Robbie's Drams
3 Sandgate, Ayr
South Ayrshire KA7 1BG
Phone: +44 (0)1292 262 135
www.robbiesdrams.com
A whisky specialist with over 600 whiskies available in store and over 900 available from their on-line shop, including a large range of Irish, Japanese and American Bourbons. Specialists in single cask bottlings, closed distillery bottlings, rare malts, limited edition whisky and a nice range of their own bottlings. Worldwide shipping.

Single Malts Direct
36 Gordon Street
Huntly AB54 8EQ
Phone: +44 (0)845 6066145
www.singlemaltsdirect.com
Very good assortment including an exciting range of own bottlings. Good selection of whisky literature. Emphasis on on-line orders, shipping worldwide.

Luvian's Bottle Shop (2 shops)
93 Bonnygate, Cupar
Fife KY15 4LG
Phone: +44 (0)1334 654 820

66 Market Street, St Andrews
Fife KY16 9NT
Phone: +44 (0)1334 477752
www.luvians.com
Wine and whisky merchant with a very nice selection of more than 600 malt whiskies.

The Maltman
(S. R. & E. Barron (Dyce) Ltd.)
119 Victoria Street, Dyce
Aberdeen AB21 7BJ
Phone: +44 (0)1224 722208
www.maltman.co.uk
A good range with over 350 malts in
stock, including a 'Collector's Corner'
with some very rare malts. There is
a mail order service, but not on-line.
Only shipping within the UK.

Robert Graham Ltd (2 shops)
194 Rose Street
Edinburgh EH2 4AZ
Phone: +44 (0)131 226 1874

Finlay House
10-14 West Nile Street
Glasgow G1 2PP
Phone: +44 (0)141 248 7283
www.whisky-cigars.co.uk
Established in 1874 this company
specialises in Scotch whisky and cigars.
They have a nice assortment of malt
whiskies and their range of cigars is
impressive. On-line ordering with shipping all over the world

Whisky Castle
Main Street
Tomintoul
Aberdeenshire AB37 9EX
Phone: +44 (0)1807 580 213
www.whiskycastle.co.uk
Whisky specialist situated in the heart
of malt whisky country. With over 500
single malts, the specialisation is in
independent bottlings. There is also a
mail order shipping worldwide with
the exception of USA.

John Scott & Miller
15-19 Bridge Street, Kirkwall
Orkney KW15 1HR
Phone: +44 (0)1856 873146
www.jsmorkney.co.uk
A very large range of whisky from all
over the world and a special selection
from Orkneys' two distilleries. There
is also a range of Havana, Dominican
Republic and Dutch cigars.

Scotch Malt Whisky Society
www.smws.com
A society with more than 20 000 members worldwide. They are specialised
in own bottlings of single casks and
release between 150 and 200 bottlings
a year. Orders on-line for members
only. Shipping only within UK.

SWITZERLAND

P. Ullrich AG
Schneidergasse 27
4051 Basel
Phone: +41 (0)61 338 90 91
Another two shops in Basel:
Laufenstrasse 16
Unt. Rebgasse 18
www.ullrich.ch
A very large range of wines, spirits,
beers, accessories and books. Over 800
kinds of whisky with almost 600 single
malt. On-line ordering.

Eddie's Whiskies
Dorfgasse 27
8810 Horgen
Phone: +41 (0)43 244 63 00
www.eddies.ch
A whisky specialist with more than
650 different whiskies in stock with
emphasis on single malts (more than
500 different). Also arranges tastings.

World of Whisky
Via dim Lej 6
7500 St. Moritz
Phone: +41 (0)81 852 33 77
www.world-of-whisky.ch
A legendary shop situated in the Hotel
Waldhaus Am See which has an even
more legendary whisky bar, the Devil's
Place. It was created by Claudio Berna-
sconi, owner of the hotel and a whisky
aficionado. With over 2,500 different
whiskies, the bar even appears in the
Guinness Book of Records. The shop,
run by Christian Lauper, stocks almost
1,000 different whiskies and has a
good range of other spirits such as
rum, cognac and armagnac. There is
also a World of Whisky Malt Club and
mail order.

Glen Fahrn
Fahrnstrasse 39
9402 Mörschwil
Phone: +41 (0)71 860 09 87
www.glenfahrn.com
A wide range of spirits, fortified wines
and champagnes. A large selection of
whisky, with over 600 from Scotland.
On-line ordering. Ships within
Switzerland and to adjacent countries.

Monnier
Büetigenstrasse 30
2557 Studen
Phone: +41 (0)32 373 43 53
www.whiskytime.ch
A large range of whisky including
600 single malts. Also grappas and
champagnes. On-line ordering.
Shipping mainly within Switzerland.

Scot & Scotch
Wohllebgasse 7
8001 Zürich
Phone: +41 44 211 90 60
www.scotandscotch.ch
A whisky specialist with a great
selection including c 560 single malts.
Mail orders, but no on-line ordering.

Angels Share Shop
Unterdorfstrasse 15
5036 Oberentfelden
Phone: +41 (0)62 724 83 74
www.angelsshare.ch
A combined restaurant and whisky
shop. More than 400 different kinds
of whisky as well as a good range
of cigars. Scores extra points for
short information and photos of all
distilleries. On-line ordering.

Cadenhead's Whisky & More
Mittlere Gasse 15
5400 Baden
Phone: +41 (0)56 222 04 44
www.cadenheads.ch
A new member of the chain of Caden-

head's stores with a nice range of
whiskies, especially Cadenhead's. Also
rum, cognac and other spirits.

USA

Binny's Beverage Depot
5100 W. Dempster (Head Office)
Skokie, IL 60077
Phone:
Internet orders, 847-581-3186
Whisky Hotline, 888-817-5898 (toll free)
www.binnys.com
A chain of no less than 22 stores in
the Chicago area, covering everything
within wine and spirits. Some of the
stores also have a gourmet grocery,
cheese shop and, for cigar lovers, a
walk-in humidor. The whisk(e)y range
is impressive with 700 single malts, 120
bourbons, 40 Irish whiskeys and more.
Among other products almost 200
kinds of tequila should be mentioned.
Online mail order service.

Traverso's
2097 Stagecoach Road,
Santa Rosa, CA 95404
Phone: +1 707 542-2530
www.traversos.com
Traverso's Gourmet Foods was established by Charles Traverso in 1922 and
today specialises in food, wine and
liquors. They have a very nice range of
malt whiskies with regular tastings in
the shop.

The Whisky Shop
360 Sutter Street
San Francisco, CA 94108
Phone: +1 415-989-1030
www.whiskyshopusa.com
Whisky specialist with 600 different
whiskies of which over 400 are single
malts. Mail order with delivery to most
states.

The Wine Specialist
2115 M St. NW
Washington, DC 20037
Phone: +1 202 833 0707
www.winespecialist.com
Wines but also complete when it comes
to spirits with over 300 different single
malts. Another exciting part of the
range is 100 different kinds of sake and
soju. Mail order within the USA.

Park Avenue Liquor Shop
292 Madison Avenue
New York, NY 10017
Phone: +1 212 685 2442
www.parkaveliquor.com
Legendary whisky shop already established in 1934. A very large assortment
of wine and spirits with 400 different
expressions of single malt.

McScrooge's Wines and Spirits
307 N. Peters Rd
Knoxville, TN 37922
Phone: +1 865 691 6463
www.mcscrooges.com
Extensive assortment of wines, spirits
and beer. More than 350 different
single malts from over 80 distilleries.

Statistics

The following pages cover statistics and fore-casts on production, sales, exports, consumption and capacity. Please read the footnotes on these pages carefully as some of the figures have been calculated differently compared to last year. The pages have been made possible thanks to kind cooperation from three sources - Euromonitor International, The Scotch Whisky Industry Review and Scotch Whisky Association.

Euromonitor International
is the world's leading independent provider of business intelligence on industries, countries and consumers. Founded in 1972, it is a privately owned company with offices in London, Chicago, Singapore, Shanghai and Vilnius. In this edition of the Yearbook, they gave us their kind permission to use their figures on sales forecast, market share and world consumption.
More information on **www.euromonitor.com**

The Scotch Whisky Industry Review 2009
is written and compiled by Alan S Gray, Sutherlands Edinburgh. It is now in its 32nd consecutive year and provides a wealth of unique business critical information on the Scotch Whisky Industry. Copies can be obtained from Sutherlands Edinburgh, 61 Dublin Street, Edinburgh EH3 6NL. Details also on the website **www.scotchwhiskyindustryreview.com**

Scotch Whisky Association (SWA)
is the trade association for the Scotch Whisky industry. Its members account for more than 95% of production and sales of Scotch Whisky. Their main objective is to promote, protect and represent the interests of the whisky industry in Scotland and around the world. They also produce a plethora of statistical material covering production and sales of Scotch whisky. More information can be found on **www.scotch-whisky.org.uk**

Whisk(e)y forecast (volume & value) by region and sector 2008-2013

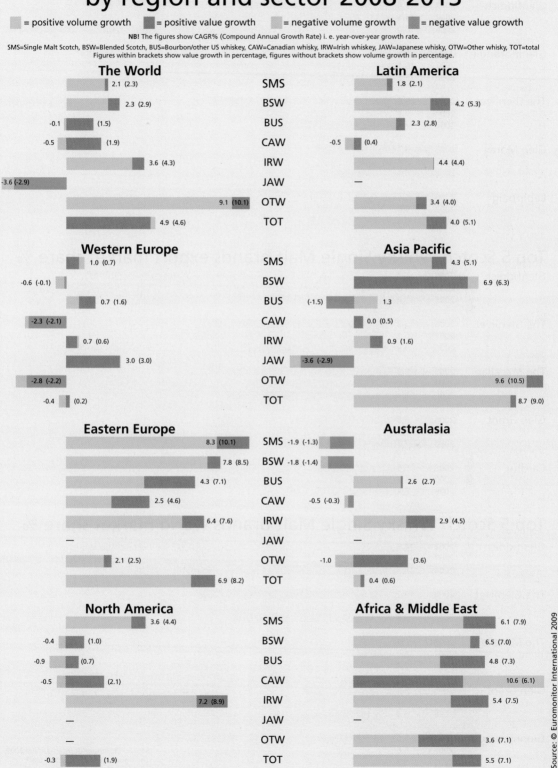

= positive volume growth   = positive value growth   = negative volume growth   = negative value growth

NB! The figures show CAGR% (Compound Annual Growth Rate) i. e. year-over-year growth rate.

SMS=Single Malt Scotch, BSW=Blended Scotch, BUS=Bourbon/other US whiskey, CAW=Canadian whisky, IRW=Irish whiskey, JAW=Japanese whisky, OTW=Other whisky, TOT=total
Figures within brackets show value growth in percentage, figures without brackets show volume growth in percentage.

The World

SMS	2.1 (2.3)
BSW	2.3 (2.9)
BUS	-0.1 (1.5)
CAW	-0.5 (1.9)
IRW	3.6 (4.3)
JAW	-3.6 (-2.9)
OTW	9.1 (10.1)
TOT	4.9 (4.6)

Latin America

SMS	1.8 (2.1)
BSW	4.2 (5.3)
BUS	2.3 (2.8)
CAW	-0.5 (0.4)
IRW	4.4 (4.4)
JAW	—
OTW	3.4 (4.0)
TOT	4.0 (5.1)

Western Europe

SMS	1.0 (0.7)
BSW	-0.6 (-0.1)
BUS	0.7 (1.6)
CAW	-2.3 (-2.1)
IRW	0.7 (0.6)
JAW	3.0 (3.0)
OTW	-2.8 (-2.2)
TOT	-0.4 (0.2)

Asia Pacific

SMS	4.3 (5.1)
BSW	6.9 (6.3)
BUS	(-1.5) 1.3
CAW	0.0 (0.5)
IRW	0.9 (1.6)
JAW	-3.6 (-2.9)
OTW	9.6 (10.5)
TOT	8.7 (9.0)

Eastern Europe

SMS	8.3 (10.1)
BSW	7.8 (8.5)
BUS	4.3 (7.1)
CAW	2.5 (4.6)
IRW	6.4 (7.6)
JAW	—
OTW	2.1 (2.5)
TOT	6.9 (8.2)

Australasia

SMS	-1.9 (-1.3)
BSW	-1.8 (-1.4)
BUS	2.6 (2.7)
CAW	-0.5 (-0.3)
IRW	2.9 (4.5)
JAW	—
OTW	-1.0 (3.6)
TOT	0.4 (0.6)

North America

SMS	3.6 (4.4)
BSW	-0.4 (1.0)
BUS	-0.9 (0.7)
CAW	-0.5 (2.1)
IRW	7.2 (8.9)
JAW	—
OTW	—
TOT	-0.3 (1.9)

Africa & Middle East

SMS	6.1 (7.9)
BSW	6.5 (7.0)
BUS	4.8 (7.3)
CAW	10.6 (6.1)
IRW	5.4 (7.5)
JAW	—
OTW	3.6 (7.1)
TOT	5.5 (7.1)

Source: © Euromonitor International 2009

Top 5 Scotch Whisky Single Malt brands UK market share %

Glenfiddich	2008	15,4
	2007	16,1
	2006	18,0
Glenmorangie	2008	15,1
	2007	15,1
	2006	15,5
The Glenlivet	2008	9,8
	2007	9,1
	2006	7,0
Glen Moray	2008	5,7
	2007	5,4
	2006	5,0
Laphroaig	2008	5,4
	2007	5,6
	2006	5,9

Top 5 Scotch Whisky Single Malt brands export market share %

Glenfiddich	2008	14,7
	2007	14,8
	2006	15,4
The Glenlivet	2008	10,2
	2007	10,1
	2006	9,9
The Macallan	2008	8,8
	2007	8,8
	2006	9,1
Glen Grant	2008	6,6
	2007	7,1
	2006	7,7
Cardhu	2008	5,8
	2007	6,2
	2006	6,8

Top 5 Scotch Whisky Single Malt brands world market share %

Glenfiddich	2008	14,9
	2007	15,1
	2006	15,3
The Glenlivet	2008	10,1
	2007	9,5
	2006	8,8
The Macallan	2008	8,1
	2007	8,0
	2006	7,8
Glen Grant	2008	6,1
	2007	6,4
	2006	6,4
Glenmorangie	2008	5,5
	2007	5,6
	2006	5,7

Source: Euromonitor International 2009
The figures exclude grey and black
market and duty free / travel retail.
2008 shares are provisional.

Top 5 Scotch Whisky Blended brands UK market share %

Bell's
2008	18,7
2007	18,7
2006	16,1

Famous Grouse
2008	17,4
2007	16,9
2006	16,6

High Commissioner
2008	7,3
2007	4,8
2006	3,5

Grant's
2008	7,0
2007	6,8
2006	6,4

Teacher's
2008	6,4
2007	7,4
2006	7,8

Top 5 Scotch Whisky Blended brands export market share %

Johnnie Walker
2008	18,8
2007	18,8
2006	18,0

J&B
2008	7,9
2007	8,1
2006	8,4

Ballantine's
2008	7,6
2007	7,4
2006	7,7

Chivas Regal
2008	5,4
2007	5,3
2006	5,2

Grant's
2008	5,4
2007	5,3
2006	5,0

Top 5 Scotch Whisky Blended brands world market share %

Johnnie Walker
2008	17,2
2007	17,0
2006	16,2

J&B
2008	7,2
2007	7,4
2006	7,6

Ballantine's
2008	6,9
2007	6,7
2006	7,0

Grant's
2008	5,5
2007	5,5
2006	5,2

Chivas Regal
2008	4,9
2007	4,8
2006	4,7

Source: Euromonitor International 2009
The figures exclude grey and black
market and duty free / travel retail.
2008 shares are provisional.

World Consumption of Scotch Whisky

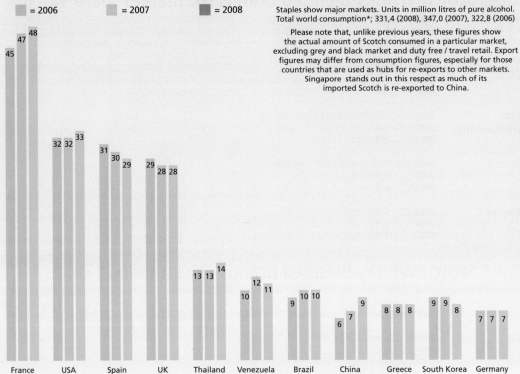

▉ = 2006　▉ = 2007　▉ = 2008

Staples show major markets. Units in million litres of pure alcohol.
Total world consumption*; 331,4 (2008), 347,0 (2007), 322,8 (2006)

Please note that, unlike previous years, these figures show
the actual amount of Scotch consumed in a particular market,
excluding grey and black market and duty free / travel retail. Export
figures may differ from consumption figures, especially for those
countries that are used as hubs for re-exports to other markets.
Singapore stands out in this respect as much of its
imported Scotch is re-exported to China.

Source: Euromonitor International 2009 and for* Scotch Whisky Industry Review 2009

Exports of Scotch Whisky

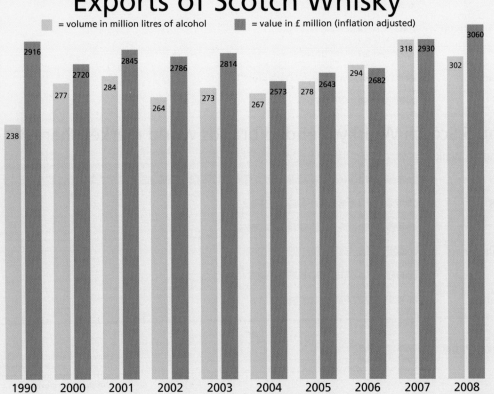

▉ = volume in million litres of alcohol　▉ = value in £ million (inflation adjusted)

Source: Scotch Whisky Association and Office for National Statistics

Distillery Capacity

Litres of pure alcohol, Scottish, active distilleries only

Distillery	Capacity	Distillery	Capacity	Distillery	Capacity
Glenfiddich	10 000 000	Bowmore	2 000 000	Ardbeg	1 000 000
Roseisle	10 000 000	Speyburn	2 000 000	Glen Garioch	1 000 000
Glenlivet	8 700 000	Inchgower	1 990 000	Tobermory	1 000 000
Macallan	8 000 000	Talisker	1 940 000	Arran	750 000
Ailsa Bay	6 000 000	Glen Elgin	1 830 000	Glengyle	750 000
Glenmorangie	6 000 000	Auchentoshan	1 750 000	Glen Scotia	750 000
Glen Grant	5 900 000	Cragganmore	1 520 000	Springbank	750 000
Dufftown	5 800 000	Bruichladdich	1 500 000	Oban	670 000
Balvenie	5 600 000	Knockando	1 500 000	Speyside	600 000
Glenrothes	5 600 000	Knockdhu	1 500 000	Benromach	500 000
Miltonduff	5 500 000	Scapa	1 500 000	Royal Lochnagar	450 000
Ardmore	5 200 000	Glencadam	1 400 000	Glenturret	340 000
Glen Ord	5 000 000	Glendronach	1 400 000	Bladnoch	100 000
Tomatin	5 000 000	Glenspey	1 390 000	Kilchoman	100 000
Kininvie	4 800 000	Balblair	1 330 000	Edradour	90 000
Glentauchers	4 500 000	Glenglassaugh	1 100 000	Daftmill	65 000
Aberlour	4 200 000	Glengoyne	1 100 000	Abhainn Dearg	20 000
Clynelish	4 200 000				
Glenburgie	4 200 000				
Tormore	4 100 000				
Allt-a-Bhainne	4 000 000				
Loch Lomond	4 000 000				
Tamnavulin	4 000 000				
Tamdhu	4 000 000				
Teaninich	4 000 000				
Royal Brackla	3 900 000				
Braeval	3 800 000				
Caol Ila	3 800 000				
Craigellachie	3 600 000				
Dalmore	3 600 000				
Auchroisk	3 580 000				
Aberfeldy	3 500 000				
Linkwood	3 500 000				
Longmorn	3 500 000				
Dailuaine	3 370 000				
Glendullan	3 360 000				
Tomintoul	3 300 000				
Mannochmore	3 220 000				
Macduff	3 200 000				
Deanston	3 000 000				
Glenfarclas	3 000 000				
Glenallachie	3 000 000				
Pulteney	3 000 000				
Cardhu	2 980 000				
Mortlach	2 910 000				
Aultmore	2 900 000				
Laphroaig	2 900 000				
Benriach	2 800 000				
Tullibardine	2 700 000				
Benrinnes	2 540 000				
Blair Athol	2 500 000				
Bunnahabhain	2 500 000				
Glenkinchie	2 500 000				
Highland Park	2 500 000				
Strathisla	2 400 000				
Fettercairn	2 300 000				
Strathmill	2 300 000				
Lagavulin	2 250 000				
Dalwhinnie	2 200 000				
Jura	2 200 000				
Glenlossie	2 140 000				
Glen Moray	2 100 000				
Balmenach	2 000 000				
Ben Nevis	2 000 000				

Summary of Malt Distillery Capacity by Category

Category	Litres of alcohol	% of Industry	Average capacity
Speyside (45)	171 850 000	59,9	3 819 000
Islands (7)	9 910 000	3,5	1 416 000
Rest of the Highlands (30)	76 360 000	26,6	2 545 000
Islay (8)	16 050 000	5,6	2 006 000
Lowlands (5)	10 415 000	3,6	2 083 000
Campbeltown (3)	2 250 000	0,8	750 000
Total (98)	**286 835 000**	**100**	**2 927 000**

Summary of Malt Distillery Capacity by Owner

Owner (number of distilleries)	Litres of alcohol	% of Industry
Diageo (28)	83 440 000	29,1
Pernod Ricard (12)	49 400 000	17,2
William Grant (4)	26 400 000	9,2
Edrington Group (5)	20 440 000	7,1
Bacardi (John Dewar & Sons) (5)	17 100 000	6,0
Whyte and Mackay (4)	12 100 000	4,2
Pacific Spirits (Inver House) (5)	9 830 000	3,4
Beam Global (2)	8 100 000	2,8
Moët Hennessy (Glenmorangie) (2)	7 000 000	2,4
C L Financial (Burn Stewart) (3)	6 500 000	2,3
Campari (Glen Grant) (1)	5 900 000	2,1
Tomatin Distillery Co (1)	5 000 000	1,7
Suntory (Morrison Bowmore) (3)	4 750 000	1,7
Loch Lomond Distillers (2)	4 750 000	1,7
Angus Dundee (2)	4 700 000	1,6
Benriach Distillery Co (2)	4 200 000	1,5
J & G Grant (Glenfarclas) (1)	3 000 000	1,0
Tullibardine Distillery Ltd (1)	2 700 000	0,9
La Martiniquaise (Glen Moray) (1)	2 100 000	0,7
Nikka (Ben Nevis Distillery) (1)	2 000 000	0,7
Bruichladdich Distillery Co (1)	1 500 000	0,5
J & A Mitchell (2)	1 500 000	0,5
Ian Macleod Distillers (Glengoyne) (1)	1 100 000	less than 0,5
Scaent Group (Glenglassaugh) (1)	1 100 000	- " -
Isle of Arran Distillers (1)	750 000	- " -
Speyside Distillers Co (1)	600 000	- " -
Gordon & MacPhail (Benromach) (1)	500 000	- " -
Co-ordinated Developm. (Bladnoch) (1)	100 000	- " -
Kilchoman Distillery Co (1)	100 000	- " -
Signatory Vintage (Edradour) (1)	90 000	- " -
Francis Cuthbert (Daftmill) (1)	65 000	- " -
Mark Thayburn (Abhainn Dearg) (1)	20 000	- " -

Do you want to find out more in detail where the different distilleries are situated? We suggest that you pay a visit to www.maltmaps.com. There you will find not only Scottish distilleries but all the other distilleries presented in Malt Whisky Yearbook. For Scottish distilleries there is also a nice, new interactive map to be found at www.maltmadness.com/whisky/map/Scotland/

ORKNEY ISLANDS

Wick

NORTH HIGHLANDS

Isle of Lewis

SKYE

Barra

Kyle of Lockalsh

Inverness

SPEYSIDE

Loch Ness

Aberdeen

Fort William

CENTRAL HIGHLANDS

EAST HIGHLANDS

Pitlochry

Dundee

Oban

MULL

WEST HIGHLANDS

Loch Tay

Loch Lomond

Perth

St. Andrews

Stirling

JURA

ISLAY

Glasgow

Edinburgh

ARRAN

Campbeltown

Ayr

THE LOWLANDS

Dumfries

Stranraer

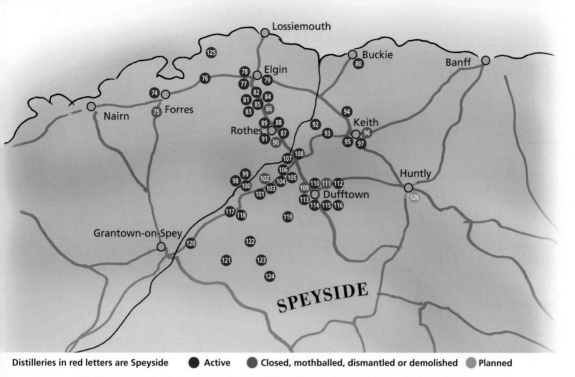

Lossiemouth · Buckie · Banff · Elgin · Nairn · Forres · Rothes · Keith · Huntly · Dufftown · Grantown-on-Spey

SPEYSIDE

Distilleries in red letters are Speyside ● Active ● Closed, mothballed, dismantled or demolished ● Planned

NB. This year I have decided to omit two planned distilleries, Blackwood and Ladybank, as the future for these seems very uncertain. Instead four new projects have been included - Annandale, Barra, Falkirk and Kingsbarns.

39 Aberfeldy	126 Duncan Taylor	114 Kininvie	1 Barra	45 Deanston	89 Glenrothes
106 Aberlour	38 Edradour	100 Knockando	2 Highland Park	46 Loch Lomond	90 Caperdonich (mb)
129 Abhainn Dearg	130 Falkirk	21 Knockdhu	3 Scapa	47 Inverleven (d)	91 Glenspey
127 Ailsa Bay	32 Fettercairn	56 Ladyburn (dm)	4 Pulteney	48 Littlemill (d)	92 Auchroisk
119 Allt-a-Bhainne	13 Glen Albyn (d)	63 Lagavulin	5 Brora (c)	49 Auchentoshan	93 Glentauchers
131 Annandale	105 Glenallachie	64 Laphroaig	6 Clynelish	50 Glengoyne	94 Aultmore
62 Ardbeg	116 Glendullan	79 Linkwood	7 Balblair	51 Kinclaith (d)	95 Strathmill
25 Ardmore	85 Glen Elgin	48 Littlemill (d)	8 Glenmorangie	52 Glen Flagler (d)	96 Glen Keith (mb)
58 Arran	35 Glenesk (dm)	46 Loch Lomond	9 Ben Wyvis (c)	53 Rosebank (c)	97 Strathisla
49 Auchentoshan	101 Glenfarclas	36 Lochside (d)	10 Teaninich	54 St Magdalene (dm)	98 Tamdhu
92 Auchroisk	112 Glenfiddich	84 Longmorn	11 Dalmore	55 Glenkinchie	99 Cardhu
94 Aultmore	52 Glen Flagler (d)	107 Macallan	12 Glen Ord	56 Ladyburn (dm)	100 Knockando
7 Balblair	24 Glen Garioch	20 Macduff	13 Glen Albyn (d)	57 Bladnoch	101 Glenfarclas
120 Balmenach	18 Glenglassaugh	81 Mannochmore	14 Glen Mhor (d)	58 Arran	102 Imperial (c)
113 Balvenie	50 Glengoyne	15 Millburn (dm)	15 Millburn (dm)	59 Springbank	103 Dailuaine
19 Banff (d)	87 Glen Grant	77 Miltonduff	16 Royal Brackla	60 Glengyle	104 Benrinnes
1 Barra	60 Glengyle	115 Mortlach	17 Tomatin	61 Glen Scotia	105 Glenallachie
30 Ben Nevis	96 Glen Keith (mb)	33 North Port (d)	18 Glenglassaugh	62 Ardbeg	106 Aberlour
82 Benriach	55 Glenkinchie	40 Oban	19 Banff (d)	63 Lagavulin	107 Macallan
104 Benrinnes	122 Glenlivet	111 Pittyvaich (d)	20 Macduff	64 Laphroaig	108 Craigellachie
74 Benromach	31 Glenlochy (d)	128 Port Charlotte	21 Knockdhu	65 Port Ellen (dm)	109 Convalmore (dm)
9 Ben Wyvis (c)	83 Glenlossie	65 Port Ellen (dm)	22 Glenugie (dm)	66 Bowmore	110 Dufftown
57 Bladnoch	14 Glen Mhor (d)	4 Pulteney	23 Glendronach	67 Bruichladdich	111 Pittyvaich (d)
37 Blair Athol	8 Glenmorangie	53 Rosebank (c)	24 Glen Garioch	68 Kilchoman	112 Glenfiddich
66 Bowmore	78 Glen Moray	125 Roseisle	25 Ardmore	69 Caol Ila	113 Balvenie
124 Braeval	12 Glen Ord	16 Royal Brackla	26 Speyside	70 Bunnahabhain	114 Kininvie
5 Brora (c)	89 Glenrothes	27 Royal Lochnagar	27 Royal Lochnagar	71 Jura	115 Mortlach
67 Bruichladdich	61 Glen Scotia	54 St Magdalene (dm)	28 Glenury Royal (d)	72 Tobermory	116 Glendullan
70 Bunnahabhain	91 Glenspey	3 Scapa	29 Dalwhinnie	73 Talisker	117 Tormore
69 Caol Ila	93 Glentauchers	88 Speyburn	30 Ben Nevis	74 Benromach	118 Cragganmore
90 Caperdonich (mb)	41 Glenturret	26 Speyside	31 Glenlochy (d)	75 Dallas Dhu (c)	119 Allt-a-Bhainne
99 Cardhu	22 Glenugie (dm)	59 Springbank	32 Fettercairn	76 Glenburgie	120 Balmenach
6 Clynelish	28 Glenury Royal (d)	97 Strathisla	33 North Port (d)	77 Miltonduff	121 Tomintoul
86 Coleburn (dm)	2 Highland Park	95 Strathmill	34 Glencadam	78 Glen Moray	122 Glenlivet
109 Convalmore (dm)	80 Inchgower	73 Talisker	35 Glenesk (dm)	79 Linkwood	123 Tamnavulin
118 Cragganmore	47 Inverleven (d)	98 Tamdhu	36 Lochside (d)	80 Inchgower	124 Braeval
108 Craigellachie	71 Jura	123 Tamnavulin	37 Blair Athol	81 Mannochmore	125 Roseisle
42 Daftmill	68 Kilchoman	10 Teaninich	38 Edradour	82 Benriach	126 Duncan Taylor
103 Dailuaine	51 Kinclaith (d)	72 Tobermory	39 Aberfeldy	83 Glenlossie	127 Ailsa Bay
75 Dallas Dhu (c)	43 Kingsbarns	17 Tomatin	40 Oban	84 Longmorn	128 Port Charlotte
11 Dalmore		121 Tomintoul	41 Glenturret	85 Glen Elgin	129 Abhainn Dearg
29 Dalwhinnie		117 Tormore	42 Daftmill	86 Coleburn (dm)	130 Falkirk
45 Deanston		44 Tullibardine	43 Kingsbarns	87 Glen Grant	131 Annandale
110 Dufftown			44 Tullibardine	88 Speyburn	

Index

Bold figures refer to the main entry in the distillery directory.